Morgan County Tennessee

Cemetery Inscriptions

Compiled by Lee M. Cross
and
Edited by Larry R. Spurling

HERITAGE BOOKS
2012

HERITAGE BOOKS

AN IMPRINT OF HERITAGE BOOKS, INC.

Books, CDs, and more—Worldwide

For our listing of thousands of titles see our website
at
www.HeritageBooks.com

Published 2012 by
HERITAGE BOOKS, INC.
Publishing Division
100 Railroad Ave. #104
Westminster, Maryland 21157

International Standard Book Numbers
Paperbound: 978-1-55613-018-2
Clothbound: 978-0-7884-9329-4

INTRODUCTION

This major collection of cemetery inscriptions from numerous large and small cemeteries throughout Morgan County, Tennessee contains about 9,700 inscriptions from over seventy cemeteries, including the large old cemetery at Wartburg, the county seat, and the newer Wartburg Memorial Gardens.

The data were originally collected by the late Lee M. Cross and have been edited for publication by Larry R. Spurling. The field work was completed in 1973, and was supplemented by data from obituaries until 1983. In a few cases maiden names or other data has been added from other sources, but for the most part the information presented here comes directly from the tombstones.

For convenience the inscriptions have been arranged in alphabetical order. A cross-index has been provided for spouses and others whose name appears out of alphabetical order. Each record ends with a three letter code indicating the cemetery. A short list of Morgan County veterans of various wars has been incorporated into the text. In a few cases the place of burial could not be determined, and these records have been assigned a special code.

GUIDE TO CEMETERY ABBREVIATIONS AND LOCATIONS

ADC Adcock - no location given

ADK Adkinson - Turn off Highway 80 at Coal Hill. At Williams Chapel sign go .2 mile on rough road; about 100 yards to left of road on hill. About 10 more graves with unmarked stones.

ADM Adams - no location given

ALB Albertson - Between Pleasant Ridge and Burrville. Were 12 unmarked graves.

AMS Amos - On Back Valley Road about 2 miles from junction of Highway 62 at Middle Creek Church; 250 yards north of road on hill.

ARM Armes Chapel - no location given. Were 10 graves with illegible small markers mostly by Schuberts Funeral Home. Copy of this cemetery made in 1971.

BCF Beech Fork - On wooded hill west of Beech Fork Creek about 300 yards north of ridge near Kelly house. Before 1840 there was a church. Were 25 or more unmarked graves; two were covered by housetop-shaped stone.

BRD Byrd - no location given. Were 15 illegible stones. Record taken 1971.

BRN Branstetter/High Point - no location given

BRR Burrville - no location given

BRW Brewster - Turn south off Highway 52 about 1.5 miles west of Rugby; after 1 mile turn right; after .25 mile turn right; go 250 yards. Were 20 illegibly marked stones.

BRZ Brazel - no location given

CBJ C B Jackson - no location given. 30 illegibly marked stones

CHN Chaney - East of Sunbright 5.2 miles on Mill Creek Road.

CLC Clear Creek - no location given

CLH Coal Hill - South of Coalfield 4 miles. 32 unmarked graves, mostly children.

CRO	Crab Orchard - no location given
CVN	Covington - no location given
DDN	Diden - From Sunbright 3.4 miles east on Mill Creek Road; then 100 yards north of road on hill. Family cemetery; no church.
DRL	Deer Lodge - no location given
DRM	Deermont/Camp Austin - no location given. Were 35 illegibly marked stones. Copy of cemetery taken May 1972; additions taken 6 Aug 1975.
DVD	Davidson (see also Fostner/Davidson) - no location given
DVS	Davis - no location given
ELZ	Elizabeth - no location given
EST	Estes - no location given
FGN	Fagan - From Coalfield 3 miles south; .2 mile west of highway. Were 3 graves without legible markers; no church; cemetery well kept.
FLF	Flat Fork - no location given
FLR	Flat Rock - West of Lancing 16 miles on Highway 62.
FRC	Friends Chapel - East of Morgan & Fentress County line about 2 miles on Highway 62.
FRN	Frankford - no location given
FRV	Fairview - West of Lancing 6 miles on Highway 62 in back of church.
FST	Fostner/Davidson (see also Davidson) - no location given
HCK	Hicks - On Solomons Hollow Road near Coalfield.
HLL	Hall - East of Sunbright about 2 miles & north of the old Jim Gasnell Farm. Were 15 graves with unmarked stones.
HWN	Hawn - West of Lancing on Highway 62. In June 1972 were 4 graves without legible markers.
ISF	Island Ford - no location given
JCJ	John C Jackson - Turn south off Highway 62 to Davis Cemetery. After about .5 mile the road turns right and crosses a branch and ends at the cemetery on top of the hill.
JHG	John Goddard - North of Stevens 1.2 miles on old Petros Road
LBR	Liberty - no location given
LNC	Lancing - no location given
LNE	Lane - no location given
LNG	Langley/Mt Zion - no location given
LST	Lester - At Pilot Mountain turn west on north side of bridge & go about 400 yards. Family cemetery.

LVN Lavender - no location given. Were 6 graves without legible markers when copied 5 Nov 1975.

MCD Macidonia - In Little Emory Valley about 9.5 miles east of Highway 27 on hillside north of road. Were 50 graves without legible markers.

MCR McCartt - no location given

MLC Mill Creek - apparently the community had placed metal markers on all graves giving as much data as possible.

MNT Montgomery - no location given

MRR Morris - no location given. Were 40 graves not marked when copied July 1972.

MSG Mossy Grove - no location given

MST Meister - no location given

NDK Nydick/Carpenter - West of Glenmary about 4 miles. One grave covered by a native stone about 4' x 7' x 5'. Perhaps a Carpenter; deceased 21 Jan 1875, ae 94y.

NWP New Petros - no location given. Were about 30 unmarked graves when copied Apr 1971, corrected Aug 1974.

OLP Old Petros - Adjacent to Petros School. About 100 graves not legibly marked.

OOO Soldiers without a burial location.

PLR Pleasant Ridge - no location given

PNY Piney - no location given

PTC Potters Chapel - no location given

RGB Rugby - no location given. Were 56 illegible markers.

RTT Ritter - no location given. Were about 20 graves not legibly marked when copied 14 June 1974.

SHD Shadeland/Greenwood - West of Glades about .5 mile & about 100 yards south of road at Greenwood Chapel. Copied Nov 1972.

SNB Sunbright - no location given

STC Stringfield Chapel - On Pea Ridge Road about 1 mile south of the Sunbright Cemetery. Estimated 8 graves were not legibly marked when copied 19 Sept 1974. Concrete block church recently built; cemetery is poorly kept.

STP Stephens/Byrge - no location given

THR Thornton - From Coalfield about 1 mile on Back Valley Road; turn right; go 1/8 mile. Were 5 graves with illegible markers when copied Apr 1975.

UNG Union Grove - no location given

UNH Union Hill/Neely - About 1 mile south of Scott &
     Morgan County Line go onto road that turns west off
     Highway 27; is 1 mile from Highway. Were about 30
     graves without legible markers when copied 20 Sept
     1974. It is level & well kept; no church.
UNN Union - no location given
WBB Webb - no location given. Copied 20 Sept 1974.
WHO White Oak - Near an old log church in fairly good
     condition but not used recently. Were 3 graves
     without legible markers when copied 1 July 1972.
WMG Wartburg Memorial Gardens - no location given
WRC Wartburg - no location given
WRJ Wm R Jackson - no location given. Were 15 graves
     with illegible markers.

ABBOTT, Mary E, d 16 Feb 1899, ae 92y, DRL

ABSTON, Mrs Carylon, d 7 July 1944, CBJ

Tommie, b 15 Apr 1913 - d 4 June 1970, CBJ

ACRES, Andie, d 6 June 1977, PLR

Dimple, b 1915 - d 1958, PLR

ADAMS, ----, b&d 20 Feb 1907, ELZ

A T, b 16 June 1885 - d 20 Feb 1899, LVN

Albert Lincoln, b 4 Apr 1894 - d 11 Feb 1938, DRL

Anna Elizabeth, d 6 July 1976, ae 81y, ALB

Calvin, b 2 Feb 1873 - d 8 Sept 1920, ELZ

Duglas K, b 16 Jan 1944 - d 31 Oct 1971, BRN

Glenn Scott, b 13 June 1915 - d 30 May 1959, WRC

Harold, d 1 June 1980, ae 81y, DRL

Maggie, d 5 Oct ----, ae 82y, BRN

Martha Scott, b 13 Apr 1877 - d 4 Jan 1941, ELZ

Michael Lee, b 1 Oct 1965 - d 7 Oct 1965, BRN

Myrtle, b 11 March 1899 - d 1 Aug 1900, LVN

Myrtle Perkins, b 20 Jan 1898 - d 21 Dec 1959, DRL

Otis Eugene, b 30 March 1926 - d 29 Jan 1964, DRL

William Reed, b 22 Feb 1908 - d 9 May 1974, WRC

ADCOCK, Calvin & Alvin, b&d 1933, ADC

Corp Archibald, b 4 Jan 1847 - d 4 Aug 1898, ADC

ADCOCK (continued)

Dewey, b 8 Apr 1899 - d 12 July 1968, EST

Gladys Irene, b 19 Sept 1911 - d 23 Apr 1951, ADC

H N, b 20 Nov 1894 - no death date, EST

Hazel, b 19 Jan 1901 - no death date, EST

Laurence & Lenora, b&d 1927, ADC

Lula, b 9 Aug 1877 - d 28 Jan 1937, ADC

Martha, b 4 Jan 1847 - d 2 Aug 1883, ADC

Pleasant, Co B 3rd TN, Inf d 29 March 1864, ae 28y, HCK

R H, b 28 Mar 1897 - d 7 Feb 1916, ADC

W M, b 12 Jan 1871 - d 14 May 1928, ADC

ADCOX, Dora Bryant, b 12 Sept 1873 - d 28 May 1951, EST

Ernest, b 1920 - d 1936, UNN

Infant, d 16 July 1956, EST

James T, b 3 July 1867 - d 23 July 1941, ADC

Joe Ralph, b 1934 - d 1937, UNN

Loyd A, b 12 June 1901 - d 6 March 1958, EST

Mickey Joey, b 13 Oct 1953 - d 15 Oct 1953, ADC

Minner E, b 6 Sept 1891 - d 31 Oct 1917, ADC

Rena, b 23 Nov 1910 - d 24 Nov 1943, ADC

Susan Ann, b 22 Dec 1968 - d 9 March 1934, ADC

Walter J, d 27 Aug 1901, ae 68y, EST

ADDINGTON, Meshack L, b 8 June 1860 - d 5 March

1

ADDINGTON (continued)
1889, DRL
Sarah H, b 22 Feb 1850 - d
9 Aug 1924, DRL
ADELOTT, Andy, d 4 Feb 1980
ae 67y, WRC
ADKINS, Carrie Louise, b 22
Aug 1924 - d 6 Sept
1939, SNB
Etta, d 21 Apr 1979, ae
84y, DRL
Judy Diane, 10 June 1951,
SNB
Lacy B, b 20 Jan 1896 - d
16 March 1964, WMG
Lennie J, d 5 July 1975,
ae 86y, FLR
Martha C, d 13 June 1981,
ae 84y, SNB
Nolan, Tec 5 206 Mil Pol
WWII b 22 Nov 1915 - d
2 Oct 1969, DRL
Rosaline Polly, b 1936 - d
31 July 1973, BRN
Ross, b 1913 - d 1974, DRL
Tony C, b 1945 - d 1946,
DRL
ADKINSON, Catherine, b 19
May 1791 - d 19 Oct
1846, ADK
Catherine, b 30 June 1848
- d 27 Aug 1849, ADK
Jessy, b 7 Oct 1828 - d 4
Apr 1837, ADK
ADKISSON, Artelia, b 3 Nov
1873 - d 1 March 1959,
DVS
Carlton, b 5 May 1931 - d
6 Aug 1969, UNN
Charles, b 16 Aug 1901 - d
22 March 1945, UNN
Clarence, b 1 Oct 1906 - d
12 June 1933, UNN
Ella Mae, b 15 May 1902 -
d 15 Jan 1953, CRO
Eunice M, b 28 Aug 1891 -
d 22 Feb 1904, DVS
Georgia M, b 4 Oct 1925 -

ADKISSON (continued)
no death date, EST
Gertie, b 13 May 1883 - d
8 Nov 1891, WRJ
Infant Dau, b&d 20 Jan
1915, WRJ
James Willis, b 23 Jun
1928 - d 9 March 1940,
CLH
L Thurston, b 4 Sept 1900
- no death date, CRO
Leonard A, b 15 Dec 1899 -
d 3 Nov 1966, NWP
Lillie Mae, b 17 Apr 1905
- d 14 Aug 1946, NWP
Meredith Davis, b 15 Apr
1912 - d 14 Oct 1918,
DVS
Nancy Ann, b 17 May 1849 -
d 11 Oct 1934, WRJ
Nina Ceneva, b 17 June
1895 - d 16 Oct 1918,
DVS
Ollie, b 10 May 1894 - no
death date, UNN
Raymond Hicks, b 21 Dec
1916 - d 3 March 1951,
EST
Ronnie Leon, b 19 Dec 1940
- d 18 Jan 1941, NWP
Roy O, b 17 Feb 1885 - d
17 Nov 1885, WRJ
Sallie T, b 12 June 1874 -
d 15 March 1945, CRO
Sherman, b 20 June 1870 -
d 18 Aug 1950, CRO
Susie, b 16 Aug 1964 - d
18 Sept 1948, UNN
Tressie R, b 21 Jan 1893 -
d 13 Aug 1976, EST
Vernon, b 15 May 1890 - d
25 Dec 1976, EST
Victor J, d 2 Apr 1977, ae
77y, DVS
W F, b 13 Nov 1851 - d 26
May 1937, WRJ
Walker, b 13 Sept 1865 - d
6 Nov 1947, DVS

ADKISSON (continued)

Walton, d 28 June 1964, ae 2y 24da, CLH

William, b 23 June 1894 - d 27 Nov 1972, UNN

Yerb, b 6 June 1907 - d 15 March 1952, UNN

ADSMOND, Anna Julia, b 9 July 1895 - d 17 June 1910, DRL

Mary Margaret, b 17 March 1858 - d 26 Apr 1928, DRL

O Theodore, b 14 July 1897 - d 1 Aug 1897, DRL

William S, b 26 March 1834 - d 18 Feb 1927, DRL

AINSCOUGH, Georgina, b&d 30 Aug 1896, RTT

Hannah, b 1856 - d 28 Apr 1926, RTT

Peter, b 1856 - d 1954, RTT

Sarah Alice, b 9 Apr 1890 - d 10 July 1891, RTT

AKINS, Andrew, b 1891 - d 1962, MSG

Bertha E, b 1 Aug 1894 - d 14 Sept 1937, MSG

Charles E, b 2 July 1931 - d 12 May 1957, MSG

Infant s/o Andrew & Bertha b&d 1934, MSG

ALBERTSON, Arabelle, b 6 Aug 1873 - d 25 June 1927, ALB

Ida Clark, b 1862 - d 1916, WRC

Javan G, b 12 Feb 1897 - d 14 Dec 1909, NDK

John Denton, d 4 March 1911, ae 8.5hr, ALB

Millard F, b 17 Oct 1869 - d 7 Oct 1943, ALB

ALBRITTON, Maggie Chaney, b 21 Aug 1898 - d 13 Feb 1941, MLC

ALDERSON, E S, b 17 Jan

ALDERSON (continued)

1939 - no death date, OLP

James B, b 25 Aug 1882 - d 7 Oct 1882, WRC

Lucy, d 22 Oct 1980, ae 91y, WMG

Lucy P, b 13 Dec 1888 - d 22 Oct 1980, WRC

T J, b 7 Nov 1831 - d 21 Jan 1916, OLP

ALEXANDER, Ernest Vernon, b 13 Sept 1863 - d 26 Feb 1956, RGB

Giles, b 22 July 1867 - d 23 Sept 1943, RGB

Mary Helen, b 10 Feb 1892 - d 23 Feb 1928, RGB

ALLCOCK (or Hallcock), James, b 1825 - d 4 May 1889, RTT

ALLEN, Arnold, b 20 June 1915 - d 24 March 1917, UNN

Bonnie L Butler, b 29 Oct 1898 - no death date, UNN

Chas Garfield, b 2 Nov 1919 - d 14 July 1950, UNN

Edward, s/o W C & M E, b 7 Dec 1916 - d 16 March 1980, WRC

Gary D, b 20 Feb 1954 - d 17 May 1954, SNB

George W, b 20 Apr 1854 - 1938, UNN

James, b&d 11 Nov 1969, CRO

James D, b 18 Sept 1889 - d 20 Nov 1972, UNN

James M, b 23 Sept 1870 - d 1 Jan 1947, UNN

James M, b 23 Sept 1870 - d 1 Jan 1947, WRJ

John W, b 28 Apr 1887 - d 12 Dec 1963, UNN

Latha L, b 14 Jan 1869 - d

ALLEN (continued)
1 Jan 1949, UNN
Latha L, b 14 Jan 1869 - d
2 Jan 1949, WRJ
Loyal, b 30 Jan 1926 - d
25 Jan 1955, UNN
Marilen E, b 28 Sept 1878
- d 15 Dec 1945, WRC
Murmie, b 29 Apr 1897 - d
10 Dec 1967, NWP
Nancy E, b 1857 - d 1921,
UNN
Ronnie, 1951, LBR
Samuel J, d 10 March 1977,
ae 94y, UNN
William C, b 9 July 1897 -
d 16 Aug 1955, WRC
ALLENDER, Clyde J, Tec 5 78
Sta, Hosp WWII - b 2
June 1918 - d 4 May
1963, LNC
ALLEY, D C, b 7 Aug 1881 -
d 6 Aug 1929, CRO
David Rowland, b 11 Aug
1893 - d 14 Feb 1933,
CRO
G F, b 29 March 1879 - d 8
Aug 1888, CRO
George W, b 21 Aug 1859 -
no death date, CRO
Grace, b 10 Apr 1883 - d 9
March 1933, CRO
J A, b 12 Oct 1874 - d 19
Jan 1888, CRO
J C, b 1870 - d 1931, CRO
James, b 26 Dec 1820 - d
12 March 1905, CRO
James Newton, b 31 March
1889 - d 3 June 1930,
CRO
Lee N, b 21 June 1882 - d
3 Sept 1903, CRO
Lena Gauden, b 30 Sept
1882 - d 18 Nov 1968,
CRO
Louise, b 7 Feb 1849 - no
death date, CRO
Martha Vailes, b 25 Sept

ALLEY (continued)
1850 - d 21 Aug 1933,
CRO
Matilda A, b 26 Oct 1815 -
d 17 Jan 1879, CRO
Mattie, b 8 Jan 1868 - d
10 May 1904, CRO
Nora, b 6 May 1880 - d 10
Sept 1880, CRO
Norina Carinne, b 11 Aug
1949 - d 25 July 1951,
CRO
W C, b 3 Feb 1877 - d 8
Aug 1888, CRO
William, b 16 Dec 1846 - d
26 Jan 1921, CRO
William Garland, b 13 July
1910 - d 30 May 1959,
CRO
ALLISON, Ernest D, d 3 Sept
1974, WRC
ALVARD, Curtis, M, b 15
July 1831 - d 6 Sept
1907, DRL
AMOS, Ellen, b 27 Apr 1879
- d 19 May 1952, AMS
AMRINE, Della M, b 31 March
1905 - no death date,
NWP
Horace B, b 10 Apr 1875 -
d 11 Nov 1970, NWP
ANDERSON, Addie Gertrude, b
6 May 1906 - d 10 May
1906, UNG
Adra L, b 1893 - d 1962,
UNG
Albert, b -- March 1918 -
d 12 Apr 1958, DVS
Alfred, Pvt 38 Reb US, Vol
Inf b 25 Oct 1878 - d
16 Dec 1952, UNG
Amanda W, b 11 Sept 1917 -
no death date, WRC
Barbara, b 10 May 1840 - d
15 Oct 1895, ELZ
Callie E, b 18 July 1895 -
d 25 Nov 1913, UNG
Clara J, b 4 Feb 1888 - d

ANDERSON (continued)
16 March 1970, WRC
Dorien, b 25 June 1936 - d
22 Nov 1966, DRL
Franklin S, b 1860 - d
1937, WRC
Fred J, b 1882 - d 1971,
CLC
Geo B, b 9 Nov 1888 - d 14
Jun 1930, DVS
Henry, b 23 Nov 1976, ae
58y, ALB
Henry W, b 23 Apr 1882 - d
29 Sept 1965, WRC
Henry W, b 1862 - d 1938,
WRC
Henry Walter, Tenn WWII, b
4 Apr 1917 - d 9 May
1956, WRC
Imagene E, b 1 Aug 1912 -
d 31 Aug 1936, WRC
Ina, b 16 Nov 1890 - d 8
July 1917, MRR
Infant, no dates, UNG
John A, b 20 Aug 1832 - d
8 Apr 1898, ELZ
Leonia, b 24 Jan 1881 - d
7 Apr 1941, BRR
Linda K, b 18 Sept 1928 -
4 Apr 1929, WRC
Liza Ann, b 26 July 1855 -
d 19 June 1929, UNG
Luan, b 15 Oct 1866 - d 12
Jan 1958, SNB
Marion B, b 4 March 1924 -
d 22 Apr 1925, WRC
Martha, b 1874 - d 1944,
MLC
Mary A, b 6 Feb 1875 - d
30 May 1876, LBR
Mary E, b 5 May 1886 - d
12 Apr 1912, UNG
Mitchell H, b 16 Apr 1886
- d 11 Nov 1918, MRR
Nellie R, b 1860 - d 1945,
WRC
Ollie M, b 1885 - d 1963,
CLC

ANDERSON (continued)
Parzeda, b 8 Aug 1886 - d
27 June 1949, DVS
Perry F, b 5 Dec 1882 - d
10 July 1945, UNG
Ray R, b 8 March 1899 - d
23 Dec 1966, CRO
Ray S, b 3 Dec 1916 - d 11
May 1934, MRR
Roscoe, b 31 July 1897 - d
4 Jan 1922, BRR
Smith, b 2 Oct 1872 - d 13
Dec 1942, BRR
T L, b 11 March 1876 - d
25 March 1900, SHD
Tennessee Hall, b 12 March
1887 - d 15 Apr 1976,
ALB
Thomas A, b 1908 - d 1941,
MLC
William H, b 16 Apr 1854 -
d 10 Nov 1921, UNG
William J, b 1889 - d
1961, UNG
William Rufus, d 5 May
1975, ae 65y, DRL
ANGEL, Wanda Jane, b 1928 -
d 1972, CRO
APLEGATE, Mary Joyce, b 28
June 1905 - d 2 July
1905, SNB
ARCHER, Charlotte M, b 8
Apr 1843 - d 26 Nov
1907, DRL
Pearcy E, b 16 Dec 1845 -
d 6 Feb 1903, DRL
ARK, Frank A, b 12 Sept
1888 - d 18 Feb 1942,
CRO
ARMES, A Florence, b 20 Aug
1890 - no death date,
LNE
Aaron, b 23 Sept 1883 - d
21 Apr 1958, LNE
Albert, b 22 Feb 1903 - no
death date, NWP
Alvin, 1951, MLC
Arbania G, b 22 Aug 1903 -

ARMES (continued)
no death date, NWP
Ardelia, b 3 June 1888 - d
20 Dec 1950, NWP
Ava, b 13 Dec 1913 - d 19
Feb 1976, NWP
Bard, b 23 May 1907 - d 5
Aug 1933, UNN
Bard, b 23 May 1907 - d 5
Aug 1933, UNN
Beverly, 25 May 1960 , NWP
Blanche, b 9 Oct 1910 - d
6 May 1955, NWP
Carlie, d 7 Apr 1978, ae
69y, NWP
Casey J, b 1922 - d 1949,
NWP
Charles Finley, d 27 June
1981, ae 62y, NWP
Clara, b 8 Jan 1868 - d 6
Jan 1937, UNN
Clarence Benton, d 10 Oct
1977, ae 78y, NWP
Cora Lee, b 25 Jan 1892 -
d 26 Oct 1902, OLP
Delbert, b 12 Oct 1940 - d
24 Feb 1944, UNN
Devinia F, b 1859 - d
1882, OLP
Dolph P, b 6 Sept 1902 - d
2 May 1958, NWP
Donald, d 11 March 1952,
NWP
Dora, b 10 June 1908 - no
death date, NWP
Elbert, b 27 Feb 1904 - d
31 May 1969, NWP
Elizabeth, b 1863 - d
1952, OLP
Frances, b 4 Feb 1906 - d
6 May 1958, BRZ
Frank, b 7 June 1903 - d
16 Aug 1904, OLP
Fred J, b 10 Jan 1855 - d
3 Aug 1906, OLP
Grant, b 28 Aug 1915 - d
31 July 1969, FRV
Harlan, b 18 Jan 1917 - d

ARMES (continued)
21 March 1967, NWP
Harrison R, b 1888 - d
1967, NWP
Hillie, b 1913 - d 1966,
NWP
Hiram, b 1858 - d 1938,
OLP
Ira, b 17 Dec 1885 - no
death date, NWP
James B, no dates, OLP
James F, b 8 May 1902 - d
19 June 1902, OLP
James H, b 1881 - d 1965,
BRZ
James Kirlie, d 12 Dec
1979, ae 57y, NWP
Jane, b 7 June 1906 - no
death date, OLP
John C, b 6 June 1884 - d
10 May 1940, NWP
John S, b 1 Feb 1895 - d
25 Nov 1961, NWP
Julia, b 18 May 1876 - d
19 June 1970, NWP
Kirlen, Cpl H Co, 46th Inf
WWI b 19 Nov 1894 - d 5
Jan 1968, LBR
Lillie Mae, b&d 18 Nov
1946, MLC
Lonas C, d 29 March 1977,
ae 80y, PTC
Louis Edward, BM3 USNR,
WWII b 16 March 1919 -
d 3 March 1951, NWP
Lucinda, b 5 June 1907 -
no death date, LBR
Madie, b 1 Feb 1910 - no
death date, NWP
Mahala C, b 6 June 1870 -
d 21 Sept 190, OLP
Martha J, b 26 May 1884 -
d 17 Aug 1953, NWP
Mary T, b 29 March 1834 -
d 25 Nov 1903, OLP
Matilda F, b 25 March 1861
- d 15 Jan 1888, OLP
Mattie, b 22 Feb 1923 - no

ARMES (continued)
    death date, NWP
  Mitchell, b 1 May 1898 - d
    8 Sept 1963, NWP
  Morgan L, b 1913 - d 1966,
    NWP
  Morgan L Jr, b 1942 - d 31
    Oct 1973, NWP
  Nellie, b 6 June 1904 - d
    14 June 1905, OLP
  Pat, d 8 July 1879, ae
    67y, NWP
  Perry, b 1881 - no death
    date, NWP
  Polly, d 2 March 1938, NWP
  Randolph, b 1962 - d 1964,
    EST
  Raymond, b 1902 - d 1945,
    OLP
  Rexie Leo, b 27 Nov 1945 -
    d 15 Nov 1966, UNN
  Robert L, b 1934 - d 1975,
    NWP
  Rosa L, b 1888 - d 1959,
    NWP
  Roxie A, b 1894 - d 1970,
    NWP
  Ruth, d 22 Apr 1981, ae
    79y, NWP
  Sabe, b 23 May 1906 - d 19
    May 1963, NWP
  Sarah L, 1962, LBR
  Sidney, b 4 Apr 1946 - d
    17 Feb 1963, NWP
  Smith, b 15 Nov 1915 - d
    28 March 1973, NWP
  Steve, b 16 Jan 1945 - d
    17 Feb 1963, NWP
  Tennessee, b 1887 - d
    1969, LBR
  Thos J, b 14 May 1910 - d
    8 Aug 1944, UNN
  W P, b 8 March 1868 - no
    death date, NWP
  Weldon, d 15 March 1978,
    ae 59y, LBR
  Wiley, b 8 Apr 1876 - d 4
    Feb 1940, NWP

ARMS, Charlie M, d 25 Feb
    1970, ae 73y, BRZ
ARNOLD, Henry C, b 1883 -
    no death date, SNB
  Sybl Hood, b 4 Oct 1915 -
    d 24 Aug 1949, LNE
ASHE, Jennie, b 8 Dec 1864
    - d 18 Aug 1924, SNB
ASHER, Mary, d 4 Apr 1911,
    ae 60y, FLF
  Samuel, b 1833 - d 15 Apr
    1907, FLF
ASHLEY, 2 Infants, no
    dates, MSG
  Alvin Hill, b 3 Apr 1919 -
    d 28 March 1964, MSG
  Angeline, b 10 Jan 1887 -
    d 28 July 1916, OLP
  Charles, Pfc 21 Inf 24 Div
    Korea b 11 Apr 1929 - d
    19 Oct 1951, NWP
  David, b 27 Apr 1859, PNY
  Ernest, b 17 Feb 1905 - d
    11 June 1941, NWP
  Flora, b 11 Sept 1891 - d
    11 Jan 1891, MSG
  Harry H, b 25 Oct 1884 - d
    22 Dec 1960, NWP
  Ira Lee, d ae 46y, NWP
  Joseph Ray, b 25 July 1931
    - d 16 Apr 1953, NWP
  Lillie V, b 6 Aug 1896 - d
    20 March 1969, NWP
  Maggie L, b 25 July 1884 -
    d 22 July 1974, UNG
  Matilda, b 1853 - d 1926,
    DRM
  N M, b 24 May 1838 - d 29
    Aug 1901, PNY
  Ollis, b 9 June 1886 - d
    18 Apr 1907, OLP
  Samuel P, b 29 June 1876 -
    d 27 March 1952, UNG
  Sarah A, b 3 March 1834 -
    d 21 Aug 1914, PNY
  Treely J, b 1884 - d 1963,
    PNY
ASLINGER, Alice, b 8 Sept

ASLINGER (continued)
1922 – no death date, LBR

Alice, b 8 Sept 1922 – no death date, LBR

Henry, b 31 March 1917 – d 15 Jan 1975, LBR

ATKINSON, Lourd Eugene, b&d 10 July 1943, UNG

AURIN, J W, b 4 Apr 1855 – d 22 July 1883, LBR

Martha J, b 18 Dec 1825 – d 26 July 1904, LBR

AUSTIN, Mother, b 1863 – d 1937, CRO

AYTES, Amos, b 6 July 1880 – d 16 July 1943, PTC

Charles M, b 1886 – d 1956, BRN

Clayton M, b 26 Jan 1907 – d 6 Feb 1973, FRN

Eli H, b 13 Feb 1883 – d 15 March 1957, BRN

F M, b 5 Oct 1850 – d 21 June 1893, BRN

Flossie, b 7 March 1909 – no death date, FRN

Grace S, b 11 Sept 1880 – d 31 Dec 1912, PTC

Inas L, b 5 Aug 1888 – d 5 Dec 1971, BRN

Jerry Ray, b 30 June 1949 – d 12 Oct 1974, FRN

Johnny Mack, b 21 July 1952 – d 17 Aug 1952, PTC

Larry E, b 2 Dec 1962 – d 23 Feb 1963, PTC

Libbie, b 16 Sept 1888 – d 10 March 1920, PTC

Perry O, b 8 Jan 1877 – d 6 March 1957, CLC

Rita F, b 1 Aug 1961 – d 7 Nov 1961, PTC

Ronald Marion Jr, d 22 Jan 1978, ae 71y, FRN

S A, b 16 Dec 1846 – d 3 Jan 1923, BRN

AYTES (continued)
Stephen S, b 13 March 1956 – d 14 March 1956, PTC

Susie L, b 2 Dec 1880 – d 23 Dec 1934, CLC

Willard Adams, b 12 Aug 1917 – d 5 July 1949, BRN

Wright, b 1918 – d 8 Sept 1976, BRN

BABB, Arthur L, b Feb 1881 – d 20 May 1963, WRC

Fanni Tishner, b 10 Nov 1893 – no death date, WRC

BABCOCK, Cevalla L, b 30 Oct 1844 – d 29 Sept 1915, BRR

Clarence E, b 24 July 1882 – d 20 May 1949, BRR

George C, b 14 Apr 1880 – d 30 Sept 1959, BRR

George W, b 25 June 1844 – d 17 March 1922, BRR

Hannah A, b 10 Feb 1886 – d 30 Oct 1959, BRR

Mary Bullard, b 7 May 1882 – d 2 May 1967, BRR

Orlon, no dates, BRR

Phenie C, b 23 Sept 1846 – d 27 Dec 1921, BRR

BAGWELL, Charles Henry, b 14 March 1887 – d 9 Aug 1952, CLH

Lizzie Gribble, b 19 July 1878 – d 3 Aug 1934, CLH

Margaret, b 23 Nov 1847 – d 24 Nov 1934, CLH

BAILEY, Edward, b 25 May 1876 – d 20 Feb 1910, CBJ

BAKER, Fanden, b 27 May 1860 – d 27 July 1883, WRC

BALES, Artelia, b 10 Dec 1883 – d 6 Feb 1906, EST

Bert Jr, b&d 27 Nov 1923, JCJ

BALES (continued)
Bert W, b 5 Apr 1901 - d 24 Oct 1970, EST
Carolyn Sue, b 1 Apr 1941 - d 15 Feb 1944, LNE
Charles O, b 21 June 1892 - d 7 Sept 1945, DRL
Ida, b 11 July 1899 - no death date, EST
Isabella, b 10 May 1869 - d 2 Nov 1900, DRL
Jessie K Ryon, b 30 May 1900 - no death date, DRL
BALLINGER, John C Jr, b 17 Sept 1925 - d 8 Nov 1931, MRR
Sarah P, b 13 Jan 1825 - d 5 Dec 1910, SNB
BANYARD, Mary W, d 19 Feb 1898, DRL
BARBER, Mildred M, b 19 Feb 1918 - d 6 Dec 1976, EST
Wiley, b 8 June 1908 - no death date, EST
BARDILL, Albert D, b 5 June 1922 - no death date, WMG
Alfred E, b&d 15 Nov 1930, WRC
Andrew J, b 1877 - d 1936, WRC
Anna Kate, b 20 Apr 1845 - d 5 May 1902, WRC
Anna M, b 1879 - d 1963, WRC
Annie, b 28 Jan 1881 - 2 Feb 1947, WRC
Benjamin, Sgt Co B Tenn Inf Sp/Am War, WRC
Betty Ann, b Jan 1808 - d 11 Aug 1885, WRC
Christian, b 16 June 1852 - d 18 Feb 1950, WRC
Christian G, b 8 May 1960 - d 8 Oct 1960, WRC
Christian, s/o Christian & Ida, b 7 Apr 1894 - d 28

BARDILL (continued)
May 1894, WRC
Deborah Lynn, b 19 Oct 1954 - d 20 Oct 1954, WRC
F M (Fritz), b 3 Jan 1877 - d 11 July 1974, WRC
Fred G, b 9 Dec 1906 - d 11 March 1966, WRC
Gus C, b 28 March 1886 - d 7 Nov 1956, WRC
Ida, b 19 Dec 1851 - d 1 Apr 1930, WRC
John Sr, s/o Peter & Mary, b 6 July 1892 - d 9 March 1931, WRC
Lena, b 26 Jan 1910 - d 4 June 1970, WRC
Margaret A, d/o Christian & Ida, b 23 July 1879 - d 16 March 1897, WRC
Margaret Mitz, b 1 Jan 1822 - d 20 Aug 1902, WRC
Mary N, b 2 May 1886 - d 13 Jan 1961, WRC
Pauline Goldberg, b 29 May 1859 - d 30 March 1945, MSG
Peter L, b -- Dec 1849 - d 24 July 1915, MSG
Rosa L, d/o Christian & Ida, b 14 Aug 1889 - d 20 Oct 1899, WRC
Walter John, TN WWI Pvt Bty E 76 Fld Art, b 15 Dec 1895 - d 6 Feb 1957, WRC
Willie Kate, b 9 Dec 1922 - d 27 Sept 1972, WMG
BARDLEY, G C, b 1881 - d 1960, NWP
BARGE, Wm, Co A 1st TN Inf, no dates, DVS
BARGER, Betty Lou, b 31 March 1950 - d 3 Apr 1950, PLR
Bobby Laura, b 22 Nov 1937

9

BARGER (continued)
- d 2 Apr 1938, UNN
Elizabeth, b 27 May 1853 -
d 23 Oct 1928, UNN
Frank C, b 1 May 1916 - d
10 Aug 1929, UNN
Ida, b 11 Sept 1878 - d 21
Sept 1921, UNN
J P, b 15 Nov 1879 - d 16
July 1958, UNN
James A, b 24 Feb 1876 - d
18 Dec 1954, UNN
Lenora Bran, b 9 Sept 1887
- d 15 Nov 1968, BRN
M Loururnia, b 25 June
1880 - d 24 Feb 1952,
UNN
Malinda Williams, b 1 May
1881 - d 19 Dec 1970,
UNN
Martha T, b 25 July 1856 -
d 20 Nov 1911, UNN
Maude Ellen, b 26 July
1902 - d 26 Dec 1911,
MNT
Nobis, b 1898 - d 1978,
PLR
Oliver M, b 26 Aug 1904 -
d 14 Sept 1973, MNT
Robert, b 28 Jan 1923 - d
29 May 1946, PNY
Ross Ray, d 23 Sept 1977,
ae 60y, LBR
Sam, b 3 June 1887 - d 4
Aug 1915, PNY
Samuel, b 14 Oct 1843 - d
11 Jan 1903, UNN
Samuel M, b 4 May 1883 - d
24 Oct 1936, UNN
Sarah, b 5 Aug 1894 - d 23
Nov 1945, PNY
Sarah F, b 5 July 1877 - d
30 Dec 1918, MNT
Vernon, b&d 25 Apr 1915,
MNT
W H, b 1 Aug 1877 - d 3
May 1932, MNT
William C, b&d 6 June

BARGER (continued)
1917, MNT
William Floyd, b 5 July
1911 - d 12 May 1912,
MNT
Z T, b 5 Nov 1848 - d 30
June 1921, UNN
BARGES, Elmo Duncan, b 28
Feb 1900 - d 27 March
1938, UNN
Francis, b 14 May 1872 - d
16 Sept 1941, BRR
H C, b 3 March 1872 - d 15
Jan 1939, BRR
Nannie E, b 22 June 1914 -
d 14 Oct 1939, MNT
BARGETSEE, Catherine, d 19
Oct 1867, ae 78y, WRC
BARGETZY, Docia, b 30 Dec
1883 - no death date,
UNN
John, b 7 Apr 1874 - d 4
Apr 1952, UNN
Louise, b 11 March 1903 -
d 3 Oct 1904, UNN
Simeon, b 1 Apr 1852 - d
10 July 1874, UNN
BARKLA, Dovie, b 1883 - d
1963, CRO
BARNAWELL, Lawrence W, b
1902 - d 1961, EST
BARNES, Fred J, d 1 Sept
1953, ae 6y, PLR
Helen Gould, b 7 Oct 1921
- d 8 July 1928, SNB
John Columbus, Sgt 7 Inf,
3 Div WWI b 13 Feb 1874
- d 18 Jan 1947, SNB
BARNETT, Arthur Buck, b 10
Oct 1895 - d 5 May 1952,
UNG
Bessie, b 1896 - no death
date, BRN
Bessie, b 30 Oct 1925 - d
19 June 1926, ELZ
Denny Lee, b 25 June 1940
- d 10 June 1942, DRL
Fehcia Joy Our Baby, 1966,

BARNETT (continued)
FLR
G W Sr, b 9 March 1855 - d
15 Sept 1929, PTC
Harry, b 1937 - d 1966,
BRN
James Thomas, b 23 Sept
1895 - d 22 Apr 1955,
PTC
Oma, b 24 Feb 1929 - d 27
Aug 1931, ELZ
Paris S, d 25 Jan 1976, ae
88y, RGB
Ritta, b 3 May 1854 - d 25
Oct 1920, PTC
Shirley Gene, b 7 Nov 1938
- d 30 Jan 1937, ELZ
Sylvan, b 1881 - d 1961,
BRN
BARNS, Flora, b 8 June 1916
- d 7 Nov 1956, WRC
Floyd Russel, b 1940 - d
1941, CRO
Jackson I, b 24 May 1852 -
d 6 July 1924, CRO
John, b 24 Nov 1839 - d 22
Nov 1937, PLR
Juda F, b 6 May 1868 - d
21 Feb 1927, CRO
Lucy B, b 27 July 1865 - d
29 Dec 1945, PLR
Luther F, b 6 June 1888 -
d 1 Jan 1931, CRO
Rufus M, 26 March 1938 -
no other date, LNE
Stella Mae, b 1890 - d
1966, LNE
BARRY, Dennis F, b 24 Apr
1851 - d 12 March 1928,
OLP
Florence D, b 5 June 1879
- d 19 Apr 1956, DVS
Frank, Pvt 55th Inv 7th,
Div 5 June 1930, OLP
Howard L, Pvt Co A 423 Inf
WWII b 24 July 1923 - d
29 Jan 1970, NWP
James T, b 9 Aug 1889 - d

BARRY (continued)
7 Nov 1960, DVS
Manie, d 15 Feb 1980, ae
85y, NWP
Margaret, b 13 June 1868 -
d 31 Oct 1921, OLP
BARTON, Addie, b 1874 - d
1946, WRC
Amy Garrett, d 29 July
1977, ae 76y, ELZ
Earl, b 1900 - d 19 July
1973, ELZ
Oscar, b 1871 - d 1943,
WRC
BASLER, Ann Wilson, b 30
Aug 1902 - d 23 Nov
1921, UNN
Anna, b Germany - d 12
March 1898, WRC
Bonnie Metcalf, b 2 Aug
1908 - d 23 Feb 1939,
OLP
Carolyn Sue, b 9 Sept 1936
- d 25 March 1938, NWP
Fred, b 1 Jan 1901 - d 1
Sept 1973, WRC
Fred W, d 1 Sept 1973, ae
72y, WRC
Harry, b 1889 - d 1966,
BRZ
Harvey A, b 16 Dec 1887 -
d 20 May 1858, WRC
Jerry David, b 1 Sept 1944
- d 29 Nov 1949, WRC
John, b - 3 Oct 1824 - d
23 Aug 1898, WRC
John O, b 5 Oct 1879 - d 2
Oct 1920, WRC
John T, d 22 Aug 1977, WRC
Martin G, b 18 June 1903 -
d 15 March 1971, NWP
Millie L, b 9 March 1894 -
d 27 March 1944, WRC
Nora, b 20 Aug 1913 - d 19
Sept 1953, NWP
Ovette Elaine, b 30 Apr
1942 - d 1 May 1942, NWP
Velda Kay, b 15 Nov 1946 -

BASLER (continued)
  d 17 Feb 1947, WRC
  William Dean, d 25 May
    1973, ae 53y, WRC
  Willis Dean, b 5 Jan 1920
    - d 26 May 1973, NWP
BASTAIN, Lila M, b 10 Nov
  1880 - no death date,
  NWP
  Rubin R, b 18 Sept 1880 -
    d 13 Oct 1943, NWP
BATE, Edith, b 1872 - d
  1962, DRL
  Joseph C, b -- Sept 1850 -
    d -- Sept 1910, DRL
BATES, Betty Ann, b 15 Oct
  1887 - d 16 July 1943,
  WRC
  Charles O, b 15 Feb 1883 -
    d 18 June 1930, MNT
BAUGHMAN, George W, b 13
  May 1881 - d 23 Sept
  1961, PNY
  Iva W, b 10 Jan 1910 - no
    death date, PNY
  Patricia, b 1 Nov 1936 - d
    12 July 1940, PNY
BAYLESS, Gertrude L, d 20
  Jan 1980, ae 66y, CRO
BEACH, Artie D, d 4 May
  1950, ae 22y, PLR
BEARD, Ada, b 1965 - d
  1972, MSG
  Infant Dau, 6 Jan 1946,
    MSG
  Mary, b 26 July 1944 - d 5
    Feb 1945, MSG
  Pauline, 17 March 1948,
    MSG
BEASLEY, Andrew, b 1892 - d
  1950, WRC
  Andrew Jack, d 2 Nov 1974,
    51y, WMG
  Bessie, b 1892 - d 1969,
    WRC
  Ida, d 30 March 1976, ae
    72y, DRL
  John W, b 1854 - d 1938,

BEASLEY (continued)
  DRL
  Marie, b 12 June 1948 -
    stone broken, WRC
  Mary E, b 1971 - d 3 July
    1973, FLR
  Nancy E, b 1847 - d 1896,
    DRL
  Ray, b 6 Feb 1927 - d 28
    Sept 1928, OLP
BEATLY, Alma D, b 6 June
  1906 - d 24 Nov 1969,
  UNG
  Eliza Jane, b 16 Jan 1881
    - d 22 Jan 1966, UNG
  Eva June, b 7 July 1940 -
    d 4 Oct 1940, UNG
  Infant, 8 May 1939, UNG
  Jess C, b 24 May 1907 - no
    death date, UNG
  John M, b 16 Jan 1867 - d
    22 Jan 1945, UNG
  Lois Mogene, b 20 Sept
    1936 - d 14 Oct 1936,
    UNG
BEATTY, Doyle R, d 16 July
  1978, ae 34y, UNG
BEATTY, Marcus, b 1961 - d
  1968, CHN
BEATY, Annie Webb, b 6 July
  1895 - d 2 Oct 1974, WBB
  Jones, b 1896 - d 1945,
    DRL
  Maj Dave, b 6 June 1872 -
    d 11 Dec 1958, WBB
  Olive A, b 28 Apr 1933 - d
    3 Aug 1935, BRD
BECK, Edwin E, b 1910 - d
  1963, WRC
  Ollie Hatcherson, b 1888 -
    d 1956, SNB
  Vera, b 1916 - no death
    date, WRC
BEDFORD, Forbett C, MO MM
  WWII, b 27 March 1913 -
  d 7 Jan 1968, OOO
  Lillie L, b 22 July 1897 -
    d 24 May 1970, CBJ

BEDFORD (continued)

Torbett C, b 27 March 1913
- d 7 Jan 1968, WMG

William R, b 4 Aug 1911 -
no death date, CBJ

William T, b 3 Apr 1887 -
d 25 July 1955, CBJ

BEECH, Leola, d 13 Oct
1941, ae ?, PLR

Piney ?, d 28 Jan 1941, ae
84y 7mo, PLR

BEENE, Curtis Ray, b 1940 -
d 31 Aug 1973, NWP

George T, b 18 Nov 1888 -
d 14 March 1952, DRL

Georgie Parker, b 5 Aug
1880 - d 19 Feb 1968,
NWP

John, b 22 March 1857 - d
23 March 1924, OLP

John Blive, b 19 Oct 1883
- d 11 May 1974, OLP

Kirk D, b 1891 - d 1967,
WMG

Kittie, b 19 Dec 1859 - d
6 Feb 1946, OLP

Luke, b 27 Jan 1901 - d 3
May 1927, OLP

Lula A, b 1891 - d 24 Aug
1977, WMG

Mart R, b 12 March 1886 -
d 11 Jan 1913, OLP

Mary Florence, b 15 Feb
1884 - d 16 Apr 1974,
OLP

Minnie Elizabeth, d 5 Feb
---- - ae 57y, WRC

William Jacob, b 27 March
1879 - d 28 Jan 1939,
NWP

Wilta, b 19 Aug 1891 - no
death date, DRL

BEKKEDAHL, Amiel M, d 22
Dec 1900, ae 26y 4mo,
PTC

Knut K, d 26 Apr 1901, ae
75y, PTC

BENNETT, Edd, b 25 May 1889

BENNETT (continued)
- 15 Aug 1912, OLP

BENSTED, John Theodore, ae
67y, RGB

BENTLED, Benj Thomas, b
1855 - d 1925, RGB

BERGMAN, Esther, b 1951 - d
1971, UNG

BERRY, Anna May Tilley, b
1843 - d 1925, RGB

Charles E, b 8 Apr 1929 -
d 17 Jan 1957, RGB

Eva, d 5 Oct 1952, ae 80y
2mo, RGB

George W, Co B 46 MS Mil
Inf b 17 Feb 1837 - d
24 Aug 1928, RGB

James, b 7 Feb 1876 - no
death date, BRW

Jeremiah, Co F 7th TN Mtd
Inf Mil Stone, RGB

Lines s/o Geo W, dates
illegible, RGB

Nancy C, b 12 Aug 1842 - d
14 Nov 1908, RGB

Polly, b 11 Jan 1880 - d
25 Jan 1951, BRW

Rosie, b 4 Apr 1932 - no
death date, RGB

BERTRAM, Alvin Willard,
1937, RGB

Bene L, b 1 Dec 1876 - d
18 Jan 1899, RGB

Benedict J, b 15 Feb 1897
- d 21 Feb 1959, SNB

Deborah K, b 2 Jan 1879 -
d 21 Jan 1933, RGB

Edward M, b 21 Sept 1885 -
d 1 May 1954, RGB

Elbert Willard, b 1928,
RGB

Electa A, b 10 July 1874 -
d 21 Nov 1951, SNB

George Adam, 1931, RGB

Howard, b 1890 - d 1951,
RGB

Infant Baby, b&d 21 June
1939, RGB

13

BERTRAM (continued)
Jack H, b 21 June 1926 - d
31 Oct 1927, RGB
James L, b 21 March 1923 -
d 27 March 1933, RGB
Jessie, b 24 Feb 1898 - d
26 Dec 1940, RGB
Juanita R, b 25 Jan 1922 -
no death date, RGB
Lena Imogene, b 1925 - d
1926, RGB
Mary Ellen, b 23 Aug 1943
- d 5 Aug 1945, RGB
Maudie, b 1896 - d 1931,
RGB
Nettie, b 11 Feb 1887 - no
death date, RGB
Othnel, S2 USNR WWII, b 1
Sept 1920 - d 26 Feb
1964, RGB
Samuel Adkins, b 24 Apr
1871 - d 18 Nov 1945,
SNB
Spencer, b 8 Apr 1882 - d
8 Apr 1955, RGB
Velma B, b 1916 - d 1969,
RGB
Vera Katherine, b 13 Jan
1919 - d 10 Aug 1938,
SNB
Wm Dennis, b 2 Oct 1888 -
d 23 March 1967, RGB
Zelphy Cath, b 20 Feb 1923
- d 9 May 1923, RGB
BERTRAND, Cora Ellen, b 1
Nov 1896 - no death
date, RGB
BILBREY, Otis J, b 22 Dec
1917 - d 1 Oct 1918, SNB
BINESH, Bernard, b 17 Aug
1892 - d 11 Sept 1964,
BRR
BINGHAM, Adra, b 27 July
1885 - d 15 June 1923,
LBR
Avery, b 22 Feb 1931 - d
24 Jan 1938, MNT
Barbara Ann, b 15 Sept

BINGHAM (continued)
1916 - d 12 Feb 1956,
WRC
Ben David, b 1915 - d
1971, WRC
Ben F, b 9 Sept 1878 - d
28 Feb 1941, WRC
Bertie (farmer), b 30 Nov
1887 - d 6 Feb 1974, CRO
Carl W, b 1920 - d 1963,
LBR
Carr, b 23 Sept 1919 - d
15 Dec 1970, CRO
Charles Frederick, d 31
Jan 1955, ae 64y, CRO
Charles T, b 5 May 1890 -
d 31 Jan 1955, CRO
Ellis E, b 3 July 1906 - d
10 March 1972, CRO
F F, b 5 June 1886 - d 10
July 1886, CRO
Helen K(or R), b 24 Jan
1921 - no death date,
CRO
Henry, b 28 Apr 1888 - d 8
Oct 1963, CRO
Hersatul E, b 19 Apr 1922
- d 7 Aug 1939, CRO
Hue, s/o John & Bertie,
------, CRO
Ida, d 14 Apr 1980, ae
82y, CRO
Ida Grasham, b 15 Sept
1897 - d 14 Apr 1980,
CRO
Ida Mae, b 6 June 1875 - d
14 Apr 1980, CRO
Infant, d/o John & Bertie,
b&d 23 March 1912, CRO
Infant, s/o John & Bertie,
b&d 21 Feb 1921, CRO
Jack, d 11 Sept 1978, ae
68y, WRC
James Harry, b 17 Sept
1895 - d 19 Jan 1974,
CRO
John, b 20 Apr 1886 - no
death date, WRC

BINGHAM (continued)
John H, b 2 Feb 1880 - d 31 May 1963, CRO
John W, b 1858 - d 1939, CRO
Judson A, b 16 July 1859 - d 10 Sept 1935, CRO
Lee Annah, b 13 Dec 1868 - d 5 March 1939, CRO
Lee, s/o John & Bertie, ------, CRO
Lilin R, b 12 May 1892 - no death date, WRC
Maggie, b 24 Feb 1894 - d 29 March 1912, CRO
Marie, b 22 Dec 1907 - no death date, CRO
Mary Goldston, b 1863 - d 1939, CRO
Mattie M, b 6 Jan 1893 - 2 27 Sept 1976, CRO
Minnie, d 26 Oct 1975, ae 93y, WMG
Minnie Bardell, b 12 Oct 1882 - d 26 Oct 1975, WRC
Myrtle Vesper, b 13 Nov 1896 - d 3 March 1967, WRC
Nellie, b 1896 - d 1923, LBR
Patsey, b 10 Oct 1865 - d 3 July 1942, CRO
Perry, b 2 Aug 1923 - d 5 March 1938, CRO
Rice, b 18 March 1861 - d 9 Feb 1936, CRO
Susan, b 1 Aug 1837 - d 6 Feb 1903, MNT
W A, b 1 Nov 1883 - d 3 Feb 1884, CRO
William G, b 8 Nov 1891 - d 11 March 1951, WRC
BISHOP, ----, broken stone, PTC
A M, b 15 May 1858 - d 20 March 1917, PTC
Florence A, b 30 July 1894

BISHOP (continued)
- d 21 Oct 1898, PTC
Helen, d 30 July 1975, ae 58y, DRL
Kelvin Shawn, b&d 9 Nov 1965, DRL
Maynard C, d 27 Dec 1975, ae 76y, PTC
Michael Allen, d 12 Apr 1964, ae 1da, DRL
Nellie, b 5 Oct 1892 - d 8 Apr 1879 (error?), DRL
Rebecca J, b 19 Feb 1863 - d 23 Sept 1914, PTC
William A, b 29 Aug 1889 - d 10 June 1954, DRL
BLACK, Colquitt T, b 20 Nov 1875 - d 14 Apr 1914, WRC
Thomas, b 12 June 1899 - d 16 Aug 1912, WRJ
BLAIR, Benton O, d 22 Feb 1980, ae 62y, PLR
Felix, b 7 Feb 1930 - d 19 Aug 1936, PLR
Gertrude Jones, b 26 Sept 1895 - no death date, PLR
Glenn, b 17 June 1925 - d 19 Feb 1926, PLR
Infant d/o N R & Gertrude, 13 Apr 1919, PLR
Infant s/o NR & Gertrude, 19 Jan 1920, PLR
James Irwin, d 8 Jan 1977, ae 53y, PLR
Niram R, b 12 June 1894 - d 28 June 1963, PLR
BLAKE, Rosia, b 21 Nov 1834 - d 6 Sept 1929, CRO
Sarah, b 1867 - d 1938, MSG
BLAKELY, D R, b 1865 - d 1966, BRR
Sarah E, b 23 Sept 1876 - d 19 July 1939, BRR
BLALOCK, Henry C, b 7 March 1890 - d 17 March 1953,

BLALOCK (continued)
UNN
BLAZERR, Leland D, d 2 Nov 1976, ae 70y, WMG
BLB, Father (Bowlin?), no dates, PTC
Mother (Bowlin?), no dates, PTC
BLEVINS, Laura, b 1866 - d 1953, NWP
Madaline Beat, b 12 Feb 1899 - d 7 July 1899, NDK
Millard, b 1861 - d 1947, NWP
Orlena E, b 7 Oct 1879 - d 30 June 1899, NDK
Thomas C, b 15 Dec 1845 - d 1 May 1910, DVS
BOLES, Leon Clifton, b 1917 - d 1972, BRN
BOLIN, Haywood S, b 1877 - d 1956, RGB
BOLTON, Etta Honeycutt, b 25 March 1868 - d 5 July 1926, LBR
BONHAM, Anna Marie, d 2 Oct 1973, ae 66y, LNC
Edgar F, Pvt 46 Inf, 9 July 1936 - no other date, LNC
Elvira, b 20 June 1875 - d 6 Aug 1951, LNC
F G, b 28 Jan 1872 - d 24 July 1958, LNC
Felix Edward, Pvt 28 QM Co 28 Div b 12 March 1926 - d 4 Oct 1953, LNC
Gerald R, d 21 Apr 1977, ae 46y, LNC
Ola, GM 3 USNR WWII, b 15 Nov 1911 - d 13 Feb 1968, LNC
Richard, 1968 - no other date, LNC
Vester H, b 19 Jan 1902 - d 18 Feb 1963, LNC
BONIFACIUS, Anna Bardill, b

BONIFACIUS (continued)
5 June 1875 - d 21 July 1943, WRC
Carl W, d 19 Apr 1979, ae 82y, WRC
Carl W Jr, b 17 Oct 1921 - d 14 July 1933, WRC
Christina, b 24 July 1898 - d 20 Dec 1900, WRC
Daniel, b 1856 - d 1919, WRC
Daniel C Sr, b 31 July 1898 - d 21 Jan 1965, WRC
Ed H, b 12 Oct 1899 - d 20 July 1960, WRC
Elizabeth, b 1877 - d 1903, WRC
Ethel Howard, b 8 May 1900 - d 15 March 1972, WRC
George, Mess Sgt 61st Inf 5 Div WWII, d 20 July 1923, WRC
Gordon, b 4 June 1860 - d 30 Aug 1939, WRC
Henrietta C, d 20 July 1979, ae 40y, WRC
Inf Boy, b 6 Dec 1923 - d 7 Dec 1923, WRC
Inf Girl, b 9 Nov 1921 - d 9 Nov 1921, WRC
Jacob, b 15 Dec 1853 - d 4 May 1914, WRC
Patsy, b 18 Sept 1902 - no death date, WRC
Rebecca, b 12 Sept 1859 - d 22 Jan 1901, WRC
BOONE, Addie, b 16 Mar 1877 - d 10 Sept 1955, WRC
John, b 31 May 1852 - d 30 May 1926, UNN
Mary, b 16 Sept 1859 - d 6 Aug 1930, UNN
W N, b 15 July 1881 - no death date, WRC
BORDEN, Mary Ellen, b 26 Oct 1877 - d 17 Jan 1919, RGB

BOSHEARS, James Franklin, b
4 Oct 1886 - d 12 June
1964, DVS
Lawrence M, b 26 Oct 1911
- d 22 Jan 1929, DVS
BOSLAIN, Delia A, b 12 Nov
1917 - no death date,
NWP
Willie E, b 26 Sept 1910 -
d 21 Jan 1977, NWP
BOSTICH, Beatrice C, d 18
Oct 1975, ae 67y, CRO
BOSTON, Bessie Louie, b 26
May 1935 - d 12 July
1936, NWP
BOUHAM, Frances T, USA b 31
Jan 1879 - d 28 Apr
1911, DRL
BOURKHARD, Anna, b 8 Dec
1872 - d 17 Sept 1938,
DRL
Infant s/o H O, b&d 25
July 1909, DRL
BOURNE, Jennie, b 1878 - d
1926, CRO
BOWDEN, John, b 19 Nov 1842
- d 5 June 1912, BRR
BOWLES, A J, b 28 June 1886
- d 16 March 1951, WRC
Mamie Lee, b 23 Sept 1892
- d 5 Feb 1961, WRC
Nina, b 1867 - d 1947, WRC
BOWLIN, David, b 3 May 1883
- d 9 Sept 1948, PNY
Infant, b&d 1967, MSG
John Hayden, b 8 March
1894 - d 12 Sept 1961,
PTC
Willie, b 1881 - d 1966,
DRM
BOWMAN, John M, b 24 June
1900 - d 25 Jan 1948,
WBB
Johnnie Sue, b 1 June 1934
- d 4 Oct 1941, WBB
Sarah A, b 29 Feb 1916 -
no death date, WBB
Vina, b 29 Dec 1879 - d 22

BOWMAN (continued)
Oct 1918, WRC
BOWMER, Buster, b 19 Jan
1885 - d 5 Sept 1972,
DRL
Elmira, b 3 Oct 1877 - d 1
Apr 1954, DRL
Gilbert R, b 6 Oct 1891 -
d 16 June 1892, DRL
Infant d/o W & L J, b 4
Aug 1894, DRL
John H, b 31 March 1824 -
d 20 June 1891, DRL
Lucinda J, b 26 July 1851
- d 21 Aug 1914, DRL
Martha, b 1915 - d 1936,
DRL
Ollie, b 1922 - d 1968,
DRL
Parilda, b 25 June 1860 -
d 14 March 1930, BRR
Thomas, b 6 Jan 1856 - d 4
Apr 1934, BRR
William, b 26 Apr 1848 - d
27 July 1917, DRL
Wm Patrick, b 1905 - d
1970, DRL
BOYD, Arthur Allen, d 30
Dec 1975, ae 73y, UNN
Frank D, b 1902 - d 1942,
DVS
BRADEN, Rachel, b 1852 - d
1925, DVS
Robert M, b 1844 - d 1924,
DVS
William I, b 7 May 1877 -
d 7 Nov 1905, DVS
BRADLEY, Infant s/o S M, no
dates, OLP
Judson D, d 1 May 1977, ae
70y, NWP
Robert T, d 12 March 1978,
ae 65y, NWP
BRADSHAW, C T, b 1920 - d
1968, NWP
Hannah, b 30 March 1872 -
d 24 March 1956, WRC
John C, b 1875 - d 1953,

BRADSHAW (continued)
WRJ
Joseph, b 2 March 1817 - d
31 Jan 1897, UNN
Lenora J, d 19 Aug 1888,
ae 40y 2mo, UNN
Maggie D Jones, b 4 Dec
1885 - d 14 June 1967,
WRJ
Mary A, d 16 May 1889, ae
40y 4mo, LBR
Saluda, b 10 July 1826 - d
29 Jan 1897, UNN
Samuel, b 1905 - d 1907,
PNY
Samuel C, b 14 Feb 1834 -
d 16 May 1911, UNN
Sarah J, b 14 Aug 1880 - d
29 Sept 1880, LBR
William H, b 8 Oct 1828 -
d 10 Oct 1879, LBR
BRANNON, Lonnie, b 12 Jan
1895 - d 14 Oct 1971,
LBR
BRANSTETTER, Addie, b 17
Apr 1918 - no death
date, BRN
Albert M, b 14 Dec 1872 -
d 14 Nov 1949, BRN
C S, b 2 Aug 1813 - d 29
Nov 1889, BRN
Charles, b 16 Jan 1917 - d
31 Oct 1970, BRN
Clayton E, b 3 June 1915 -
d 28 Jan 1917, BRN
Clifford D, b 24 Apr 1937
- d 12 Apr 1939, BRN
Clifford D, Sfc USN b 24
March 1927 - d 3 Aug
1946, OOO
Della J, b 29 July 1907 -
no death date, BRN
Didle, b 31 Jan 1909 - d
18 May 1909, BRN
Donna M, b 16 May 1960 - d
1 Feb 1963, FLR
Earl R, b 13 June 1903 - d
6 Feb 1967, BRN

BRANSTETTER (continued)
Ellis C, b 24 March 1927 -
d 3 Aug 1946, BRN
Esther Elaine, b 1 May
1946 - d 8 June 1963,
BRN
Franklin, b 15 March 1933
- d 17 May 1933, BRN
G W, b 7 July 1874 - d 7
Sept 1908, BRN
H L, b 19 Jan 1841 - d 24
June 1900, BRN
Infant, b&d 16 July 1907,
BRN
Infant, b&d 16 Oct 1973,
BRN
Infant Dau, b&d 16 Nov
1936, BRN
Infant Dau, b&d 10 May
1949, BRN
Infant Dau, b 24 Apr 1951
- d 28 Apr 1951, BRN
Infant Son, b&d 7 June
1928, BRN
James K, d 1964, BRN
Jessie Doyle, b&d 17 June
1924, BRN
John, b 20 Sept 1882 - d
27 Dec 1954, BRN
Larry Keith, b 7 Dec 1952
- d 3 Sept 1953, BRN
Leona, b 1883 - d 1969,
BRN
Lizzie, b 24 Oct 1871 - no
death date, UNG
M H, b 19 Apr 1894 - d 14
March 1941, BRN
Margaret F, b 6 May 1873 -
d 2 Nov 1949, BRN
Martha, b 29 March 1922 -
no death date, BRN
Mary L, b 2 Apr 1865 - d
12 Jan 1867, CLC
Mary R L, b 18 June 1894 -
d 22 Jan 1902, BRN
Mavis Mae, b 1 May 1923 -
d 16 May 1923, BRN
Mayme L, b 25 July 1927 -

BRANSTETTER (continued)
d 24 March 1938, BRN
Menferd M, b 25 Sept 1911
- d 12 Sept 1955, BRN
Merdie, b 11 March 1884 -
d 3 March 1948, BRN
Monroe, b 25 May 1846 - d
14 June 1926, UNG
Orlena, b 13 Oct 1876 - d
24 March 1942, BRN
Otis I, d 29 Aug 1979, ae
59y, BRN
R R, b 7 Mar 1862 - d 28
July 1940, BRN
Rachael, b 30 Oct 1895 - d
18 Nov 1895, BRN
Rebecca, b 10 March 1838 -
d 3 March 1924, BRN
Roy Virgil, d 10 Aug 1979,
ae 70y, BRN
Rozene, b 1930 - d 12 Feb
1977, BRN
Sarah Hester, b 16 Dec
1874 - d 31 Aug 1937,
BRN
Travis, b 1883 - d 1951,
BRN
W D, b 31 March 1868 - d
29 Apr 1943, BRN
William E, d 11 Nov 1978,
ae 87y, BRN
Willie, b 10 May 1884 - d
17 Jan 1904, BRN
BRASEL, Dr A C, b 19 Sept
1874 - d 20 Nov 1902,
BRZ
C H, b 15 Apr 1873 - d 12
March 1916, BRZ
Claud, b 19 Sept 1912 - d
1 Nov 1973, UNN
Glenn, b 1900 - d 1972,
LBR
Ida A, d 18 Oct 1894, ae
14y 7mo, BRZ
Infant, d/o Leon & Rena,
b&d 1961, WRC
J C, b -- July 1868 - d 6
Nov 1891, BRZ

BRASEL (continued)
James, b 24 May 1861 - d
21 July 1863, BRZ
Levi, b 29 Dec 1849 - d 15
Sept 1935, BRZ
Malinda Kelly, b 6 Dec
1847 - d 11 Aug 1901,
BRZ
Mildred, b 27 Oct 1910 -
no death date, UNN
Millie, b 1 Aug 1863 - d
14 Sept 1946, BRZ
Myrtle, b 4 Sept 1883 - d
11 Feb 1963, LBR
Perry, b 28 Jan 1880 - d
16 Oct 1925, LBR
Randall H, b 8 Nov 1887 -
d 18 Sept 1918, BRZ
V L, b 15 Nov 1889 - d 1
Nov 1920, BRZ
BRAWNER, Jerry M, b 13 July
1875 - d 31 July 1931,
CRO
Rosie Rittrell, b 8 Dec
1872 - d 29 May 1952,
CRO
BRAY, Eva, b 31 March 1896
- d 12 May 1970, NWP
Louise Trammel, b 1909 - d
11 Apr 1978, UNN
Montie, d 30 Sept 1981, ae
75y, UNN
BRAYLES, Felix E, b 1923 -
d 1925, BRR
Patton R, b 24 Aug 1879 -
d 5 Nov 1957, BRR
BRAZEL, Benjamin, b 15 Nov
1855 - no death date,
BRZ
Benjamin, Corp Co G 3 TN
Inf Sp/Am War, no dates,
OOO
D Witt, b 25 Sept 1858 - d
20 Sept 1859, BRZ
Jesse, b 24 Oct 1816 - d
24 June 1875, BRZ
Joseph, b 19 Nov 1875 - d
16 Jan 1879, BRZ

BRAZEL (continued)

Mary, b 26 March 1890 - d 11 March 1892, BRZ

Nicholas, b 6 Apr 1883 - d 25 Jan 1884, BRZ

Susannah, b 30 Nov 1829 - d 13 Feb 1923, BRZ

BREEDLOVE, Greely, b 1888 - d 1971, LBR

Infant, b&d 12 Dec 1898, LBR

Martha, b 28 March 1824 - d 27 June 1906, LBR

R I, b 6 June 1854 - d 10 Apr 1893, LBR

Rufus Edgar, b 3 Aug 1893 - d 27 Feb 1913, LBR

BREVARD, Frank E, b 21 Aug 1859 - d 27 Apr 1914, WRC

BREWER, Arzelia, b 1 Oct 1899 - d 25 Jan 1919, WRC

Eliza C, b 10 Apr 1875 - d 19 Oct 1940, LBR

Hansford, b 1885 - d 1959, WRC

John, b 25 March 1911 - d 26 Oct 1912, OLP

John F, b 22 May 1921 - d 18 Jan 1923, OLP

Peggy Jean, b 7 May 1950 - d 9 May 1950, LBR

Ray, b 6 Oct 1926 - d 26 July 1928, OLP

William Jr, Sgt 318 Inf, 80 Div WWII, 8 Oct 1944, 000

William Jr, TN WWI, d 8 Oct 1944, WRC

William M, b 26 Apr 1870 - d 30 March 1931, LBR

BREWSTER, Averdia, b 30 May 1904 - d 29 Nov 1960, BRW

Charles E Jr, b&d 7 July 1966, BRW

Charles R, 1956, BRW

BREWSTER (continued)

Clara A, b 10 March 19-- - d 9 Oct 1914, BRW

Ellen H, b 17 Sept 1905 - d 28 Feb 1980, BRW

J Thomas, b 1855 - d 26 Oct 1941, NDK

J W, b 28 July 1861 - d 5 May 1934, NDK

Jessie W, Pfc 166 Inf 42 Rainbow WWI, b 15 Oct 1893 - d 15 Oct 1966, BRW

John S, b 4 Apr 1875 - d 15 June 1963, BRW

Lorenda, b 7 May 1895 - d 5 Sept 1914, BRW

Manda, b 15 July 1888 - d 13 Dec 1918, BRW

Martha S, b 2 Jan 1881 - d 13 Aug 1913, NDK

Mary C, b 1852 - d 16 Jan 1917, NDK

Miney, b 13 Jan 1884 - d 3 June 1954, BRW

Nancy, b 1882 - d 1957, RGB

Onvie Ray, b 1923 - d 9 Aug 1975, PLR

Willey, b 3 Feb 1912 - d 4 Feb 1912, BRW

William A, b 29 March 1884 - d 16 Nov 1957, BRW

BRIENT, John H, b 11 Jan 1811 - d 28 Dec 1870, MNT

Minerva J, b 16 July 1821 - d 5 Oct 1873, MNT

Minerva T, b 10 Sept 18-- - d 3 Feb 1881, MNT

Sarah Ann, b 9 June 1811 - d 18 Oct 1849, MNT

BRIGGS, April, 1968, DVD

Dewey F, d 3 July 1978, ae 64y, LNC

Elmer C, b 16 Aug 1911 - d 14 Jan 1951, LNC

Fred F, b 1877 - d 1966,

BRIGGS (continued)
LNC
James Carl, b 1 Nov 1918 –
d 3 Feb 1942, LNC
W N, b 1907 – d 1967, LNC
BROCK, Dellie, b 24 June
1892 – d 8 Aug 1892, LNE
Dixie Alley, d 25 July
1976, ae ------, CRO
Elmer L, d 6 June 1975, ae
76y, RTT
Lina, b 21 Nov 1903 – d 7
July 1929, PNY
Lula Langley, b 6 Dec 1889
– no death date, DVS
Malissa, b 3 March 1873 –
d 7 July 1898, LNE
Mary A, b 2 July 1888 – d
4 June 1898, LNE
Sarah J Frye, b 19 Sept
1889 – d 4 Jan 1939, RTT
Susie J, b 15 Jan 1880 – d
5 Jan 1909, WRC
Virgil, d 18 Aug 1977, ae
75y, WRC
William H, b 13 March 1890
– d 12 Jan 1959, DVS
William M, b 8 Feb 1879 –
d 26 June 1941, DVS
William R, b 8 Sept 1873 –
d 14 Sept 1960, WRC
BROOKS, Aaron, b 1852 – d
1939, PLR
B M, b 11 Sept 1888 – d 8
May 1968, PLR
Bobby H, b 1941 – d 1955,
PLR
Charles C, b 1878 – d
1947, RGB
Fred H, b 15 Feb 1892 – d
16 Aug 1934, PLR
Ina Mae, b 16 Apr 1893 – d
25 Apr 1971, PLR
John L, b 28 Nov 1875 – d
8 Nov 1918, CRO
Julia, d 19 Feb 19--, CRO
Mary J, b 1861 – d 1941,
PLR

BROOKS (continued)
Mrs Fred H, d 21 July
1979, ae 84y, WMG
Nellie D, b 1874 – d 1958,
RGB
Nora L, b 28 Sept 1885 –
no death date, CRO
Theodore, b 7 Apr 1905 – d
3 Sept 1905, SHD
BROTHERTON, A J, b 22 Feb
1840 – d 14 July 1908,
SNB
Nannie, b 1840 – d 1893,
SNB
BROWN, A C, b 1901 – d
1967, WRC
A E, b 13 Feb 1856 – d 24
June 1930, BRR
Alfred E, d 13 Nov 1978,
ae 75y, BRR
Arthur, b 15 March 1885 –
d 17 Apr 1919, PLR
Artie Fairchilds, d 5 Sept
1975, ae 74y, BRR
Baby, b&d 12 Sept 1909,
SHD
Belle, d 11 May 1941, ae
57y, DRL
Bertha C, d 26 July 1896,
ae 14mo 3wk, WRC
Betty Lou, b 14 March 1930
– d 26 March 1934, PLR
Boyd, b 7 Apr 1908 – d 29
May 1909, WRC
Carl, b 14 Feb 1895 – d 2
Jan 1966, LBR
Charles, b 28 Sept 1847 –
d 16 Mar 1918, WRC
Rev Charles H, d -- Apr
1979, ae 83y, LN
Charlie, b 13 Feb 1883 – d
4 March 1913, PLR
Clara Shannon, b 24 July
1879 – d 24 June 1934,
SNB
Clarence, d 6 Dec 1979, ae
79y, BRR
Clementine, b 13 Sept 1861

BROWN (continued)
- no death date, BRR
Cora, b 30 Sept 1904 - no
death date, DRL
Curthe, b 9 Nov 1900 - d
10 Sept 1901, SHD
David B, b 22 Feb 1898 - d
21 Oct 1899, OLP
Delphia H, b 21 March 1894
- d 28 Dec 1962, UNG
Doyle F, d 4 Aug 1981, ae
75y, NWP
Easter, b 20 Dec 1849 - d
20 Nov 1905, CRO
Edward L, b 1888 - d 1958,
WRC
Elmer H, d 10 Dec 1903, ae
76y, NWP
Elsie S, b 1910 - no death
date, UNG
Ernest F, d 5 May 1980, ae
75y, BRR
Eva P, b 25 May 1908 - d
12 Aug 1978, NWP
Francis Victoria, b 26 Apr
1883 - d 13 March 1968,
PLR
Gleneva Jones, d 5 March
1977, ae 44y, BRR
Grace W, b 4 Dec 1917 - d
11 June 1918, PLR
Grady, b 28 July 1903 - d
10 Jan 1904, LVN
Grely C, b 18 Nov 1892 - d
9 Aug 1893, CRO
Harry O, b 17 Dec 1876 - d
11 March 1958, WRC
Harvy C, b 29 July 1897 -
d 16 Feb 1917, WRC
Henry, d 2 Jan 1978, ae
73y, FLR
Ida H, d 21 Aug 1981, ae
81y, CRO
Irene, d 6 Nov 1980, ae
79y, WRC
Irene, d 29 Aug 1974, ae
80y, UNG
Irvin M, d 7 May 1980, ae

BROWN (continued)
68y, PLR
J M, b 23 Apr 1860 - d 17
Jan 1892, PLR
J R, dates faded, SHD
Jack, b 6 Feb 1878 - d 16
Apr 1927, DRL
Jackie Ray, b 16 Apr 1932
- d 18 Apr 1958, NWP
Jake C, b 11 July 1899 - d
7 Dec 1974, CRO
James E, b 24 May 1910 - d
23 May 1955, CRO
James William, b 11 July
1911 - d 7 Oct 1958, WRC
Jesse V, b 27 Sept 1903 -
d 2 Nov 1962, DRL
Laura Lou, b 18 Apr 1854 -
d 15 Oct 1872, MNT
Lillie, b 20 June 1897 - d
29 Apr 1926, CRO
Lillie, d 1 May 1907, ae
67y, NWP
M, b 1876 - d 1926, CRO
Mable, b 23 Dec 1916 - d
24 March 1918, PLR
Madeline, b 31 March 1919
- d 6 Apr 1926, WRC
Maggie, b 1889 - d 1941,
WRC
Mary Edwards, 24 Feb 1888
LBR
Mary Jane, b 6 Apr 1886 -
d 15 Feb 1968, MSG
Mary, w/o N B, d 28 Apr
1915, CRO
N B, d 7 May 1904, ae
about 50y, CRO
Nellie Marie, b 3 Dec 1922
- d 17 Nov 1927, LNC
Nellie T, Inf d/o Chas & J
A, no dates, WRC
Newel, b&d 9 Oct 1964, MSG
Robert Wilson, b 18 Sept
1913 - d 8 Nov 1972, MSG
Roy, b 23 June 1889 - no
death date, UNG
Ruth Augusta, b 4 Feb 1924

BROWN (continued)
- d 26 Sept 1926, BRR
Samuel W, b 19 May ---- -
d 15 Oct 1875, PTC
Samuel Wayne, d 17 July
1977, ae 39y, UNG
Sarah D, b 19 July 1858 -
d 29 Nov 1922, LNE
Sim Carson, Pfc USA WWI, b
15 May 1893 - d 22 Jan
1971, BRR
Steril, d 29 Apr 1979, ae
71y, UNG
Tilie, b 10 Dec 1881 - d
17 Apr 1904, LVN
Tom C, b 29 June 1905 - d
23 March 1965, NWP
Travis Patrick, d 10 May
1977, ae 56y, WMG
Tyndale H, b 28 Jan 1873 -
d 16 Apr 1922, SNB
Vauerie McCartt, b 13 Aug
1884 - d 24 Feb 1972,
WRC
Vester, d 15 Oct 1975, ae
87y, UNG
W, b 1848 - d 1926, CRO
W C, b 19 Apr 1897 - d 15
Jan 1918, BRR
Walter, b 1889 - d 16 July
1973, MSG
Walter O, b 28 Jan 1886 -
d 13 July 1930, WRC
Wilborn L, b 1883 - d
1956, UNG
William B, d 11 July 1981,
ae 70y, PLR
William David, b 28 May
1939 - d 8 July 1968,
BRN
Willie Barger, b 20 June
1889 - no death date,
WRC
Zora, b 23 Feb 1884 - d 9
Apr 1932, SHD
BROYLES, Cora L, b 17 Dec
1893 - d 21 July 1968,
CRO

BROYLES (continued)
Fred C, b 21 June 1898 - d
16 Aug 1955, CRO
Mrs Harold, d 6 Feb 1976,
ae 87y, BRR
BRUMBALOUGH, Cecil Ottila,
b 25 Feb 1926 - d 21 Dec
1934, ELZ
Mildred, b 9 Feb 1921 - d
11 Jan 1922, ELZ
Ruby Dimple, b 25 Feb 1923
- d 15 Nov 1928, ELZ
BRUMMET, Mary E, b 13 June
1876 - d 23 July 1955,
DVS
William, b 29 Oct 1874 - d
6 Sept 1963, DVS
BRUMMETT, Catherine, b 27
Feb 1856 - d 7 Apr 1923,
DVS
BRUMMIT, J V, b 15 Nov 1930
- d 3 Jan 1931, CRO
BRYANT, ------, d 14 Nov
----, ae 15y, DVS
Lettie, b 13 Apr 1843 - d
13 Jan 1902, PLR
William Sr, b 2 Sept 1880
- d 10 Feb 1960, DVS
BRYS, Jane (BONIFACIUS), b
14 Oct 1922 - no death
date, WRC
William A, b 30 Jan 1900 -
d 13 Feb 1965, WRC
BUCANNAN, Pearl Johnson, d
1 Jan 1977, WRC
BUCK, Cythia M, b 2 Jan
1907 - 5 Oct 1975, PLR
Dollie Hall, d 15 May
1981, ae 78y, PLR
Don, b 2 July 1904 - d 8
Dec 1970, PLR
Gertie M, b 30 May 1884 -
d 18 May 1938, PLR
Infant Son, b&d 16 Dec
1946, PLR
James J, b 20 Sept 1875 -
d 21 Feb 1960, PLR
Shirley K, b&d 29 Dec

BUCK (continued)
1943, PLR
Spencer Jr, b&d 2 Apr 1967, SNB
Wanda L, b 9 June 1941 - d 7 June 1942, PLR
BUKNELL, Elizabeth H M, b 19 May 1859 - d 22 May 1896, SHD
BULLARD, Clara, b 16 July 1906 - d 16 May 1907, SNB
Clarence, b 16 July 1906 - d 14 May 1907, SNB
Elizabeth Jett, b 31 May 1858 - d 30 Nov 1895, BRR
Faye Elizabeth, b 22 Apr 1921 - d 14 Aug 1936, CRO
William, b 7 Aug 1860 - d 11 Apr 1932, BRR
William Harvey, b 25 Feb 1887 - d 10 Feb 1969, CRO
BULLEN, Carson, b 6 June 1915 - d 30 June 1943, LBR
Cleveland E, b 15 May 1888 - d 5 July 1950, LBR
Cornie V, b 30 Aug 1950 - d 2 Apr 1967, LBR
Hugh C, d 2 Nov 1979, ae 54y, LBR
BULLOCK, Lillian Brumby, d 18 May 1978, ae 87y, WRC
BULLRED, Fred H, b 27 Oct 1889 - d 12 Aug 1953, WRC
BUNCH, ------, no other ID, DVS
Angie, b 4 June 19-- - d 22 Oct 1958, NWP
Bessie, d 29 Nov 1980, ae 87y, NWP
Bud, d 9 Aug 1980, ae 81y, UNN
Carson E, b 1 Feb 1927 - d

BUNCH (continued)
15 Sept 1946, ELZ
Castio, b 14 May 1935 - d 10 Nov 1967, MSG
Dewey Lee, b 14 Dec 1898 - d 24 May 1966, EST
Edward Bay, d 9 Dec 1950, ae 61y, SNB
Edward H, b 19 Dec 1943 - d 25 Sept 1973, NWP
Ellen, b 26 Dec 1903 - d 13 Aug 1955, UNN
Fisher, d 21 Nov 1976, ae 67y, NWP
Flora, b 17 Sept 1907 - d 21 June 1970, MSG
Garland H, b 4 Jan 1901 - d 30 Nov 1951, MSG
General, d 7 Nov 1975, ae 86y, LBR
General M, b 31 Jan 1889 - d 14 Apr 1975, UNN
Granville B, Pvt USMC, VN b 8 Apr 1951 -d 3 Nov 1972, NWP
Greesie, b 8 Sept 1907, no death date, EST
Harold C M, b&d 26 June 1975, CBJ
Harry, b 28 Aug 1950 - d 18 Feb 1951, UNN
Isaac, b 18 July 1870 - d 19 Oct 1912, DVS
James A, d 4 May 1979, ae 56y, UNN
James Franklin, b 10 Jan 1895 - d 4 July 1964, EST
Janie, b 1962 - d 1963, NWP
Jessie Halburnt, b 15 Feb 1903 - d 5 Oct 1952, EST
Jimmy R, b 10 Jan 1952 - d 29 May 1974, UNN
Joseph Walter, b 12 Sept 1893 - d 16 Jan 1971, DVS
Lavatia Sue, b 13 Nov 1943

BUNCH (continued)
- d 29 Apr 1961, NWP
Leslie D, b -- Apr 1902 -
d 1 Oct 1975, UNN
Lonas M, b 13 Nov 1896 - d
29 March 1972, LBR
Lula Peters, b 16 Oct 1898
- d 16 Sept 1971, DVS
Mary, d 7 Dec 1979, ae
69y, UNN
Mary Ann, b 17 June 1867 -
d 28 March 1922, OLP
Mary S, b 29 July 1944 -
no death date, NWP
Mattie E, b 23 Dec 1892 -
d 29 July 1970, UNN
Miller, b 14 March 1880 -
27 Apr 1919, DVS
Neda A, d 21 Jan 1981, ae
65y, DVS
Nettie P, b 10 June 1898 -
d 12 Aug 1980, LBR
Ralph, b 1914 - d 1970,
NWP
Ramsey Jr, b 17 Apr 1929 -
d 17 July 1959, UNN
Ramsey Sr, b 15 Feb 1882 -
d 2 Nov 1962, NWP
Roger Dean, b 25 March
1950 - d 27 Apr 1968,
NWP
Ronnie, d 12 Apr 1975, ae
26y, LNE
Ruth, b 1905 - d 1971, SNB
Vina, b 14 Apr 1885 - d 4
May 1921, OLP
Virgie, d 20 Dec 1977, ae
78y, PTC
BUNN, Anna Rheba, b 12 June
1920 - d 15 Apr 1923,
WBB
Anna Webb, b 28 March 1864
- d 20 Feb 1920, WBB
Delores, b 8 June 1905 - d
7 March 1936, WBB
Ernest L, b 1 Dec 1904 - d
11 Dec 1973, WBB
John F, b 16 Feb 1893 - d

BUNN (continued)
18 Nov 1911, WBB
Larkin, b 3 May 1854 - d 5
June 1928, WBB
Nell, b 24 Aug 1907 - no
death date, WBB
Samuel C, b 6 Nov 1886 - d
10 June 1917, WBB
Virgil C, b 7 Feb 1897 - d
29 Dec 1921, WBB
BURCHETT, William C, b 1903
- d 1972, WRC
BURGE, F M Waits, b 6 Dec
1891 - d 17 Feb 1920,
LNC
May Hester, d 2 Oct 1969,
ae 69y 5mo, NWP
BURGER, Minerva L, b 30 May
1868 - d 21 March 1944,
LBR
BURGESS, Edith Dora Lane, d
-- Sept 1962, ae 66y,
DVS
Ethel L, b 22 July 1897 -
d 8 Sept 1962, DVS
Ethel L, d 3 Feb 1978, ae
84y, UNN
Lillian, b&d 13 Oct 1965,
STP
Patricia Ann, b 25 June
1964 - d 13 Oct 1965,
STP
Sib E, b 20 July 1892 - d
11 July 1943, DVS
BURKES, John Duncan, b 28
Sept 1893 - d 13 Jan
1963, WRC
BURNETT, Letha, b 5 Oct
1879 - d 23 March 1903,
DRL
Occi, b 11 Oct 1895 - d 8
May 1937, UNG
BURNS, Henry W, Co B 5th TN
Inf, military stone no
dates, LNC
John W, b 10 Aug 1860 - d
27 Aug 1920, LNC
Mary Jane, b 28 June 1881

BURNS (continued)
- d 13 March 1940, LNC
Rosa Mae, d 16 May 1978, ae 75y, FLR
William F, b 1894 - d 1972, FLR
BURRESS, Harve Hannah, b 30 March 1904 - d 6 May 1905, DVS
Mary J, b 23 Apr 1915 - d 12 July 1942, LBR
BURRETT, Mary J, b 16 Nov 1872 - d 9 May 1956, LBR
BURRIS, Roy F, b 4 May 1916 - d 6 Feb 1941, CBJ
BURROUGHS, Andrew B, b 6 Dec 1850 - d 27 March 1886, RGB
BURTON , Everett Henry, d 7 Nov 1965, ae 53y 6mo, CRO
Herbert S, b 31 Dec 1937 - d 22 Dec 1959, WBB
Ida, b 12 March 1890 - d 24 Feb 1953, WBB
Mona, b 22 Jan 1904 - d 31 July 1959, WBB
Raymond C, d 17 June 1979, ae 77y, WBB
BUSBY, Ellen Morgan, d 7 Dec 1977, ae 71y, UNN
Lottie Ellen M, b 15 Oct 1906 - d 7 Dec 1977, UNN
BUSH, Tim F, b 20 Feb 1912 - d 15 July 1913, BRR
BUTLER, ------, cn/o J B, no dates, DVS
Albert (stone turned upside down by vandals; name given by Mr Carson who lived nearby), no dates, AMS
Arvil s/o Albert & Martha, b 26 March 1908 - d 26 Sept 1908, AMS
Bonie, b 29 Dec 1886 - 10 June 1897, DVS
C J, b 8 Apr 1866 - d 17

BUTLER (continued)
Oct 1939, DVS
Cleary, b 16 May 1897 - d 6 July 1898, DVS
Harlan L s/o Albert & Martha, b 10 July 1913 - d 8 Oct 1913, AMS
Isabella, b 29 Aug 1796 - d 20 Aug 1867, DVS
J B, no dates, DVS
James, b 1931 - d 1969, PNY
Laura, b 29 July 1874 - d 25 Apr 1904, DVS
Martha (stone turned upside down by vandals; name given by Mr Carson who lived nearby) , no dates, AMS
Matilda, b 10 Apr 1872 - d 19 Dec 1934, DVS
Maud, b 10 Feb 1909 - no death date, DVS
Mecie, b 8 Apr 1873 - d 30 Nov 1944, EST
Owen Willis, b 29 Oct 1909 - d 13 July 1945, DVS
Preston, b 28 March 1902 - d 4 July 1902, DVS
Savannah Georgia, b 17 Nov 1918 - d 6 March 1919, WRJ
Wilburn s/o Albert & Martha, b&d 18 Nov 1918, AMS
BUXTON, Abe Lee, b 26 Feb 1881 - d 7 July 1952, WRC
Bertha Bargess, b 3 Oct 1887 - d 16 Feb 1977, WRC
Elizabeth, b 9 Oct 1829 - d 8 June 1878, MNT
George H Sr, b 7 Dec 1882 - d 25 Feb 1971, WRC
Hulda, b 9 Nov 1864 - d 4 Apr 1956, WRC
J H, b -- Oct 1889 - d --

BUXTON (continued)
    July 1959, LNC
    John F, Cpl HQ WWI b 28
        Apr 1887 - d 4 July
        1964, WMG
    John Michael, b 6 July
        1871 - d 18 July 1971,
        WMG
    Joseph, STC Bty WWI, b 12
        Jan 1886 - d 4 Sept
        1967, WMG
    Laurence, b 28 March 1890
        - d 20 Aug 1927, MNT
    Lillian, d 1 Dec 1975, ae
        80y, MNT
    Louise, b 9 July 1872 - d
        4 June 1951, MNT
    Lucinda, b 8 Jan 1845 - d
        17 Dec 1918, MNT
    M W, b 2 Sept 1825 - d 16
        Oct 1916, MNT
    Mills W Sr, b 20 March
        1871 - d 19 Jan 1924,
        MNT
    Noah, b 21 Aug 1914 - d 25
        Jan 1929, MNT
    Welsey W, Pfc Bty Co WWII
        b 5 May 1918 - d 7 Dec
        1962, MNT
BYARS, Sam, no dates, FLR
BYE, Miss Eugenia, d --
    March 1976, ae 50y, WMG
BYRD, A V, b 17 March 1873
    - d 29 Nov 1948, WRC
    Anna M, b 6 Sept 1895 - d
        17 Apr 1967, LBR
BYRD, Dr Archie, b 23 Apr
    1882 - d 30 Apr 1928,
    WRC
    Dr. Archie, b 23 Apr 1882
        - d 30 Apr 1928, WRC
    Barney, b 22 Dec 1904 - d
        7 June 1913, WRC
    Belvia Hall, b 1889 - d
        1963, LBR
    Bessie G, b 1890 - d 1971,
        WRC
    Corbett S, b -- May 1892 -

BYRD (continued)
    no death date, LBR
    Cornelia, d 3 March ----,
        DVS
    Daniel Hale, b 20 Feb 1958
        - d 21 Feb 1958, CLC
    Eva, b 4 July 1910 - d 27
        May 1977, WRC
    George, no dates, DVS
    H M, b 24 Nov 1854 - d 11
        March 1929, LBR
    Hale Columbus, b 6 Sept
        1860 - d 18 March 1832,
        LBR
    Hill, b 22 Feb 1840 - d 12
        Dec 1937, LBR
    Ibbie, b 9 Aug 1899 - no
        death date, DRL
    Capt J H, b 16 Aug 1834 -
        d 16 Apr 1907, DRL
    Jackie B McCartt, b 1 Sept
        1877 - d 26 Dec 1942,
        WRC
    James, d 6 March 1888, ae
        5y 11mo, LBR
    Jeff Lee Jr, b 1923 - d
        1944, LBR
    Jeff Lee Sr, b 1888 - d
        1958, LBR
    Joe, b 7 Jan 1882 - d 10
        Jan 1958, DRL
    John R, b 1886 - d 11
        March 1973, WRC
    Kieth, 1976 (no other no-
        tation), LNE
    Lee, d 24 Apr 1973, ae
        76y, LBR
    Lewis Woods, b 14 Aug 1904
        - d 18 March 1924, UNN
    Maggie, b 24 Sept 1866 - d
        11 Dec 1951, WRC
    Mary, b 1878 - d 1908, LBR
    Mary E, b 8 Jan 1848 - d 8
        Sept 1922, DRL
    Mary Henry, b 21 March
        1852 - d 27 May 1931,
        LBR
    Mary Stringfield, b 2 Feb

BYRD (continued)
1861 - d 22 Aug 1898, LBR
Naomi R, b 23 May 1935 - d 5 Sept 1973, DRL
Odos M, b 3 March 1915 - d 15 Sept 1922, LBR
Ola May, b 8 March 1893 - d 15 Apr 1966, LBR
Oler C, b&d 28 May 1921, PNY
Orien A, b 22 Aug 1901 - d 24 Dec 1950, WRC
Oscar W, b 21 June 1890 - d 21 June 1958, LBR
Rebecca J, b 20 March 1865 - d 8 Dec 1908, LBR
Sallie, b 6 Oct 1817 - d 2 Apr 1889, LBR
Sharon Lynn, b 1951 - d 1957, WRC
Shelt L, b 21 May 1889 - d 1 Jan 1890, LBR
Troy A, b 1962 - d 1962, WRC
Victoria Elles, b 7 Apr 1902 - d 8 May 1936, LBR
W Rice, b 12 Sept 1849 - d 18 March 1925, LBR
Walter D, Pvt b 30 Dec 1925 - d 28 June 1944, LBR
William, b 30 June 1874 - d 11 June 1906, LBR
William (Buster), b 25 Aug 1927 - d 31 July 1951, WRC
William A, b 24 Oct 1885 - d 11 March 1965, DRL
Willie B, b 7 July 1892 - b 10 Feb 1962, WRC
BYRGE, Charley, d 1 March 1971, ae 46y, STP
Elsie Greasy, d 17 Oct 1980, ae 56y, STP
George, b 11 May 1906 - no death date, CRO
H E, b 25 Aug 1905 - d 1

BYRGE (continued)
Nov 1966, CRO
Henry Miller, b 29 Apr 1884 - d 16 Oct 1961, LNC
Michael, b 21 May 1886 - d 5 June 1968, NWP
Sarah, b 12 July 1889 - no death date, NWP
Savannah, b 29 June 1888 - d 16 Feb 1964, NWP
Theodore R, d ----, ae 61y, LNC
BUFF, Bille Holliday, b 18 June 1894 - d 15 Feb 1975, SNB
CADDELL, Connie Best, b 16 Aug 1940 - d 22 Oct 1966, NWP
CAGLE, Bertha I, b 1882 - d 1966, CRO
Tom, b 1880 - d 1942, CRO
Wilbur, b 9 Feb 1909 - d 28 May 1954, CRO
CALDWELL, George W, b 6 Sept 1881 - d 6 Feb 1957, DRL
John Francis, b 27 June 1911 - d 12 May 1950, DRL
Maxine Brown, d 5 Oct 1869, ae 49y, BRR
Tennie M, b 5 May 1892 - no death date, DRL
CAMILE, Emile E, b 8 July 1891 - d 20 March 1955, PLR
CAMIRE, Bertha Blair, b 8 July 1891 - d 4 Apr 1959, PLR
CAMPBELL, Ella Gones, b 13 Sept 1902 - d 7 May 1962, EST
CAMPBELL, Ethel M, b 21 May 1899 - d 15 June 1974, DVS
Gertrude, b 10 Sept 1884 - d 12 Jan 1964, WRC

28

CAMPBELL (continued)

Oliver, b 19 Feb 1896 - no death date, DVS

Polk, d -- Oct 1962, EST

W H, b 1877 - d 1939, BRR

William B, b 20 Dec 1899 - d 7 Apr 1945, EST

CAMPER, Grover C, b 8 March 1899 - d 19 March 1961, PLR

CANNON, Ralph M, b 21 Feb 1918 - d 30 June 1975, LBR

Willie Mae, b 13 Dec 1921 - d 9 March 1975, LBR

CANUP, Alpha May, b 11 Feb 1907 - d 15 June 1957, CRO

Elbert, no dates, CRO

Father, no dates, CRO

J D, b 6 July 1877 - d 13 May 1926, CRO

Lee A, d 27 Oct 1939, ae 35y, CRO

Mother, no dates, CRO

Roy A, b 19 May 1901 - no death date, CRO

Sarah, b 18 Jan 1844 - d 20 Apr 1907, CRO

CAPPS, Arthur H, Pfc 11 ABN Med, BN 11 ABN b 7 March 1936 - d 1 Oct 1955, UNG

B C, b 1862 - d 1944, UNG

Bruce, b 25 Jan 1930 - d 17 Aug 1967, UNG

Dewey, d 31 March 1977, ae 69y, UNG

Dwayne Mitchell, d 1 Aug 1975, ae 2da, UNG

Emma, d 21 June 1974, ae 60y, UNG

Mary, b 1907 - d 1958, UNG

Orlando, d 30 Oct 1974, ae 64y, UNG

CARMAN, Raymond, b 1903 - d 1961, CRO

CARNEY, Mildred Louise, b

CARNEY (continued)

31 Jan 1923 - d 25 Oct 1925, CRO

CARPENTER, Consider, b 25 July 1797 - d 22 May 1869, NDK

Dorsa Ewing, b 1 May 1884 - d 13 Oct 1947, CRO

Elizabeth T, b 1 May 1847 - d 14 July 1933, CRO

G S, b 8 Sep 1821 - d 5 Feb 1903, CRO

Geraldine, b 22 Dec 1920 - d 8 May 1931, CRO

Lula Welch, b 20 Jan 1889 - d 29 Sept 1952, CRO

Sarah M Kittrell, b 1875 - no death date, CRO

Stonewall J, b 1875 - d 1928, CRO

Susannah, b 21 Nov 1800 - d 22 Feb 1892, NDK

CARR, Ethel M, b 1 Jan 1901 - d 11 June 1964, DRM

Isaac, dates faded, DRM

James Homer, MD 1Lt Med Corps WWI b 26 Apr 1890 - d 1 March 1972, CRO

Jerry Dean, b 26 Feb 1965(or 1964) - d 11 Nov 1974, WRJ

Mona Goldston, d 29 July 1978, ae 77y, CRO

CARROL, Eva, b 5 Jan 1916 - d 16 Sept 1919, LNE

Morton, b 18 Feb 1886 - d 21 Oct 1960, DRL

CARROLL, Anna Mae, d 10 Oct 1973, ae 68y, DRL

Carolyn Sue, d 2 Nov 1965, ae 22y, THR

Charles C, d 29 Sept 1978, ae 93y, WRC

Ella P, b 18 Feb 1879 - d 20 Feb 1984, MCD

James, d 5 July 1962, ae 72y, MCD

Joanna, b 10 Aug 1839 - d

CARROLL (continued)
20 Oct 1912, MCD
Littie, b 1894 - d 1968, MCD
W M, b 20 Feb 1840 - d 6 June 1922, MCD
William E H, b 31 Jan 1915 - d 28 Nov 1966, LNE
CARSON, Beulah Human, b 13 Feb 1904 - no death date, WRC
Dora E, b 17 Oct 1885 - d 28 Nov 1973, EST
Dorothy Mae, 16 March 1928, DVS
Elizabeth J, b 6 July 1901 - d 17 March 1928, DVS
Ida Gray, b 16 July 1913 - d 10 March 1933, DVS
Isaac C, b 22 Sept 1883 - d 10 Aug 1959, EST
Jack Thomas, b 1 May 1928 - d 7 Sept 1954, EST
James Alex, b 1 Jan 1888 - d 29 Mar 1943, WRC
Johnnie Mae, b 5 July 1930 - d 31 Oct 1936, JCJ
Joseph H, Pvt, b 2 June 1893 - d 29 Sept 1918 (France), DVS
Joseph Harrison, d 4 March 1978, ae 55y, EST
Lloyd Lankford, b 27 July 1911 - d 17 July 1971, BRR
Mary Ova, b 21 June 1891 - no death date, EST
Stephen Jerry, d 1 Oct 1979, ae 30y, EST
Thomas J, b 22 Nov 1888 - d 18 Nov 1961, EST
CARTER, Dora B, b 17 March 1880 - d 3 Oct 1952, WRC
George W., b 6 March 1872 - d 17 March 1953, WRC
Georgia England, b 5 July 1919 - no death date, SNB

CARTER (continued)
J A, b 17 Apr 1857 - d 12 Nov 1923, MNT
Jennie, b 3 Oct 1872 - no death date, WRC
John , b 1 June 1828 - d 20 Aug 1903, WRC
Josie, b 25 Apr 1852 - d 18 Aug 1907, WRC
Lewis, b 5 Oct 1881 - d 13 March 1944, WRC
Mary E, b 10 Feb 1905 - d 12 Oct 1962, CLC
Mary Jane, b 1860 - d 1939, MNT
Meredith L, b 3 Oct 1923 - d 19 March 1945, UNN
Thomas R, b 4 March 1876 - d 22 Oct 1943, WRC
William Fred, b 8 Apr 1867 - d 17 Aug 1929, WRC
William C, b 15 Aug 1922 - d 4 Sept 1974, SNB
Winifred, b 18 May 1880 - d 30 June 1941, WRC
CASADA, Lillie S, b 7 Nov 1889 - no death date, CRO
CASE, Alta, 22 Aug 1943, MSG
Dewey D, b 29 March 1910 - d 9 Apr 1970, MSG
Margaretta Sue, 9 Feb 1946, MSG
Pauline, 11 Apr 1942, MSG
Zenice Honeycutt, b 7 Sept 1913 - d 1972, MSG
CASH, James Harvey, b 15 June 1862 - d 28 Jan 1952, CRO
Laura E Webb, b 28 May 1899 - d 25 June 1973, CRO
Lester Jr, b&d 7 Apr 1928, CRO
Mary Alice, 30 Jan 1829 - no other date, CRO
Mattie Elizabeth, b 19 Oct

CASH (continued)
1867 - d 26 Aug 1951,
CRO
Ralph Webster, b 29 Dec
1929 - d 30 Dec 1929,
CRO
William Evans, b 16 Feb
1923 - d 2 Sept 1933,
CRO
Wm Samuel, b 23 Dec 1894 -
d 29 Jan 1976, CRO
CASSADA, Carl O, b 8 Jan
1913 - d 12 July 1969,
CRO
Oscar, b 25 Feb 1882 - d
23 Dec 1965, CRO
Roy Albert, b 6 Dec 1918 -
d 23 March 1921, CRO
CATE, Mary J, b 4 Nov 1865
- d 2 June 1896, DVS
Sam, b 29 Apr 1889 - d 26
Jan 1945, WRC
William Henry, b 11 Sept
1895 - d 22 June 1967,
PTC
CATEN, George, b 8 Jan 1922
- d 18 Sept 1923, PLR
CATES, Anna, b&d 1971, WRC
Briant, b&d 4 Jan 1914,
WRC
Frank C, 1Sgt USA, d 10
May 1940, WRC
Myrtle M, b 22 May 1920 -
d 4 June 1978, WRC
Shirley Dean, b&d 20 Aug
1944, WRC
CHADWELL, Darlene, b&d 12
May 1954, ARM
Jerry Lee, b&d 8 May 1953,
ARM
CHADWICK, Naomi Rogers, b
18 Nov 1908 - no death
date, DVS
Ruben Herbert, b 21 June
1907 - d 16 June 1972,
DVS
CHANDLER, James R, b 25 Nov
1930 - d 13 May 1958,

CHANDLER (continued)
NWP
CHANEY, Albert S, b 15 Nov
1877 - d 7 June 1904,
CHN
Buford, b 13 Aug 1924 - d
14 June 1975, DVS
Charles, d 9 Nov 1981, ae
80y, MLC
Gertie Sims, b 1900 - no
death date, CHN
Herman H, b 6 Oct 1911 - d
23 Apr 1964, WHO
Jackie Gene, b 12 Feb 1947
- d 2 Dec 1965, DVS
Jean, 1932, MLC
Jeanette, b 10 May 1924 -
no death date, DVS
Lorena Mae, b&d 13 Apr
1941, WHO
Magel D, b 2 May 1920 - no
death date, WHO
Rachel, b 18 Oct 1908 - d
12 July 1974, DVS
Rebecca, b 7 Aug 1860 - d
5 March 1942, MLC
Wilda, 1935, MLC
William Joseph, b 1884 - d
1953, CHN
CHAPMAN, Albert, b 1863 - d
1941, DRM
Benjamin W, b&d 1 June
1956, LBR
Emlie (Langley), b 10 Aug
1863 - d 17 May 1900,
DRM
Hopey Breedlove, b 6 Sept
1856 - no death date,
UNN
James, b 1825 - dates
faded, DRM
James Henry, b 5 Aug 1861
- d 8 Jan 1942, UNN
John W, b 12 Aug 1885 - d
16 Oct 1960, LBR
Lloyd E, b 30 July 1945 -
d 24 Dec 1945, NWP
Margie L, b 7 Aug 1899 - d

CHAPMAN (continued)
16 Nov 1904, UNN
Mary E, b 22 Jan 1900 - d
10 July 1958, LBR
Michael, ae 4y, MSG
Minnie M, b 17 Jan 1900 -
d 30 May 1900, DRM
Roe, b 17 Feb 1888 - d 27
Dec 1961, LBR
Mrs Rosa A, d 28 Nov 1978,
ae 92y, DRM
Stella K, b 3 Nov 1892 -
no death date, LBR
CHARLES, Harry Richard, d 3
Aug ----, ae 54y 11mo,
NWP
CHASE, Irwin A, d 29 Dec
1980, ae 72y, WRC
CHASTEEN, Carol Anne, d/o J
E, no dates (b&d in-
fant), BRR
Ida B, b 2 Dec 1876 - d 30
March 1954, BRR
James E, b 23 Sept 1909 -
d 26 Feb 1962, BRR
James R, b 10 Jan 1883 - d
27 Jan 1958, BRR
Reba O, b 10 Dec 1913 - d
5 Sept 1976, BRR
CHATMAN, Emily Mae, b 1910
- d 1968, PNY
Oma M, b 27 July 1890 - d
4 June 1966, LBR
Sam Houston, b 10 Sept
1934 - d 12 July 1973,
LBR
CHECK, John, Co B 5th TN
Mtd Inf Civil War Mili-
tary Stone b 13 Jan
1844 - d 9 Nov 1921, CLH
CHEEK, Abbie, d 21 Apr
1976, ae 85y, DVS
Allen F, d 8 Aug 1968, ae
1da, CLH
Edith, ae (?) & inf son,
CLH
Elmere baby/ Wm C, no
dates, RTT

CHEEK (continued)
Florence J, b 1872 - d
1964, CLH
Frank M, b 19 Jan 1905 - d
25 Sept 1975, CLH
Jesey, b 13 June 1882 - d
30 Nov 1882, DVS
John H, b 25 May 1906 - d
3 Nov 1965, CLH
Lizzie Peters, b 9 Feb
1850 - d 11 Nov 1932,
CLH
Loraine G, b 24 May 1908 -
no death date, CLH
Martha, b 13 Aug 1843 - d
28 July 1898, DVS
William F, b 1871 - d
1953, CLH
CHERRY, Anna, b 7 Jan 1867
- d 5 Oct 1889, DRL
Asinath F, b 6 Dec 1836 -
d 1 March 1904, DRL
S B, b 21 Aug 1868 - d 10
Aug 1887, DRL
T M, b 28 Jan 1832 - d 28
Feb 1902, DRL
CHESTER, Bessie L, b 18 Feb
1877 - d 22 Nov 1919,
CLP
William P, b 13 Nov 1855 -
d 24 Nov 1908, CLP
CHEURUANT, Russel R, 21
March 1935, MSG
CHILDRESS, Juanita, b 16
Dec 1914 - no death
date, DVS
Lawrence, b 2 Apr 1909 - d
4 Feb 1975, DVS
Mary E C, b 1848 - d 1928,
WRC
CHILDS, Gladys Cromwell, b
9 Jan 1931 - d 31 Jan
1969, CRO
Henry H, b 17 Jan 1906 - d
22 Oct 1959, DVS
CHOATE, Christopher C, b 24
Jan 1913 - d 14 Jan
1959, WRC

32

CHOATE (continued)
Wm McKinley, b 18 Jan 1897
- d 1 July 1929, BRR
CHRISTMAS, Jennie (?Jim-
mie), FN USN Korea b 5
Jan 1930 - d 19 Sept
1971, CLH
Novella, b 1890 - d 1968,
RTT
CIBER, Winfry, b 1860 - d
1945, OLP
Clarence Jr, b&d 24 June
1955, WRC
CLAIBORNE, James Leon, b 2
July 1938 - d 23 Feb
1948, NWP
Maude E, b 1901 - d 1950,
NWP
Ona W, b 17 Feb 1896 - d 6
Sept 1955, NWP
W R Buster, b 10 Apr 1924
- d 4 Aug 1937, NWP
CLARK, Annie M, b 11 Nov
1904 - d 13 Sept 1961,
CLH
Arville R, Pvt 1232 Mil
Pol WWII, b 13 Dec 1913
- d 12 Apr 1966, LNE
Aver Ernest, b 15 Feb 1909
- d 6 Oct 1941, UNN
Calvin Coolidge, d 27 Aug
1973, ae 49y, FLR
Charles A, Co B 18th PA
Cav, Mil Stone, RGB
Charles Henry, b 17 March
1862 - d 7 Apr 1934, LNE
Charlie F, b 20 Dec 1884 -
d 6 Oct 1970, DVS
Crowder C, b 21 Oct 1907 -
no death date, DVS
Dorothy H, b 9 Sept 1907 -
d 11 Jan 1976, DVS
Elizabeth Belle, b 3 Feb
1877 - d 1970, LNE
Elizabeth Rose, b 18 Oct
1916 - d -- Oct 1916,
BRR
J S, b 25 March 1841 - d

CLARK (continued)
18 Jan 1928, BRR
James Franklin, d 16 May
1969, ae 47y 10mo, CLH
James Robert, d 5 Feb
1968, ae 74y, CLH
Jerusha C, b 13 Apr 1848 -
d 27 May 1913, BRR
Lucy M, b 30 Oct 1895 - no
death date, DVS
Mitchell, b&d 15 June
1950, UNN
Sarah E, b 17 June 1839 -
d 17 Apr 1888, RGB
Sidney, T4 2nd Inf, WWII,
b 6 Nov 1923 - d 3 July
1950, LNE
Vera Charlotte, d 26 Nov
1972, ae 47y, CLH
William A, b 12 May 1866 -
d 30 Jan 1919, CRO
William Beecher, b 16 Sept
1897 - d 1898, BRR
William J, d 19 June 1981,
ae 77y, LNE
CLAWSON, Jennie, b 27 Oct
1880 - no death date,
CRO
Norman S, b 5 May 1881 - d
19 May 1937, CRO
CLAYTON, Bernard, 4 Apr
1913, LBR
Lois M, b 24 July 1926 - d
10 Dec 1966, LBR
CLIFT, Abner Marion, b 25
Oct 1834 - d 21 Dec
1853, CRO
James Robert, b 1917 - d
1922, WBB
Mary Casey, b 8 Nov 1793 -
d 5 June 1847, CRO
William, b 10 Feb 1774 - d
22 Jan 1847, CRO
CLINTON, Eva Vickers, b 13
Feb 1887 - d 2 Dec 1935,
PNY
Herman, b 3 June 1906 - d
21 Nov 1915, PNY

33

CLOUSE, James J, b 1883 - d
 1955, RGB
CLOWERS, Bailey, b 1926 - d
 1966, LNE
 Bill, b 27 June 1892 - d 9
 Apr 1964, WRC
 Carl, d 21 Aug 1978, ae
 55y, LNE
 Estel, b 1919 - d 1966,
 LNE
 Gregory Allen, b&d 23 Nov
 1974, CRO
 Infant Dau, b&d 11 Oct
 1935, WRJ
 John F, b 1884 - d 1963,
 LNE
 Oineima, b 15 Dec 1881 - d
 31 Oct 1957, WRC
 Russell, d 30 Apr 1978, ae
 66y, LNE
 Zona, b 1887 - d 1962, LNE
COAKLEY, Elizabeth B, b 17
 Aug 1878 - d 14 Dec
 1934, RGB
 Francis J, b 5 Oct 1862 -
 d 27 June 1914, RGB
COALEY, Edna Jane, b 10 Nov
 1872 - d 9 Jan 1937, NWP
COATES, Myrtle Strutton, d
 4 June 1978, ae 58y, WRC
COCHRAN, Frank Marion, b 27
 Jan 1892 - d 17 Aug
 1973, CRO
 Sarah J, b 1 May 1895 - no
 death date, CRO
COFFEY, Clara Leon, b 22
 March 1922 - d 19 Dec
 1944, CRO
 Ernie May, b 21 Apr 1897 -
 d date eroded, SNB
 Eva Gamble, b 14 Feb 1882
 - d 28 Dec 1956, CRO
 Joe, d 17 Aug 1979, ae
 26y, CRO
 Larry James Sr, b 6 May
 1944 - d 12 July 1972,
 CRO
 Lawrence, d 9 Jan 1979, ae

COFFEY (continued)
 87y, CRO
 Leonard Edward, b 21 Apr
 1876 - d 7 Nov 1934, CRO
 M A, no dates, MRR
 M E, no dates, MRR
 Nancy, b 23 Feb 1854 - d 3
 Apr 1945, CRO
 W L, b 23 March 1853 - d
 18 Nov 1905, CRO
COFFMAN, Laurence, b 14 Oct
 1924 - d 2 March 1926,
 CRO
 Once Watson, b 11 June
 1897 - no death date,
 CRO
 T J, d 22 May 1931, ae
 83y, LNC
 Thomas E, b 1920 - d 1970,
 CRO
 Walter W, 1972, CRO
 William A, b 3 June 1876 -
 d 12 Apr 1944, CRO
COKER, Infant, no dates,
 MSG
 John H, d 25 May 1952, ae
 76y 10mo, CLH
COLE, Edward E, b 23 Jan
 1962 - d 23 March 1962,
 CRO
 Edward Wayne, d 7 June
 1980, ae 36y, FLR
 Gertrude L, b 6 June 1901
 - d 18 Aug 1970, FLR
 Hay J, b 11 March 1909 - d
 2 Feb 1953, FLR
 Lottie Lee, b 12 Dec 1922
 - d 1 May 1944, FLR
 Mack, b 12 Sept 1896 - no
 death date, FLR
COLEMAN, Mark Edward, b 19
 Oct 1947 - d 27 Oct
 1969, LBR
 William G, b 9 May 1907 -
 d 26 Oct 1959, WRC
COLLINS, Alf, b 15 Feb 1882
 - d 29 Oct 1954, LNC
 Anne F, b 1 May 1892 - d

34

COLLINS (continued)
25 Feb 1973, LNC

Annie, d 29 Aug 1952, ae 63y, DVD

Billy Ray, BT3 USN, b 1 Aug 1947 - d 2 Sept 1968, DVD

Charles Madison, b 16 Oct 1879 - d 15 Dec 1962, CLC

Chester Edwin, b 30 Dec 1941 - d 16 Dec 1942, DVD

Edith Marie, b 22 Apr 1922 - d 25 July 1957, LVN

Ethel Land, b 3 July 1888 - d 9 Nov 1937, CLC

Frank, b 8 Oct 1875 - d 5 Feb 1944, LVN

George W, b 10 July 1887 - d 25 Nov 1958, LNC

Glena June, b&d 12 Apr 1941, LNC

Infant Dau, b&d 22 May 1940, LNC

Jerry C, b 13 Aug 1915 - d 27 Apr 1964, CLC

John Astor, b 18 March 1919 - d 6 May 1972, MSG

Leota, b 23 Oct 1915 - d 7 May 1957, CLC

Lillie, b 14 Oct 1888 - d 22 Jan 1922, LNC

Lloyd H, b 17 Jan 1917 - d 20 Jan 1973, FST

Mark Anthony, b 15 Nov 1946 - d 27 Feb 1947, CLC

Martha, b 21 May 1921 - no death date, FST

Martha Jane, b 28 Dec 1950 - d 5 Jan 1951, LNC

Mary Jane, b 10 Jan 1947 - d 30 May 1949, LVN

Nellie Newby, d 7 May 1981, ae 59y, LNC

Robert (Bob), d 22 July 1981, ae 70y, WRC

COLLINS (continued)
Ruth Ann, b 28 Nov 1941 - d 12 Sept 1947, LNC

Samuel A, b 12 Apr 1912 - d 6 Sept 1957, LVN

Sarah Louise, b&d 31 May 1920, LVN

Tennessee J, b 22 June 1882 - d 15 Aug 1953, LVN

Tommie W, b 14 May 1914 - d 11 Apr 1970, LVN

Virgil, d 18 Aug 1978, ae 59y, LNC

Virginia Ashley, b 19 Sept 1916 - no death date, MSG

Wilburn E, b 2 July 1907 - d 18 Dec 1965, LVN

Willard Ben, d 5 Oct 1974, ae 56y, LNC

Wm Edgar, no dates, ELZ

COLSTON, Charles J, b 29 Nov 1920 - d 5 Apr 1936, DVS

James A, b 11 Feb 1882 - no death date, DVS

Vennie, b 21 Feb 1895 - d 3 Nov 1956, DVS

COLVIN, Leonard J, b&d 18 Jan 1926, DVS

COMER, Beulah Barges, b 6 June 1906 - d 11 Oct 1974, UNN

Clyde H, b 15 Apr 1910 - d 26 Feb 1970, UNN

Luretha M, b 25 Oct 1914 - no death date, UNN

Odeva, b 13 Dec 1918 - no death date, UNN

COMPTON, Jackie Farrell, d 20 Apr 1978, ae 15y, LBR

CONASTER, Leland S, b 16 Jan 1908 - d 16 Nov 1977, LNE

Lewis Alfred, b 8 July 1931 - d 27 Oct 1932, WBB

CONASTER (continued)
Lewis Sr, b 13 May 1894 -
d 12 Feb 1951, WBB
Mary Agnes, b 23 Jan 1923
- d 22 Sept 1923, WBB
Raymond, b 1 Oct 1952 - d
26 Aug 1956, LNE
Scott, b 13 May 1865 - d
27 May 1946, WBB
Vince R, b 9 Aug 1871 - no
death date, WBB
CONNER, Billy, SA USN
Korea, b 2 July 1934 - d
19 Dec 1953, NWP
Hallie J, d 21 Jan ----,
ae 58y, NWP
Ham, HA 2 USNR WWII, b 15
Apr 1923 - d 23 Feb 1967
(or 1951), NWP
Thomas E, b 20 Dec 1921 -
d 2 June 1961, CRO
COOK, Mr Bob, no dates, SHD
Mrs Bob, no dates, SHD
Cassie Drake, b 17 Aug
1875 - d 10 May 1957,
PLR
DeWitt, d 25 May 1976, ae
77y, CRO
H P, b 27 March 1865 - d
10 March 1930, PLR
Robert, b 11 Aug 1913 - d
28 Nov 1975, CRO
Robert (Bob), b 1884 - d
1957, CRO
COOLEY, Doris, b 18 Dec
1928 - d 2 Feb 1933, WRC
Joseph H, b 30 Aug 1896 -
15 Dec 1962, WRC
Madge M, b 10 May 1910 -
no death date, WRC
COOPER, Alexander, b 15 Feb
1910 - d 16 Feb 1910,
MNT
Annie L, b 1 June 1904 -
no death date, LBR
Arvel L, b 20 Jan 1899 - d
24 Sept 1962, EST
Barbara A, b 9 March 1949

COOPER (continued)
- no death date, LNE
Birdie M, b 8 Feb 1895 - d
18 June 1896, MNT
Christeen, b&d 1915, SNB
Cleo Vaden, b 9 March 1923
- d 19 March 1923, LVN
Clifford, b 21 Jan 1932 -
d 16 May 1934, DVD
Clovis A, d 22 Oct 1978,
ae 65y, BRR
Clyde J, b 25 May 1890 - d
7 Oct 1963, CRO
D L (Fate), b 13 March
1878 - d 14 Oct 1967,
LVN
Dr D W, b 7 Apr 1851 - d 8
March 1910, WRC
Daniel P, b&d 25 Jan 1956,
LNE
David, b 12 Jan 1891 - d 6
Dec 1959, WRC
David, 4 Sept 1942 - no
other dates, DVD
David E, b 24 March 1876 -
no death date, DRL
Delia A, b 12 Apr 1877 - d
30 July 1962, LBR
Della, b 1910 - d 1912,
SNB
Donald, b 26 May 1941 - d
9 May 1947, PLR
Edsel Willis, b 25 Aug
1929 - d 1 May 1944, DRL
Everett R, b 26 June 1910
- d 15 Sept 1910, LVN
Florence J, b 14 Nov 1885
- d 14 July 1948, EST
Forrest, b 27 Aug 1902 - d
26 July 1968, PNY
Frances B, b 29 Sept 1872
- d 30 Apr 1952, SNB
Geo W, b 15 Sept 1883 - d
11 Nov 1895, LVN
Gertie Edmonds, d 2 July
1979, ae 73y, EST
Harold Lee, b 8 June 1933
- d 17 May 1934, PLR

COOPER (continued)

Henry, b 23 Sept 1955 - d 21 Oct 1928, DVD

Ira Hayes, d 10 Feb 1977, ae 48y, EST

J G, b 10 May 1869 - no death date, SNB

J R, b 23 Dec 1872 - d 18 Nov 1898, LVN

James F, b 20 Jan 1849 - d 2 Nov 1905, LVN

James O, b 1882 - d 1956, WRC

Jefferson F, d 26 Aug 1975, ae 49y, DRL

John P, b 9 May 1878 - d 6 Nov 1964, LBR

Joseph H, b 1884 - d 1940, WRC

Joseph R Jr, b 5 Aug 1929 - d 28 June 1931, DVD

Kate Alley, b 11 March 1890 - d 11 Sept 1922, CRO

Lola G, b 20 Apr 1911 - d 12 Feb 1932, LVN

Louisa A, b 1 March 1854 - d 27 Oct 1909, LVN

Mary, b 2 Apr 1861 - d 11 Feb 1935, WRC

Mary J, b 1 Apr 1881 - d 18 Apr 1947, PNY

Mary L Honeycutt, b 9 June 1900 - d 15 March 1945, DVD

Mattie E, b 4 May 1888 - d 25 Sept 1969, LVN

Nevada Morgan, b 12 Apr 1891 - d 5 Dec 1955, WRC

Nina King, b 15 Feb 1870 - d 27 Oct 1939, PTC

Polly Ann, b 22 Nov 1874 - d 13 Jan 1957, PNY

Randy Lee, b 25 June 1949 - d 24 Jul 1968, LNE

Rhoda, b 20 Jan 1854 - d 15 Dec 1925, DVD

Rittie M, b 6 Jun 1886 - d

COOPER (continued)

3 Apr 1958, DRL

Roy L, b 1905 - d 1970, PNY

Russel T, b 30 March 1912 - d 21 May 1935, CRO

Sherman L, b 24 May 1899 - d 12 May 1961, LBR

Tecumseh (Tee), d 7 Oct 1981, ae 79y, CLC

Thomas G, b 1 Dec 1867 - d 30 Oct 1953, PNY

W A, b 20 Nov 1885 - d 18 July 1915, LVN

Walter H, b 8 Nov 1896 - d 3 March 1966, LBR

Wm Riley, 24 May 1884, ae 24y 5mo, LBR

COPAS, Ida R, b 1926 - d 18 June 1975, DRM

Ola Lee Evans, b 2 May 1907 - d 27 May 1974, DRL

COPELAND, Ida M, b 24 Oct 1888 - d 20 Oct 1912, OLP

Ida M, b 24 Oct 1888 - d 20 Oct 1912, OLP

CORMACK, Barlow J, d 24 Aug 1977, ae 62y, FST

CORUM, Rev R L, b 24 June 1862 - d 22 Apr 1914, LVN

Sarah A, b 17 Apr 1842 - d 19 Sept 1913, LVN

COUTERIER, Mary Ellen, b 17 Feb 1907 - d 16 Nov 1973, WRC

COUTURIER, Mary Emily, d 16 Nov 1973, ae 66y, WMG

COVENTRY, Elizabeth Flo, b 16 Dec 1892 - d 2 March 1894, BRR

COVINGTON, Mrs Bertha, d 2 Nov 1979, ae 80y, CVN

COX, A M, b 25 June 1867 - d 2 March 1906, CLC

Abadah Fate, b 23 Nov 1889

COX (continued)
- d 3 Apr 1975, MSG
Ainy Brown, b 11 March 1889 - d 12 June 1964, UNG
Anna Howard, b 12 Jan 1842 - d 6 Nov 1925, CLC
Arie H, b 1 July 1890 - d 25 Apr 1973, CLC
Baby Girl, 1971, MSG
C M, b 13 May 1873 - d 29 Dec 1922, UNG
Rev C M, b 3 May 1908 - d 14 July 1948, WRC
Charles, d 5 June 1880, ae 39y, CLC
Charles, b 1942 - d 1945, NWP
Charles, b 14 Aug 1917 - d 25 Feb 1970, NWP
Conner, s/o M A & Sarah, d 22 March 1881, CLC
Dean, b 15 Oct 1946 - d 24 Oct 1946, MSG
Della, b 20 Sept 1889 - d 29 Dec 1966, UNG
Elizabeth, b 14 Sept 1886 - d 31 May 1916, CLC
Ellen, b 9 May 1885 - d 17 Oct 1974, NWP
Fred L, b 13 Oct 1883 - d 4 May 1867, CLC
George B, b 21 Oct 1882 - d 22 Aug 1922, UNG
Halie, b 1884 - d 1970, WRC
J M, b 13 Oct 1881 - d 4 Feb 1910, CLC
Jammie, 15 Nov 1947, MSG
John A, b 2 Oct 1832 - d 23 May 1895, CLC
Margaret M, b 6 June 1899 - d 8 Jan 1979, MSG
Martin A, b 1 May 1842 - d 29 June 1919, CLC
Monroe, b 6 Jun 1874 - d 29 Mar 1948, WRC
Myrtle, b 17 Oct 1906 - d

COX (continued)
1 June 1926, CLC
Nancy, b 7 Sept 1840 - d 8 Aug 1890, CLC
Noah, b 17 July 1879 - d 6 May 1965, UNG
Perry, b 15 Dec 1876 - d 12 Nov 1921, CLC
Rosa E, b 28 March 1884 - d 13 March 1913, CLC
Roy C, d 1 May 1977, ae 62y, WMG
Ruby, b 30 Apr 1910 - d 11 March 1924, CLC
Sarah, b 23 Dec 1846 - d 10 Apr 1910, CLC
Mrs W M, b 2 May 1863 - d 24 Nov 1912, OLP
William, b 29 July 1865 - d 8 Apr 1938, NWP
CRABTREE, Dillard, b 1897 - d 1960, CRO
Doris, b 1900 - d 5 Dec 1974, CRO
Frank, b&d 7 Apr 1914, DRM
Infant, d 28 May 1886, RGB
Mack, b 3 March 1946 - d 14 Sept 1967, EST
Ruby H, b 4 May 1924 - d 6 July 1924, DRM
Willie Lou, d 4 Apr 1977, ae 41y, CRO
CRAIN, Bertie Nelson, b 1889 - no death date, WRC
Homer O, b 1883 - d 1962, WRC
Mrs Bertie, d 28 Nov 1975, ae 85y, WRC
CRAINE, James M, b -- Oct 1886 - d 24 Dec 1958, JCJ
CRANE, Henry M, b 23 June 1831 - d 4 May 1900, DRL
CREEKMORE, Dawes H, b 1856 - d 1931, CRO
Don L, d 8 Oct 1979, ae 78y, WRC

CREEKMORE (continued)

Floyd H, 11 Oct 1933, OLP

Henrietta, b&d 30 Oct 1923, CRO

Louise D, b 6 Apr 1926 - d 16 Dec 1960, NWP

Willitti, b 19 June 1928 - no death date, NWP

CRENSHAW, Agnes H, d June 1901, ae 6y 9mo 1da, WRC

Benton, b 25 Apr 1908 - d 11 June 1933, WRC

Diha C, b 9 July 1871 - d 16 March 1904, CLC

Edna Wamta, b 9 July 1914 - d 25 Jan 1915, WRC

Elizabeth Ellen, b 28 Oct 1887 - d 11 Sept 1974, WRC

Infant, d 12 Feb 1862, ae 1mo, MNT

John W, b 16 March 1811 - d 2 Aug 1858, MNT

W B, b 1835 - d 1879, MNT

W B, b 12 Apr 1869 - d 15 Feb 1934, WRC

CRISP, A B, b 8 Apr 1891 - d 18 July 1920, PLR

Cenith, b 24 Dec 1851 - d 6 July 1928, PLR

Daisy, b 18 July 1884 - d 21 Aug 1914, PLR

George W, b 2 Feb 1853 - d 14 Aug 1926, PLR

Isaac Lawson, d 14 July 1975, ae 65y, BRR

J L, b 11 Oct 1876 - d 7 Aug 1954, PLR

Joe, b 2 May 1884 - d 8 Sept 1962, PLR

CROCKETT, Billie W, b 1909 - d 1968, WMG

Lois, b 1932 - no death date, WMG

CROMWELL, Amos, b 20 July 1916 - d 5 Aug 1916, MNT

Anna, b 12 March 1810 - d 7 July 1891, ELZ

CROMWELL (continued)

Artie Mae, b 5 Nov 1919 - d 19 Nov 1941, CRO

Benny Edward, b 11 July 1946 - d 12 Dec 1946, CRO

Bily Glenn Jr, b&d 25 Apr 1959, UNG

Carl F, b 14 March 1912 - d 18 Dec 1956, BRR

Clyde E, b 10 March 1906 - d 18 Feb 1967, BRR

Della, d 15 Sept 1971, ae 65y 5mo, CRO

Dora Edna, b 7 June 1915 - d 5 Nov 1925, CRO

Elmer Franklin, d 22 May 1966, ae 65y, CRO

Gertie Lee, d 3 Dec 1978, ae 85y, WRC

J B, b 1 Nov 1851 - d 14 March 1915, ELZ

J H, d 31 Dec 1975, ae 94y, WRC

J O, b 18 Oct 1871 - d 11 Apr 1944, SHD

J Walter, b 25 Apr 1917 - d 8 Apr 1968, UNG

James, b 9 Jan 1855 - d 19 March 1934, CRO

James A, b 7 Feb 1818 - d 12 Sept 1901, SHD

James Brooks, b 21 May 1938 - d 14 Feb 1971, UNG

James S, b 1 Nov 1864 - d 5 Apr 1945, UNG

Jane, b 17 May 1820 - d 21 Feb 1910, ELZ

John J, b 13 Apr 1799 - d 10 May 1885, PLR

John Marcus, b 22 Dec 1963 - d 9 June 1964, UNG

Louise Holloway, b 31 March 1886 - d 30 July 1916, MNT

M B, b 27 May 1839 - d 10 Jan 1908, SHD

CROMWELL (continued)
Mae R, b 16 Sept 1915 - d
28 Aug 1929, CRO
Marlyn Eugenia, b 6 May
1937 - d 6 June 1937,
BRR
Martha J, b 18 Apr 1918 -
no death date, BRR
Marvin G, b 29 March 1971
- d 4 Aug 1971, WHO
Matilda, b 11 May 1857 - d
23 Aug 1875, ELZ
Parthina Webb, b 26 Feb
1859 - d 14 Feb 1932,
CRO
Pearl, d 3 Jan 1894, CRO
Ralph Lloyd, d 9 Oct 1979,
ae 62y, CRO
Robert Charles, b 9 Aug
1877 - d 10 May 1918,
ELZ
Rose, 30 Sept 1905, CRO
Sadie L, b 1 June 1888 - d
3 June 1960, WHO
Sam W, b 20 Dec 1872 - d
11 Dec 1957, WHO
Sarah Cox, b 22 Feb 1866 -
d 3 March 1938, UNG
Sarah Louise, d 6 Apr
1978, ae --, BRR
Stephen, 29 Aug 1907, CRO
William, b 11 Nov 1889 - d
27 Oct 1981, CRO
Willie Mae, b 30 July 1917
- d 10 Oct 1918, ELZ
Wynna Rose, b 7 May 1962 -
d 3 Oct 1969, CRO
CROSS, Abraham, b 13 Feb
1869 - d 11 July 1869,
UNN
Bessie, b 1897 - d 9 Sept
1973, EST
Churchwell, b 1 Jan 1883 -
d 29 Dec 1960, UNN
Clarence, b 6 June 1925 -
d 8 Oct 1965, EST
Clifford, b 12 Aug 1930 -
d 13 Apr 1930, MSG

CROSS (continued)
Delia Langley, b 21 March
1870 - d 17 Jan 1949,
MSG
Flilchea Leon, b 25 Dec
1941 - d 31 Jan 1968,
EST
Floyd, b 4 Aug 1918 - d 12
Oct 1940, PNY
Gladys A, b 1 July 1909 -
d 18 Sept 1947, WRC
Henry, b 19 March 1896 - d
29 July 1896, UNN
Hollis B, b 24 July 1907 -
d 25 Sept 1910, MSG
Ivory, b 22 Feb 1897 - no
death date, UNN
James, b&d -- Sept 1874,
UNN
James Edward, b 26 Apr
1926 - d 31 Dec 1926,
MSG
James M Civil War Vet, b 4
Apr 1837 - d 22 Aug
1875, UNN
Jane Hall, b 18 May
1842(1845) - d 8 Aug
1918(1924), MSG
Jenifer Grace, b 30 Dec
1978 - d 1 Jan 1979, WMG
Kathleen, b 8 Jan 1927 -
no death date, EST
Lelia, 8 July 1907, ae
4mo, PNY
Linda Rae, b 14 Apr 1944 -
no death date, EST
Maggie, b 11 Jan 1893 - d
3 Nov 1912, OLP
Mary A, b 7 July 1858 - d
4 May 1897, UNN
Matilda G, b 13 Feb 1876 -
d 27 Feb 1954, MSG
Nellie Honeycutt, b 4 Aug
1887 - d 11 Oct 1957,
PNY
Romona Lee, b&d 14 June
1924, MSG
Rufus A, b 4 May 1872 - d

CROSS (continued)
9 Feb 1963, MSG
Rufus A Jr, b 6 June 1916 - d 15 Oct 1916, MSG
Susan Daphene, b 19 July 1951 - d 14 Nov 1954, WRJ
Thomas J, b 17 Feb 1870 - d 23 July 1951, MSG
Tina Lorene, d 12 June 1962, ae 1da, EST
Vera, b 25 Oct 1872 - d 20 March 1900, UNN
Wiley C, b 1890 - d 1964, EST
William M, b 7 March 1884 - d 6 Dec 1970, PNY
CROUCH, Alta Green, b 3 Aug 1897 - d 25 March 1973, BRR
Emma, b 9 March 1938 - d 28 June ----, BRR
Harold C, d 5 Dec 1974, BRR
Hazel R, b 13 Sept 1919 - no death date, BRR
John D Jr, b 7 July 1909 - d 26 Dec 1959, BRR
Joyce, b 19 Jan 1923 - d 16 Aug 1924, BRR
Sarah B, b 5 May 1877 - d 23 Aug 1951, BRR
Thomas O, b 29 Aug 1893 - d 1 Sept 1942, BRR
Travis, b 16 Nov 1917 - d 12 Dec 1917, BRR
CROWE, Nancy Massengill, b 26 June 1893 - d 16 Nov 1951, DVS
CUNDIFF, Elmer Chester, b 23 May 1882 - d 2 Feb 1951, WRC
Josee White, b 25 March 1889 - no death date, WRC
CURBOW, Harry, b 1918 - d 1934, PNY
Newt M, b 11 Aug 1888 - 6

CURBOW (continued)
Feb 1933, PNY
CURTAIN, Dewey L, Pvt USA WWII, b 13 Jan 1920 - d 19 June 1965, CLH
Larry C, b 8 July 1972 - no death date, CLH
Mattie C, b 20 July 1891 - no death date, CLH
Muriel C, b 1 Jan 1923 - no death date, CLH
Thomas J, b 15 Aug 1887 - d 27 Oct 1973, CLH
Tom Jr, TN Tech 5 1397 Mil Pol WWII, b 7 June 1925 - d 25 May 1963, DVS
CURTIS, Bessie Stennett, b 17 Apr 1900 - d 5 Dec 1934, ELZ
James Andy, d 8 Apr 1977, ae 81y, ELZ
Oscar, d 12 Nov 1975, ae 43y, WMG
CURTISTREW, William, b 29 July 1866 - d 5 Aug 1915, PLR
CZARNY, John W, b 17 May 1907 - d 27 July 1964, BRR
Oma M, b 24 Apr 1913 - no death date, BRR
CZURNEY, Gleneva D, 12 Apr 1937, UNG
Johnny, b 16 Oct 1933 - d 29 Dec 1933, UNG
D, F H, b -- March 1829 - d 23 Apr 1906, SNB
D'ARY, Dr Ralph, b 21 Apr 1844 - d 7 Oct 1904, WRC
Roslaf LeRoy, b 24 Nov 1867 - d 20 Jan 1915, WRC
D----, Mary, b 3 Oct 1828 - d 15 Aug 1886, CLC
DAGAN, Joseph Patrick, b 29 Jan 1893 - d 6 Sept 1963, WRC
DAGLEY, Clyde, b 1916 - d

DAGLEY (continued)
1966, NWP
Eldridge Kenneth, b 24 Feb
1924 - d 24 May 1927,
WRC
George W, b 22 July 1892 -
d 28 Nov 1956, WRC
Ina B, b 13 Aug 1906 - no
death date, WRC
J, b 14 June 1898 - d 19
Apr 1972, WRC
James S, b 28 March 1874 -
d 1 Oct 1965, WRC
John H, b 3 March 1881 - d
12 Sept 1944, NWP
L S, b 29 Feb 1884 - d 25
Oct 1938, WRC
Louis S, d 13 May 1981, ae
59y, WRC
Maggie R, b 21 Apr 1889 -
d 14 July 1979, WRC
Marlene, b 8 Aug 1949 - d
21 Aug 1949, WRC
Nila Litton, w/o L S, no
dates, WRC
Nina Edith, d 11 March
1969, ae 78y, NWP
Reba C, b 7 Apr 1900 - d
28 Aug 1964, WRC
Robert, b 28 July ---- d 4
Jan ----, WRC
Roy J, b 24 May 1902 - d 1
Jan 1978, WRC
Russell S, b 2 June 1837 -
d 28 Dec 1907, OLP
DAGNEY, Lee Chester, b 12
Sept 1924 - d 16 Oct
1974, WRC
DANIEL, Amanda, d 30 Sept
1881, ae 49y, UNN
Benny J, d 29 Apr 1980, ae
46y, DRL
Clara Jean, b 23 May 1938
- d 7 Sept 1938, BRD
Hope Alice, b 16 May 1892
- d 17 Dec 1970, LNE
Nora E, b 10 May 1926 - d
9 Oct 1926, LNE

DANIEL (continued)
William Calvin, b 23 May
1885 - d 29 June 1953,
LNE
DANIELS, Agnes, d 30 May
1979, ae 68y, NWP
Betty June, b 28 Dec 1926
- d 31 Oct 1927, NWP
DANTEL, Ann E Emerson, b
1865 - d 1948, WRC
DAUGHERTY, Bobby Jean, d 3
March 1981, ae 44y, NWP
Burl, b 2 June 1899 - no
death date, THR
Columbus L, b 17 March
1894 - d 5 Sept 1957,
NWP
Della Taylor, b 29 Nov
1877 - no death date,
CRO
Dennis Ray, d 7 March
1865, ae 1mo 16da, NWP
Dora Ruth, d 1 March 1969,
ae 30y, STP
Flossie S, b 11 Nov 1910 -
d 13 Nov 1968, NWP
Francis, d 18 Feb 1949, ae
32y 7mo, NWP
Grace, b 28 July 1903 - no
death date, RTT
Henry, d 20 May 1981, ae
45y, NWP
Hooper, b 11 Sept 1911 - d
6 March 1951, DVS
Jodie P, Pfc USA WWII, b
13 Dec 1921 - d 26 Aug
1962, NWP
John William, b 6 March
1876 - d 17 Sept 1934,
CRO
Mary E, b 6 Sept 1848 - d
2 Aug 1923, PNY
Nancy Jane, b 1 Dec 1897 -
d 26 May 1971, THR
Noah, b 28 Sept 1905 - d
25 March 1974, NWP
Otis Dewey, Pfc 1903 SVC
Cmd WWII, b 9 Jan 1915 -

DAUGHERTY (continued)
d 12 Sept 1965, NWP
Paul, b 8 Feb 1900 - d 12
Aug 1907, OLP
Paul, b 8 Feb 1900 - d 12
Aug 1907, OLP
Rhoda Helen, d 28 Sept
1977, ae 76y, NWP
Rittie, b 2 Sept 1876 - d
18 Aug 1943, NWP
Susie J, b 20 May 1874 - d
30 Sept 1937, UNN
Velma, b 16 Aug 1913 - no
death date, NWP
Daniel, b 28 May 1872 - d
7 Dec 1957, BRZ
Ruby, b 5 Sept 1908 - d 1
Nov 1910, OLP
William, b 20 Apr 1897 - d
6 Oct 1907, OLP
William, b 20 Apr 1897 - d
6 Oct 1907, OLP
DAUTEL, Anglea M, b 25 June
1855 - d 3 May 1956, WRC
Rachel, b 1886 - d 1964,
WRC
DAVENPORT, Cove D, b 17 Apr
1837 - d 14 Apr 1908,
SHD
Martha J, b 8 Sept 1840 -
d 19 July 1911, SHD
DAVIDSON, Annie K, b 7 May
1881 - d 19 Apr 1951,
BRR
Arthur J, b 2 March 1899 -
no death date, CLC
B S, b 7 June 1846 - d 14
Aug 1897, DVD
Charles Terry, b 11 Dec
1934 - d 4 Oct 1953, WRC
Charlie, d 5 Apr 1975, ae
74y, WMG
Della, b 1886 - d 1970,
WMG
Dewey T, b 6 May 1901 - d
14 Aug 1902, CLC
Dillar, d 29 Nov 1976, ae
71y, MCR

DAVIDSON (continued)
Effie Arena, b 19 Feb 1906
- d 17 Jan 1968, CLC
Eliza Ann Goad, b 29 June
1860 - d 21 Feb 1943,
CLC
Elma, b 2 Feb 1915 - d 11
March 1915, CLC
Elva D, b 26 July 1894 - d
-- Feb ----, DVD
Ephriam, no dates, MNT
Ephriam M, b 1856 - d 18
June 1902, MNT
Ethel, d 31 July 1979, ae
81y, CLC
Georgia, b 1943 - d 1970,
RGB
Hannah, b 18 Feb 1828 - d
4 Aug 1907, BRR
J C, b 12 Apr 1866 - d 5
March 1946, BRR
J D, b 1889 - d 1969, CLC
James, b 20 July 1824 - d
-- Oct 1866, BRR
Jean, d 4 Jan 1951, ae 13y
6mo, CRO
Jeanette Banks, b -- June
1867 - d -- Sept 1904,
DRL
Johnnie W, b 1 May 1879 -
d 24 May 1908, CLC
Joseph P, b 4 Oct 1884 - d
13 Feb 1963, DVD
Justina, b 24 Apr 1908 - d
17 March 1958, BRR
Lois, d 3 March 1981, ae
55y, FST
M J, b 19 June 1825 - d 14
Jan 1906, LVN
M T, b 10 May 1847 - d 8
Jan 1917, CLC
Martha, d 5 Nov 1975, ae
79y, CLC
Mary Ann, b 1805 - d 1903,
DVD
Mary Ella, b 30 March 1906
- d 17 Nov 1906, DVS
Mary J, b 4 July 1871 - d

DAVIDSON (continued)
    12 July 1871, MNT
  Menan, b 6 March 1820 - d
    5 July 1902, BRR
  Minerva, b 28 Feb 1824 - d
    12 Sept 1900, LVN
  Otis Sr, b 21 March 1903 -
    no death date, BRR
  Rebecca, b 10 May 1825 - d
    30 Oct 1869, BRR
  Rebecca M, b 22 March 1862
    - d 26 Dec 1965, MNT
  Sarah Owen, b 21 May 1871
    - no death date, BRR
  W L E, b 8 Apr 1811 - d 7
    May 1890, DVD
  Wilburn, b 15 Sept 1849 -
    d 12 Oct 1928, DVD
  William Lee, Col Rev War,
    b 1746 - d 1828, DVD
  William R, b 29 March 1873
    - d 15 May 1957, BRR
DAVIS, A D, no dates, DVS
  Addie McCartt,   b 6   March
    1881 - d 16 Sept 1968,
    SNB
  Albert C, b 24 Apr 1915 -
    d 3 Sept 1971, WRC
  Albert G, b 16 June 1890 -
    d 25 Sept 1974, LBR
  Albert G, b 29 Jan 1876 -
    d 28 May 1902, LBR
  Alva L, d 30 Aug 1975, ae
    71y, DVS
  Alvin C, b 25 June 1884 -
    d 25 Aug 1951, MSG
  Amanda, b 15 Feb 1867 - d
    4 Apr 1887, LBR
  Amy C Crenshaw, b 4 July
    1873 - d 11 Jan 1926,
    LBR
  Amy E, d 12 Oct 1976, ae
    82y, WRC
  Ann Walker, d 4 Oct 1981,
    ae 85y, BRD
  Anna W, b 25 March 1874 -
    no death date, LBR
  Arthur H, b 4 Sept 1902 -

DAVIS (continued)
    d 17 Apr 1949, CLC
  Baby, b 12 Oct 1907 - d 25
    Nov 1907, UNG
  Ballerma, b 1864 - d 1946,
    UNG
  Blanche D, b 16 March 1895
    - d 27 Jan 1940, DVS
  Boyd C, b 17 March 1916 -
    d 16 May 1975, LNE
  Carl L, b 20 June 1900 -
    no death date, CLC
  Carlos W, b 27 Jan 1910 -
    d 18 Feb 1954, CRO
  Caster, b 3 June 1909 - d
    25 June 1909, WRC
  Charles, b 23 Feb 1897 - d
    25 May 1898, CLC
  Charles H, b 18 Jan 1872 -
    d 22 Aug 1948, WRC
  Charles W, b 12 Apr 1914 -
    d 18 Oct 1916, SNB
  Charlotte, b 1 Jan 1822 -
    d 10 July 1904, DVS
  Claude, b 20 Jan 1916 - d
    2 March 1916, SNB
  Daniel E, b 25 Feb 1869 -
    d 14 June 1949, CLC
  David K, b 28 Nov 1869 - d
    2 Oct 1933, LBR
  Dora Toney, b 11 Oct 1880
    - d 1 Jan 1940, WRC
  Doshia G, b 23 June 1904 -
    d 25 March 1971, CLC
  Douglas Lynn, b 10 Oct
    1941 - d 28 Oct 1963,
    DVD
  Edith J, b 5 July 1903 - d
    11 May 1953, EST
  Elgie L, b 5 Sept 1905 - d
    25 Nov 1905, UNG
  Enith I, b 13 June 1924 -
    no death date, LBR
  Ethel Pauline, b 15 Aug
    1873 - d 16 Aug 1924,
    BRR
  Etta P, b 9 Oct 1896 - d 4
    Jan 1978, MSG

44

DAVIS (continued)

Eva C, b 21 Dec 1899 - d 9 Aug 1955, EST

Evan S, b 11 Dec 1879 - d 21 May 1948, UNN

F B, b 12 Aug 1838 - d 8 June 1913, NDK

Flora Mae, b 3 Feb 1899 - d 13 Oct 1977, SNB

Florence Jone, b 26 Aug 1890 - no death date, UNN

Frances, b 1876 - d 1967, UNG

Garteaux, b 3 June 1909 - d 17 Sept 1909, WRC

Gerude L, b 16 Dec 1959 - d 7 Jan 1960, LBR

Gifford Leon, b 6 May 1912 - d 8 Dec 1922, MLC

Grady L, b 4 July 1935 - d 28 Aug 1972, LBR

Granville, b 19 Mar 1893 - d 8 Oct 1953, WRC

H C, Co B 11th TN Cav, no dates, DVS

H D, no dates, DVS

Harold, no dates, CLC

Harold Blain, b 4 Aug 1930 - d 21 Jan 1932, SNB

Henry H, b 5 Feb 1871 - d 23 March 1945, DVS

Hobart G, b 1897 - d 1933, DVS

Hubert L, b 25 July 1911 - d 22 Jan 1934, CLC

Hugh R, b 29 Oct 1913(?) - d 29 Aug 1859(?), DVS

Hugh R, b 26 May 1873 - d 15 Feb 1934, DVS

Ida B, b 22 June 1879 - d 26 Jan 1927, DVS

Infant, no dates, CLC

Infant, no dates, CLC

Infant, b 31 July 1898 - d 3 Aug 1890, DVS

J A, b 1895 - d 1908, BRD

Jake C, b 10 Apr 1895 - d

DAVIS (continued)

3 June 1965, EST

James Nelson, b 28 June 1870 - d 15 March 1930, BRR

James Roddy, b 20 Jan 1902 - d 18 March 1972, SNB

Jason M, d 15 Apr 1980, ae 73y, FST

Jennie Mae, b 3 March 1897 - d 24 Apr 1970, CLC

Jessie M, d 20 Oct 1981, ae 75y, MLC

John, b 12 Nov 1836 - d 23 Jan 1898, BRR

John M, b 1777 - d 19 Nov 1851, DVS

John M, b 13 Dec 1861 - d 2 Apr 1944, LBR

John M, b 8 Nov 1873 - d 15 Nov 1918, NDK

John P Sr, b 27 May 1866 - d 25 Aug 1950, SNB

Johnnie L, b 7 July 1928 - d 24 May 1964, CLC

Josephine F, b 5 Apr 1873 - d 11 Oct 1940, DVS

Joyce Ann, b 12 June 1936 - d 1 Aug 1936, CLC

June, b 10 July 1902 - d 1 Dec 1958, DVS

Katie J, b 14 July 1897 - d 9 Apr 1960, LBR

L Sena, d 3 Nov 1904, ae 4y, DVS

Lane C, b 27 Jan 1910 - d 18 Aug 1946, CRO

Laura Scott, b 6 Jan 1878 - d 20 Apr 1926, WRC

Lawrence C, b 30 Oct 1886 - d 18 Oct 1963, WRC

Lea, b 28 Sept 1878 - d 19 Dec 1881, LBR

Lillie, b 21 Aug 1876 - d 21 March 1910, SNB

Lizzie, b 9 March 1871 - d 19 Apr 1892, NDK

Lloyd G, b 28 Apr 1913 - d

DAVIS (continued)
4 Dec 1943, CLC
Lucinda, b 19 May 1837 - d
19 May 1927, LBR
Lucinda, b 10 March 1821 -
d 22 Sept 1861, BCF
Luin Elmer, b 5 Jan 1888 -
d 19 Dec 1937, WRC
M A, no dates, DVS
Major Col, d 10 May 1880,
ae c 70y, DVS
Mamie, b 10 Oct 1904 - d 4
Apr 1907, LBR
Mary A, b 1 Feb 1837 - d
20 July 1922, DVS
Matilda A Liles, b 15 Feb
1874 - d 9 Dec 1952, DVS
Mildred, d Aug 1975, ae
62y, WRC
Mildred, b 19 Sept 1898 -
d 3 Aug 1902, CLC
Minnie Alice, b 18 Dec
1882 - d 16 Jan 1969,
DVS
Nellie L, b 2 June 1909 -
d 24 Nov 1909, UNG
Nettie, b 5 July 1895 - d
25 Jan 1959, LBR
O A, no dates, DVS
Patterson, b 26 July 1928
- d 29 Dec 1929, LBR
Perry E, b 23 May 1928 - d
15 July 1929, UNG
Pollie, b 6 Jan 1835 - d
17 June 1909, NDK
R A, b 11 Apr 1832 - d 6
March 1895, LBR
Rachel E, b 1 Apr 1850 - d
25 Feb 1901, UNH
Ralph, b 29 July 1908 - d
29 Sept 1909, CLC
Ralph L, b 13 July 1910 -
d 26 July 1937, WRC
Ray W, Pfc 360 Ftr Gp, AAF
WWII, b 18 July 1917 - d
12 Aug 1956, CLC
Raymond, d 18 Aug 1979, ae
66y, FRV

DAVIS (continued)
Reubin, d 18 July 1981, ae
57y, SNB
Rhoda Mae, b 10 Jan 1953 -
d 5 Sept 1958, PTC
Richard, b 11 June 1870 -
d 16 Oct 1873, DVS
Roger, b 11 Jan 1954 - d
13 March 1954, MSG
Rose, b 10 July 1910 - no
death date, CLC
Roy D, b 16 Oct 1922 - d 4
Aug 1952, CLC
Ruben A, b 2 Oct 1892 - d
28 June 1939, LBR
S A, no dates, DVS
Sam Huston, b 28 Feb 1910
- d 16 June 1910, SNB
Sam L, b 17 Dec 1868 - d
21 Jan 1955, DVS
Sarah A (Hall), b 4 May
1848 - d 2 Feb 1918, LBR
Sarah Adeline C, b 8 Sept
1871 - d 2 May 1927, CLC
Susie Branstetter, b 3
March 1885 - d 16 Feb
1944, CLC
Thomas Ellis, d 18 June
1979, ae 70y, DVS
Thomas H, d 6 Dec 1903, ae
85y, DVS
Thomas H Jr, b 1 Nov 1828
- d 15 Nov 1910, DVS
Thurman Jr, b 16 Oct 1933
- d 3 Apr 1940, LNC
W D, b 14 July 1895 - d 8
Oct 1944, CLC
W M, no dates, DVS
Walter Reed, b 18 Dec 1929
- d 4 June 1973, SNB
William, b 8 Sept 1843 - d
2 Feb 1912, DVS
William, b 6 Nov 1854 - d
10 March 1898, DVS
William H, b 1871 - d
1957, LBR
X, no dates, DVS
DAWN, Sarah Elizabeth, b 30

DAWN (continued)
Oct 1856 - d 4 Dec 1937, LNE
William Jasper, b 13 Apr 1849 - d 13 Apr 1921, LNE
DAWSON, Dora Dean, b 8 Oct 1899 - d 7 --- 1899, SNB
DEARMOND, Matilda Estes, b 12 Apr 1852 - d --- Aug 1880, EST
Samuel J, Co B 32d WWI, b 16 Apr 1877 - d 2 June 1900, EST
DEBIEUX, Amelia, b 27 Apr 1828 - d 16 July 1906, WRC
Emily Isabella, b 25 Nov 1867 - d 1 Jan 1901, WRC
Jerlen Theresa, b 1 Feb 1851 - d 17 Aug 1908, WRC
Ostavia Mary, b 4 July 1855 - d 27 July 1928, WRC
Paul J, b 25 Jan 1859 - d 1 Jan 1940, WRC
Mrs Paul, b 19 Nov 1828 - d 9 Feb 1896, WRC
Siciler Marie, b 1847 - d 1935, WRC
DEDFORD, Charles Chifton, b 7 March 1904 - d Feb 1938, WRC
DEFORD, James Floyd, b 20 Sept 1901 - d 23 May 1973, FST
Sophrinia A, b 26 Feb 1897 - no death date, FST
DELANEY, Charles C, b 21 July 1895 - d 24 Dec 1958, NWP
Eliza Matilda, d 14 Oct 1974, ae 86y, NWP
George P, b 10 May 1914 - d 22 Apr 1955, NWP
Horace, d 5 Sept 1977, ae 53y, NWP

DELANEY (continued)
Louise, b 1887 - d 1976, NWP
Lula Louise, d 30 Sept 1967, DVS
Myrtle E, b 17 Aug 1896 - no death date, NWP
DELIUS, Blanch Caroline, b 5 March 1910 - d 17 June 1911, CRO
Caroline J, b 15 Dec 1853 - d 20 Jan 1934, CRO
Carrie, b 16 Aug 1877 - d 9 March 1879, WRC
Charles A, b 30 Aug 1874 - d 29 Sept 1959, CRO
Charles W H, b 17 Feb 1837 - d 5 Nov 1882, WRC
Daisy Morgan, b 3 Oct 1891 - no death date, CRO
Dorcas Ruth, b 4 July 1931 - d 23 July 1931, CRO
Eunice Lorene, b 18 July 1923 - d 11 Jan 1938, CRO
Mae, b&d 10 Jan 1939, CRO
Mary, b 18 July 1873 - d 25 Aug 1873, WRC
Peter Oscar, b 9 Sept 1848 - d 15 Sept 1938, CRO
DELK, Murchison, b 27 Apr 1908 - d 28 June 1934, UNG
DELOZIER, Betty J, b 13 Sept 1932 - no death date, NWP
Charles H, b 17 Apr 1916 - d 17 Feb 1972, NWP
Mary D, b 10 Sept 1905 - d 2 Jan 1969, WMG
DELUIS, Charles Mac, d 23 Dec 1980, ae 26y, CRO
DENMAN, Alma J, b 1932 - d 1964, WMG
DENNIS, Angenett B, d 17 May 1901, ae 72y, DRL
G W, d 5 May 1903, ae 89y, DRL

47

DEPORTER, E L, d 28 Sept 1979, ae 82y, CRO

DIAL, Annie, d 21 Sept 1975, ae 87y, PTC

Jackson, d 20 June 1975, ae 79y, PTC

DIDEN, Ada, b 25 Aug 1923 - d 8 Sept 1923, MCD

Anna, b 1875 - d 1963, DDN

Ashury, b 1901 - d 1972, WMG

Della C, b 6 Nov 1890 - d 18 Feb 1953, MLC

Dorothy, b 7 Feb 1914 - d 24 Sept 1944, MCD

E R Sr, b 1804 - d 1871, DDN

Ester R, b 1801 - d 1886, DDN

James M, 8 May 1920, DDN

James W, b 20 Jan 1867 - d 1 March 1937, MCD

John A, b 24 June 1881 - d 8 June 1967, MLC

John S, b 1845 - d 1964, DDN

John T, b 22 Oct 1942 - d 26 Sept 1945, MCD

Joseph P, b 8 May 1920 - d 11 May 1920, DDN

Josha A, b 16 Sept 1876 - d 24 May 1953, WRC

Kimberly A, b 1964 - d 1969, WHO

Martha J, b 1845 - d 1924, DDN

Rosa, b 1876 - d 1966, DDN

Solomon E, b 1877 - d 1881, DDN

Sylvia June, b&d 28 March 1937, LVN

DILBECK, George W, b 13 Aug 1924 - d 24 Jan 1971, LBR

Wilmer, b 11 Feb 1903 - d 6 March 1961, LBR

Winnie, b 30 June 1906 - no death date, LBR

DILLON, Edith Mae, b 1 Apr 1887 - d 19 Nov 1972, WMG

Isabell, b 28 Feb 1877 - d 22 March 1949, WRC

John, b 31 Oct 1864 - d 11 Nov 1946, WRC

John R, d 7 Nov 1981, ae 74y, WMG

Kate, b 10 May 1860 - d 27 Jan 1899, WRC

Mary, b 13 March 1870 - d 11 Jan 1943, WRC

Thomas C, b 4 March 1863 - d 4 March 1922, WRC

DIMLING, Grace E, b 25 Sept 1884 - d 29 Sept 1885, RGB

John A, b 1855 - d 15 Dec 1882, RGB

DIXON, Ervin J, b 7 Apr 1896 - d 11 Sept 1968, DRL

Infant d/o S W, 7 Aug 1914, SHD

Julia, b 22 July 1880 - d 11 Apr 1918, MLC

Parelda V, b 30 May 1871 - d 10 Sept 1950, SHD

Samuel W, b 18 July 1870 - d 13 March 1940, SHD

DODSON, Edd Ross, b 15 Nov 1874 - d 25 March 1953, WRC

Ethel Anderson, b 26 Aug 1877 - d 29 Apr 1962, WRC

Mary E d/o E R & Ethel, no dates, MNT

Raymond, b 20 Dec 1908 - d 28 Dec 1909, MNT

Robert Ed, d 18 Oct 1975, ae 73y, PTC

DOGAN, Joe P, d 12 June 1980, ae 53y, MNT

Joseph Patrick, Pfc Bty F 13 Fld Art WWI, b 29 Jan 1893 - d 6 Sept 1963,

DOGAN (continued)
OOO
DOKEYNE, Osmond Fred, b 28 March 1851 - d 14 Aug 1881, RGB
DONAHUE, Buena, b 1887 - d 1961, PNY
Peter, b 1886 - d 1963, PNY
DORMODAL, Francis Smith, b 9 March 1853 - d 4 Feb 1931, DRL
DORSCHEID, Mary M, b 17 March 1859 - d 26 Feb 1919, DRL
Matt, b 14 Dec 1854 - d 12 March 1919, DRL
DOSSETT, George, b 19 Apr 1888 - d 1 Apr 1962, LBR
Mossie, b 24 Nov 1893 - d 1 Jan 1942, LBR
DOUGLAS, Edith P, b 1883 - d 1914, RGB
Eleanor M, b 1880 - d 1918, RGB
Floyd, b 1921 - d 1967, SNB
Harry L, d 14 Feb 1976, ae 67y, ELZ
J C, b 19 June 1839 - d 14 March 1917, SHD
Leona S, d 4 March 1968, ae 67y, ELZ
Lonzo, no dates, ELZ
Malinda Isabelle, b 8 Jan 1861 - d 2 May 1937, SHD
Mary, b 3 Aug 1839 - d 17 Feb 1902, SHD
Thomas Franklin, d 11 Feb 1977, ae 86y, ELZ
Thurman, b 1925 - d 1946, ELZ
DRAKE, Elizabeth, b 6 March 1856 - d 12 Feb 1937, PLR
Marshall, b 20 Oct 1852 - d 5 May 1936, PLR
DRORE, J MD, b 1836 - d

DRORE (continued)
1907, WRC
DUCCNOV, Megley, d 4 Apr 1950, ae 83y, WRJ
DUDLEY, Eva, no dates, SNB
Laura, no dates, SNB
DUFFY, Glena Mae, d 1 Sept 1978, ae 42y, CLC
DUGGAR, Albert, no dates - infant son, LBR
Alley, b 13 Feb 1890 - d 28 May 1890, LBR
Cordelia, b 1892 - d 1902, LBR
Frank, b 1857 - d 1989, LBR
Lillie, b 8 Apr 1896 - no death date, LBR
Malley, b 25 July 1886 - d 13 June 1914, LBR
Mary Emma, b 2 Aug 1887 - d 21 Jan 1963, LBR
Matilda, b 1855 - d 1898, LBR
Perly, b 5 Nov 1888 - d 7 July 1889, LBR
DUNAWAY, John S, b 8 Nov 1901 - d 28 March 1958, SNB
Johnnie Mae, b 14 March 1929 - d 31 Jan 1931, SNB
W H, b 21 Feb 1868 - d 2 Jan 1935, SNB
DUNCAN, Abba, b 22 Sept 1822 - d 3 Jan 1900, UNN
Annie Joyner, b 20 Dec 1876 - d 12 June 1957, UNN
Bery Burl, b 1921 - d 1944, UNN
Bessie, b 21 June 1907 - no death date, NWP
Beulah, b 14 Dec 1902 - d 30 Apr 1959, WRC
Charles, d 31 Jan 1978, ae 60y, UNG
Christine T, d 18 Jan

DUNCAN (continued)
1979, ae 91y, NWP
Cinda, b 5 Nov 1891 - d 15
Apr 1967, UNG
Clarence, d 23 Apr 1976,
ae 61y, NWP
Craven, b 1798 - d 1873,
WRC
Drefus, d 9 Nov 1979, ae
77y, NWP
E R, b 16 July 1832 - d 9
May 1910, PLR
Edna M, b 14 March 1892 -
d 30 Aug 1892, PLR
Elizabeth R, b 17 Dec 1838
- d 9 May 1900, PLR
Emanuel R, b 13 Apr 1906 -
d 21 July 1973, NWP
Flord A, b 1912 - d 1966,
NWP
Fred B, b 21 May 1888 - d
6 Oct 1956, PNY
George W, b 16 Aug 1903 -
d 9 Nov 1903, UNN
Gertie S, b 10 Oct 1890 -
no death date, PNY
Rev Harley, d 21 March
1976, ae 56y, UNG
Henrietta Jones, b 11 May
1863 - d 7 Apr 1944, PNY
Horace, b 30 Oct 1930 - d
27 Aug 1965, UNN
Horace G, b 12 May 1900 -
no death date, UNN
Hubert, b 28 Dec 1905 - d
4 July 1936, NWP
Isaac, d 3 Jan 1979, ae
59y, NWP
J F, b 9 Apr 1843 - no
death date, OLP
J F, b 15 July 1886 - d 29
June 1887, UNN
Jasper A, b 6 July 1888 -
d 25 Aug 1953, WRC
Joe S, b 19 Apr 1890 - d
20 March 1909, PLR
John, b 6 March 1783 - d
27 Sept 1836, HLL

DUNCAN (continued)
John K, b 23 Apr 1861 - d
3 Sept 1941, UNN
John Richard, b 26 Oct
1908 - d 4 Jan 1966, UNN
M A, b 2 Apr 1892 - d 15
Nov 1892, UNN
Margaret Byrd, b 26 Nov
1841 - d 16 Oct 1917,
UNN
Martha J, b 3 Apr 1878 - d
14 Jan 1942, UNN
Mary, b 29 May 1875 - d 12
Feb 1917, UNN
Mary, b 3 Jan 1895 - d 6
Jan 1971, UNN
Mary, b 1810 - d 1891, WRC
Mary A, b 2 July 1853 - d
20 July 1917, OLP
Mary Ethel, b 1895 - d
1915, UNN
Mrs Nancy, b 14 Feb 1862 -
d 14 July 1912, WRC
Noah, b&d 17 June 1936,
NWP
Paul, d 10 June 1975, ae
42y, NWP
Polly Ann, b 11 June 1857
- d 6 Oct 1941, UNN
Rachel Kelly, b 28 July
1874 - d 5 May 1919, UNN
Randal R, b 18 June 1919 -
d 5 Feb 1971, UNN
Robert Fay, b 29 July 1895
- d 27 March 1951, WRC
Robert Lee, b&d 10 Aug
1920, PNY
Ruby E, b 19 March 1928 -
no death date, UNN
Samuel H, b 5 June 1887 -
d 30 Sept 1924, UNN
Susie J, b 11 Aug 1902 -
no death date, UNN
T J, b 14 March 1835 - d 1
May 1912, UNN
Thomas, d 29 Dec 1977, ae
38y, NWP
Vertie E, b 7 July 1903 -

DUNCAN (continued)
d 14 Oct 1966, PNY
W Ernest, b 1 Oct 1892 - d
8 Dec 1976, UNN
W H C, b 25 Dec 1869 - d
27 Dec 1905, UNN
W Houston, b 11 Aug 1863 -
d 11 Sept 1940, UNN
Wiley A, Mex War Vet, b 7
Apr 1828 - d 1 May 1914,
UNN
Willard F, d 28 March
1979, ae 74y, NWP
William, d 19 June 1980,
ae 80y, UNN
Wm Ray, b 10 May 1905 - d
19 Nov 1934, PNY
Wm Wiley, b 7 March 1866 -
d 8 Sept 1950, PNY
DUNLAP, Lonnie, b 1887 - d
1937, DRM
Millis, b 1888 - d 1968,
LNC
DUNN, George W, b 1901 - d
1973, FLR
Marion Johnson, d 4 Jun
1963, WRC
Mary Belle, d 25 Nov 1975,
ae 70y, UNG
Robert Fay, CMM USN WWI, b
29 July 1895 - d 27
March 1951, OOO
DUNNING, Frank Herbert, b 2
Oct 1856 - d 7 March
1903, SNB
Frank Herbert, b 2 Oct
1856 - d 7 March 1903,
SNB
DUNNINGTON, Granville, d 7
Sept 1974, ae 68y, BRD
DUNSMORE, James, d Deer
Lodge, ae 78y, DRL
DUPEE, Elizabeth, b 1876 -
d 1942, CRO
Robert, b 13 Feb 1835 - d
4 Feb 1913, CRO
Sarah, b 26 Apr 1844 - d 5
July 1918, CRO

DURHAM, Lula M, b 11 May
1917 - no death date,
FLR
Virgil P, b 15 Apr 1902 -
d 6 Jan 1967, FLR
William Dudley, d 10 Oct
1978, ae 55y, FRC
DYE, Grice, b 1894 - d
1970, CRO
DYER, Albert, b 1893 - d
1950, MCD
Arizona, b 4 July 1868 -
no death date, MCD
Elsie Hamby, d 31 Aug
1978, ae 83y, MCD
Mildred Terry, d 28 Nov
1980, ae 59y, LBR
Sarah, b 16 March 1840 - d
25 Nov 1917, SNB
William, b 26 Oct 1861 - d
12 Aug 1946, MCD
DYLE, Haron Ann, d 25 Oct
1969, ae 1mo 19da, PTC
EARLEY, Rachel, b 4 Feb
1876 - d 4 Sept 1941,
LNC
EARNEST, Otha R, b 12 Oct
1902 - d 21 Dec 1904,
SNB
EASTHAM, Iwendalyn Gale,
d/o Alvin, b&d 4 June
1943, WRC
Lloyd E, b 16 June 1900 -
d 14 March 1980, WRC
Weline Mae, b 29 June 1905
- d 19 Jan 1961, WRC
EASTRIDGE, Albert K, d 30
March 1975, LBR
C H, b 16 Apr 1892 - d 18
Aug 1964, EST
Charles Z, b 22 Sept 1889
- d 28 Nov 1943, LBR
Delbert R, b 5 Feb 1933 -
d 14 Oct 1945, EST
Eugene B, b 18 Aug 1915 -
no death date, EST
Harry O, b 1918 - d 1939,
LBR

EASTRIDGE (continued)
James D B, b 25 Sept 1862
- d 13 May 1864, HCK
Lillie M, b 19 Apr 1894 -
d 14 March 1973, LBR
Lola Jones, b 22 Aug 1896
- d 14 Sept 1973, EST
Lucy R, b 6 Apr 1895 - d
19 Jan 1944, EST
Mary E, b 4 Sept 1864 - d
23 March 1943, LBR
Maxine N, b 18 Jan 1919 -
d 15 March 1977, EST
Samuel M, b 17 July 1885 -
d 14 Apr 1943, EST
EBLE, Harold Vincent, b 9
Feb 1925 - d 21 July
1925, PNY
Mart, b 28 June 1898 - d
24 Aug 1969, PNY
Mattie, b 14 Nov 1891 - d
25 Jan 1967, PNY
Robert Martin, b 22 Aug
1920 - d 30 Apr 1934,
PNY
Walter, WWI, b 6 June 1892
- d 8 July 1941, PNY
EDMONDS, Ben F, b 1884 - d
1958, NWP
Beulah W, b 19 Sept 1884 -
no death date, NWP
Charles H, b 14 Sept 1883
- d 24 Feb 1952, NWP
Charlie, b 28 July 1882 -
d 3 Aug 1916, EST
Eugene, b 22 Aug 1914 - d
6 Feb 1915, STP
Maggie, b 1891 - no death
date, NWP
Milda, b 15 Aug 1885 - 19
Nov 1907, WRC
Odis E, b 24 May 1912 - d
2 Nov 1913, EST
Sallie, b 11 Apr 1886 - d
22 Jan 1976, EST
EDWARDS, Anna J, b 21 June
1845 - d 14 Aug 1945,
WRC

EDWARDS (continued)
Bettie, b 1864 - d 1936,
OLP
Charles L, d 19 March
1980, ae 56y, WRC
Cyrus, Co B 13 KY Cav Mil
Stone, no dates, WRC
Ed S, b 25 July 1887 - d
15 Oct 1967, CRO
Evelyn L, b 27 Aug 1972 -
no other date, EST
Everett Jr, b 5 Nov 1903 -
d 22 Aug 1955, WRC
General, b 20 Sept 1908 -
d 18 Oct 1930, CRO
Henry D, b 18 Nov 1862 - d
1 Apr 1932, CRO
John, no dates, LBR
Johnie, b 30 May 1934(?) -
d 20 May 1934(?), WRC
Klondike, b 25 July 1898 -
d 20 March 1911, CRO
Luther, b 14 Feb 1936 - d
2 Feb 1940, WRC
Mary S, b 1869 - d 1933,
CRO
Perley, Co B 3 TN Inf
Sp/Am War, no dates, WRC
Robert, b 1864 - d 1931,
OLP
Ruth S, b 17 Aug 1881 - no
death date, CRO
Stella Phillips, d 14 May
1979, ae 84y, UNH
T N, b 1871 - d Sept 1931,
WRC
ELDRETH, Elizabeth, b 1889
- d 8 July 1973, DRL
ELDRIDGE, Gertrude, d 7 Oct
1981, ae 84y, WBB
Joe V, b 7 Feb 1906 - d 13
Jan 1975, BRN
Lila Eilley, b 1902 - d
1931, CRO
Oma, b 28 Feb 1914 - no
death date, BRN
ELGIN, George, b 1859 - d
1920, ELZ

ELIME, Billie B, b 1903 - d 1957, CRO

ELLINGHAUSEN, Emilie, b 15 June 1862 - d 18 March 1956, DRL

William, b 28 Jan 1856 - d 8 Apr 1929, DRL

ELLIS, Burl, d 1 Dec 1980, ae 84y, WRC

Burl, b 12 Dec 1895 - no death date, WRC

Ellen Jones, b 17 Feb 1903 - d 26 Jan 1974, DVS

Laura Kennedy, b 5 Jan 1910 - d 2 Mar 1945, WRC

Leonard M, b 9 May 1900 - d 1 Oct 1976, LNE

Linda, b 18 June 1903 - no death date, LNE

Mary Louise, d 15 Apr 1970, ae 45y 5mo, PNY

Roger N, b 4 Nov 1900 - d 1 Aug 1901, BRR

Wilham Edward, b 30 Nov 1921 - d 23 Dec 1959, WRC

ELLISON, Michelle, b&d 11 Jan 1971, NWP

ELY, Bruce, b 8 March 1931 - d 15 Feb 1970, DRL

Charlie W, b 10 Apr 1889 - d 22 March 19--, ae 78y, UNG

Eula, b 21 May 1928 - no death date, DRL

Frankie, b 25 May 1889 - d 14 Aug 1969, UNG

EMERY, Joseph, b 1858 - d 1889, BRR

Helen L, b 1916 - d 1951, DVS

Henry Guy, b 17 May 1870 - d 3 July 1933, UNN

Mellie, b 15 Apr 1888 - d 25 Nov 1968, DVS

Noah, b 19 Apr 1885 - d 12 Mary 1948, DVS

ENGERT, Augusta, b 6 June

ENGERT (continued) 1845 - d 31 Oct 1910, WRC

Charles, b 6 Sept 1883 - d 1 Jun 1953, WRC

Etier Louise, b 17 Oct 1918 - d 19 Oct 1918, WRC

Etta, b 18 Feb 1890 - no death date, WRC

Frederick, b 11 Jan 1834 - d 7 Dec 1891, WRC

Maria F, b 1 Feb 1845 - d 20 Apr 1887, WRC

Mary Alled, b 23 Mar 1928 - d 28 Jun 1928, WRC

Thelma C, b 7 March 1912 - d 8 July 1912, WRC

William F, d 12 Oct 1974, ae 85y, WRC

ENGLAND, Bennie H, b 27 Feb 1913 - d 7 Sept 1929, SNB

Cal F, d 24 Oct 1978, ae 71y, WHO

Cecil Alex, b 5 July 1901 - d 12 Oct 1963, EST

Charley H, b 17 Aug 1879 - d 13 Jan 1899, SNB

Mrs Dora E, d 13 Aug 1974, ae 86y, WHO

Elmer, b 18 May 1898 - d 16 Aug 1968, EST

Eva E, d 18 Oct 1981, ae 68y, SNB

Ezra, d 2 Apr 1905, ae 17y, SNB

Flora, b 17 Apr 1900 - d 28 March 1932, UNG

George Wash, b 5 June 1880 - d 2 May 1965, SNB

Grace K, b 6 May 1895 - d 28 Aug 1960, BRR

Harry, b 1899 - d 1967, UNG

Jack Ritchie, b 24 July 1926 - d 8 Nov 1974, SNB

James R, b 30 May 1854 - d

ENGLAND (continued)
1 Sept 1936, DRL
James W, b 11 Feb 1838 - d
22 May 1921, SNB
John, Co K 5th TN Inf, b
c1816 - d 21 Dec 1902,
LVN
Julian Howard, d 18 Dec
1979, ae 52y, SNB
Malinda, b 22 Feb 1890 - d
22 March 1938, UNG
Nannie J McCartt, b 11 Oct
1884 - d 12 Oct 1962,
SNB
Rebecca P, b 7 Nov 1850 -
d 7 Sept 1909, SNB
Robert, buried 27 May
1977, PLR
Robert J, d 24 May 1977,
ae 64y, LNE
Robert M, b 3 Oct 1887 - d
23 July 1971, BRR
Rusaw, b 27 Feb 1917 - d 7
May 1950, MLC
Sarah E, b 23 March 1856 -
d 11 March 1937, DRL
Stanley, b 24 Aug 1903 - d
25 March 1904, SNB
W A, b 22 Nov 1885 - d 20
May 1916, SNB
W T, b 26 Oct 1850 - d 26
Dec 1914, SNB
Wiley Sr, b 11 Oct 1886 -
d 7 Aug 1936, UNG
William E, b 1969 - d
1970, UNG
ENTSMINGER, H R, b 7 Oct
1875 - d 22 Nov 1959,
WRC
Nancy Byrd, d 18 May 1979,
ae 39y, WRC
Robert H, b 15 Feb 1918 -
d 26 May 1944, WRC
ERICKSON, Audrey Ann, b 14
May 1927 - d 25 March
1933, UNN
Dalton M, b 8 July 1943 -
d 4 Jan 1944, UNN

ERICKSON (continued)
Ernest G, b 22 Dec 1895 -
d 24 May 1961, UNN
Lewis, b 29 Oct 1924 - d 6
Jan 1929, UNN
Lillian A, b 16 March 1935
- d 19 Feb 1936, UNN
Lillian G, b 8 July 1900 -
d 12 June 1977, UNN
Mary McPeters, b 21 May
1862 - d 12 Apr 1933,
UNN
Ole B, b 4 June 1955 - d 9
March 1924, UNN
Rudolph, b 25 Feb 1903 - d
19 June 1920, UNN
ERNEST, George W, b 1853 -
d 1924, DRL
Mary E, b 1863 - d 1931,
DRL
ERVIN, Barbara, b 17 March
1827 - d 17 Dec 1872,
PTC
Nancy M, b 2 Sept 1837 - d
29 Aug 1893, PTC
ERWIN, Amanda Williams, b 1
June 1836 - d 25 May
1914, ELZ
ESL, foot stone, SNB
ESTES, Annie Butler, b 9
Jan 1871 - d 27 Apr
1966, EST
Annie M, b 28 Nov 1855 - d
27 Aug 1921, EST
Dorcas, b 6 March 1917 -
no death date, EST
George W, b 9 March 1858 -
d 13 Oct 1933, EST
Jane Justice, b 22 Dec
1822 - d 23 March 1906,
EST
Jennie, 15 Jan 1865 - no
other date, EST
Lawrence L, b 19 Sept 1909
- d 24 Jan 1964, EST
Matilda F, b 26 Aug 1881 -
d 22 Dec 1898, EST
Nora Elizabeth, b 29 Apr

ESTES (continued)
1889 - d 17 May 1958, CHN
Peter, b 1830 - d 19 July 1864, EST
R T, b 22 March 1855 - d 9 July 1960, EST
Sarah A, d c1912, ae 62y, EST
William A, b 26 Sept 1846 - d 19 June 1904, EST
William Elmer, b 21 July 1896 - d 7 Aug 1954, CHN
EVANS, Amy, b 1921 - d 1973, MSG
Betty Jane, b 24 Oct 1925 - d 11 Dec 1926, CRO
Bill W, Pvt, b 20 July 1925 - d 27 Feb 1945, PNY
Etta C, b 15 Nov 1895 - no death date, PNY
John W, b 7 March 1884 - d 16 March 1961, PNY
Martha M, b 5 March 1914 - d 22 Sept 1967, BRR
Mary Joyner, b 30 Aug 1894 - d 14 May 1964, WRC
Ruth Aileen, b 28 Nov 1948 - d 25 Aug 1967, MSG
EVERHARD, Harold H, F1 USN WWII, b 4 Nov 1919 - d 12 Sept 1971, WRC
J C, b 3 Nov 1879 - d 30 Oct 1937, WRC
Mary, b 6 May 1879 - d 4 July 1954, WRC
EZELL, J H, b 26 May 1875 - d 29 July 1912, CBJ
FAGAN, Daniel, d 18 March 1967, ae 58y, FGN
Ida G, b 6 Aug 1869 - d 7 June 1945, FGN
James A, b 13 Feb 1867 - d 31 Jan 1940, FGN
James D, b 5 Oct 1899 - d 31 May 1926, FGN
Jane, b 4 Jan 1829 - d 18

FAGAN (continued)
June 1899, FGN
Leonard A, b 30 Oct 1895 - d 29 July 1920, FGN
Sadee M, b 20 Nov 1891 - d 8 July 1973, EST
Walter D, b 21 Oct 1891 - d 20 Feb 1956, EST
William Fred, b 10 Apr 1890 - d 18 Aug 1954, FGN
FAIRCHILD, David (Andy), b 5 Nov 1913 - d 6 March 1978, LBR
George, b 22 June 1878 - d 14 Sept 1919, OLP
Gilbert, b 1899 - d 1968, MLC
Henrietta, b 29 May 1901 - d 9 July 1912, MLC
Herbert Obies, b 29 Apr 1918 - d 14 Feb 1919, MLC
Little Nath, b 28 Apr 1918 - d 10 Nov 1918, OLP
Martha E, b 2 June 1922 - d 17 June 1922, MLC
Sam Houston, b&d 2 June 1922, MLC
Samuel O, b 1932 - d 1972, SNB
Walter H, d Feb 1940, WRC
William F, b 9 Apr 1880 - d 3 Aug 1952, MLC
FAIRCHILDS, Betty J, b 6 Aug 1924 - d 21 Jan 1929, MLC
Dorothy, b 15 Aug 1918 - d 10 Sept 1918, MLC
Eli, b 11 Oct 1823 - d 25 Aug 1881, UNN
Hattie, d 1960, ae 68y, DDN
James, b 1869 - d 1942, UNN
James, b 3 Feb 1854 - d 11 Sept 1915, UNN
John C, b 9 Oct 1863 - d 8

FAIRCHILDS (continued)
Feb 1935, BRR
L C, b 25 March 1922 - d
15 May 1923, MLC
Louis, b 1916 - d 1929,
UNN
Lydia M, b 25 Nov 1893 - d
13 Dec 1928, MLC
Martha A, b 6 March 1874 -
d 19 Jan 1964, MLC
Mary, b 6 Aug 1833 - d 22
March 1913, UNN
Mary S, b 7 March 1852 - d
21 Aug 1931, UNN
Maud, b 1883 - d 1959, UNN
Melvinia, b 16 Feb 1830 -
d 9 July 1874, UNN
Savanah J, b 19 Feb 1869 -
d 21 June 1934, BRR
Walter Lonzo, b 9 Dec 1912
- d 20 Jan 1929, MLC
Worth, no dates - Civil
War stone, UNN
Worth, Co B 3rd TN Inf, no
dates, UNN
FALLS, John Bob, d 5 Sept
1976, ae 84y, UNN
FARICHILD, David A, b 17
Aug 1867 - d 15 Nov
1944, LBR
Martha A, b 29 July 1880 -
d 5 Oct 1963, LBR
FARICHILDS, Lewis C, b 20
Feb 1868 - d 23 Aug
1938, MLC
FARINGTON, Effie, b 4 Jan
1869 - d 7 Aug 1888, DRL
FARMER, Carl Houston, b 13
July 1915 - d 22 Jan
1952, CRO
Charles C, b 13 Apr 1897 -
no death date, NWP
Donald, b 11 Feb 1935 - d
8 March 1975, LBR
E C, b 25 March 1879 - d
14 Jan 1935, CRO
H C, b 9 May 1849 - d 6
Dec 1933, CRO

FARMER (continued)
Rebecc Aytes, b 1 May 1857
- d 26 Sept 1923, CRO
Ruth B, b 25 Aug 1899 - d
9 Dec 1966, NWP
Wanda, b 16 July 1932 - no
death date, LBR
FARR, Brenda Sue, b&d 9 Nov
1953, DVS
Carl Joseph, b 9 May 1954
- d 12 May 1954, DVS
Joe, Pvt 119 Inf 30 Div,
WWI, b 4 March 1888 - d
21 Aug 1951, DVS
Laura Bell, b 28 March
1895 - d 3 Jan 1917, CRO
Linda Sue, 1951, CRO
Pearl, b 11 Oct 1901 - d
24 June 1965, DVS
FARRIN, Dorothy Cox, b 1892
- d 1964, UNN
FARRIS, Ancil , b 1878 - d
1959, PNY
Charlie R, b 27 Feb 1913 -
d 21 March 1914, PNY
Harold, b 21 May 1903 - d
18 Dec 1925, PNY
Margie, b 10 Jan 1915 - d
29 Dec 1915, PNY
Nell, b 1882 - d 1961, PNY
FARSTNER, Amalie
Fawlewieke, b 22 July
1837 - d 30 Oct 1913,
WRC
FELTS, Arminda, b 13 Aug
1910 - d 16 Nov 1965,
WRC
Herschel, b 12 Nov 1902 -
no death date, WRC
FERGUSON, John, Sgt Bty A
42 Art WWI, b 18 Oct
1885 - d 20 Sept 1953,
CRO
Martin W, b 28 Aug 1850 -
d 22 Jan 1934, PLR
Reba Melissa, b 24 Jan
1908 - d 5 Oct 1910, BRR
FERMAN, Laura T, b 7 May

FERMAN (continued)
  1883 - d 1 Feb 1923, CRO
FINCHER, Bash, b 26 June
  1888 - d 27 Dec 1967,
  NWP
FINK, Amanda Lee, b 15 Oct
  1883 - d 22 Oct 1948,
  THR
  Eugene Franklin, b 22 Aug
  1914 - d 1 Nov 1928, THR
  John Larkin, d 26 Dec
  1960, ae 78y, THR
FINKS, Crystal Irene, b 28
  Apr 1921 - d 6 Jan 1948,
  ADC
FISHER, George A, b 6 May
  1855 - d 20 May 1885,
  MRR
FITZGERALD, Henry, b 27 Oct
  1893 - d 13 Feb 1896,
  MNT
FLETCHER, Carl L, b 11 Sept
  1936 - d 25 May 1938,
  RGB
  Charlie, b 4 Feb 1913 - d
  8 Feb 1913, RGB
  Eva L, b 30 Aug 1906 - no
  death date, RGB
  Harry E, b 16 June 1906 -
  d 20 Aug 1964, RGB
  John W, Co L 117 Inf, b 18
  Feb 1894 - d 7 Oct 1918
  (in France), RGB
  Lottie, b 10 Apr 1874 - d
  13 Apr 1951, RGB
  Minerva J, b 8 Dec 1867 -
  d 28 March 1961, WRC
  Tommy Joe, d 8 Feb 1974,
  ae 10y, RGB
  Walter, b 2 Jan 1863 - d 8
  Dec 1937, RGB
FLOWERS, Alta, d 7 Oct
  1975, ae ----, PLR
  Oplas G, b 7 Oct 1889 - d
  24 Apr 1930, PLR
FOGLEMAN, Jake, s/o Ernest,
  ------, CRO
FORD, Bill, b 10 June 1890

FORD (continued)
  - d 6 Dec 1963, LBR
  Bill, b 12 May 1895 - d 6
  Feb 1958, NWP
  Cordie E, b 16 Apr 1864 -
  d 13 Feb 1948, UNG
  Essie, b 9 Feb 1898 - d 8
  Dec 1950, NWP
  J B, b 24 Dec 1937 - d 9
  Jan 1938, LBR
  James Henderson, d 7 July
  1973, ae 82y, UNG
  Kenneth Lee, d 4 Nov 1978,
  UNG
  Mary, b 25 July 1903 - no
  death date, LBR
  Robert F, b 3 Apr 1928 - d
  24 Nov 1941, LBR
  Vicey Graves, d 18 Nov
  1977, ae 83y, UNG
FORRESTER, Elizabeth, b 15
  Aug 1841 - d 9 Aug 1917,
  SNB
FOSTER, ----, no dates, DDN
  Edna Laura, b 23 Dec 1904
  - d 30 Aug 1966, SNB
  Elbert T, d 24 Nov 1979,
  ae 79y, SNB
  Ida Lee, b 3 June 1877 - d
  4 March 1911, OLP
  Infant Dau, b&d 5 Oct
  1902, OLP
  Nolan R, d 24 July 1981,
  ae 47y, NWP
  Wilma L, b 5 Dec 1918 - d
  7 Jan 1965, LBR
FOUST, Lillian E, b 25 May
  1909 - d 5 Sept 1942,
  MRR
FOWLER, Edgar, d 30 Apr
  1980, ae 73y, UNG
  Ella, b 1910 - d 1964, UNG
  Frank W, b 22 Jan 1881 - d
  20 Jan 1961, DRL
  Lillian E, b 12 July 1886
  - d 9 March 1968, DRL
  Lizzie, b 2 Aug 1880 - d
  20 March 1950, STC

FOWLER (continued)
Lula Ann Chamb, b 12 Apr
1846 - d 2 Dec 1934, SNB
Orin P, Co E 89 NY Inf,
Mil Stone, SNB
FRANCIS, Anna Jackson, b 28
Oct 1880 - d 24 Aug
1940, LBR
Bertha Rich, d 29 July
1975, ae 75y, ARM
Carl N, b 28 July 1902 - d
21 Nov 1902, LBR
Charles S, b 30 Nov 1871 -
d 5 Jan 1930, LBR
Charlotte, b 2 Aug 1868 -
d 14 March 1923, LBR
Claude B, b 28 Feb 1905 -
no death date, CRO
Earl Eugene, d 23 June
1957, ae 4mo, LBR
Edith, b 29 Jan 1906 - d 8
June 1976, CRO
Elmer, d 29 Aug 1981, ae
48y, ARM
Julie M, b 5 Feb 1890 - d
23 June 1912, CRO
Margaret Love, b 11 Jan
1861 - d 17 Oct 1948,
LBR
Ollie, b 20 Dec 1906 - no
death date, LBR
Ray, b 23 Aug 1908 - d 10
Dec 1939, LBR
Raymond A, b 13 May 1915 -
d 2 March 1945, LBR
W R, 3rd Reg Co G Vol Inf
Sp/Am, b 28 March 1867 -
d 15 Jan 1899, LBR.
FRANKLIN, John A, b 21 Apr
1899 - d 23 Dec 1963,
WRC
Nellie B, b 6 Apr 1902 -
no death date, WRC
FREDERICK, Grace H, d 14
July 1978, ae 73y, NWP
John B, b 15 May 1864 - d
28 Dec 1928, PNY
John B, b 25 Apr 1866 - d

FREDERICK (continued)
4 Oct 1938, PNY
FREELS, Casper E, b 19 Oct
1897 - d 8 Feb 1900, ALB
Chas B, b 22 Feb 1896 - d
29 Nov 1921, PLR
Clara Ruth, b 11 July 1941
- d 14 July 1941, SNB
Delia L, b 30 Oct 1891 -
no death date, LNE
Donald Dean, b 4 Apr 1941
- d 8 June 1963, MLC
Edward L, b 27 Oct 1921 -
d 10 June 1925, ELZ
Edward Theodore, b 9 Aug
1906 - d 1 Sept 1976,
SNB
Ella Mae Jennings, d 5 Feb
1979, ae 59y, LNE
Ella May, b 1 May 1887 - d
1 May 1910, WRC
Emlie, b 9 Feb 1852 - d 28
Apr 1935, MLC
Enoch Floyd, Sgt USA, WWI,
b 12 Aug 1893 - 29 Nov
1961, LNE
Flora E, b 12 Nov 1899 - d
9 Feb 1900, ALB
George, b 1907 - d 1921,
MLC
Guy F, b 14 March 1902 - d
6 Jan 1937, PLR
Henry H, b 1848 - d 1962,
MLC
J L, b 12 Oct 1952 - d 27
Oct 1918, MLC
J W, b 3 Aug 1884 - d 5
March 1912, PLR
Jesse, b 15 Apr 1824 - d 2
July 1898, PLR
Jesse M, b 19 Feb 1855 - d
28 June 1918, SNB
Joe Edward, b 17 June 1890
- d 24 May 1965, SNB
John R, b 25 March 1909 -
d 13 Feb 1958, WRC
John W, b 13 Feb 1908 - d
29 Feb 1908, PLR

FREELS (continued)

Jonathan, 1977, LBR

Julia Ann, b 15 March 1870 - d 1 Sept 1946, SNB

Kermet Clifton, d 6 Aug 1978, ae 67y, SNB

Laura M, b 1920 - no death date, LNE

Lucy Human, 11 March 1895, SNB

Lulu, b 5 Dec 1893 - d 7 Sept 1953, SNB

Magnus, b 1918 - d 1 Apr 1973, LNE

Margaret Johnson, b 13 Sept 1907 - no death date, SNB

Mary F Jones, b 9 Oct 1866 - d 8 Feb 1959, PLR

Mary Jo, b 12 May 1857 - d 1 Feb 1910, SNB

Marye, b 2 Jan 1886 - d 29 March 1886, PLR

Minnie, b 12 Feb 1877 - d 26 July 1919, WBB

Monroe T, Pvt 23 Inf 2 Div WWI, b 29 Apr 1891 - d 4 Jan 1959, LNE

Nancy E, b 1 Apr 1828 - d 9 July 1901, PLR

Nell Freels, b 30 Jan 1906 - d 4 Aug 1938, PLR

Nellie C, b 16 Mar 1902 - d 22 Sept 1955, WRC

Nora A, b 1902 - no death date, MLC

Rebecca Ann, b 29 Oct 1880 - d 4 Jan 1953, LNE

Rosa M, b 23 Mar 1914 - no death date, WRC

Russell, b 17 Aug 1860 - d 24 Apr 1929, PLR

Samuel W, b 3 Nov 1878 - d 2 Oct 1893, PLR

Terry E, b 25 March 1954 - d 26 Jan 1955, LNE

Wanda Maurine d/o Hubert, 2 Oct 1930, PLR

FREELS (continued)

William Clifford, d 20 Sept 1972, ae 71y, CLC

FREEMAN, Edward, d 21 Jan 1977, ae 52y, EST

Ralph Garfield, d 9 May 1978, ae 67y, EST

William G, b 13 Apr 1913 - d 26 Feb 1964, EST

FRELS, Rosetta J, b 4 July 1874 - d 19 Dec 1899, ALB

FREY, Oscar N, b 24 Oct 1885 - d 20 June 1960, EST

FREYTAG, A M, b 2 Dec 1836 - d 29 June 1921, WRC

Albert Jr, d 28 June 1980, ae 62y, WRC

Albert L, b 26 Apr 1885 - d 8 Apr 1955, WRC

Audrey C, b 20 Jan 1908 - d 5 Feb 1929, WRC

August A, b 16 March 1888 - d 17 Nov 1961, WRC

Bertie E, b 14 July 1890 - d 25 Nov 1973, WRC

Burton, b 29 Jan 1927 - d 15 March 1939, WRC

Burton H, b 20 Apr 1901 - d 10 Feb 190-, WRC

C D, b 11 Jan 1860 - d 10 Apr 1948, WRC

Charles, b 1879 - d 1972, WRC

Clair Davis, b 11 Oct 1881 - d 26 July 1927, WRC

Clara Lou, d 28 May 1944, WRC

Edd C, b 21 July 1882 - d 19 May 1927, WRC

Edna, d 6 Sept 1917, ELZ

Ernest H, b 29 Nov 1887 - d 1967, LBR

Francis, b 1813 - d 1886, WRC

Frederic R, b 2 March 1893 - 4 Oct 1898, WRC

FREYTAG (continued)
Gus, b 1 May 1888 - d 15 Dec 1945, WRC
Ironer H, b 30 July 1894 - d 22 Feb 1969, WRC
J D, b 15 Nov 1898 - d 11 July 1925, WRC
Jack Jr, b 12 Jan 1946 - d 22 Mar 1946, WRC
Julia, b 23 Dec 1889 - d 13 Jan 1929, WRC
Larry Ray, b 24 Aug 1947 - d 6 Feb 1948, WRC
Lena, b 12 Apr 1892 - d 2 Oct 1932, WRC
Leon, b 1 June 1909 - d 19 Jan 1949, WRC
Louise G, b 1 May 1833 - d 29 Dec 1904, WRC
Louise Kamer, b 27 Dec 1858 - d 9 Apr 1934, WRC
Mary, b 9 March 1835 - d 9 March 1872, WRC
Mattie, b 11 Jan 1889 - d 6 June 1903, LBR
Maud Bales, b 18 June 1908 - d 2 Aug 1963, WRC
Maud Neil, d 2 Jan 1981, ae 93y, WRC
Reba Shelton, d 21 Sept 1973, ae 64y, WRC
Rivera Duncan, b -- March 1853 - d 17 Sept 1938, WRC
Shelia Diane, d 23 Sept 1979, ae infant, MNT
Miss Thelma, d 25 July 1975, ae 77y, WRC
W M, b 27 July 1850 - d 12 Sept 1938, WRC
William A, b 6 Aug 1907 - d 11 Nov 1912, WRC
FRITTS, Ben, b 17 Oct 1853 - d 16 Nov 1918, DRM
Mrs Emily, d c 1978, ae 75y, ISF
William Sr, d -- Feb 1906, in 66th y, LBR

FRITTS (continued)
Winnie O, b 1900 - d 1960, LBR
FROGG, Andrew Marion, d 10 March 1973, ae 64y, MLC
Ethel A, b 25 Jan 1906 - d 7 Oct 1926, BRR
Henry M, b 27 Oct 1904 - d 18 Sept 1941, MRR
Hulda, b 1864 - d 23 May 1921, MRR
FROGGE, Charles A, b 30 March 1967 - d 31 March 1967, MLC
Charles Oscar, d 10 Feb 1974, ae 33y, MLC
Dock P, b 15 Jan 1882 - d 6 June 1964, RGB
Everett, b 1898 - d 1962, RGB
Gertrude, b 1897 - no death date, RGB
Gladys Mary, b 15 Aug 1923 - d 29 Oct 1950, RGB
Laura Hamby, d 28 Aug 1977, ae 63y, MLC
Lawrence A, d 19 Feb 1978, ae 52y, RGB
Louis, 1951, MLC
Nancy Ann, b 6 Jan 1871 - no death date, RGB
Sallie A, b 29 Jan 1880 - d 24 March 1978, RGB
Timothy A, b 11 March 1870 - d 12 Feb 1946, RGB
Vernon Pete, b 12 March 1935 - d 30 Aug 1955, RGB
FRY, Charlotte E, b 15 Oct 1865 - d 11 Aug 1896, RTT
Harlan, b 13 June 1917 - d 18 Oct 1919, ADC
Melvin A, b 10 Oct 1851 - d 14 Dec 1910, RTT
FUDGE, Carol Sue Wilson, d 9 Feb 1979, ae 34y, UNN
FULCO, Hazel Hamby, b 21

FULCO (continued)
July 1926 - d 26 Oct
1954, WRC
FULLER, Bessie Jeffers, d 2
Feb 1978, ae 71y, SNB
FULTON, T J, b 24 March
1959, CRO
Tillie, b 29 Feb 1851 - d
12 Aug 1912, CRO
FUTRELL, Ethelridge Sr, d
29 March 1884, ae 83y,
RTT
Albert, b 2 June 1892 - d
14 Aug 1964, ADC
Bonnie Lee, Pvt Co H 8 Inf
Rgt, b 25 Feb 1933 - d 8
Oct 1955, OOO
Clarence, b 18 May 1900 -
d 22 Sept 1971, THR
Conrad, b 11 Sept 1903 - d
25 Sept 1979, EST
Ethelridge Jr, Co H 3rd TN
Inf Mil Stone, RTT
Francis S Thornton, b 11
Aug 1902 - d 1 Oct 1978,
THR
Georgia Eva, b 1 Oct 1913
- d 15 Oct 1918, RTT
Kenneth Lloyd, b 19 Dec
1933 - d 17 Jan 1934,
RTT
Lela, b 1 Jan 1895 - no
death date, ADC
Margaret L, b 20 Sept 1879
- d 5 Aug 1935, RTT
Sadie, b 31 Dec 1909 - no
death date, EST
William R, b 13 June 1874
- d 29 March 1939, RTT
Winfred Lenice, d 11 July
1979, ae 63y, ADC
GALLEGLY, E H, b 19 Feb
1900 - d 3 Jan 1903, CBJ
GALLION, Emma Webb, b 12
June 1880 - d 1 Jan
1922, WBB
Wm Earnest Jr, b 29 Dec
1921 - d 12 Jan 1922,

GALLION (continued)
WBB
Wm Earnest MD, b 8 Feb
1880 - d 25 May 1951,
WBB
GALLOWAY, A P (Edley), b 26
Feb 1833 - d 15 June
1912, BRD
Adra, b 5 Jan 1895 - no
death date, SNB
Annie Lou, b 17 Nov 1938 -
d 16 March 1940, PLR
Anwailiza, b 1829 - d
1907, PLR
Arlo, b 23 June 1912 - d
25 Oct 1928, SHD
C Arthur, b 9 June 1886 -
d 13 Sept 1911, BRR
Rev Charles, b 16 Apr 1866
- d 30 Jan 1902, UNG
Charles P, Cpl TN 433 AFF
WWII, b 3 Apr 1928 - d
19 June 1948, PLR
Charles W, d 26 Oct 1978,
ae 79y, PLR
Cleatus, b 5 July 1904 - d
25 Dec 1921, SHD
Clemia, b 21 Feb 1878 - d
19 July 1901, SHD
Cora E, b 15 Apr 1894 - d
17 Apr 1895, PLR
Danna Denise, b 26 Aug
1961 - d 14 Nov 1961,
SNB
Donley, b -- Oct 1912 - d
-- July 1913, BRR
Edie England, b 21 Nov
1867 - d 1 Dec 1944, PLR
Edith I, b 1906 - d 1963,
PLR
Francis Marion, b 21 July
1890 - d 4 March 1958,
SNB
George F, b 8 Jan 1893 - d
8 July 1972, BRR
Gertrude, b 13 Feb 1918 -
d 20 Apr 1921, SHD
Gertrude K, b 22 March

GALLOWAY (continued)
1908 - d 24 Jan 1968,
UNG
Hannah B, b 20 Aug 1830 -
d 22 July 1913, PLR
Infant, 8 March 1933, UNG
Infant, no dates, SHD
Infant s/o Charles &
Edith, 16 Aug 1937, PLR
Infant s/o HW & Ruby, 7
July 1937, PLR
J O, b&d 18 Jan 1935, PLR
James H, b 26 Jan 1858 - d
7 Jan 1918, BRR
James Martin, b 2 March
1885 - d 28 Apr 1959,
SNB
James W, b 14 March 1855 -
d 28 Feb 1885, PLR
John B, d 23 May 1889, ae
29y 5mo, BRR
John W, b 1824 - d 1908,
BRR
Josephine, b 1856 - d
1920, BRR
Josie E, b 16 Sept 1894 -
d 22 May 1974, BRR
Kenneth, b 1919 - d 1922,
BRD
Laura A, b 13 June 1861 -
d 12 Aug 1932, BRR
Laura F, b 20 June 1862 -
d 24 Feb 1901, BRR
Leander C, b 7 Apr 1865 -
d 21 Oct 1926, PLR
Lee, d 29 Nov 1974, ae
59y, PLR
Lee Oden, b 5 Oct 1903 - d
10 Jan 1968, UNG
Levi P, b 20 June 1828 - d
11 Jan 1894, PLR
Lillian, no dates, BRR
Lucille, b 25 Feb 1914 - d
20 Jan 1935, PLR
Lucy, b 18 Feb 1837 - d 8
Apr 1889, BRD
Miss Mary, ae 79y, BRR
Mary Ann, b 1826 - d 1917,

GALLOWAY (continued)
BRR
Mary Jane, b 7 Nov 1882 -
no death date, SNB
Maryville Ray, b 26 Jan
1921 - d 22 June 1943,
PLR
Maurice Arlo, b&d 1 Jan
1938, SNB
Minor A, b 13 Jun 1889 - d
6 Apr 1965, WRC
N C, b 18 July 1877 - d 24
May 1958, WRC
Nickie Lynn d/o Larry, 16
Oct 1963, PLR
Nora Bell, b 25 Nov 1881 -
d 31 Oct 1964, SNB
Orville W, d -- Feb 1975,
BRD
Osa B, b 22 Feb 1870 - d
26 Aug 1939, UNG
Judge Samuel J, b 9 Apr
1925 - d 26 July 1972,
BRR
Timothy C, b 1848 - d
1940, BRR
Vard Clifton, b 14 March
1951 - d 17 March 1951,
UNG
Wilma Jean, b 17 Feb 1928
- d 11 Apr 1928, UNG
GAMBELL, Johnnie V, b 4 Aug
1904 - d 19 Nov 1905,
CBJ
GANN, J R, b 1923 - d 1933,
PNY
Josephine M, b 1881 - d
1958, PNY
Willian b, b 1873 - d
1966, PNY
GARDNER, Walter, b 9 Sept
1850 - d 23 Apr 1885,
RGB
GARLEWSKI, Antonina, b 1863
- d 17 Nov 1918, DRL
GARNAR, Minnie Lee, b 26
March 1886 - d 26 July
1887, DVS

GARRET, Josie C, b 6 Apr 1885 - d 7 Dec 1970, LNE

Malinda, b 2 Oct 1832 - d 5 Feb 1867, ELZ

Tim, b 10 Feb 1917 - d 10 Dec 1969, LNE

GARRETT, Albert, b 2 Feb 1870 - d 2 Nov 1957, ELZ

Alfred, b 14 Oct 1864 - d 13 Apr 1965, ELZ

Alice, b 5 Nov 1853 - d 11 Sept 1915, ELZ

Annie, b 3 Jan 1875 - d 23 Aug 1960, ELZ

Annie Stonecipher, b 13 Sept 1854 - d 8 Aug 1930, ELZ

Arona A, b 7 Apr 1902 - no death date, DRL

Ben, b 30 Sept 1871 - d 6 Jan 1940, DRL

Bessie L, b 2 June 1906 - no death date, ELZ

Bobby Lee, b 4 Aug 1933 - d 18 Aug 1933, ELZ

Caroline, b 6 Oct 1856 - d 16 June 1858, ELZ

Charles H, b 11 Jan 1904 - no death date, ELZ

Clifford M, d 16 Oct 1977, ae 62y, ELZ

Daniel, b 30 July 1865 - d 9 July 1937, ELZ

E B, b 1826 - d 1903, CRO

Earl, b 29 Aug 1897 - no death date, ELZ

Edward Ray, d 10 Aug 1977, ae 75y, ELZ

Elijah, d 9 Oct 1975, ae 75y, ELZ

Elisha, b 10 March 1901 - d 13 Apr 1936, ELZ

Elizabeth Jane, b 28 March 1858 - d 28 Sept 1862, ELZ

Elizabeth Pearl, b 10 Nov 1930 - d 16 Nov 1932, DRL

GARRETT (continued)

Ethridge, b 29 July 1898 - d 31 March 1959, ELZ

Etta S, b 11 Dec 1896 - no death date, ELZ

Everett H, b 13 Aug 1895 - d 2 March 1968, DRL

Everett Leroy, d 24 Dec 1977, ae 53y, DRL

Flossie, d 31 May 1978, ae 76y, WHO

Geir, Sgt Co B 1st Inf WWI, b 15 May 1896 - d 30 May 1963, DRL

Gertrude Nash, d 28 March 1978, ae 68y, DRL

Guy D, b 6 July 1904 - d 8 Jan 1973, ELZ

James, b 22 Apr 1873 - d 29 Sept 1962, ELZ

James H, b 1870 - d 1930, DRL

Joe O, b 14 Jan 1880 - d 22 Aug 1940, ELZ

Laura Alice J, b 24 Nov 1870 - d 28 March 1947, ELZ

Laura Byrd, b 2 Sept 1869 - d 2 March 1941, DRL

Luther N, d 15 Sept 1981, ae 85y, ELZ

Mae S, b 20 Oct 1903 - d 13 Sept 1949, ELZ

Malinda, d 1964, ae 8y, ELZ

Martha Cromwell, b 5 Dec 1832 - d 9 July 1915, ELZ

Mary E w/o Will, no dates, ELZ

Mary S, b 1875 - d 1935, MSG

Mary S L Jones, b 7 June 1873 - d 6 Apr 1952, ELZ

Nancy C, b 22 Dec 1885 - d 28 Feb 1952, ELZ

Oda W, b 27 Nov 1913 - d 7 Oct 1966, ELZ

63

GARRETT (continued)

Organ W, Cook 117 Inf 30 Div WWI, b 14 Oct 1890 - d 24 Sept 1949, WHO

Pearl, b 13 Nov 1900 - d 4 Jan 1901, ELZ

Ray L, d 12 Sept 1981, ae 54y, SNB

Squire, b 1 Nov 1831 - d 13 Oct 1861, ELZ

Thomas J, b 9 Sept 1883 - d 9 Dec 1961, ELZ

Velford, b 4 Oct 1854 - d 13 March 1935, ELZ

W R, b 28 March 1858 - d 7 Nov 1881, ELZ

Will, b 22 Apr 1880 - no death date, ELZ

William Hines, b 21 July 1827 - d 3 Nov 1913, ELZ

GASKIN, Everett Ray, d 24 Jan 1980, ae 79y, LBR

Russell Thomas, b 18 March 1937 - d 12 Jan 1938, LBR

GASNELL, Joe D, b 11 Feb 1905 - no death date, SNB

Thelma Ruth, b 25 March 1913 - d 1 Dec 1969, SNB

GASTON, Georgia, d 15 Nov 1980, ae 85y, CHN

Gerald Eugene, b 14 Sept 1935 - d 10 March 1937, CHN

John J, b 28 Oct 1874 - d 29 July 1956, CHN

GATHER, Ethel, b 18 Sept 1904 - no death date, LBR

H, b 29 Nov 1902 - d 26 Sept 1969, LBR

GAUDIN, Geo Frederick, b 1 March 1827 - d 7 May 1901, UNN

Rhoda, b 5 Aug 1832 - d 30 Oct 1897, UNN

GAUGE, Matilda Jackson, b

GAUGE (continued)

25 Aug 1873 - d 18 Oct 1943, EST

GAVEL, Joseph, b 1 Jan 1892 - d 22 Jan 1904, DRL

Vincent G, b 10 July 1888 - d 7 Oct 1937, DRL

GAYHART, Carl E, d 26 Aug 1976, ADM

Luna, d 27 Jan 1977, ae 63y, ADM

GEBERUANT, Annie, b 1910 - d 1962, WRC

GEIER, Antoni, b 16 Feb 1860 - d 2 March 1936, CLC

Eliza, b 18 July 1900 - d 1 Aug 1961, WRC

Infant, d/o A & Minerva, no dates, CLC

John R, Pvt 503 CML Stor Co WWII, b 2 Apr 1902 - d 2 Nov 1965, CLC

Minerva Williams, b 16 Apr 1866 - d 2 June 1945, CLC

GEORGE, A S, Cpl Co H 1st WI Inf, no dates, BRR

Linda Hegbee, b 15 June 1841 - d 13 June 1903, BRR

GERARDI, Edith, b 1910 - d 1929, DRL

John, b 1866 - d 1946, DRL

John W, d 21 July 1981, ae 80y, DRL

Mary, b 1874 - d 1948, DRL

GIBSON, Alvin W, b 1900 - no death date, RGB

Andrew J, Pvt Co H 117 Inf 30 Div WWI, b 11 March 1899 - d 4 Dec 1966, LNE

Billy Joe, b 7 Feb 1945 - d 23 July 1945, PLR

C A, no dates, PNY

Edith Mae, b 1909 - d 1965, RGB

Emet E, Pvt Ord Dpt WWII,

GIBSON (continued)
b 19 Jan 1894 - d 13
June 1970, RGB
Lenora C, b 6 Aug 1897 - d
15 May 1972, LNE
Marilyn S, b 28 Feb 1932 -
d 2 Oct 1970, LNC
GILBERT, Lindsay B, Pvt
USAF ME WWII, b 2 Jan
1930 - d 16 Jan 1973,
CRO
GILES, Horace W, b 17 May
1871 - d 5 Aug 1918, RGB
Mary, b 1846 - d 1907, RGB
S H, Co B 21 NY Cav, Mil
Stone, RGB
William J, d 10 Jan 1887,
ae 1mo 17da, DVS
GILLETTE, Sarah, b 20 Oct
1825 - d 12 Jan 1914,
DRL
GILLIAT, Bessie, d 29 Jan
1888, RGB
Ellen McDaniel, b 1838 - d
1906, RGB
Leila C, b 1883 - d 1906,
RGB
Wm Henry, b 1830 - d 1898,
RGB
GILLIS, Ada Todd, b 10 Nov
1877 - d 27 March 1969,
CRO
Andrew, b 10 May 1889 - d
21 Feb 1940, CRO
Clifford Quillen, b 9
March 1903 - d 27 Nov
1922, CRO
Eliza J, b 21 Jan 1848 - d
7 Aug 1931, CRO
Hessie S, b 25 Aug 1927 -
no death date, CRO
Jessie, b 1 July 1878 - d
21 July 1941, CRO
Joe W, b 4 May 1908 - d ---
Apr 1964, CRO
Marie, d 4 July 1978, ae
83y, CRO
R W, b 2 Apr 1842 - d 14

GILLIS (continued)
Apr 1919, CRO
Ralph, b 6 Apr 1900 - d 12
July 1901, CRO
GILLISPIE, Clyde B, b 1885
- d 1957, LBR
Martha, b 1894 - no death
date, LBR
GILMORE, Gertrude, b 23 Feb
1891 - d 24 July 1948,
WRC
John C, b 10 March 1882 -
d 23 Feb 1970, WRC
GILREATH, Elbert, b 28 Dec
1901 - d 7 Aug 1974, CRO
Mattie, b 18 Aug 1904 - no
death date, CRO
GISI, Catharine, no dates,
DVS
Mary, no dates, DVS
Philip, Co E 5th IN Cav,
no dates, DVS
GLEVINS, Millar, b 1861 - d
1947, NWP
GOAD, A L, b 26 Jan 1891 -
d 4 Feb 1912, CLC
Arrona, b 11 Oct 1878 - d
4 Nov 1897, CLC
Berry, b 18 Apr 1865 - d 8
May 1948, LNE
Bessie Lee, b 27 Sept 1897
- d 4 Apr 1902, OLP
Clifford, d 29 Sept 1975,
ae 60y, NWP
Cynthia, b 27 June 1884 -
d 11 Feb 1858, NWP
Elizabeth, b 17 June 1866
- d 17 June 1909, CLC
Elizabeth, b 11 Jan 1857 -
d 11 June ----, CLC
Estel (Ed), d 16 Apr 1978,
ae 46y, NWP
Imogene Russell, d 1 June
19811, ae 57y, NWP
Infant, b 8 June (il-
legible), CLC
J M (Dock), b 8 June 1852
- d 21 Jan 1928, CLC

GOAD (continued)

James Frederick, d 9 Feb 1973, ae 21y, PTC

Jim, b 1829 - d 1909, MLC

Rev John, b 4 Feb 1817 - d 22 June 1904, CLC

John L, b 25 March 1883 - d 8 Apr 1904, CLC

Lottie, b 9 June 1906 - no death date, SNB

Lucinda, b 10 Feb 1857 - d 10 Feb 1942, CLC

M M, b 1874 - d 1964, WMG

Martha, b 15 March 1840 - d 14 March 1948, MLC

Mary, b 15 Sept 1897 - d 20 Sept 1951, NWP

Maryetta, b 1 Nov 1913 - d 2 Feb 1920, CLC

Merida M, b 1874 - d 1964, WMG

Micky Lynn, 1970, LNE

Millard F, b 22 Aug 1873 - d 12 May 1955, NWP

Ollie Cox, d 23 May 1976, ae 98y, WMG

Perry C, b 8 Nov 1902 - d 12 Feb 1976, SNB

Robert, d 6 July 1980, LNE

W R, b 5 June 1907 - d 27 Apr 1943, NWP

William, d 6 July 1980, LNE

William, b 8 Oct 1833 - d 14 Jan 1925, MLC

GODDARD, Annie Elizabeth, b 13 June 1903 - d 16 July 1968, JHG

Celia Langley, b 22 Nov 1844 - d 17 May 1918, LNG

Charles C, b 29 May 1888 - d 17 Dec 1904, OLP

Charlotte E, d 30 July 1966, ae 102y, DVS

David R, b 7 Sept 1836 - d 26 Aug 1912, DVS

E R, b 13 June 1854 - d 20

GODDARD (continued)

Oct 1959, JHG

Esther Irene, d 12 Sept 1976, ae 82y, EST

Frances M, Co F 5th TN Inf, d 9 May 1883, LNG

James H, b 20 Sept 1859 - d 29 Aug 1918, EST

James M, b 30 Nov 1870 - d 25 July 1899, LNG

Joseph Walter, b 3 Aug 1884 - d 3 Nov 1956, JHG

Kenneth, b 23 Apr 1930 - d 28 Nov 1970, JHG

Leroy, b 16 July 1925 - d 22 Oct 1926, LBR

Margaret, b 4 March 1922 - d 17 March 1925, OLP

Mart, b 4 Aug 1873 - d 11 May 1947, EST

Mary R, b 24 March ---- - d 11 Dec 1917, DVS

Nan, b 21 May 1878 - d 9 Jan 1955, EST

Nancy, b 18 Feb 1829 - d 28 Oct 1908, DVS

Nancy C, b 14 May 1934 - no death date, JHG

Nancy C, b 23 Jan 1862 - d 25 Jan 1916, EST

Nancy J, b 11 Aug 1852 - d 14 Aug 1928, JHG

Ora, b 21 March 1897 - d 11 Jan 1900, EST

Prince Albert, d 4 Sept 1978, ae 88y, EST

Raymond, b 23 Aug 1906 - d 12 Sept 1932, EST

Samuel, b 17 Feb 1829 - d 4 Feb 1863, UNN

Theresa May, d 24 Feb 1977, ae 92y, DVS

Thomas W, b 2 Feb 1829 - d 23 Sept 1863, DVS

Vesta W, b 9 Sept 1881 - d 20 June 1966, NWP

W A, b 18 Aug 1893 - d 23 Feb 1929, LBR

GODDARD (continued)
William B, b 15 Feb 1800 -
d 27 Nov 1881, LNG
GODSEY, Nellie A, b 26 June
1910 - no death date,
PNY
W O B, b 20 Sept 1895 - d
19 Nov 1961, PNY
GOE, Laura Sexton, d 22 Aug
1980, ae 44y, LNE
GOFF, Barton W, b 8 March
1887 - no death date,
BRR
Bessie F, b 16 June 1891 -
d 1 Apr 1955, BRR
Caroline, b 3 March 1853 -
d 7 Apr 1939, BRR
Mary S, b 18 May 1838 - d
16 Apr 1877, NDK
Neavel H, b 15 Apr 1831 -
d 17 Feb 1912, BRR
GOFORTH, Eugene, b 1928 - d
1929, CRO
GOGGINS, Hurst W, b 1905 -
d 1923, BRR
Maggie, d 22 Oct 1979, BRR
Ocie O, b 3 July 1877 - d
15 Jan 1868, BRR
GOINS, Dave P, b 29 Jan
1856 - d 12 Oct 1940,
CRO
Link C, b 16 May 1890 - d
15 Feb 1923, CRO
Martha J Buttram, b 29 Apr
1862 - no death date,
CRO
GOLDBERG, Charles L, b 29
Apr 1883 - d 15 Aug
1960, PNY
Charles W, b 10 Apr 1852 -
d 19 July 1917, LBR
Edward, b 1870 - d 1920,
LBR
Givan, b 27 June 1913 - d
4 Oct 1959, PNY
Larry R, b 13 March 1939 -
d 20 July 1964, PNY
Linda W, b 28 June 1945 -

GOLDBERG (continued)
d 31 May 1963, PNY
Minnie H, b 13 Apr 1894 -
no death date, PNY
Pauline, b 1870 - d 1964,
LBR
Walter, b 23 Feb 1885 - d
11 Apr 1960, PNY
GOLDBERT, Mary (Brazel), b
9 Oct 1856 - d 15 Jan
1886, LBR
GOLDSTON, Alex P, b 1879 -
d 1936, CRO
Amanda Norman, b 9 March
1874 - d 18 Apr 1937,
CRO
Belva Ray, b 2 Jan 1895 -
d 10 March 1917, CRO
C F, b 25 Aug 1850 - d 1
Oct 1908, CRO
Donald, b 1908 - d 1929,
CRO
Donald D, b 28 March 1913
- d 24 Sept 1967, CRO
Florence C, b 2 Aug 1880 -
d 25 July 1956, CRO
Frances M, b 12 July 1927
- no death date, CRO
Gladys C, b 26 Sept 1906 -
d 15 Oct 1920, CRO
Henry Norman, b 6 Jan 1906
- d 29 July 1917, CRO
Howard, b 3 Nov 1905 - d
14 May 1945, CRO
Huston, b 1872 - d 1931,
CRO
J L, d 12 June ----, ae
21y 7mo, CRO
James B, b 11 July 1910 -
d 17 Oct 1973, CRO
James M, b 9 July 1877 - d
1 Jan 1931, CRO
Rev John D, b 22 Nov 1915
- d 10 Feb 1974, CRO
Julia, b 1883 - d 1926,
CRO
Kate, b 187- - d 1947, CRO
Louverne, b 1875 - d 1939,

GOLDSTON (continued)
CRO
M T, b 1 May 1881 - d 5
July 1885, CRO
Mack Donald, b 27 Nov 1860
- d 25 Sept 1933, CRO
Maggie, b 1877 - d 1968, CRO
Minnie, b 14 Aug 1880 - d
29 Jan 1921, CRO
Nancy Sturges, w/o Wiley
L, d 28 Sept 1913, CRO
Newel, b 30 Dec 1916 - d
23 Oct 1918, CRO
Pauline, b 9 June 1895 - d
15 Oct 1974, CRO
W Albert, b 24 Aug 1876 -
d 11 Aug 1955, CRO
Wiley L, b 9 May 1820 - d
15 Feb 1885, CRO
William, b 3 Aug 1924 - d
3 Aug 1944, CRO
William D, b 1908 - d
1937, CRO
William Horace, b 29 Sept
1876 - d 12 Nov 1931,
CRO
Wilma Leah, b 7 Dec 1907 -
d 14 May 1962, CRO
GOLDTON, Larkin, b 1867 - d
1941, CRO
GOOCH, Darrel, d 1963, WRC
Ernest Earl, b 21 March
1893 - d 16 Feb 1967,
DVD
Gurnie A, b 18 Sept 1889 -
no death date, DVD
John Richard, b 12 June
1953 - d 30 Oct 1953,
WRC
Lena K, b 4 Aug 1879 - d
26 Apr 1963, WRC
Harry Milton, b 1 Apr 1914
- d 2 Jan 1956, FRV
Joe P, b 2 May 1860 - d 20
Feb 1949, FRV
John M, b 20 Jan 1897 - d
15 May 1974, FRV
Lizzie B, b 20 Jan 1894 -

GOOCH (continued)
d 7 Feb 1973, FRV
Minnie Alice, b 28 Dec
1870 - d 31 Jan 1943,
FRV
GOODMAN, ----, b 18 June
---- - d 7 Jan 197-, WRC
Anna J B, b 2 May 1933 - d
12 Apr 1977, WRC
Easter, b 25 Sept 1865 - d
20 Feb 1945, WHO
Franklin, b 13 May 1892 -
d 8 Dec 1971, MNT
Jaqueline Ann, b 26 May
1855 - d 6 June 1958,
WRC
Johnnie L, b 7 Aug 191- -
d 20 Sept 19--, WRC
Maude C, b 20 Feb 1900 - d
29 Jan 1967, MNT
Pearlie, b 9 Nov 1892 - d
30 June 1971, ELZ
Will, b 1 Jan 1892 - d 27
March 1958, ELZ
GOODWIN, Dixer Anna, b 18
July 1883 - d 21 Apr
1961, CRO
Edward W, Pvt 1570 SVC Co
MD WWI, b 6 June 1918 -
d 24 July 1966, CRO
Jessie Virgil, b 25 Oct
1910 - d 15 Feb 1942,
CRO
Lowel Bingham, b 6 March
1938 - d 26 July 1942,
CRO
Thomas M, b 18 March 1883
- d 11 June 1955, CRO
GORDY, Flora Jean, d 2 Oct
1975, ae 69y, WRC
GORMAN, Rev W D, d 6 Apr
1901, ae 55y, SNB
GOSNELL, Emily, b 14 Dec
1877 - d 19 Aug 1963,
SNB
Martha, b 12 Jan 1926 - d
3 March 1952, OLP
Sam, b 2 Aug 1899 - d 29

68

GOSNELL (continued)
Nov 1902, OLP
William Howard, b 24 Feb
1908 - d 1 March 1928,
SNB
Zander, b 15 Oct 1870 - d
19 Nov 1926, OLP
GOUGE, Betty J, no dates,
CBJ
Harvey C Sr, d 28 Jan
1975, ae 83y, DVS
Hugh, d 24 March 1977, ae
75y, CBJ
James Oliver Sr, b 17 June
1904 - d 21 Sept 1972,
CBJ
Rena Eileen, b 30 Aug 1910
- no death date, CBJ
Vanissa, d 14 March 1978,
ae 2.5y, CBJ
GRACE, Beulah R, b 1 June
1915 - d 19 Aug 1971,
WRC
Cecil, b 12 March 1907 - d
6 Dec 1969, PNY
Herbert L, b 6 Feb 1896 -
d 29 Feb 1952, CRO
Ralph Cole, Cpl Gen Hosp
MD WWII, b 19 Dec 1923 -
d 27 Nov 1968, CRO
Ruby, b 23 Aug 1913 - no
death date, PNY
Vesta R, b 4 July 1922 -
no death date, CRO
Walter A, b 12 Jan 1902 -
d 30 Dec 1976, WRC
GRANES, Dorine Hall, b 16
Dec 1916 - d 20 Feb
1948, PTC
GRAVES, Carl Zane, b 26 May
1950 - d 19 Oct 1950,
UNG
Claude, b&d 1950, UNG
James, b 10 Oct 1891 - d 7
Apr 1964, UNG
Judy Faye, b 13 Sept 1948
- d 26 Apr 1949, UNG
Minnie A, b 10 Jan 1904 -

GRAVES (continued)
no death date, UNG
Veline, b 14 Apr 1952 - d
15 March 1954, UNG
Wilham, ae 23y, UNG
GRAY, Cleo Patra, b 2 May
1886 - d 5 July 1970,
DVS
W C, b 17 May 1872 - d 11
Nov 1940, DVS
GRAYSON, Marion F, b 18 Nov
1861 - d 22 June 1930,
PNY
May Belle, b 4 Nov 1879 -
d 2 Dec 1958, PNY
Roger, b 23 Apr 1908 - d
10 July 1909, PNY
GREEN, Bruce, b 1911 - d 10
May 1972, LBR
C V, d 12 Feb 1873, ae 15y
8mo, BCF
E R, d 21 Dec 1883, ae 62y
11mo, BCF
Joseph LeRoy, b 1879 - d
1963, LBR
Julia Dori, b 1891 - d
1933, LBR
Mossie Thomas, b 11 Nov
1918 - d 9 June 1958,
FRV
Rebecca, b 5 Nov 1805 - d
31 July 1900, CLC
GREENE, Ada Marie, b 1923 -
d 1925, NWP
Ernest H, b 10 Jan 1920 -
d 2 Aug 1970, LBR
John F, b 10 June 1923 - d
7 March 1972, LBR
L C Hank, b 12 March 1884
- d -- Dec 1965, LBR
Lillie Ann, b 10 Sept 1885
- d 3 Nov 1965, LBR
Reuben H, d 16 Nov 1976,
ae 67y, NWP
GREER, Benj F, b 9 Nov 1835
- d 10 June 1910, BRR
Emma Dayhuff, b 27 Nov
1883 - d 24 May 1973,

GREER (continued)
BRR
James S, b 22 Jan 1868 - d
25 Oct 1945, BRR
Lillian, b&d 27 Jan 1909,
BRR
Mollie, b 12 June 1869 - d
1 July 1913, BRR
Rosetta, b 21 Oct 1871 - d
27 Jan 1909, BRR
Talitha A, b 11 Nov 1841 -
d 11 March 1929, BRR
GREGG, James G Sr, b 20
June 1907 - d 26 Oct
1956, WRC
Mrs James (Ola), d 21 Oct
1949, ae 37y, MNT
GRIER, Bertha C, b 26 July
1899 - d 6 Oct 1967, FLR
Bonnie Lee, b 9 June 1937
- no death date, FLR
Charles C, b 13 Jan 1931 -
d 5 July 1964, FLR
Robert E, b 22 Sept 1897 -
no death date, FLR
GRIFFIN, Eunice Hurtt, b
1912 - d 1935, WBB
John J, b 16 July 1840 - d
23 Oct 1926, SNB
John Luther, b 24 Aug 1886
- d 23 June 1956, SNB
Lillian Rogers, b 8 Oct
1872 - d 30 Dec 1952,
DVS
Martha, b 19 March 1897 -
d 6 Oct 1980, SNB
Martha V, b 29 Nov 1869 -
d 28 Oct 1938, SNB
GRIFFIS, Edgar, d 28 March
1976, ae 95y, NWP
GRIFFITH, Abraham M, b 1891
- d 1 July 1978, LNE
Alex S, b 1858 - d 1940,
PLR
Alice, b 1845 - d 1937,
PLR
Arden C, b 18 Dec 1926 - d
24 Dec 1936, BRR

GRIFFITH (continued)
Arthur Lee, b 14 Dec 1925
- d 12 May 1941, LNE
Baily B, b 15 March 1857 -
d 28 March 1945, LNE
Batrice, b 26 Dec 1916 - d
20 Jan 1972, UNH
Charleen, b 9 June 1928 -
d 6 June 1930, LNE
Christina M, d 29 Sept
----, ae 4y, NWP
Clara, b 23 March 1885 - d
17 Oct 1958, ELZ
Clara Jone, b 1904 - d
1964, ELZ
Clyde, b 28 May 1891 - d
17 July 1964, BRR
Daisy Scott, d 18 Oct
1980, ae 72y, LNE
Douglas E, b 28 Oct 1915 -
d 19 Aug 1924, UNH
Earl, Cpl USA Korea, b 22
Oct 1931 - d 17 Sept
1972, BRR
Earl G, d 29 June 1975, ae
75y, EST
Easter Sexton, b 19 March
1867 - d 18 Dec 1953,
LNE
Eli, b 15 July 1851 - d 4
Nov 1909, MLC
Eliz Ann Garrett, b 30
July 1879 - d 4 Aug
1947, ELZ
Freeman H, b 16 Oct 1896 -
d 22 March 1898, PLR
Geneva I, b 21 July 1914-
d 8 Sept 1962, BRR
George Pat, b 4 Jan 1883 -
d 10 March 1970, PLR
Isabelle, b 1867 - d 1946,
PLR
Jane, b 15 Oct 1872 - no
death date, ELZ
Joel, b 9 Feb 1873 - d 19
May 1954, ELZ
John, b 9 Feb 1869 - d 30
Sept 1936, ELZ

GRIFFITH (continued)
John R, Pvt Co D 210 Inf
WWII, b 13 Oct 1908 - d
26 March 1964, UNH
Leonard, d 14 Dec 1980, ae
64y, ELZ
Levi, b 25 Jan 1882 - d 7
Aug 1914, MLC
Loma, b 13 Jan 1927 - d 20
June 1928, LNE
Margaret, no dates, MLC
Martha V, b 23 June 1888 -
d 20 March 1968, LNC
Nettie C, b 10 Dec 1891 -
no death date, BRR
Nettie E, b 17 Feb 1889 -
d 11 Aug 1936, UNH
Patricia Ann, b 5 July
1952 - d 4 Dec 1976, WRC
Raymond Kenneth, b 21 Dec
1927 - d 5 Sept 1949,
LNE
Sylvester, b 28 Jan 1905 -
d 6 May 1923, LNE
Thomas W, b 7 March 1879 -
d 17 Dec 1943, BRR
Troy, b 1925 - d 1972, MCD
W W, b --- - d 1965, PLR
Wanda Frye, b 12 Aug 1929
- d 19 Jan 1972, WRC
GROSMAN, George W, d 1 Dec
1959, ae 87y 4mo, CRO
GRYDER, Levi E, b 11 June
1905 - d 8 Apr 1946, LNE
GSCHWEND, John Joseph, b
1818 - d 15 June 1904,
WRC
Susannah, b 22 May 1832 -
d 23 Feb 1908, WRC
GUBERNANT, Bertha, b 24
March 1889 - d 26 May
1958, DRL
Frank, b 1889 - d 1969,
DRL
GUFFEY, Alice M Douglas, b
9 Dec 1860 - d 8 Dec
1941, SHD
Blanche Lee, b 14 March

GUFFEY (continued)
1907 - d 6 Aug 1948, PNY
Enoch S, b 6 Nov 1924 - no
death date, BRR
Glenice M, b 8 Aug 1926 -
d 16 March 1947, BRR
Jemima, b 13 Nov 1826 - d
14 March 1890, UNG
Mary C, b 1881 - d 1968,
UNG
Mary Jane, b 24 July 1838
- d 9 May 1897, UNG
Smith, b 6 Nov 1822 - d 5
May 1889, UNG
GUION, Elizabeth, b 6 Dec
1845 - d 1 Nov 1902, RGB
GUNNELS, Ethel C, b 1 Jan
1889 - d 12 June 1957,
PLR
G W, marked by field
stone, PLR
Joe R, b 1897 - d 3 May
1973, PLR
GUNTER, Abe, b 12 Aug 1914
- d 26 Jan 1918, MNT
Alice, b 10 Sept 1878 - d
23 Sept 1966, MNT
Betty Barger, b 23 Nov
1906 - no death date,
MNT
Carl, d 20 Jan 1977, ae
78y, WRC
Carol Sue, b 11 Sept 1947
- d 15 Sept 1947, MLC
Charles M, b 7 Jan 1871 -
d 26 Mar 1949, WRC
Cora B, b 1917 - no death
date, MSG
Cordelia, b 1876 - d 1962,
DDN
David Ray, b 14 Dec 1961 -
d 19 Dec 1961, MLC
Dillard Goodpasture, b 27
March 1875 - d 13 Nov
1947, BRR
Edward H Sr, b 1903 - d
1972, MSG
Floyd, d 6 Apr 1980, ae

GUNTER (continued)
68y, LNE

Freeman, b 1947 - d 1948, MLC

Glennis M, b 8 Sept 1924 - d 30 May 1971, FLR

Hilliard F, d 1 June 1972, ae 49y 1mo, MLC

Lee E, b 17 May 1898 - d 6 Aug 1974, MNT

Little Earl, b 19 July 1926 - d 17 Oct 1936, WRC

Margaret A, b 19 March 1876 - d 25 Oct 1965, WRC

R C H, b 23 Jun 1841 - d 31 May 1913, WRC

Ralph, b 16 Apr 1908 - d 25 Aug 1938, MNT

Ruby Mae, b 20 Apr 1950 - d 25 March 1965, EST

Ruhr Peters, b 20 May 1880 - d 7 Feb 1942, BRR

S C (Doc), d 31 Jan 1974, ae 77y, WMG

Steve, b&d 1931, MSG

Tommis, b&d 1947, MLC

Tommy Lee, b 11 Oct 1943 - d 17 Dec 1944, WRC

Walter E, b 1 March 1916 - d 8 March 1971, EST

Will W, b 5 Feb 1865 - d 21 Jan 1964, DDN

William Harvey, b 15 March 1876 - d 10 Feb 1947, MNT

GURST, Calvin, b 1855 - d 1929, BRR

GUTH, George N, b 1888 - d 1971, WBB

Lillian Margaret, b 8 Aug 1912 - d 22 July 1914, WBB

Lois Ireta, b 24 June 1923 - d 22 July 1924, WBB

Myrtle W, b 1893 - no death date, WBB

GUTHRIE, J T, b 10 Feb 1854 - d 14 May 1893, SNB

HAAG, Annie H, b 14 July 1882 - d 2 March 1954, WRC

Baby, 1943, LBR

Charlies, b 19 Sept 1859 - d 18 Sept 1937, WRC

Walter C, Pfc Co K 2nd VN, 5th Cav Korea, b 17 Dec 1932 - d 23 Feb 1951, LBR

HAGWOOD, J M, b 10 Oct 1858 - d 30 Jan 1944, EST

Laura A, b 7 July 1882 - d 9 July 1960, EST

HAIL, Bridget V, b 3 Apr 1889 - d 28 May 1910, SNB

HALBURNT, Arthur M, b 16 July 1901 - d 8 Dec 1976, EST

Camila H, b 9 Oct 1858 - d 18 March 1955, EST

Flossie B, b 23 Sept 1905 - no death date, EST

Jennie, b&d 24 May 1900, EST

William A, b 27 March 1872 - d 11 Nov 1905, EST

HALE, Infant, b&d 12 Dec 1888, DRL

Jewel, b 4 May 1891 - d -- Sept 1892, DRL

Martha, b 20 Apr 1907 - no death date, NWP

Raymond, b 29 Aug 1905 - d 9 Apr 1975, NWP

HALL, Adeline McPeters, b 16 Feb 1861 - d 21 Oct 1943, LBR

Albert, b 15 Sept 1905 - no death date, ELZ

Albert, b 26 Nov 1872 - d 6 Sept 1900, ELZ

Alexander, b 1 Dec 1851 - d 6 Aug 1860, ELZ

Alice, b 22 May 1866 - d

HALL (continued)
14 Nov 1886, ELZ
Allene, b 1908 - d 1967, WMG
Alvin E, b 15 May 1927 - d 2 Jan 1929, ELZ
April, no dates, DVS
Arnold Lane, b 18 Dec 1915 - d 31 Jan 1969, WRC
Audrey May, b 28 May 1924 - d 13 May 1929, LBR
Barbara, b 14 Aug 1793 - d 19 Apr 1865, ELZ
Barbara W, b 16 May 1884 - d 9 Aug 1973, WRC
Bernard G, d 22 Aug 1975, ae 75y, LBR
Bertha (Breedlove), b 9 Aug 1890 - no death date, LBR
Bruce, b 29 May 1885 - d 13 Apr 1948, LBR
Calvin, dates faded, FLR
Carl Thomas, b 13 Nov 1937 - d 21 Oct 1968, UNN
Carrie K, b 2 Feb 1883 - d 26 Aug 1951, WRC
Cherrie B, b 1936 - d 1950, LNC
Chester E, 3 June 1948 - no other dates, LBR
Clarence, b 20 Feb 1916 - d 18 Dec 1931, PTC
Clinton Sr, b 23 May 1952 - d 2 July 1978, WRC
Cloah Scott, b 21 Nov 1834 - d 24 Aug 1922, MNT
Con D, b 13 July 1883 - d 13 Sept 1962, WRC
Cora E, b 12 Feb 1919 - no death date, LBR
Daniel M, b 12 July 1855 - d 16 Apr 1881, FLF
Dave, b 25 Dec 1794 - d 19 May 1860, ELZ
David, b 22 Dec 1858 - d 26 Nov 1940, LBR
David E, b 25 Feb 1858 - d

HALL (continued)
31 Dec 1935, FLR
David L, b -- Nov 1869 - d 22 Oct 1907, WRC
David L, b 9 Oct 1871 - d 29 Oct 1905, WRC
Dempsie Scott, b 21 Dec 1963 - d 10 Jan 1964, CRO
Dollie V, b 19 Apr 1909 - d 15 Feb 1910, MNT
Dora, b 9 March 1903 - d 23 May 1906, WRC
Dora, dates faded, FLR
Doris Lualie, b 15 May 1933 - d 2 Aug 1941, UNN
Edwin, b 28 Aug 1880 - d 1 Aug 1882, WRC
Elbert, d 7 Feb 1978, ae 80y, NWP
Elder G M, b 16 March 1892 - d 15 Nov 1938, LVN
Elisha, b 1 Jan 1799 - d 4 March 1878, ELZ
Elisha, Co 6 4th TN Cav, b 27 Nov 1827 - d 11 Feb 1896, MRR
Eliza J, b 1876 - d 1958, PLR
Elmer C, b 8 May 1911 - d 1 Aug 1934, WRC
Emily J, b 25 Oct 1845 - d 2 Jan 1916, WRC
Ervin, no dates, UNN
Estel, b 22 March 1928 - d 9 Oct 1966, LNC
Flora, d 25 Nov 1896, ae 2mo, ELZ
Florence Gunter, b 21 Aug 1900 - d 16 July 1959, WRC
Frank D, b 9 Sept 1913 - d 25 Jan 1919, ELZ
Frank R, b 1883 - d 1963, LBR
Fred E, d 19 Jan 1978, ae 56y, DRL
G L, b 29 Oct 1865 - d 7

HALL (continued)
July 1915, MNT
Garrett, b 15 Sept 1882 –
d 10 Jan 1929, ELZ
Garrett, b 5 March 1810 –
d 28 Feb 1869, LBR
Gary Ronald, d 25 Apr
1963, ae 2y, DVS
Genell, b&d 1936, FLR
George, no dates, LNC
George W, b 12 Dec 1854 –
d 11 May 1931, FLF
Gilbert W, Pvt 309 Inf,
78th Div, 27 Sept 1939 –
no other date, LBR
Harry H, b 11 March 1892 –
d 23 Feb 1936, LNC
Henry, b 27 Aug 1892 – d
14 Dec 1909, BRN
Hugh Cooper, b 31 Mar 1900
– d 11 July 1918, WRC
Hugh Haskell, b 9 Aug 1920
– d 19 June 1975, LBR
Infant, b 20 Aug 1911 – d
25 Dec 1911, ELZ
Infant, b&d 15 Oct 1903,
ELZ
Infant, b&d 12 May 1941,
BRN
Infant, b 18 Nov 1950 – d
18 Nov 1950, WRC
Infant, b 2 Apr 1953 – d 2
Apr 1953, WRC
Infant, d 22 Apr 1895, ae
3mo, ELZ
Infant, no dates, LVN
Inman G, b 8 Nov 1909 – d
3 Feb 1910, ELZ
J T, b 3 March 1894 – d 16
Nov 1894, ELZ
James M, b 1847 – d 1927,
LBR
Jane, b 15 June 1824 – d
15 July 1880, UNN
John, b 16 Apr 1842 – d 8
Dec 1900, WRC
John, b 11 July 1872 – d 8
Jan 1914, ELZ

HALL (continued)
John B, b 1865 – d 1936,
PLR
John D, b 12 June 1915 – d
7 Dec 1968, LNC
John Samuel, b 22 Feb 1896
– d 9 March 1896, ELZ
John Sr, b 10 June 1818 –
d 27 May 1884, ELZ
Johnny, b 25 Dec 1887 – d
5 Sept 1905, LVN
Joseph Lee, Pvt 10 AA Rpl
Tng BN, b 9 July 1925 –
d 7 Feb 1951, WRC
Julia, b 26 Apr 1873 – d
21 Aug 1875, WRC
Julia B, b 12 Apr 1899 – d
4 Feb 1905, WRC
Kenneth, d 1 July 1875, ae
57y, BRN
Leona, b 2 Sept 1890 – no
death date, FLR
Leonard, d 21 Nov 1978, ae
88y, FLF
Linday H, d 2 Nov 1969, ae
76y, SNB
Lizzie Howard, d 8 Oct
1977, ae 81y, WRC
Lizzie J, b 27 Aug 1871 –
d 3 Dec 1912, WRC
Louis E, b 1907 – d 1963,
LBR
Louisa Scott, b 24 Aug
1875 – d 1 March 1940,
ELZ
Lucy M, b 6 Aug 1922 – d
11 March 1968, LBR
Luke, b 5 Jan 1879 – d 6
Dec 1956, FLR
Luster, b 19 Dec 1889 – d
23 Nov 1907, LVN
Luther W, b 1898 – d 1968,
LBR
M Doric, b 12 March 1879 –
d 25 Nov 1931, ELZ
Mae H, b 6 May 1918 – no
death date, LNC
Mamie Townsend, d 8 Dec

74

HALL (continued)
1977, ae 67y, NWP
Marcella M, b 20 July 1911
- d 10 July 1977, NWP
Margaret, b 18 March 1860
- d 1 Jan 1890, FLF
Martha Chapman, d 8 May
1977, ae 80y, UNN
Martha Elizabeth, b 1852 -
d 1927, LBR
Martha F, b 25 May 1833 -
d 31 March 1884, MRR
Martha Jane, d 30 July
1925, WRC
Martha M, b 1895 - d 2
July 1968, BRR
Mary, b 1 May 1815 - d 15
Apr 1883, ELZ
Mary B, b 4 July 1887 - d
24 Jan 1963, LBR
Mary Sexton, b 12 Oct 1896
- d 1977, WRC
Matilda A, b 1887 - d
1931, LVN
Millie (Asher), b 1 Apr
1865 - d 14 Apr 1942,
FLF
Minnie M Thornton, b 12
June 1898 - no death
date, LNC
Myrtle, b 1910 - d 1933,
LBR
Nancy, b 11 Jan 1847 - d
11 Jan 1929, ELZ
Nancy B, b 20 June 1892 -
no death date, LBR
Nancy Byrd, d 30 Dec 1977,
ae 83y, WRC
Nellie Hazel, b 10 Nov
1904 - d 1 Dec 1909, ELZ
Nellie M, d 22 May 1981,
ae 74y, WRC
Nettie, b 11 July 1886 - d
13 May 1943, SNB
O B, b 5 Nov 1883 - d 24
Oct 1910, LBR
Parlee, b 31 Aug 1873 - d
28 March 189-, SNB

HALL (continued)
Paul H, b 21 May 1907 - d
26 Dec 1907, ELZ
Rebecca, b 23 March 1816 -
d 22 Nov 1888, ELZ
Robert Homer, b 24 Nov
1897 - d 11 June 1901,
WRC
Robert L, b 28 Aug 1918 -
no death date, LBR
Robert, Pvt 11 Inf 5 Div,
WWII, b 20 Dec 1897 - d
16 Jan 1952, LNC
Roy H, Pvt 57 Pioneer Inf,
b 14 Dec 1936, MNT
Rutilia, b 12 March 1832 -
d 12 Feb 1890, UNN
Sam E, b 27 March 188- - d
18 July 1937, SNB
Samuel, b 25 March 1760 -
d 9 June 1819, ELZ
Samuel, b 24 Aug 1864 - d
1 Jan 1944, ELZ
Samuel L, b 15 Nov 1853 -
d 24 Aug 1860, ELZ
Samuel M, b 23 Jan 1880 -
d 10 Aug 1961, LBR
Steven Phillip, d 20 June
1977, ae 26y, LBR
Taft, b 3 Nov 1882 - d
1943, ELZ
Tempe, b 1 Jan 1875 - d 15
Aug 1945, ELZ
Tennessee M, b 19 Feb 1866
- d 14 May 1938, LVN
Tenya Denise, 1972, DRL
Thomas A, b 20 Jan 1890 -
d 27 Oct 1944, WRC
Thomas K, b 18 May 1875 -
d 19 Apr 1927, CBJ
Thurman L, b 31 Dec 1924 -
d 26 May 1967, WRC
Vess, b 14 Dec 1926 - no
death date, NWP
Virginia Lynn, d 7 Apr
1962, ae 1y, ARM
W C, b 16 Sept 1868 - d 14
July 1902, BRN

HALL (continued)

W J, b 22 Nov 1857 - d 9
Oct 1886, FLF

Walter, b 9 Apr 1898 - d
14 Nov 1963, LNE

William E, b 1893 - d
1964, BRR

William L, b 1886 - d
1927, LVN

William M, d 13 Aug 1974,
ae 76y, ALB

Wylie A, b 10 July 1865 -
d 25 June 1895, UNN

Z T, d 20 March 1936, ae
90y, ELZ

HALLCOCK, Walter, b 29 June
1890 - d 31 Aug 1899,
RTT

HALLCOX, Elsie Lee, b 10
Apr 1914 - d 1 Oct 1923,
RTT

Floyd E, b 7 Feb 1901 - d
25 July 1928, EST

Maggie Bryant, b 16 Sept
1874 - d 25 June 1960,
RTT

Ollie, b 19 July 1881 - d
17 Feb 1977, EST

Ray, b 30 July 1912 - d 3
Oct 1912, EST

Sam, b 4 Oct 1870 - d 18
May 1941, RTT

Sewell, b 12 July 1881 - d
5 Feb 1965, EST

HALLOWAY, Agnes, b 11 June
1918 - d 23 Feb 1936,
MNT

Crimson B, b 19 Apr 1888 -
d 5 Oct 1960, WRC

Jennie, b 8 March 1925 - d
7 Aug 1926, MNT

Joe Preston, b 15 May 1883
- no death date, WRC

Martha, b 15 Aug 1849 - d
13 Dec 1939, WRC

P O, b 13 Aug 1836 - d 24
Nov 1892, MNT

HALSTON, Charlotte Eliza-

HALSTON (continued)

beth, b 18 Feb 1885 - d
12 Feb 1972, UNN

Willie, b 4 Oct 1882 - d 4
Feb 1919, UNN

HAM, Moses, Co I 8th Vol
NH, b 17 May 1833 - d 17
Aug 1902, SNB

HAMBRIGHT, Betsy, d 12 Jan
1888, ae 5y, PLR

H D, b 18 Oct 1851 - d 11
Jan 1932, PLR

Henry D, b 31 July 1888 -
d 3 Jan 1909, PLR

Infant Son, b&d 6 Apr
1887, PLR

John B, b 17 Nov 1878 - d
26 July 1948, PLR

John D, b 12 June 1891 - d
14 Oct 1967, PLR

Mark, b 30 June 1896 - d
18 March 1920, PLR

Mary Duncan, b 27 Apr 1858
- d 7 Feb 1936, PLR

HAMBY, Adam N, d 26 May
1977, ae 17mo, UNN

Alberta D, d 7 Aug 1916,
CRO

Alex, b 5 Dec 1860 - d 7
Oct 1921, MCD

Alfred Aytes, b 16 Jan
1874 - d 24 Aug 1964,
WRC

Alma E, b 9 July 1893 - no
death date, DRM

Anderson, b 27 June 1857 -
d 13 Sept 1930, WRC

Artie, b 6 Feb 1911 - no
death date, ELZ

Augusta, b 1886 - d 1927,
MLC

Baby, d 1967, LNE

Balford, b 1909 - d 1949,
LBR

Beatrice, b 3 Apr 1896 - d
2 Sept 1900, CLC

Brenda B, b 10 Apr 1951 -
d 8 Aug 1961, ARM

76

HAMBY (continued)

Burtha, b 4 May 1895 - d 19 June 1901, ELZ

Calvin, b 1872 - d 1939, MCD

Caroline Jean, b 23 Jan 1947 - d 24 March 1947, PNY

Clara L (Ruppe), b 19 Feb 1899 - d 15 March 1976, DRM

Cora, b 1886 - d 1962, ELZ

David, b 31 Aug 1953 - d 27 Dec 1953, ELZ

Dempsie, b 5 Sept 1935 - d 11 March 1948, ELZ

Earnie, b 10 Sept 1890 - d 26 July 1981, LNE

Edith, b 25 Oct 1908 - no death date, BRD

Edna, b 15 Nov 1868 - d 15 Mar 1958, WRC

Edward H, b 8 Jan 1923 - d 27 Feb 1966, PNY

Edward Lee, b 19 July 1948 - d 13 July 1949, WRC

Electric, b 13 May 1874 - d 2 Sept 1896, CLC

Eliza, b 1847 - d 1928, MLC

Eller, b 1921 - d 1952, ELZ

Emily Catherine, b 18 June 1844 - d 14 Apr 1866, ELZ

Era, b 4 Apr 1904 - d 23 June 1913, MCD

Etta Hall, d 16 Jan 1976, ae 85y, ELZ

Finley, b 13 Apr 1906 - d 15 Jan 1971, LNE

Frank, d 23 Dec 1894, ae 59y, MCD

Franklin, b 8 Nov 1837 - d 7 March 1901, MCD

French, d 29 Sept 1976, ae 77y, WRC

Gertie D, b 17 Apr 1887 -

HAMBY (continued)

d 20 June 1960, MCD

Gus Henry, d 20 Jan 1979, ae 60y, WMG

Harlin, b 2 Nov 1886 - d 26 March 1968, SNB

Helen M, b 7 Apr 1921 - no death date, PNY

Henderson, b 1887 - d 1936, MCD

Infant Dau, b 23 March 1912 - d 30 March 1912, SNB

Ivory F, b 8 Nov 1876 - d 3 Nov 1945, MLC

J W, b 17 Aug 18-- - d 17 Jan 1912, MCD

Jake, b 24 March 1882 - d 20 Feb 1961, LNE

James M, b 10 Sept 1850 - d 25 July 1918, WRC

Janie, b 18 Oct 1874 - d 21 Oct 1962, PTC

Jean R, b 8 Dec 1934 - no death date, LNE

Jeremiah, b 1835 - d 5 Aug 1907, MCD

Julia Rader, b 15 March 1885 - d 16 March 1940, ELZ

Julia S, b 7 Oct 1913 - no death date, LNE

Katie J, b 8 March 1920 - d 2 Dec 1922, DRM

Kenley, b 4 Oct 1923 - d 13 Dec 1969, ARM

Ladusky, b 28 Feb 1869 - d 18 Jan 1943, ELZ

Lake, 13 Apr 1874 - d 30 July 1940, ELZ

Larry, d 1972, UNN

Leonard, b 11 July 1908 - d 7 Oct 1955, ELZ

Lewis, b 9 May 1878 - d 20 May 1932, LBR

Lewis, b 15 Dec 1878 - d 9 Nov 1957, WRC

Lous, b 9 Jan 1932 - d 10

HAMBY (continued)
Feb 1964, ELZ
Lucinda, b 30 March 1867 -
d 22 Sept 1900, MCD
Mahalah, b 14 Jan 1879 - d
26 Jan 1936, LBR
Manda, b 13 Feb 1866 - d 9
March 1939, WBB
Mary, b 1867 - d 1939, MCD
Maudie, b 1911 - d 1913,
MLC
Rev Merle, d 14 June 1975,
ae 49y, LNE
Mersly D, b 20 Feb 1926 -
d 14 June 1975, LNE
N Clenice, b 9 May 1890 -
d 9 June 1964, DRM
Nela, b 10 Apr 1910 - d 24
Apr 1911, MCD
Permelia, b 1875 - d 1962,
MCD
Persie R, Pfc 117 Inf 30
Div WWI, b 9 Sept 1894 -
d 17 Aug 1964, SNB
Rebecca, b 6 May 1860 - d
8 Jan 1917, WRC
Rebecca Shaver, b 26 Dec
1879 - d 19 Feb 1930,
WRC
Rema, d 1931, MCD
Riley, b 1887 - d 1965,
ELZ
Robert, b 1915 - d 1917,
MLC
Ronnie L, b 5 Jan 1947 - d
15 Jan 1947, LNE
Samuel M, d 23 March 1961,
ae 88y, MCD
Sarah E, b 8 Oct 1878 - d
27 July 1964, MLC
Selina, b 7 June 1891 - no
death date, SNB
Sherman, b 21 Sept 1867 -
d 3 Feb 1941, PTC
Sylvester, b 18 June 1897
- d 27 March 1965, BRD
Sylvester, b 21 June 1888
- d 27 Apr 1907, SNB

HAMBY (continued)
Talbert, b 26 March 1907 -
d 3 March 1966, ELZ
Vergis, b 1 Sept 1908 - d
18 Nov 1909, MCD
Vilia, b 13 Apr 1919 - d
22 July 1923, LBR
W H, b 8 March 1880 - d 6
Jan 1956, ELZ
W M, b 2 Apr 1852 - d 17
Jan 1910, ELZ
William Lester, Cpl USA
WWII, b 2 May 1920 - d
21 July 975, CRO
William, b 15 May 1842 - d
19 March 1887, MCD
William, b 1847 - d 1911,
MLC
William R, d 28 May 1981,
ae 69y, LNE
William R, b 13 Jan 1892 -
d 5 Nov 1947, DRM
Zra, b 4 March 1907 - d 5
March 1907, MCD
HAMLIN, Henry Conrad, d 9
Oct 1976, ae 66y, RGB
HAMMOND, Alina E, b 16 Apr
1885 - d 28 Nov 1967,
PLR
Charity M, b 8 July 1873 -
d 22 June 1919, PLR
Charles Lance, d 24 Aug
1981, ae 70y, PLR
Christine, b 11 Jan 1919 -
d 23 June 1919, PLR
Fred, d 30 Aug 1980, ae
67y, PLR
Glen B, b 1919 - d 1941,
CRO
Harry E, b 26 March 1876 -
d 14 May 1905, PLR
Harry Levi, b 25 Aug 1874
- d 22 Nov 1947, PLR
Leon, b 17 July 1921 - d 9
July 1922, PLR
Lloyd L, b 24 Feb 1905 - d
9 July 1977, PLR
M, b 22 Dec 1833 - d 15

HAMMOND (continued)
July 1913, DRL
Mary Ann Davis, b 31 March 1920 - d 8 Jan 1977, PLR
Nellie, b 5 Oct 1904 - d 15 March 1905, PLR
Nellie, b 25 Oct 1904 - d 15 Dec 1905, PLR
Nilis, b 19 Sept 1909 - d 7 Apr 1933, RGB
O K, b 19 Feb 1880 - d 19 Apr 1911, PLR
Sarah Ellen, b 7 May 1844 - d 20 Nov 1929, PLR
Verdon P, b 13 July 1914 - d 3 Feb 1971, PLR
HAMMONS, Callie, b 25 Oct 1877 - d 23 Feb 1964, NWP
Fred J, b 20 Sept 1897 - d 11 July 1916, OLP
J F, b 8 March 1869 - d -- May 1916, OLP
Jessee, b 27 Oct 1844 - d 30 Dec 1915, OLP
Magdaline, b 25 Oct 1922 - d 8 Feb 1926, OLP
HAMON, E C, b 23 June 1896 - d 26 Dec 1922, SHD
E S, b 23 Jan 1894 - d 16 Nov 1896, SHD
HAMPTON, Charles Ramon, b 12 Feb 1923 - d 18 Feb 1923, WRC
Horace S, b 1890 - d 1965, WMG
Mary Ruth, b 20 Sept 1938 - d 12 Dec 1938, ELZ
Nancy J, d 19 Apr 1975, ae 84y, WMG
HANEY, Era, b 10 March 1905 - d 4 May 1925, LNE
HANKINS, Clara, d 1960, WRC
T J, b 3 May 1881 - d 10 June 1910, MSG
HANNAH, A R, b 28 Mar 1899 - d 7 July 1963, WRC
Samuel F, b 29 Nov 1943 -

HANNAH (continued)
d 19 May 1961, WRC
HANNAHAN, Archie Wayne, b 28 Dec 1928 - d 4 Apr 1956, FLR
B Monroe, b 9 Feb 1873 - d 16 Feb 1955, FLR
Lindale Paul, b 11 Dec 1944 - d 24 Nov 1965, FLR
Lou Vernia, b 4 Oct 1873 - d 5 Nov 1940, FLR
Louis E, no dates, FLR
HANSON, John M, b 22 Apr 1874 - d 29 Jan 1906, DRL
Tellie D, b 19 Oct 1879 - no death date, DRL
HARDEE, Helen M, b 1913 - d 1971, CRO
Howard B, T5 USA WWII, b 8 Jan 1912 - d 3 Apr 1973, CRO
HARDIE, Charles J, b 21 March 1868 - d 21 Jan 1922, CRO
Harry, b 1905 - d 1949, CRO
Mary, no dates, CRO
William J, b 30 March 1909 - d 27 June 1948, CRO
HARDWICK, Dock, d 24 Oct 1979, ae 86y, WMG
Emily Cath, d 24 Feb 1980, ae 37y, FST
HARGES, Donald I, d 9 July 1979, ae 55y, WMG
Fannie Ellen, b 7 Dec 1884 - d 12 July 1964, WRC
Isaac Burton, b 15 Jan 1887 - d 12 Feb 1962, WRC
Kellie Ray, b 19 Nov 1918 - d 19 Nov 1937, WRC
Larry R, b 12 July 1942 - d 25 June 1970, WMG
Mertie, b 19 Feb 1947 - d 19 Feb 1947, WRC

HARGES (continued)
Paul, b 3 Jan 1926 - d 2
Sep 1926, WRC
HARGIS, Billy Ray, d 4
March 1977, ae 31y, MCR
Faye M, b 6 June 1922 - no
death date, CRO
Herbert Lee, d 27 Aug
1977, ae 55y, MCR
Kenneth L, b 7 Jan 1916 -
d 11 Oct 1964, CRO
Randall Richard, b 3 Dec
1946 - d 17 Apr 1950,
CRO
HARLAN, Thelma, d 5 Apr
1979, ae 69y, DRL
HARNESS, Belle, b 5 June
1896 - d 25 June 1965,
WMG
Margaret N, b 31 Oct 1935
- no death date, SNB
R D, b 23 Feb 1934 - d 22
July 1966, SNB
Rose Lee, b 1946 - d 1965,
PTC
HARNEY, Edna McCartt, d 29
June 1979, ae 64y, FRV
Infant s/o T L Harney, 9
June 1950, FRV
HARNSBY, Ellen French, d 24
Dec 1977, ae 77y, WRC
HARPER, William H, b 9 Feb
1894 - d 20 Nov 1963,
WRC
HARRIS, Audrey, b 1911 - d
1958, WRC
Kenneth, d 20 Aug 1974, ae
28y, NWP
Meady, b 8 Feb 1906 - no
death date, NWP
Mollie, b 1 Sept 1883 - d
7 May 1973, WRC
Owen C Jr, b 21 Aug 1923 -
d 3 May 1966, NWP
Regina Davidson, b 24 Jan
1858 - d 30 Oct 1924,
DVD
Robert, b 9 Feb 1892 - d

HARRIS (continued)
29 June 1976, NWP
Robert D, b 12 Oct 1884 -
no death date, WRC
Ruth, d 30 Dec 1974, ae
48y, NWP
Steven Randy, b 28 June
1976 - d 30 June 1976,
LBR
HARRISON, M E, b 6 March
1861 - d 16 March 1861,
OLP
HART, Arnold C, b 1908 - d
14 Sept 1976, WRC
James Alvin, b 11 June
1919 - d 17 May 1951,
WRC
James Edgar, b 1 Sept 1895
- d 4 March 1953, WRC
Thelma Chapman, b 1911 - d
1940, LBR
HARTSFIELD, James A, b 4
Dec 1850 - d 3 Apr 1882,
LNE
HATFIELD, Bettie Carrol, b
13 Feb 1874 - d 27 May
1915, LNE
G D, b 1 May 1898 - 15 Dec
1964, WRC
Jennie, b 6 Oct 1894 - d
24 May 1919, WRC
John F, b 11 May 1881 - d
8 Apr 1849, LNE
Joseph, b 1869 - d 1923,
LBR
Minnie C, b 27 June 1907 -
no death date, WRC
Myrtle, b 1894 - d 1913,
LBR
Ruby, Inf d/o G D & Min-
nie, no dates, WRC
Sallie, b 1865 - d 1908,
LBR
HATHAWAY, Lula G, d 20 May
1975, ae 92y, PTC
HATMAKER, Bernard Lee, b 20
Aug 1925 - d 15 Sept
1946, LNE

HATMAKER (continued)
Christiena, b 20 Sept 1914
- d 17 Dec 1917, LNE
D C, b 24 July 1883 - d 26
Nov 1937, LNE
Emma Goad, b 14 Oct 1892 -
no death date, LNE
HAWN, A A, b 1879 - d 1950,
CLC
A Wayne, d 1911, ae 70y,
PTC
Albert J, b 11 June 1866 -
d 22 Oct 1946, HWN
Arnold A, b 26 Feb 1896 -
d 19 Aug 1917, HWN
Belle, b 1876 - no death
date, CLC
Bertha, no dates, MLC
Callie, b 15 Feb 1888 - d
28 Dec 1933, DVD
Carl, b 8 Apr 1906 - d 11
March 1930, DVD
Cecil W, d 15 Feb 1975, ae
69y, PTC
Charles LaMar, b 4 Feb
1967 - d 24 Dec 1974,
LNE
Charles Lawson, b 4 Feb
1867 - d 24 Dec 1974,
PLR
Clyde A, b 15 Oct 1907 - d
20 July 1941, CLC
Earl M, d 28 Apr 1976, ae
69y, PTC
Edward J, d 9 March 1975,
ae 88y, DRL
Elnora, b 11 Dec 1882 - d
8 Jan 1960, PTC
Florence R, b 1906 - d
1942, PTC
G W, b 19 June 1882 - d 19
March 1929, DVD
H N, b 6 March 1855 - d 16
Apr 1882, PTC
Herma Anita, b 28 Apr 1916
- d 24 Apr 1966, DRL
Hunt Raymond, b 25 Dec
1910 - d 17 March 1935,

HAWN (continued)
DRL
Ida Essie, d 17 March
1976, a 81y, CLC
Infant Baby, no dates, PTC
Irene, b 7 March 1931 - d
12 Aug 1931, DRL
James, b 1880 - d 1967,
CLC
James H, b 1884 - d 1943,
PTC
Jane, b 23 Jan 1844 - d 23
Nov 1882, CLC
Jennie G, b 16 Apr 1873 -
d 6 Dec 1895, WRC
John, no dates, MLC
Joseph, b 1876 - d 1968,
PTC
Joyce Emma, b 23 May 1926
- d 3 Sept 1926, DRL
Lazarus P, d 15 Jan 1977,
ae 74y, PTC
Leonard J, b 3 May 1895 -
d 25 March 1963, DRL
Louis J, b 1900 - d 1945,
PTC
M, b 3 Sept 1860 - d 31
May 1922, WRC
M E, b 26 March 1874 - d
17 May 1886, PTC
Maggie, d 3 March 1980, ae
75y, LNE
Martha J, b 23 Dec 1880 -
d 30 March 1911, PTC
Nancy M, d 8 Oct 1876, ae
48y 2mo, MNT
Norman J, b 4 Dec 1922 - d
6 Jan 1945, DRL
Octavia Bunch, b 1933 - d
17 Sept 1980, MSG
Randale Jr, d 1908, NWP
Robert Pace, b 13 Jan 1887
- d 14 July 1957, PTC
Sarah Amanda, b 3 June
1867 - d 4 Oct 1926, HWN
Sarah Potter, d 1908, ae
65y, PTC
Sina, b 1908 - d 1964, LNC

HAWN (continued)
Sylvia Scott, d 1 Apr
1952, ae 65y, HLL
Telle H, b 20 Sept 1898 -
no death date, DRL
Virgil, b 1904 - d 1964,
ARM
William M, b 1877 - d
1962, ARM
HAYES, Iva Lee, d 2 July
1968, ae 21y, BRR
HAYMOND, Elijah Gren, b 16
Apr 1834 - d 8 Aug 1895,
SNB
HAYNER, Rev J E, d 10 May
1980, ae 84y, WMG
HAYNES, C A, d 24 Dec 1978,
ae 57y, NWP
Joe Billie, b&d 28 March
1932, ELZ
HAYWORTH, Doctor F, b 3 Aug
1856 - d 9 March 1922,
DRL
Estella M, b 12 May 1892 -
d 20 March 1922, DRL
Marie E, b 16 Oct 1913 - d
25 March 1938, DRL
Roberta Betty, d 4 Aug
1980, ae 69y, DRL
Sarah E, b 24 Apr 1858 - d
3 May 1932, DRL
Thomas T, b 25 July 1884 -
d 21 Aug 1964, DRL
Wilson W, b 26 March 1912
- d 28 Oct 1914, DRL
HAZELWOOD, Martha B, b 22
May 1908 - d 9 June
1942, BRN
HEADDEN, Lorenz G, b 3 Sept
1902 - d 14 May 1964,
CRO
HEADEN, Arta Phillips, b 18
Feb 1909 - d 3 July
1945, CRO
HEADRICK, ----, b 24 July
1952 - d 12 Sept 1952,
DRM
Charles, b 14 Dec 1848 - d

HEADRICK (continued)
3 Oct 1852, DRM
Edith L, b 14 Apr 1892 - d
14 March 1976, CRO
Edward G, b 13 June 1900 -
no death date, DRM
Elbert Ray, b 14 Feb 1937
- d 16 Sept 1965, DRM
Elizabeth, b 27 Jan 1863 -
d 5 Jan 1934, DRM
Emma Langley, b 7 Sept
1885 - d 20 Sept 1959,
CRO
Ethel L, b 18 June 1903 -
d 27 Nov 1972, DRM
Fran Gott, b 18 Aug 1855 -
d 17 Oct 1859, DRM
J G, b 20 June 1862 - d 13
Jan 1925, DRM
J M, b 7 Oct 1816 - d 31
July 1896, DRM
Jo Ann, b 21 March 1940 -
no death date, DRM
John R, b 16 May 1925 - d
24 Feb 1966, DRM
Lois (Mathis), b 14 Feb
1898 - d 5 Nov 1937, DRM
M R, b 12 Nov 1825 - d 23
Dec 1893, DRM
Minnie Kamer, b 2 July
1877 - d 17 Apr 1975,
DRM
Susan, b 11 Sept 1840 - d
8 Dec 1906, LBR
William L, b 27 Sept 1888
- d 5 Dec 1972, CRO
HEADRICKS, Sam, b 12 June
1871 - d 2 Dec 1930, CRO
HEATH, L O, b 1893 - d
1969, PNY
HEDRICK, Caroline, b 3
March 1860 - d 22 July
1861, DRM
Caroline -, b 29 June 1856
- d 2 July 1889, DRM
Charles J, b 20 Feb 1899 -
d 25 Feb 1899, DRM
Edward, b 18 Oct 1857 - d

HEDRICK (continued)
17 Oct 1859, DRM
F H, b&d 19 Apr 190, DRM
Fredrich,   b 21 Dec 1867 -
d 28 May 1868, DRM
Fritz,   b 31 July 1853 - d
8 Oct 1932, DRM
Hannah,   b 31 Dec 1873 - d
17 Feb 1948, DRM
John Henry, b 16 July 1870
- d 24 March 1872, DRM
Louis, b 28 March 1847 - d
13 July 1931, DRM
Mable C, 25 Sept 1911, DRM
Pauline,   b -- June 1851 -
d 24 Oct ----, DRM
HEIDEL,   Alex   E,   b 20 Nov
1868 - d 22 June 1920,
WRC
Alex F Jr, b 13 Aug 1902 -
d 17 Jan 1962, WRC
Alvin H,   d 27 March 1977,
ae 72y, WMG
Amanda R,   b 17 March 1875
- d 18 Apr 1968, WRC
Anna Marie,   b 19 Oct 1873
- d 4 March 1961, WRC
Arthur L, b 6 Feb 1922 - d
11 Nov 1940, WRC
Barbara Jee,   b 9 Nov 1941
- d 3 March 1942, UNN
Bell F,   b 31 March 1881 -
d 29 Dec 1951, WRC
Charles F,   b 1 Jan 1859 -
d 26 Oct 1926, WRC
Christine,   b 3 Dec 1913 -
d 3 Oct 19--, WRC
Clarence,   22 Aug 1910 - d
23 Aug 1965, WRC
Clayton, b 25 Feb 1916 - d
19 Feb 1940, WRC
Dora R,   b 1883 - d   1958,
WRC
Edgar,   b   1896 - d   1970,
WMG
Edward,   b 13 Dec 1856 - d
28 March 1931, WRC
Eunice,   b 28 Oct 1912 - d

HEIDEL (continued)
23 Dec 1912, UNN
Frank E, d 21 Dec 19074,
ae 71y, WMG
Fred J,   b 1886 - d   1965,
WMG
Georg, Maj, d 12 Nov 1980,
ae 90y, WRC
Grace McDowell, d 9 Feb
1980, ae 77y, WRC
Gustavus J,   b 12 Dec 1866
- d 4 Sept 1955, WRC
Harold Loyd, b 18 Oct 1943
-d 30 Oct 1945, UNN
Hazel,   b 12 Sept 1920 - d
7 Feb 1942, WRC
Henry L, b 28 Jan 1908 - d
28 Apr 1951, WRC
Herbert M,   b 18 Sept 1917
- d 27 July 1918, WRC
Hurchel Wm, b 4 Dec 1915 -
d 1 May 1916, WRC
Ida, b&d 21 Jan 1901, DRM
Jaycelyn F,   b   1937 - d
1966, WMG
Johann,   b 15 Dec 1828 - d
24 Jan 1914, WRC
John Fred, b 2 Sept 1914 -
d 12 Sept 194-, WRC
John Gilbert, b 27 June
1905 - d 14 Feb 1906,
WRC
Lucy May, b 31 July 1924 -
d 15 March 1925, WRC
Martha Louise, d 28 Apr
1981, ae 15y, WMG
Minnie C,   b 23 Oct 1882 -
d 22 May 1939, WRC
Paula F, b 1893 - no death
date, WMG
Reece,   b&d -- March 1915,
UNN
Rosa, b&d 21 Jan 1901, DRM
Rosa (Kramer), b 13 Oct
1862 - d 8 July 1949,
WRC
Rosa Lee, b 26 Sept 1927 -
d 6 July 1929, WRC

HEIDEL (continued)
Sam, b 18 Feb 1926 - d 30 March 1963, WRC
Valora M, b 1960 - d 1966, WMG
HEIDLE, Amanda A, b 5 July 1891 - d 23 May 1970, LBR
Charles Thomas, b&d 1 Jan 1930, LBR
Ernest D, b 13 March 1892 - no death date, LBR
Gus E, b 16 June 1885 - d 15 Sept 1967, LBR
Lola Ruth, b 2 Feb 1885 - d 31 Jan 1923, LBR
Pansy Matilda, b 18 July 1916 - d 16 Oct 1918, LBR
Roy, b 31 Oct 1908 - d 28 Apr 1928, LBR
HELMS, A C, b 7 Sept 1890 - d 1 Sept 1973, MST
Della Finch, d 5 March 1979, ae 85y, MST
HELTON, Ishmael W, b 20 June 1912 - d 28 May 1971, EST
Sally M, b 25 June 1909 - no death date, EST
Terrie Renna, b 18 Feb 1960 - d 14 Nov 1963, EST
HEMBREE, Clifton, b 1898 - d 1978, NWP
Elmer Holmer, b 15 May 1901 - d 25 Oct 1942, EST
John H Sr, d 12 Oct 1981, ae 77y, LNC
John Paul, b 1941 - d 22 Apr 1978, NWP
Rufus Elmore, b 25 Apr 1930 - d 9 Apr 1975, NWP
HENDERSON, Homer P, b 1880 - d 16 Jan 1968, BRR
Mary Ellender, b 10 June 1847 - d 6 Sept 1874,

HENDERSON (continued)
UNN
HENDRICK, Fred G, b 29 Oct 1885 - d 15 Dec 1975, CRO
HENLEY, Naomi F Lyons, b 19 July 1885 - d 21 Aug 1969, DRL
HENRY, Augusta Kreis, b 14 May 1855 - d 19 Apr 1892, WRC
Ben Jacob, b 22 Feb 1875 - d 10 June 1962, WRC
Carolyn, d 7 July 1954, ae 6y 3mo, LNE
Charles D, b 24 June 1887 - d 1951, WRC
Ellen, b 12 Aug 1825 - d 13 Dec 1897, LBR
Ernest Keith, d 18 Nov 1978, ae 21y, NWP
Ida Kaufman, d 10 Feb 1978, ae 88y, WRC
Kenneth, d 17 June 1951, PTC
Oscar, b 9 Apr 1891 - d 13 Aug 1954, PTC
Owen, b 1907 - d 1967, WRC
Peter, b 9 Mar 1845 - d 21 Sept 1926, WRC
Peter Jr, b 5 Oct 1897 - d 18 Feb 1900, WRC
Samuel, d 11 Feb 1869, ae 21y 11mo, LBR
Sarah Ann, b 25 Feb 1870 - d 8 Feb 1943, BRN
Sarah Leona, b 14 March 1882 - d 28 Sept 1964, WRC
HENSLEY, Alva G, d 7 June 1980, ae 81y, UNG
Cas, b 9 Feb 1902 - d 2 Sept 1963, NWP
Clarence, b 22 Jan 1900 - no death date, NWP
Clifton, d 27 Apr 1978, ae 80y, NWP
Clyde E, b 1 Jan 1915 - d

HENSLEY (continued)
6 Sept 1968, NWP
Frederick, b&d 10 March 1947, NWP
Hannah, b 1877 - d 1943, NWP
Hazel, b 6 Nov 1903 - no death date, NWP
Henry Clay, b 1875 - d 1943, NWP
Jackie Ray, b 15 Nov 1931 - d 15 Nov 1933, OLP
Mae, d 28 June 1879 - d 70y, NWP
Travis, b 10 July 1925 - d 15 Feb 1967, NWP
HESTER, M F, b 9 March 1852 - d 21 Feb 1933, BRN
HEYDEL, Christian F, b 30 Aug 1816 - d 26 Nov 1884, WRC
Ella S, b 14 Oct 1908 - no death date, LNE
T Otto, b 22 Nov 1894 - no death date, LNE
HICKMAN, Catherine, b 11 Jan 1859 - d 19 Apr 1929, PTC
Dennis W, b 19 Sept 1882 - d 30 Dec 1960, CLC
George L, b 30 Jan 1879 - d 8 Dec 1942, CLC
Herbert H, d 27 May 1980, ae 70y, CLC
Hilva C, b 16 Feb 1904 - d 12 June 1974, BRN
Lenora S, b 16 June 1880 - d 18 Sept 1942, CLC
Leo Dinton, b 11 Feb 1912 - d 16 May 1944, CLC
Lucille L, b 9 Aug 1928 - d 28 June 1970, CLC
Mack, d 18 Jan 1974, ae 77y, PTC
Mary A, b 18 Jan 1885 - d 2 Jan 1962, CLC
Melvin C, b 6 March 1940 - d 22 May 1958, PTC

HICKMAN (continued)
Nellie O, b 14 Feb 1912 - no death date, BRN
Ova Glenice, b 15 Aug 1922 - d 9 June 1944, CLC
Phyllis Ann, b 24 May 194- - d 22 July 1944, CLC
Scott, b 8 Aug 1861 - d 30 Aug 1959, PTC
T F, b 22 May 1905 - d 2 Oct 1905, CLC
HICKS, Austin, no dates, DRL
Dora E Blair, b 8 Feb 1887 - d 11 Aug 1938, PLR
Helen, b 1928 - d 1964, LNC
James, WWI, b 18 Apr 1889 - d 22 Feb 1941, RGB
Joel Deanie, b 10 March 1885 - d 23 June 1960, PLR
Mary Northrup, d 19 Dec 1978, ae 83y, PLR
Millie, b 9 Feb 1865 - d 27 Sept 1949, LNE
HIGGINS, Oma, b 1897 - d 1963, LNE
Patsy Joan, d 24 June 1980, ae 26y, LNE
HILL, Aaron D, b 1 March 1909 - d 17 Dec 1973, RTT
Allen, b 31 March 1888 - d 27 March 1974, RTT
Charlie, baby, no dates, MLC
Earl, b 3 Oct 1911 - d 14 Aug 1968, RTT
Ella, b 2 Aug 1898 - 31 Dec 1914, MSG
Fred, b&d 6 Apr 1906, RTT
Gertrude, b 28 Nov 1898 - d 4 June 1953, RTT
Glenn A, b 4 Sept 1916 - d 17 Feb 1947, RTT
J S, b 2 July 1852 - d 30 March 1926, MSG

HILL (continued)
John Wisley, b 7 Sept 1865
- d 28 Aug 1948, RTT
Johnnie Levy, b 29 Sept
1915 - d 27 Nov 1921,
CBJ
Mamie, b&d 6 Apr 1906, RTT
Mary Louise, b 21 Dec 1865
- d 14 Dec 1957, RTT
Mary M, b 17 Feb 1888 - d
17 Apr 1962, RTT
Sailer Dyer, b 1 Jan 1861
- d 9 June 1932, MSG
Theodore, no dates, MSG
Victor S (Dick), b 1 March
1892 - d 13 May 1973,
MSG
HILTON, Daniel Eugene, b 11
Dec 1950 - d 12 March
1973, LBR
Eloise Williams, no dates,
WRC
Linda Lou, b&d 20 Dec
1940, LBR
William James, b 1901 - d
1962, WRC
HINES, Billy, b 1927 - d
1937, WRC
Dora, b 1880 - d 1946, WRC
George, b 1904 - d 1939,
WRC
Ina Marie, d 30 Aug 1978,
ae 69y, WRC
Lace, b 1874 - d 1930, WRC
Raymond Jr, b 10 Nov 1933
- d 14 Apr 1967, LNC
Raymond M, d 17 Jan 1981,
ae 68y, LNC
Robert Dale, b 22 May 1937
- d 27 Jan 1938, LNC
Virgil C, d 19 June 1977,
ae 58y, WMG
Wayne Rogers, b 31 Dec
1940 - d 8 Oct 1941, LNC
HINKLE, Allen L, Sgt USMC
WWII, b 23 Nov 1925 - d
9 May 1973, NWP
HINSLEY, Edith, b 22 May

HINSLEY (continued)
1904 - d 18 July 1905,
CBJ
HIXON, Elizabeth Walls, b 4
Feb 1886 - d 17 Sept
1920, DVS
Ervin L, b 24 Apr 1914 - d
28 July 1914, LNC
J S, b 12 May 1884 - d 12
Aug 1914, LNC
HOBBS, Irene M Koontz, d 4
Jan 1980, ae 75y, OLP
Lorenzo, b 17 Nov 1870 - d
24 Apr 1929, OLP
Matilda Jane, b 9 Oct 1874
- d 10 Oct 1965, OLP
HODGE, Gracy, d 1 March
1942, ae 37y, LNC
HOLBERT, S H, b 12 Aug 1863
- d 3 July 1933, UNH
Tennessee, b 6 July 1866 -
d 28 July 1954, UNH
HOLDER, Anna May, date des-
troyed, LBR
Carl G, b 1905 - d 22 Apr
1977, LBR
Dollie, b 5 May 1881 - no
death date, WRC
Earl, d 1 Oct 1978, ae
83y, FLF
Elizabeth M, b 22 March
1885 - no death date,
PNY
Mrs Geneva S, d 9 Sept
1978, ae 69y, LBR
Georgiana, d 11 July 1876,
ae 8mo 28da, RTT
Haigia, 1945, LBR
J V, b 16 Feb 1879 - d 6
June 1948, WRC
Jennie A, d 10 Jan 1961,
ae 93y, FLF
John, b 13 Aug 1886 - d 3
Feb 1976, LBR
Martin, b 25 Oct 1875 - d
22 Oct 1961, PNY
Nannie Morgan, b 1883 - d
1963, WRC

86

HOLDER (continued)

Robert, b 11 March 1916 – d 4 March 1951, FLF

Virginia, b 11 Dec 1945 – d 26 June 1949, LBR

W A, b 3 June 1876 – d 21 March 1941, WRC

HOLLADAY, Dudley, Pvt Co C 4th Cas Rgt, b 1 Sept 1892 – d 9 Oct 1965, WRC

Forest Lee, b 10 Apr 1918 – d 17 May 1931, SNB

J Henry, b 12 Feb 1884 – d 4 Aug 1954, SNB

Lee C, b 1882 – d 1932, SNB

Lewis J, b 1877 – d 1933, SNB

Margaret B, d -- Feb 1973, ae 79y, WMG

Margaret B, b 4 Nov 1893 – d -- Feb 1973, WRC

Mary E, b 1858 – d 1936, SNB

Robert A, b 1848 – d 1894, SNB

Robert Steel, b 18 July 1880 – d 5 Sept 1889, SNB

HOLLEY, Billy Eugene, b 18 May 1932 – d 23 July 1973, CRO

George C, d 2 June 1981, ae 80y, CRO

George E, b 29 Jan 1918 – no death date, CRO

Georgia McGill, d 31 Dec 1980, ae 62y, CRO

HOLLOWAY, Audrey, b 1908 – d 1919, MLC

Lizzie, b 1848 – d 1910, MLC

Myrtle, b 1898 – d 1920, MLC

Pauline, b 1910 – d 1928, MLC

HOLLOWELL, Laura M, b 1875 – d 1953, BRR

HOLLOWELL (continued)

Oren W, b 1876 – no death date, BRR

HOLLY, Mrs G W, d 9 Feb 1926, CRO

HOLMER, Anna W, d 6 March 1974, ae ----, DRL

David B, d 22 March 1977, ae 88y, DRL

HOLMES, David William, b 3 Dec 1947 – d 19 July 1966, DRL

HONEYCUTT, Amanda, b 1 Dec 1851 – d 24 Dec 1903, PNY

Arnold H, b 1919 – d 1965, MSG

Audery Arleen, b 11 Feb 1928 – d 30 Apr 1928, PNY

Ben M, b 1875 – d 1930, PNY

Bess, b 1893 – d 1967, WMG

Carrie, d 3 Oct 1973, ae 91y, WMG

Carrie, b 9 Mar 1882 – d 3 Oct 1973, WRC

Clarence Lee, b 22 Aug 1915 – d 10 March 1925, PNY

D C, Co D 2nd TN Inf, b 1843 – d 16 Oct 1875, LBR

Daisy Alice, b 1 May 1891 – d 6 Jan 1916, PNY

David Meshack, b 11 Apr 1868 – d 29 June 1887, LBR

Devine P, b 1917 – d 1943, PNY

Douglas, no birth date – d 22 Dec 1941, PNY

Dow L, b 8 Aug 1882 – d 25 July 1951, PNY

E G, b 31 July 1894 – d 27 Oct 1909, PNY

Effie Cooper, b 2 Oct 1895 – d 3 Aug 1952, PNY

HONEYCUTT (continued)
  Elizabeth A, b 10 May 1844
    - d 13 Jan 1919, PNY
  Emma E, b 9 Nov 1925 - d
    30 Jan 1926, PNY
  Eva Wilson, b 17 Feb 1884
    - no death date, PNY
  Harriet O, b 13 Aug 1870 -
    d 18 Dec 1870, LBR
  Hershel, d 25 Oct 1975, ae
    80y, FST
  Imer Hendrick, b 30 Oct
    1871 - d 6 Aug 1872, LBR
  Inf Dau, no dates, MSG
  J A, b 1869 - d 1949, WRC
  Laura Howard, b 6 Oct 1872
    - d 26 Nov 1968, LNC
  Lila M, b 20 Nov 1926 - d
    15 Dec 1926, PNY
  Mable Mae, b 17 June 1915
    - d 23 May 1947, PNY
  Massie A, b 23 Oct 1889 -
    no death date, PNY
  Nathan, b 15 May 1837 - d
    15 Feb 1875, LBR
  Nathan L, b 27 June 1909 -
    d 16 Oct 1939, WRC
  Paul, b 23 Apr 1852 - d 23
    March 1933, PNY
  Ricky Lynn, b&d 21 Sept
    1961, DRM
  Samuel C, Capt Co D, Rgt
    TN, b 6 Feb 1835 - d 11
    May 1872, LBR
  Samuel N, b 26 Dec 1843 -
    d 16 Jan 1923, PNY
  Sarah E Taylor, b 1878 - d
    1944, PNY
  Susan Helen, b 22 Nov 1865
    - d 29 Nov 1865, LBR
  Ted, b&d 15 Sept 1919, PNY
  Valora M, b 1905 - no
    death date, WMG
  Velia J, b 2 Feb 1894 - no
    death date, CRO
  Verried L, Pvt 15 Co Re-
    cruit Depot, WWI, b 1
    May 1893 - d 9 Aug 1961,

HONEYCUTT (continued)
  CRO
  Wiley, b 22 Apr 1880 - d 4
    Nov 1945, PNY
  William Jean, b 21 Jan
    1921 - d 1 Dec 1921, PNY
  William L, b 9 Jan 1890 -
    no death date, PNY
HONICUTT, Henrietta, d 2
    May 1868, ae 85y, BRR
HOOD, Annah J, b 28 Aug
    1931 - no death date,
    EST
  Bowers, b — Sept 1900 - d
    25 Nov 1960, CBJ
  Paul, b 17 Sept 1934 - d 2
    June 1970, EST
  Robert, b 1884 - no death
    date, LNE
  Rosa, b 1875 - d 1954, LNE
  Tessie, b 24 Sept 1899 - d
    5 Apr 1968, CBJ
  W A, b 1890 - d 1964, CBJ
HOOKS, Frank, Pfc USAAF,
    WWII, b 9 Feb 1915 - d
    11 (or 12) Feb 1974, LNE
  G Thomas, b 30 Jan 1872 -
    d 27 Feb 1955, LNE
  Glen, d 2 May 1980, ae
    73y, LNE
  Lannie, b 29 May 189- - d
    26 Dec 19--, LNE
  Laura E, b 3 Nov 1881 - d
    10 July 1949, LNE
  Opha--, b 12 June 19-- - d
    16 Apr 19--, LNE
  Tony Lynn, b&d 16 Nov
    1968, LNE
HOOPER, Eminr, b 26 Nov
    1875 - d 22 Oct 1903,
    DRL
HOPE, James, b 2 Dec 1889 -
    d 21 Nov 1890, RGB
  Richard, b 3 Apr 1885 - d
    16 July 1885, RGB
  Richard M, no dates, RGB
HOPKINS, Thurman, b 27 Dec
    1922 - d 26 March 1929,

HOPKINS (continued)
WRC
HOPPER, Anderson, b 5 Oct
1846 - d 25 May 1906,
EST
Mary E, b 13 Oct 1852 - d
6 June 1903, EST
HORNSBY, Charlie, b 1898 -
d 1945, WRC
Mayme L, b 1883 - d 1972,
WRC
HOUSE, Lona, d 16 June
1980, ae 61y, NWP
W M, b 26 Apr 1832 - d 16
July 1916, PLR
HOUSLEY, Inf, b&d 26 Oct
1963, EST
HOUSTON, Joe, d 20 Apr
1978, ae 60y, UNG
John Henry, b 2 Sept 1927
- d 14 Apr 1974, LNE
Joseph, b 1890 - d 1953,
LNE
Mamie, b 1907 - no death
date, LNE
HOWARD, Alva, d 9 Nov 1973,
ae 69y, CLC
Anil, b 1908 - d 1966, LNC
Arto H, b 12 July 1907 - d
1 Jan 1946, WRC
Arto James, d 26 Aug 1972,
ae 40y 8mo, WRC
Barbara J, b 10 Aug 1945 -
no death date, BRN
Bonnie N Dagley, d 9 Sept
1978, ae 69y, WRC
Byrd W, b 16 Dec 1936 - d
23 Jan 1969, BRN
Claud, b 27 Jan 1919 - no
death date, BRN
Caroline, b 29 March 1808
- d 18 March 1893, CLC
Charles J, b 25 May 1899 -
d 31 Oct 1906, LNC
Clayton Donald, b 6 May
1955 - d 24 June 1977,
WRC
Clyde H, d 1 May 1976, ae

HOWARD (continued)
71y, CRO
Cora, b 11 Aug 1901 - d 15
Nov 1962, CRO
Delphia Bowman, b 22 Apr
1876 - d 31 Jan 1948,
WRC
Dock G, d 15 March 1975,
ae 85y, CLC
Dollie, b 1908 - d 1962,
WRC
Dora L, b 15 Nov 1898 - d
1 Apr 1958, BRN
Elisha, b 28 March 1846 -
d 19 March 1909, LVN
Elizabeth, b 21 Sept 1831
- d 22 May 1874, CLC
Elizabeth McC, b 5 Dec
1859 - d 3 Aug 1902, CLC
Emily M, b 12 Nov 1879 - d
18 Jan 1957, CRO
General, b&d 14 May 1919,
PNY
George Ulysses, b 22 Dec
1868 - d 13 Feb 1948,
WRC
Rev Gilbert H, b 9 May
1887 - d 8 Sept 1938,
CLC
Harlan J, b 14 Oct 1902 -
d 19 Oct 1926, CLC
Henry Herchel, d 19 Aug
1981, ae 76y, WRC
Horace, b 1 Nov 1873 - d
22 Apr 1922, CLC
Infant, b&d 7 March 1877,
CLC
Infant, b&d 30 Nov 1934,
BRN
Infant, b&d 11 May 1882,
CLC
Infant, b&d 15 Nov 1868,
CLC
Infant, b&d 17 Apr 1934,
CLC
Infant, b&d 20 Feb 1925,
BRD
Infant, d 18 Jan 1888, CLC

HOWARD (continued)
Infants, two c/o Arlo H, no dates, MSG
Rev James A, Cpl Co C 4th TN Inf, b 25 Oct 1872 - d 9 Sept 1952, CLC
Jeffery Kenneth, d 8 Sept 1981, ae 26y, CLC
Jessie R, b 1 Feb 1927 - d 7 Feb 1927, BRD
Joe M, b 15 Dec 1869 - d 8 Apr 1956, BRN
John, d 25 Apr 1950, ae 79y, MSG
Jona M, b 14 May 1914 - d 12 Apr 1937, CLC
Joseph A, b 9 Nov 1933 - d 23 Apr 1935, CLC
Josie W H, b 25 Oct 1889 - d 14 Mar 1967, CLC
Julie R, b 27 March 1954 - d 28 March 1954, BRN
Kesiah, b 2 Aug 1817 - d -- Nov 1879, CLC
L J, b 1876 - d 1963, CLC
Leona, b 28 May 1888 - d 28 March 1890, CLC
Lewis S C, b 15 July 1835 - d 17 Feb 1897, CLC
Lola, b 9 Nov 1895 - d 14 Apr 1896, LNC
Louise, d 21 Oct 1981, ae 76y, CLC
Louise Bardell, d 9 June 1976, ae 77y, WRC
M E, b 22 Feb 1859 - d 28 Jan 1896, CLC
Martha, b 7 Nov 1854 - d 10 Aug 1915, CLC
Martha, b 1871 - d 1967, MSG
Mary A, b 9 July 1843 - d 2 May 1900, LBR
Mary A, b 7 Aug 1820 - d 10 Aug 1898, DRL
Mary Branstetter, b 31 Dec 1884 - d 9 Aug 1942, CLC
Mary C, b 15 June 1879 - d

HOWARD (continued)
4 Feb 1962, BRN
Matilda, b 13 Oct 1865 - d 16 Nov 1866, CLC
May Jewel, b 3 Nov 1908 - d 14 Aug 1973, BRR
Myrtle, b 26 Jan 1914 - d 13 June 1974, BRN
Nola England, b 1905 - d 1936, LNC
Pearl McGill, b 14 Sept 1908 - d 13 Nov 1966, CRO
R T, b 7 June 1864 - d 1 Jan 1903, LNC
Reid, b 10 June 1917 - d 28 Feb 1918, CRO
Richard B, b 1874 - d 1948, WRC
Robert W, b 1903 - d 1926, LNC
Rosa, b 1873 - d 1964, CLC
Ross, b 25 Jan 1910 - d 4 July 1952, WRC
Roy, Pvt USA, b 1 Oct 1902 - d 21 Feb 1940, WRC
Ruby Powell, b 24 Sept 1902 - d 26 Oct 1956, WRC
Rev Sam'l J, b 1883 - d 1954, CLC
Samuel, b 6 May 1844 - d 20 Jan 1913, CLC
Samuel, b 18 Oct 1800 - d 10 Jan 1888, CLC
Samuel, b 29 Nov 1879 - d 17 Feb 1897, CLC
Sarah Williams, b 7 June 1838 - no death date, LVN
Seivel, b 21 July 1898 - d 19 Sept 1954, CRO
Sinthia May, b 25 March 1898 - d 4 Apr 1898, PTC
Solomon N, b 29 June 1881 - d 14 July 1901, CLC
Susan, b 1 Nov 1851 - d 26 Jan 1938, CLC

HOWARD (continued)

William, 2Lt Co F 1st TN Inf, b 8 May 1831 - d 17 Oct 1916, LVN

Wm Lindsey, d 1 March 1978, ae 77y, ISF

HUCKABY, ----, b 26 Aug 1910 - d 6 July 1914, MLC

Albert Edward, d 17 May 1975, ae 38y, SNB

Edd, b 14 Aug 1875 - d 14 Jan 1944, WRC

Edward Jr, b 1901 - d 1947, WRC

Ernest C, b 1908 - d 1918, CBJ

Margaret Miller, b 17 May 1883 - d 17 July 1962, WRC

Nancy, dates illegible, WBB

Sarah D, d 19 Sept 1961, ae 53y, SNB

HUCKLEBY, Mae, b 3 Nov 1885 - d 10 Nov 1957, FRV

HUDSON, Cassie, b 12 Jan 1878 - d 25 Feb 1962, EST

Charles E, d 9 Feb 1895, ae 15y 11mo, UNN

Charles W, b 14 June 1874 - d 6 March 1943, EST

Don Edward, b 18 March 1907 - d 8 March 1917, OLP

Estella M, b 28 Aug 1917 - d 18 Jan 1919, EST

Jeannette, b 21 June 1913 - d 10 May 1916, EST

Latham G, b 10 Apr 1900 - d 6 June 1900, EST

Martha E, b 12 Oct 1842 - d 1 March 1876, LBR

N A, b 6 Feb 1844 - d 24 Apr 1915, EST

Nancy A, b 13 Oct 1831 - d 1 Oct 1899, EST

HUDSON (continued)

Richard G, b 4 Feb 1819 - d 11 Nov 1881, EST

Robert M, b 2 July 1900 - d 6 June 1906, EST

Roughton, b 4 July 1870 - d 11 May 1919, OLP

Samuel M, b 11 Apr 1854 - d 17 Aug 1879, EST

T G, b 5 July 1847 - d 2 May 1917, EST

HUFF, Bertha, b 31 Oct 1908 - d 29 June 1910, PNY

Mary Jane, b 1871 - d 1958, CRO

HUGH, Henry W, d 20 Apr 1978, ae 43y, FST

HUGHES, Flora M, b 1906 - d 1909, BRR

Margaret E, b 1797 - d 1887, RGB

Nettie M, b 1868 - d 1950, SNB

Viola Y, b 1876 - d 1919, BRR

HULING, Arthur M, MD, b 25 May 1887 - d 29 Oct 1979, ae 92y, WRC

Cassell L, b 28 March 1930 - no death date, UNG

Daniel Monroe, b 1884 - d 1943, LBR

Georgia B, b 13 May 1897 - d 11 Apr 1978, WRC

James M, b 29 Nov 1860 - d 19 Dec 1953, ALB

Nora, b 30 Sept 1865 - d 17 Jan 1957, ALB

Peggy A, b 24 Nov 1935 - d 15 Dec 1970, UNG

T E, b 25 Apr 1904 - d 2 Feb 1943, ALB

HULL, Catherine, b 18 May 1850 - d 29 Dec 1901, BRR

Clarence s/o Melvin, no dates, ALB

Clifford s/o Melvin, no

HULL (continued)
dates, ALB
Franklin Dennis, b 26 Feb 1847 - d 9 Nov 1932, BRR
Herman A, b 5 March 1880 - d 17 Sept 1902, BRR
Rev J Melvin, b 13 Apr 1873 - d 4 Apr 1905, ALB
Leonzo B, b 24 July 1875 - d 25 Dec 1878, BRR
Mary Jane Brown, b 2 June 1863 - d 23 Feb 1933, PLR

HUMAN, ---- s/o W H, no dates, MLC
Alice, b 10 Apr 1888 - d 7 March 1917, WBB
Anglie, b 15 Dec 1882 - d 28 March 1928, MLC
B H, b 6 Aug 1845 - d 13 Apr 1924, SNB
Baby s/o Chas W, 30 Aug 1919, MLC
Bonnie, b 10 Nov 1953 - d 3 Dec 1953, MLC
Calvin R, b 26 Aug 1962 (?) - d 16 Aug 1962 (?), DVD
Charles Carr, d 17 Jun 1973, ae 64y, WRC
Charles W, b 11 Jan 1873 - d -- Feb 1956, WRC
Charlie, b&d 27 Jan 1932, MLC
Christine H Cross, b 4 May 1912 - d 15 Sept 1966, MLC
E F, b 6 May 1842 - d 12 Aug 1903, MLC
Earnest, b 1903 - d 1904, MLC
Ebenezer, b 6 Nov 1851 - d 5 June 1932, SNB
Edgar, b 1909 - d 1918, MLC
Edward F, b 1878 - d 1928, MLC
Effie, b 30 Apr 1891 - d

HUMAN (continued)
26 Aug 1907, SNB
Effie Howard, b 8 Nov 1906 - no death date, FST
Eliza J, b 11 Sept 1878 - d 12 March 1912, MLC
Elizabeth, b 8 May 1893 - d 8 Aug 1975, WRC
Elizabeth Webb, b 13 Mar 1874 - d 16 Feb 1944, WRC
Ella, b 26 May 1868 - d 11 March 1932, WRC
Elmer R, b 2 Aug 1901 - d 8 Aug 1973, FST
Elmer Randolph, d 8 Aug 1973, ae 72y, LNC
Emily, b 22 Feb 1901 - no death date, DVD
Ernest W, b 14 Nov 1908 - d 29 Sept 1939, MLC
Frank, b 22 Apr 1911 - d 5 Feb 1929, WRC
Frank D, d 21 June 1977, ae 77y, SNB
Gordon, b 23 Oct 1911 - d 16 Jan 1957, WRC
Hazel, b 28 Jan 1917 - d 17 Aug 1925, WRC
Hi, b 21 Aug 1893 - d 16 Oct 1929, SNB
I J, b 1875 - d 1946, WRC
Infant, b 3 Feb 1928 - d 3 Feb 1928, WRC
Infant, b&d 1 Aug 1954, WRC
Isaac Franklin, b 18 Apr 1867 - d 13 Apr 1945, MLC
J M, b 19 Jan 1840 - d 5 Jan 1915, MLC
Jack, b 1894 - d 1912, MLC
James A, b 16 Aug 1870 - d 31 May 1894, SNB
Laurine, d 21 Oct 1976, ae 44y, MLC
Lena Burns, d 8 Sept 1981, ae 79y, WRC

HUMAN (continued)

Lydia, b 18 May 1841 - d 27 July 1910, MLC

Marie B, b 1906 - no death date, SNB

Mary Jane, b 5 Oct 1872 - d 12 March 1960, MLC

Mary Walker, b 9 Jan 1851 - d 31 May 1894, SNB

Maude Brock, b 1880 - d 1967, MLC

Mildred, b 1922 - d 1923, MLC

Minnie E, b 1881 - d 1949, WRC

Nancy A, b 11 Dec 1845 - d 5 Jan 1919, MLC

Nannie Andrew, b 1866 - d 1937, SNB

Neva, b 1915 - d 1919, MLC

P M, b 11 Nov 1873 - d 24 Feb 1905, SNB

Parthena, b 22 Apr 1853 - d 22 Feb 1927, SNB

Phoelu Victoria, b 18 Sept 1871 - d 18 Apr 1939, MLC

Ruth A, b 9 June 1900 - d 3 July 1901, DDN

Sam H, b 11 March 1872 - d 19 Apr 1941, MLC

Thos Harlan, b 17 March 1902 - d 22 Jan 1912, MLC

W L, b 4 May 1915 - d 28 Aug 1934, MLC

W Riley, b 6 Sept 1868 - d 19 Nov 1910, MLC

Walter E, b 1895 - d 1960, SNB

Willard, b 9 Feb 1905 - d 23 Nov 1906, MLC

William Alvin, b 1867 - d 1935, SNB

William J, b 9 Dec 1888 - d 5 Sept 1965, WRC

Willie J, b 8 June 1909 - d 15 Oct 1909, MLC

HUMES, Nell Woolum, d 14 March 1979, ae 80y, LBR

HUMMEL, Audrey M, b&d 10 July 1929, BRD

John E, d 5 July 1975, ae 82y, BRD

John Eugene, b 15 July 1938 - d 4 Sept 1938, BRD

HUNLEY, Harrison, b 5 May 1847 - d 19 Jan 1934, PNY

Hattie, b 6 Oct 1889 - d 24 Dec 1964, PNY

Martha, b 13 June 1866 - d 25 June 1937, PNY

Nancy A, b 1939 - d 1885, BRD

HUNLLEY, Joseph L Jr, b 23 July 1932 - d 17 March 1966, DRL

HUNT, Clinton D, b 1881 - d 1934, CRO

Martha A, b 1880 - no death date, CRO

Mattie, d 1 June 1978, ae 98y, CRO

HUNTER, Annie, b 8 May 1879 - d 5 July 1956, DVS

Herbert, b 24 Nov 1902 - d 24 March 1977, NWP

Raymond, d 2 May 1978, ae 58y, NWP

HURST, Addison Orval, b 12 March 1908 - d 7 March 1953, DRL

Billie Oscar, b&d 27 Oct 1924, DRL

Buna A, b 3 May 1918 - 19 Dec 1964, DRL

Charlie, b 16 Jan 1902 - d 2 June 1911, BRR

Charlie Floyd, b 12 Sept 1887 - d 31 May 1964, DRL

Clara M, b 19 Jan 1907 - d 11 July 1907, DRL

Dave A, b 30 May 1880 - d

HURST (continued)
20 Feb 1954, DRL
Donald L, b 8 Sept 1940 -
d 14 Apr 1959, DRL
Drucilla Hall, b 11 Aug
1853 - d 13 Apr 1935,
DRL
Edith M, b 12 March 1919 -
d 5 Jan 1933, DRL
Eliza, b 1855 - d 1917,
BRR
Ella, d 14 Oct 1976, ae
72y, FST
Ernie O, b 27 Aug 1915 - d
17 June 1963, DRL
Floyd, b 18 June 1848 - d
18 Nov 1933, DRL
Garvie C, b 28 Apr 1913 -
d 29 June 1914, DRL
H D, b 25 Feb 1934 - d 20
Feb 1950, DRL
Herman D, d 18 Oct 1975,
ae 66y, DRL
Homer, b 23 May 1895 - d 4
Sept 1895, BRR
Irene M, b 20 March 1894 -
no death date, DRL
Jack A, d 22 Oct 1977, ae
46y, DRL
James A, b 17 Apr 1894 - d
20 March 1961, DRL
Jennie L, b 14 June 1936 -
d 25 May 1954, DRL
Jeremiah, b 7 Oct 1832 - d
21 March 1902, LVN
Lester W, b 14 Nov 1914 -
d 14 Feb 1915, DRL
Lila, b&d 6 Apr 1918, BRR
Lindsay W, b 3 July 1890 -
d 25 May 1954, DRL
Lucy E Scott, b 13 Feb
1888 - d 5 Sept 1941,
DRL
Marcus, b 14 Apr 1908 - d
11 Oct 1912, DRL
Miller E, b 24 Nov 1873 -
d 7 Sept 1938, DRL
Minnie England, b 23 Oct

HURST (continued)
1891 - d 26 Sept 1978,
DRL
Nannie, b 30 Apr 1887 - d
24 Nov 1929, DRL
Ray C, d 26 May 1980, ae
58y, DRL
Walter L, b 22 May 1924 -
d 15 Sept 1929, BRR
HURTT, John Lynette, b&d 1
Apr 1969, DRL
Martha Webb, b 1892 - d
1936, WBB
Mary Ann Freels, b 7 June
1866 - d 29 March 1937,
PLR
Orlenia, b 10 Oct 1834 - d
11 Feb 1918, PLR
W A, b 16 July 1859 - d 9
Dec 1925, DVS
William E, b 7 Feb 1868 -
d 23 Apr 1937, PLR
HUSKINS, Eliza, b 11 May
1842 - d 31 Aug 1915,
OLP
Geraldine West, b 31 May
1925 - d 10 Oct 1972,
CRO
Herschel, b 8 Jan 1908 - d
1 July 1928, CRO
S M, b 18 Jan 1849 - d 9
Jan 1921, OLP
Sam L, b 18 Nov 1928 - no
death date, CRO
Samuel M, b 22 Jan 1868 -
d 30 Jan 1950, CRO
Susie Thomas, b 10 May
1881 - no death date,
CRO
HUTCHERSON, George Dewey, d
27 Oct 1973, ae 77y, SNB
Georgeann Whit, b 16 Dec
1861 - d 1 Aug 1929, SNB
Nancy P, b 1894 - no death
date, CRO
Sim E, b 1890 - d 1962,
CRO
William K, b 10 Aug 1860 -

HUTCHERSON (continued)
d 31 Jan 1915, SNB
HUTCHINS, H I, b 16 June
1860 - d 27 Jan 1919,
CLC
HUTCHISON, Bertie E, b 17
Jan 1889 - d 16 July
1922, SNB
Bessie E, b 27 Apr 1890 -
d 21 July 1972, SNB
Madge Peck, b 1910 - d
1940, SNB
William Edd, b 4 Oct 1882
- d 10 Apr 1953, SNB
William H, b 1907 - d
1944, SNB
HUTTER, Dorothy P, b 13 Oct
1903 - d 23 Feb 1939,
NWP
HYDEL, Infant, 6 March
1931, ELZ
INNESS, Cora E, b 30 Oct
1886 - d 21 Sept 1950,
SHD
George, b 13 Oct 1944 - d
4 Sept 1964, SHD
J Cullon, b 13 Aug 1874 -
d 8 Jan 1943, SHD
Wiley M, b 30 June 1906 -
d 9 Aug 1952, SHD
INNIS, Emma D, b 1883 - d 9
Oct 1973, UNG
John R, d 6 Aug 1975, ae
60y, BRR
Thomas, b 1877 - d 1858,
UNG
ISADORE, Baby Leonard, b 2
Dec 1912 - d 13 July
1913, BRR
ISHAM, Dave, b 1900 - d
1951, PNY
Mrs Dixie, d 6 Aug 1979,
ae 41y, WMG
J P, b 18 March 1855 - d 2
Feb 1910, PNY
Ollie P, b 25 March 1890 -
d 3 March 1946, CRO
ISRAEL, Dolphus, b -- Feb

ISRAEL (continued)
1902 - d -- Feb 1904,
MSG
Ira, b 12 March 1916 - d
29 May 1917, MSG
John W, b 1 Jan 1864 - d 9
March 1951, MSG
Pernina, b 5 Sept 1868 - d
16 Oct 1948, MSG
JACK, Lucinda, b 10 July
1821 - d 9 May 1822, ELZ
Samuel T, no dates, ELZ
W M, b 1 June 1836 - d 13
Jan 1919, ELZ
JACKS, Ben W, d 31 Dec
1973, ae 77y, WMG
Daniel Lee, b 3 Oct 1924 -
d 26 Sept 1944, BRR
Edgar M, b 13 June 1920 -
d 16 May 1972, BRR
Elsie H, b 22 Aug 1902 - d
11 Sept 1969, WMG
Esteline, b 7 Feb 1922 -
no death date, BRR
Ethel, d 3 Oct 1976, ae
76y, WMG
Fred M, b 12 Sept 1881 - d
11 Oct 1962, BRR
James W, b 9 May 1896 - d
28 July 1945, BRR
Kenneth V, b 18 Feb 1936 -
d 7 June 1936, BRR
Kisah Angeline, b 27 July
1856 - d 15 March 1947,
BRR
Lucretia, d 19 Feb 1980,
ae 92y, BRR
Mary Elizabeth, b 9 May
1875 - d 30 July 1958,
DRL
Mary Ella, b 30 Sept 1875
- d 29 July 1944, LNE
Nicholas, b 25 July 1877 -
d 14 March 1938, DRL
R J, b 12 July 1856 - d 2
Dec 1917, DRL
Rena Bates, d 16 June
1975, ae 93y, DRL

JACKS (continued)

Rhoda Lyons, b -- Feb 1850
- d -- Sept 1936, DRL

Ross G, b 19 Oct 1883 - d
2 Nov 1961, BRR

Virgil, b 1900 - d 1966,
WMG

Wilkes, b 11 Feb 1851 - d
8 Sept 1933, BRR

William M, b 1 Apr 1861 -
d 14 June 1949 LNE

JACKSON, Abba Duncan, b 2
Apr 1859 - d 16 July
1926, JCJ

Abbie, b 3 Aug 1880 - d 10
Sept 1934, EST

Abraham L, b 1 Dec 1901 -
no death date, EST

Andie, b 15 Jan 1918 - d
16 Dec 1918, EST

Arphie A, b 28 Dec 1877 -
d 26 Nov 1959, EST

Arthur, b 13 June 1910 - d
1 Aug 1910, MLC

Arthur L, d 12 March 1966,
ae 57y 6mo, DVS

Bert, d 7 Sept 1975, ae
58y, DVS

Bertha M, d 25 March 1967,
ae 62y, EST

Bettie, b 30 Nov 1842 - d
15 Dec 1934, BRR

C B, b 1 Aug 1848 - d 28
May 1915, CBJ

C R, Co I & D 3rd TN Inf,
no dates, LBR

Cecil E Jr, d 4 March
1967, ae 0da, EST

Charlie, b 22 Aug 1883 - d
16 Feb 1969, WRJ

Christine, b 2 June 1942 -
d 13 Feb 1959, THR

Claude H, b 19 May 1912 -
d 12 Dec 1966, THR

Clay G, b 7 Dec 1915 - d
19 Oct 1918, JCJ

Cornelius, b 6 May 1869 -
d 21 July 1894, LBR

JACKSON (continued)

David C, Sgt Co A 4th TN
CAV, b 4 Jan 1844 - d 9
May 1901, EST

Della, b 1947 - d 1948,
THR

Donie Sampsell, b 26 Jan
1878 - d 25 Oct 1955,
WRJ

Donna Gale, b 16 Sept 1946
- d 31 May 1963, NWP

Edgar, b 24 Feb 1904 - d
13 Oct 1961, DVS

Edith A, b 10 Dec 1923 -
no death date, DVS

Elizabeth, b 3 July 1842 -
d 29 June 1921, EST

Elizabeth H, d 6 Aug 1901,
ae 48y, WMG

Elizabeth M, b 16 March
1861 - d 26 Dec 1922,
EST

Elmer, b 1911 - d 1934,
DVS

Emily Jan, ae 84y, DVS

Emma, b 14 Sept 1892 - d
30 May 1930, WRJ

Ethel, d 17 Feb 1977, ae
84y, EST

Ethel M, b 14 Nov 1908 - d
19 June 1974, DVS

Ezra W, b 26 Jan 1881 - d
1 June 1901, WRJ

Fannie Jane, b 1878 - d
1961, DVS

Fred Rex, b 27 Aug 1881 -
d 1 Nov 1960, EST

G W, b 28 July 1850 - d 16
Jan 1921, EST

Gennie, b 19 Nov 1900 - d
2 Aug 1901, WRJ

George, b 19 Nov 1900 - d
10 May 1943, WRJ

H Maynard, b 11 Jan 1868 -
d 25 June 1937, DVS

Harrison B, b 1 Jan 1889 -
d 5 Nov 1918, WRJ

Hattie Adkisson, b 19 Oct

JACKSON (continued)

1883 - d 15 June 1957, WRJ

Henry D, b 19 July 1892 - d 20 June 1902, WMG

Ida May, b 26 Nov 1877 - d 20 Nov 1950, DVS

Ida T, b 24 Apr 1876 - d 13 June 1957, THR

Infant, b&d 24 Oct 1902, EST

Inf Dau, b 22 June 1897 - d 26 June 1897, WRJ

Inf Son, 31 March 1920 - no other date, WRJ

Irene, b 23 Apr 1915 - no death date, EST

Iven, d 19 May 1904, ae 18y, WRJ

Jacob M, b 3 March 1894 - d 8 Sept 1956, CRO

Jennie, b 22 Sept 1884 - no death date, EST

John, d 19 Feb 1886, ae 26y 11mo, LBR

John, b 25 Dec 1896 - d 1 July 1942, WRJ

John C, b 14 July 1842 - d 17 Oct 1910, JCJ

John C Jr, b 22 May 1872 - d 6 Dec 1928, JCJ

John F, d 11 Aug 1948, ae 76y, DVS

Joseph, b 13 Feb 1852 - d 5 July 1894, DVS

Joseph C, b 9 May 1870 - d 5 Feb 1938, EST

Joseph Sabe, b 28 Sept 1911 - d 7 July 1965, EST

Julia, b 1875 - d 1878, JCJ

Kimberly Gaye, d 26 June 1978, ae 16y, EST

L G, b 29 Feb 1878 - d 16 June 1940, EST

L M, b 4 May 1862 - d 28 July 1864, HCK

JACKSON (continued)

Lee, d 8 Jan 1978, ae 90y, EST

Lina, b 30 May 1860 - d 11 Dec 1929, WRJ

Lizzie, b 6 Nov 1883 - d 14 May 1900, LBR

Lloyd W, b 22 Aug 1902 - d 14 March 1947, JCJ

Lola C, d 31 May 1965, ae 58y, EST

Lola Maxine, d 19 Nov 1955, ae 31y 4mo, PTC

Loretta, b 3 Feb 1928 - d 7 Feb 1928, ADC

Lucinda, b 22 Oct 1864 - d 9 March 1871, HCK

M C, b 7 Sept 1872 - d 29 Dec 1872, HCK

Mable I, b 15 Feb 1915 - no death date, EST

Maggie Liles, b 22 June 1900 - d 7 Feb 1954, WRJ

Mahala, b 11 Jan 1822 - d 17 Feb 1891, WRJ

Mamie J, b 16 March 1897 - no death date, DVS

Manward W, b 30 Nov 1888 - d 30 Aug 1895, WRJ

Mark V, b 1872 - d 1939, BRR

Mary Dell, b 8 July 1902 - d 26 Sept 1960, EST

Mary Etta, b 14 Apr 1885 - d 21 June 1957, EST

Mary J Estis, b 21 Nov 1848 - d 12 Oct 1899, CBJ

Mary M, b 4 Dec 1843 - d 23 July 1893, JCJ

Micher, d 4 Apr 1950, ae 23y, WRJ

Minnie, b 23 Feb 1900, d 30 Dec 1900, DVS

N D, b 30 Jan 1864 - d 18 Oct 1882, JCJ

Noah G, b 16 March 1903 - d 11 Dec 1917, WRJ

JACKSON (continued)

Oveline, b 24 May 1889 - d 25 Aug 1895, WRJ

Phillip Roy, d -- Oct 1924, ae 5y 1mo, PTC

Phoenia Galloway, d 25 May 1977, ae 91y, BRR

R H, b 9 Jan 1879 - d 1 Feb 1952, EST

Rena, b 19 July 1889 - d 16 Feb 1966, EST

Richard H, b 8 Apr 1861 - d 31 Aug 1935, WRJ

Robert G, d 12 Apr 1975, ae 65y, THR

Robert I, b 30 July 1909 - d 17 June 1966, DVS

Roger Edward, b 9 March 1918 - d 22 Oct 1918, WRJ

Ruley Mathew, d 27 June 1974, DVS

Ruth Cooper, b 7 Aug 1912 - d 13 Feb 1959, THR

Sallie Lee, b 29 Nov 1901 - d 27 Oct 1960, EST

Sam H, b 9 Apr 1877 - d 19 Nov 1943, THR

Sam M, b 21 Apr 1888 - d 26 Nov 1963, WMG

Samuel Chris, b 13 March 1934 - d 5 Jan 1964, DVS

Samuel L, b 16 May 1858 - d 20 Jan 1930, WRJ

Sarah J, b 13 Feb 1861 - d 29 Nov 1899, WRJ

Sarah J Liles, b -- June 1856 - d 31 Oct 1932, WRJ

Susan Denice, d 4 Jan 1961, ae 15da, EST

Susan Hudson, b 14 Feb 1856 - d 22 Aug 1910, EST

Susan M, b 5 Nov 1878 - d 7 July 1962, JCJ

Thomas, b 1 Oct 1871 - d 30 Oct 1933, DVS

JACKSON (continued)

Thomas F, b 13 Oct 1856 - d 2 Nov 1884, LBR

Vera, b 2 Apr 1899 - d 23 June 1913, EST

W E, b 4 June 1876 - d 19 Nov 1913, PNY

W Staples, b 18 June 1860 - d 17 Oct 1930, WRJ

Walter, b 25 March 1890 - d 15 Feb 1966, EST

Welch, b 24 May 1908 - no death date, EST

Wiley R, b 15 Feb 1876 - d 20 Nov 1934, EST

William, b 17 Sept 1870 - d 15 Sept 1873, JCJ

William, b 9 Aug 1875 - d 21 Apr 1938, EST

William H, b 21 June 1878 - d 17 Apr 1897, WRJ

William L, b 3 Feb 1899 - d 29 Nov 1975, DVS

Rev Wm R, d 31 March 1886, ae 67y, WRJ

Zilfie, b 15 Jan 1907 - d 4 June 1907, WRJ

JACKUBOWSKI, Thomas, b 20 May 1915 - d 1 Apr 1960, DRL

JAMES, Eveline, d 17 Oct 1974, FLR

Sam Riley, b 1913 - d 1963, BRR

Stiphon Goad, 1973, SNB

JANIS, Alvin Lee, d 29 Sept 1976, ae 62y, UNG

JARNIGAN, Jennie C, b 2 Jan 1909 - d 13 Dec 1966, EST

Marlin Ralph, d 26 May 1973, ae 38y, EST

Sam, b 28 July 1907 - d 21 Feb 1978, EST

Tolbert, d 6 Jan 1977, ae 88y, EST

JARRETT, French, b 11 March 1852 - d 22 Dec 1920,

JARRETT (continued)
BRR
James, b 26 Aug 1840 - d 15 Apr 1934, BRR
Russell, b 26 July 1888 - d 28 Dec 1917, BRR
Theodore, b 1857 - d 1926, BRR
JEFFERS, A J, b 1928 - d 1972, SNB
Bessie S, b 12 June 1908 - no death date, SNB
Jerry Wayne, b 31 Dec 1951 - d 2 Jan 1952, CRO
Kevin Carl, b 1952 - d 1953, BRR
Kevin Lee, b&d 12 Sept 1975, CRO
Lee H, b 29 Dec 1894 - d 1 Feb 1973, CRO
Maggie P, b 28 July 1899 - no death date, CRO
Virgie Mae, b 10 Apr 1931 - no death date, LNE
Willard E, b 9 Apr 1903 - d 11 Dec 1966, SNB
Willard E Jr, 1Lt USA, b 22 July 1932 - d 15 June 1974, LNE
JENNINGS, Bailum, b 2 Apr 1883 - d 20 Oct 1883, MRR
Dick R, b 4 Aug 1906 - d 1 Oct 1961, SNB
Elmer, b 1908 - d 1962, SNB
Flossie, b 1926 - d 11 March 1976, SNB
Frank, d 7 Sept 1980, ae 38y, SNB
Harold, b 1937 - d 1971, SNB
Rev J T, b 16 Nov 1863 - d 16 Dec 1941, MRR
John R, b 1950 - d 31 May 1973, SNB
Joyce, d 9 March 1976, ae 51y, CRO

JENNINGS (continued)
Margaret, b 1882 - d 1972, SNB
Martha J, b 1824 - d 8 June 1896, MRR
Maxine, b 1932 - d 1966, PLR
Ruby M, b 12 June 1903 - no death date, SNB
Virgil, b 1908 - d 1964, MRR
JENNY, Earl Clifton, b 4 June 1904 - d 1 May 1976, BRN
JESTES, S Elender, b 2 Aug 1870 - d 7 Oct 1870, HCK
JESTES, Samson David, b 1 Feb 1873 - d 27 Feb 1873, HCK
JESTICE, Mahalie, b 28 Oct 1832 - d 22 March 1912, MCD
Martha Jane, b 4 Apr 1854 - d 7 Sept 1859, MCD
Mary Ann, b 17 May 1858 - d 21 Sept 1859, MCD
JETT, Erastus H, b 16 Sept 1887 - d 24 Feb 1945, SNB
JOHNSON, Albert, b 7 Dec 1867 - d 28 March 1923, CLC
Alford, b 27 Apr 1910 - no death date, PNY
Almida, b 2 Apr 1851 - d 2 Sept 1933, PNY
Aruetta, b 13 March 1964 - d 7 May 1972, CRO
Asmes Kenneth, b 20 Dec 1896 - d 24 Sept 1931, WRC
Beatrice, b 31 Oct 1898 - d 28 Oct 1900, PNY
Bertha A, b 7 March 1890 - d 8 Nov 1906, BRR
Charlie E, b 1902 - d 1970, NWP
Claude, b 25 Sept 1872 - d

JOHNSON (continued)
13 Apr 1922, DRL
Conway E Jr, b 27 May 1935 - d 14 March 1972, DRL
Earl C, b 3 July 1898 - d 17 Sept 1898, BRR
Elizabeth, b&d 2 Apr 1917, PNY
Ellen Isham, b 22 May 1889 - d 20 June 1940, PNY
Emma, d 17Apr 1976, ae 62y, CRO
Fannie, b 24 Sept 1866 - d 11 Dec 1947, WRC
Francis L, b 30 March 1934 - d 17 Aug 1934, DRL
Fred H, b 22 Nov 1913 - d 26 March 1956, PNY
Henry, b 1865 - d 1935, CRO
Henry Tom, b 20 Nov 1915 - d 23 July 1963, PNY
Imagene E, b 30 Dec 1918 - no death date, PNY
Infant, b&d 6 Feb 1890, BRR
James P, b 24 Jan 1888 - d 25 Nov 1908, CBJ
Jessie J, b&d 24 Apr 1908, PNY
John B, b 1870 - d 1874, PNY
John Van, b 3 July 1872 - d 10 July 1948, WRC
Julius S, b 27 Apr 1837 - d 14 Jan 1925, BRR
Lavernia, b 1881 - no death date, PNY
Lillian, b 27 July 1926 - d 31 March 1953, PNY
Lillie F, b 1874 - d 1960, PNY
Lona, b 1894 - d 1959, UNN
Loraine, b 24 May ---- - d 25 Nov 1926, PNY
Luverina, b 19 Apr 1845 - d 10 Sept 1933, BRR
Martin, no birth date - d

JOHNSON (continued)
1964, NWP
Melvin, no dates, BRR
Mildred A, b 29 Aug 1938 - no death date, DRL
Millard Filmore, b 7 Apr 1878 - d 9 Oct 1941, PNY
Nancy R, b 9 Jan 1871 - d 28 Dec 1905, BRR
Nannie E, b 1871 - d 1948, BRR
Opal Gaffin, b 5 Aug 1876 - d 29 Jan 1958, WRC
Oral L, b 12 June 1903 - d 1 Aug 1903, BRR
Oscar E, b 11 June 1881 - d 16 Dec 1970, DRL
Oscar Newton, b 1909 - d 5 May 1964, EST
Phyllis Karen, d -- May 1981, ae 31y, CRO
Rachel M, b 30 Sept 1888 - no death date, DRL
Rebecca Jean, b 18 May 1976 - no death date, CRO
Robert (Bob), d 10 June 1981, ae 85y, SNB
Sallie, b 1845 - d 31 July 1910, PNY
Samuel A, b 1879 - d 1953, PNY
Shaver Emmit, b 8 Oct 1883 - d 9 Sept 1912, DRL
Stella, b 1910 - no death date, EST
Vada Arms, d 23 Nov 1979, ae 88y, NWP
Velma F, b 12 Sept 1915 - no death date, PNY
W H, b 19 June 1888 - d 13 Nov 1951, PNY
W M, b 10 Apr 1864 - d 16 Dec 1900, PNY
Waldo E, b 3 June 1906 - d 6 June 1906, LBR
Walter, b 8 Aug 1907 - d 27 March 1926, PNY

JOHNSON (continued)

William G, b 8 March 1905 - d 1 Feb 1961, OLP

William R, b 1868 - d 24 June 1925, PNY

Wm Marion, b 2 Nov 1861 - d 20 Oct 1941, SNB

Zachariah T, b 4 March 1868 - d 23 March 1946, BRR

JOHNSTON, Infant, b 18 July 1907 - d 29 July 1907, OLP

Sarah A, b 9 July 1887 - d 22 July 1907, OLP

JONES, A, b 1887 - d 1969, WMG

Ada Davis, b 20 Aug 1914 - no death date, EST

Addie, b 25 March 1923 - no death date, BRN

Alice, b 26 Jan 1878 - d 20 Dec 1884, BRR

Alice C, b 24 June 1876 - d 19 Sept 1905, LNC

Allie Spurling, d 3 June 1979, ae 60y, UNG

Alva, b 25 Dec 1883 - d 28 Aug 1942, DRL

Amy, b&d 2 Sept 1906, LNC

Andrew W, b 18 May 1892 - d 11 Aug 1970, LNC

Anna, b 17 Nov 1825 - d 9 Jan 1901, CLC

Annie V, b 18 July 1890 - d 7 Apr 1909, UNN

Arthus Hurshel, d 16 July 1979, ae --, ADM

Aubrey Summers J, b 2 Oct 1901 - no death date, UNN

Baby, d 1967, LBR

Barbara Inez, b 1963 - d 1974, WRC

Barbara Inez, d 11 Aug ----, ae 11y, WMG

Belly Eason, d 26 Nov 1977, ae 27y, DRL

JONES (continued)

Ben M, b 1854 - d 1920, UNN

Bertha A, d 17 Oct 1979, ae 69y, PLR

Bessie G, b 12 Dec 1937 - d 18 Dec 1937, MRR

Bobby Gordan, b 22 July 1926 - d 21 July 1967, LBR

Buena V, b 8 Nov 1868 - d 1916, UNN

C R, b 6 Feb 1904 - d 11 Jan 1940, PLR

Carlos Eugene, b 17 May 1938 - d 21 Oct 1939, UNG

Charleen, b 22 Apr 1931 - d 18 Jan 1934, PLR

Charles, b 7 March 1886 - d 4 Jan 1931, OLP

Charlie, b 9 Sept 1899 - d 10 Oct 1899, UNN

Charlie E, b 11 Oct 1891 - d 11 Feb 1971, WRJ

Clarence V, b 9 Jan 1904 - d 4 Oct 1925, WRJ

Claude, b 29 Jan 1909 - d 12 Dec 1969, ELZ

Claude E, b 20 June 1905 - d 13 Aug 1906, RTT

Clay Evans, d 13 Apr 1980, ae 85y, DRL

Cleatus R, b 6 June 1923 - d 29 June 1923, MRR

Columbia B, b 8 Feb 1885 - d 15 Aug 1962, UNN

Columous B, b 31 Dec 1844 - d 10 Apr 1905, ELZ

Conley, b 3 July 1913 - d 20 Dec 1974, CRO

Cordelia C, b 30 Jan 1825 - d 5 Apr 1902, DRL

Cordelia Grant, b 13 Oct 1852 - d 20 Feb 1946, WRC

Dave L, d 1964, WRC

David M, b 31 Dec 1848 (or

JONES (continued)
1845) - d 27 Oct 1907,
UNN

David M, b 1866 - d 1916,
UNN

Dec Boyd, b 17 Dec 1919 -
d 4 Nov 1947, WRC

Dee Witt C, b 1875 - d
1954, ELZ

Dora May, b 16 May 1915 -
d 14 Aug 1937, NWP

Edith, b 28 Nov 1904 - d
28 March 1926, PLR

Edward R, b 13 Nov 1913 -
d 30 May 1916, WRJ

Egbert, d 1 Dec 1978, ae
76y, UNG

Eliza, b 2 Jan 1854 - d 24
Feb 1922, UNN

Eliza Lee, b 1875 - d
1957, DRL

Elizabeth, b 8 July 1883 -
d 17 Nov 1962, LBR

Elizabeth, d 11 Oct 1908,
stone broken, CLC

Elizabeth, b 26 May 1856 -
d 5 Jan 1939, UNN

Elizabeth, b 3 March 1854
- d 24 Feb 1922, UNN

Elizabeth H, b 20 March
1870 - d 10 Aug 1871,
BRR

Ella Clark, b 6 May 1871 -
d 22 Dec 1930, WRC

Ellen (Joyner), d 6 March
1974, ae 79y, LBR

Elmer, b 7 Dec 1909 - d 10
Feb 1973, EST

Elmer, b 13 May 1901 - d
12 Oct 1970, FLR

Essie B, b 15 Apr 1901 - d
14 Sept 1972, UNN

Estel Jr, b 21 Dec 1941 -
d 7 March 1942, UNG

Estel W, b 18 Apr 1908 - d
26 July 1969, UNG

Ethel M, b 29 Oct 1912 -
no death date, UNG

JONES (continued)
Flora, b 19 June 1881 - d
31 May 1904, LBR

Floyd A, b 21 Feb 1907 - d
19 Jan 1909, PLR

Fornia, b 10 March 1880 -
d 1 Jan 1963, WRJ

Fox Edward, b 22 Nov 1877
- d 13 March 1963, ELZ

Frances, b 17 Dec 1895 - d
3 March 1897, DVS

Frank, b 31 Dec 1891 - d 3
Jan 1973, UNN

Frazer, b 1879 - d 1957,
WRC

Fred O, b 7 June 1888 - d
5 March 1965, WRC

Freddie E, b 17 Nov 1895 -
d 1 May 1922, OLP

Frederick B, b 11 Aug 1880
- d 27 Sept 1881, BRR

Garfield, b 19 Oct 1881 -
d 29 Apr 1950, STP

Garfield Jr, d 5 Aug 1979,
ae 59y, LBR

Gillum H, b 22 Sept 1833 -
d 30 June 1962, ELZ

Grace Shotwell, b 4 Jan
1894 - no death date,
SNB

Gregory, d 24 Apr 1981, ae
19y, UNG

Hannah, b 7 Nov 1849 - d
10 Apr 1898, BRR

Hazel, b 14 March 1909 - d
20 Aug 1970, DVS

Henderson M, b 24 Aug 1892
- d 28 Apr 1947, UNN

Henry, Co D TN Inf Sp/Am,
b 9 May 1874 - d 26
March 1936, PLR

Herbert, b 6 Dec 1870 - d
17 Apr 1938, FLR

Herbert W, b 1 June 1889 -
d 3 Jan 1898, BRR

Howard Lee, d 27 July
1977, ae 26y, ELZ

Hugh Kinder Sr, b 24 Apr

JONES (continued)

1891 - d 18 May 1968, SNB

Ida Pearl, b 1872 - d 1963, UNN

Inazie Dant, b&d 1932, UNG

Infant, b&d 8 Apr 1909, PNY

Infant, b 4 Nov 1857 - d 9 Jan 1858, SHD

Inf Dau, b 10 Jan 1924 - d 11 Jan 1924, WRJ

Inf Dau, b&d 1 Dec 1929, WRJ

Inf Son, b&d 15 Oct 1915, WRJ

Inf Son, b&d 16 Aug 1926, PLR

Inf d/o Marie & Ira, -- Jan 1947, ELZ

Ira, d 27 Jan 1980, ae 60y, ELZ

Isabella R, b 18 Oct 1867 - d 21 Nov 1948, EST

Jack, b 15 Nov 1918 - d 3 March 1975, EST

Jackie Lee, b 19 Oct 1938 - d 5 Apr 1947, UNG

James B, b 1791 - d 13 May 1877, UNN

James C Sr, d 22 Aug 1976, ae 50y, PLR

James E, b 17 Sept 1859 - d 1 May 1946, WRJ

James M, b 15 Aug 1829 - d 3 May 1900, UNN

James S, b 4 May 1870 - d 27 Apr 1949, PLR

Jeremiah, b 26 Apr 1825 - d 9 March 1900, NDK

Jerry, b 1864 - d 3 Oct 1938, MRR

Jerry Wayne Jr, d 15 Dec 1977, ae 3da, ADM

Jesie T, b 8 Nov 1888 - d 1 June 1965, UNG

Joanne, b 22 Aug 1938 - d 13 Feb 1939, WRJ

JONES (continued)

John, b -- March 1888 - d 20 Jan 1946, EST

John A, b 12 Dec 1874 - d 29 June 1933, WRC

John C, b 12 Sept 1876 - d 4 Nov 1957, CRO

John F, b 27 Apr 1869 - d 12 Sept 1958, MRR

John W, b 4 March 1874 - d 26 Dec 1950, WRJ

John W, b 1870 - d 1940, DRL

Johnny, b 31 Jan 1948 - d 31 May 1976, EST

Joseph D, b 9 July 1841 - d 4 Sept 1919, UNN

Joseph Millu, b 1855 - d 1934, UNN

Joyce W, b 20 May 1915 - d 1 Apr 1966, DRL

Kathy (infant), no dates, MSG

Kenneth, b 20 June 1914 - d 11 Feb 1916, MRR

Kenneth C, b 11 June 1915 - no death date, UNN

L Bertha, 1883 - no other date, UNN

L H, b&d 1 March 1934, ELZ

Larry Jo, d 16 June 1962, ae 1da, LNG

Leighton, b 29 March 1912 - d 8 Dec 1956, UNN

Lena M Kittrell, b 7 March 1916 - no death date, CRO

Lenna H, b 19 Aug 1905 - no death date, WRC

Leonard, b 1894 - d 1971, DRL

Leonard Fred, b 1886 - d 1969, UNN

Leonard T, b 12 Jan 1898 - d 3 Aug 1957, FLR

Lewis J, b 6 Oct 1819 - d 20 June 1905, CLC

Lloyd, b 1909 - d 1965,

JONES (continued)
UNN

Lloyd C, b 24 March 1903 -
d 27 Sept 1954, FLR

Lois Mae, b 5 Feb 1937 - d
15 Sept 1966, DRL

Lora, b 12 Nov 1902 - no
death date, DRL

Lora, b 30 Aug 1915 - no
death date, ELZ

Lourena J, b 23 Jan 1867 -
d 29 June 1957, FLR

Loy Reid, b 1930 - d 1971,
DRL

Lucy E, b 12 Apr 1877 - d
9 Feb 1934, FLR

Lula, b 1895 - d 10 Aug
----, WMG

Lula E, b 13 March 1902 -
no death date, FLR

Lyndal Dean, b 1 Sept 1936
- d 25 May 1967, PNY

Madeline W, b 15 Nov 1915
- d 14 Jan 1973, UNN

Madison L, b 21 Dec 1898 -
d 14 Oct 1903, LVN

Mae W, b 23 Apr 1895 - no
death date, WRJ

Maggie G, b 1870 - d 1890,
DRL

Maggie Hall, b 18 June
1885 - d 1968, ELZ

Mamie, b 4 Feb 1889 - d 18
May 1907, UNN

Margaret, b 17 June 1842 -
d 17 Dec 1917, WRC

Margaret Langley, b 28 Jan
1838 - d 20 May 1909,
HCK

Margie Stephens, b 20 Apr
1922 - d 4 July 1978,
UNG

Martha, b 10 Jan 1840 - d
20 Nov 1898, WRC

Martha M Miller, b 5 Jan
1884 - d 10 June 1943,
DRL

Martin A, b 11 Apr 1853 -

JONES (continued)
d 17 Jan 1933, DRL

Mary, b 1876 - d 1972, WRC

Mary E, b 7 May 1860 - d
14 June 1941, MRR

Mary E Allen, b 1856 - d
1947, UNN

Mary E Williams, b 31 Oct
1852 - d 20 Feb 1933,
UNN

Mary Ellen, b 20 Oct 1879
- d 24 Aug 1908, WRC

Mary Galloway, b 19 May
1869 - d 10 May 1956,
FLR

Mary Jackson, b 18 Feb
1841 - d 10 Nov 1871,
HCK

Mary Jane, b 11 June 1853
- d 24 Nov 1937, SNB

Mary Lyles, b 13 July 1864
- d 7 Jan 1942, WRJ

Mary Matilda, b 21 Apr
1888 - d 15 Dec 1953,
EST

Mary Viola Parrott, b 14
Jan 1920 - d 4 July
1940, BRR

Matilda Stonecipher, b 8
Sept 1827 - d 20 Dec
1903, UNN

Maybelle M, b 1 May 1881 -
d 13 Oct 1958, CRO

Melvin, b 24 June 1912 - d
18 Aug 1967, BRN

Millie E, b 5 Apr 1873 - d
6 Sept 1949, FLR

Minerva, b 13 May 1881 - d
6 June 1948, STP

Mona Martha, b 22 Jan 1928
- no death date, LBR

Myrtle Annie, b 2 Nov 1909
- d 11 June 1925, UNG

Nancy Ann, b 12 Sept 1882
- d 6 May 1959, UNG

Nancy M, b 14 Jan 1966 - d
13 Sept 1942, UNN

Norman, d 26 Feb 1977, ae

JONES (continued)
60y, ADM

Oby Ray, b 16 March 1896 - d 31 Dec 1973, LBR

Ova E, d 7 March 1980, ae 78y, UNG

Parly L, b 7 Sept 1895 - d 11 March 1947, UNN

Patience Davidson, b 13 Dec 1851 - d 31 March 1889, BRR

Patsy, b 18 Sept 1869 - d 20 July 1872, CLC

Paul Gene, b 1 Sept 1930 - d 4 Aug 1933, WRJ

Polly, b 8 Feb 1833 - d 28 Apr 18--, SHD

R Jeannine, b 27 Sept 1954 - d 1 Jan 1955, WRC

Rachel, b 2 March 1847 - d 6 Jan 1910, ELZ

Rachel, b 1801 - d 9 July 1878, UNN

Ralph D, d 17 Nov 1980, ae 33y, WMG

Randolph B, b 25 July 1921 - d 4 Aug 1956, WRJ

Ray, b 11 Feb 1902 - d 21 Feb 1932, DRL

Ray E, b 1924 - d 1969, LBR

Ray Hubert, b 11 Aug 1892 - d 12 Oct 1959, UNN

Raymond, b 16 Aug 1905 - no death date, DVS

Raymond G, b 20 March 1918 - d 11 May 1964, UNG

Rebecca, b 28 Sept 1888 - d 17 Nov 1959, SNB

Rebecca, b 7 Feb 1858 - d 5 Feb 1860, CLC

Reid, b 24 Apr 1961 - d 19 May 1968, DRL

Robert Edward, b 3 March 1940 - d 29 Dec 1959, WRC

Roger Wilham, d 31 Dec 1976, ae 85y, LBR

JONES (continued)
Roxie J, b 23 Aug 1978 - d 13 Jan 1919, WRJ

Rufus, b 2 July 1842 - d 22 Sept 1929, SNB

Rufus H, b 2 Dec 1878 - d 6 Jan 1956, LBR

S H, MD, b 9 Sept 1874 - d 14 Dec 1953, DRL

Sadie, b 29 June 1902 - d 25 Feb 1971, EST

Sallie, b 22 Apr 1895 - d 6 Aug 1976, LBR

Sally Stonecipher, b 20 March 1824 - d 3 Nov 1909, UNN

Sally Williams, b 23 Aug 1860 - d 22 March 1949, UNN

Sam C, b 23 Feb 1867 - d 15 March 1934, PLR

Sam Huston Jr, MD, b 1911 - d 1962, DRL

Samuel, b 17 July 1820 - d 17 July 1907, UNN

Samuel B, b 7 Sept 1853 - d 24 Oct 1890, UNN

Samuel B, b 12 Feb 1889 - d 1 Aug 1963, CLH

Sarah R, b 15 Apr 1907 - d 1 Oct 1945, ELZ

Screna Barger, b 17 Feb 1847 - d 5 Dec 1939, UNN

Shadrack, b 17 Feb 1863 - d 25 Nov 1903, SHD

Sharon, inf, 8 Apr 1954, UNG

Shirley Belle, b 1939 - no death date, DRL

Stephanie K, b&d 12 June 1937, SNB

Stobert, b 21 July 1897 - d 11 Sept 1898, MRR

Stobert s/o Grant & M J, d 11 Sept 1895, MRR

Susan Jane, b 11 June 1911 - d 30 Aug 1976, CLH

Thomas, b 1897 - d 1972,

JONES (continued)
WMG

Thomas J, b 8 March 1882 –
d 21 March 1968, UNG

Verdie, no dates, UNN

Vergil J, b 13 May 1899 –
d 9 Feb 1959, WRJ

Vestie, b 1876 – d 1963,
UNN

Violet, b&d 8 Oct 1905,
LBR

W C, b 23 July 1894 – d 13
Sept 1894, MRR

W D, Co F 1st TN Inf, b 17
Jan 1844 – d 22 March
1921, WRC

W H, b 10 Aug 1871 – d 18
May 1940, WRC

W M, b 4 Apr 1840 – d 18
Sept 1901, WRC

Walter S, b 26 Aug 1884 –
d 16 Dec 1944, UNG

Walter W, b 3 June 1888 –
d 29 Aug 1965, SNB

Weltha A, b 22 Jan 1901 –
no death date, SNB

William Alex, b 2 June
1824 – d 25 Jan 1899,
UNN

William Arthur, b 12 March
1883 – d 1 July 1966,
EST

William E, d 31 Jan 1975,
ae 67y, DRL

William H, 2nd TN Mtd Inf
Musn Cherokee War, b 21
Feb 1821 – d 30 Sept
1912, OOO

William N, b 21 Feb 1821 –
d 30 Sept 1912, SNB

Willie, b 1 May 1893 – d 6
May 1893, UNN

Mrs. Willie Mae, d 29
March 1981, ae 92y, DRL

Willie Ray, b 10 Aug 1892
– d 6 March 1965, BRR

Wilma Sue, b 24 June 1946
– d 18 Sept 1962, DVS

JONES (continued)
Wm C (Red), b 21 Feb 1900
– d 26 June 1974, DRL

Zadie, b 1883 – no death
date, WRC

JORDAN, Thomas R, b 2 Feb
1891 – d 16 Oct 1918,
CLC

JOSELYN, Alice Marguerite,
d 1888, RGB

JOTINSON, Mary, b 27 June
1898 – d 5 March 1975,
SNB

JOYNER, Andy, b 3 Jan 1874
– d 26 July 1944, UNN

B F, b 2 Jan 1881 – d 1
June 1901, LBR

Bert V, b 21 Sept 1899 – d
15 Aug 1962, WRC

Calvin, Civil War Vet, b
12 Oct 1845 – d 6 May
1894, UNN

Charles W, b 1874 – d
1942, LBR

Ellis, b 4 Sept 1914 – d
25 Oct 1917, LBR

G D, d 26 June 1887, ae
75y 6mo, LBR

James A, 1870 – no other
date, UNN

Joe D, b 17 Apr 1885 – d
17 Jan 1922, UNN

John C, b 20 June 1871 – d
30 July 1903, UNN

John C, b 26 June 1877 – d
28 July 1924, LBR

Jonny F, d 19 Feb 1889, ae
1y 8da, UNN

Mary Summers, b 1 March
1848 – d 27 July 1931,
LBR

Minnie L, b 1882 – d 1942,
LBR

Nellie C, b –– Jan 1888 –
d 1954, UNN

O R, b 2 Feb 1881 – d 3
Aug 1929, UNN

R A, b 10 Aug 1840 – d 4

JOYNER (continued)
May 1914, LBR
Rachel A Kelly, b 28 July 1845 - d 22 Aug 1917, UNN
Sally, b 2 Sept 1815 - d 8 June 1874, LBR
Samuel, b -- March 1867 - d 1916, UNN
JUDKINS, Ada Mae Gibbs, d 1 Nov 1978, ae 89y, WRC
Rev Alfred T, b 9 June 1888 - d 29 June 1967, WRC
Ammon E, b 1913 - d 1970, DRL
Elza H, b 13 Nov 1909 - d 29 Jan 1968, WRC
Henry J, b 22 June 1907 - d 17 June 1948, WRC
JUMP, W R (Bill), d 10 July 1979, ae 78y, WMG
JUNE, Helene, b 29 Feb 1872 - d 6 Aug 1896, WRC
Mrs T O, b 15 March 1844 - d 19 June 1918, WRC
Rev T O, b 23 Oct 1840 - d 4 Dec 1913, WRC
JUSTICE, Andrew, b 26 May 1915 - d 12 May 1959, UNN
Bessie R Jones, b 6 Nov 1885 - d 23 March 1953, WRC
Billy Bert, b 1 July 1934 - d 16 July 1935, DVS
Blaine, T3 108 Evac, WWII, b 19 March 1913 - d 11 Apr 1967, EST
Charles R, b 12 Feb 1884 - d 9 Sept 1963, EST
Clarissa Elizabeth, b 15 March 1854 - d 1 Oct 1915, UNN
Clyde, b 16 Sept 1929 - d 29 March 1931, EST
Daisy Mae, b 12 Nov 1916 - d 22 Aug 1918, DVS

JUSTICE (continued)
Donald, b&d 1954, EST
Ellen Woods, b 18 Dec 1874 - no death date, UNN
Elsie, b 10 Apr 1909 - no death date, UNN
Eric Bert, b 9 Aug 1881 - d 23 Dec 1958, DVS
G W, b 5 Oct 1850 (?) - d 19 May 1880 (?), MRR
Gilbert Elmore, b 15 Oct 1906 - d 10 Jan 1965, UNN
Halian, d 30 Oct 1980, ae 96y, EST
Halken, b 5 Sept 1884 - d 30 Oct 1980, EST
Harve A, b 3 Jan 1881 - d 12 July 1842, UNN
Hejakiah, b 15 March 1849 - d 23 March 1886, UNN
Horace, b 1881 - d 1967, EST
Hugh, b 8 June 1901 - d 7 March 1947, UNN
Infant, d 8 Dec 1918, UNN
Infant, d 16 May 1915, UNN
Infant, 5 Nov 1939 - no other dates, DVS
John, b 24 June 1820 - d 29 July 1904, UNN
John A, b 20 May 1880 - d 15 Apr 1958, UNN
John Allen, b 16 March 1953 - d 8 Aug 1976, UNN
Lizzie, b 27 Feb 1909 - no death date, UNN
Lou Rogers, d 31 Aug 1974, ae 92y, DVS
M M, b 26 June 1850 - d 11 Apr 1951, EST
Martha, b --March 1912 - d 23 Aug 1918, UNN
Mary A, b 31 Dec 1902 - d 2 March 1908, UNN
Milly, b 27 Nov 1895 - d 28 June 1961, UNN
Nancy, d 10 Feb 1892, ae

JUSTICE (continued)
72y, UNN
Oliver V, b 29 Jan 1884 -
  d 21 Nov 1961, UNN
Ordella, b 25 Sept 1914 -
  no death date, UNN
Oscar, b 16 March 1905 - d
  2 July 1905, UNN
Robert M, b 9 Oct 1917 - d
  28 Jan 1972, DVS
Ronald, b&d 1954, EST
S H, b 2 Dec 1876 - d 29
  Apr 1957, WRC
Sadie B Lowe, b 24 March
  1906 - d 8 Aug 1976, UNN
Sallie, b 9 Oct 1881 - d
  24 Jan 1961, UNN
Samuel Houston, d 3 Apr
  1977, ae 94y, UNN
Sarah, b 22 Apr 1816 - d
  -- Feb 1861, UNN
Susan, b 24 Dec 1861 - d 6
  Jan 1924, DVS
Telethia Caroline, b 18
  May 1846 - d 3 Dec 1928,
  EST
W M, b 12 Aug 1855 - no
  death date, DVS
Wanda Jane, b&d 12 March
  1938, EST
Wayne, d 26 July 1978, ae
  60y, UNN
Wm Riley, b 10 Sept 1879 -
  d 4 March 1952, UNN
JUSTIS, Melvina D, b 1848 -
  d 1918, CLC
Nannie, b 8 Aug 1869 - d
  12 March 1940, LBR
Walter, b 14 Apr 1912 - d
  14 Dec 1912, LBR
Walter, Pfc Co E 57 Pio
  Inf, WWI, b 15 Sept 1895
  - d 6 July 1963, ARM
William, b 6 Jan 1852 - d
  10 Jan 1929, LBR
KAMER, Amos, b 26 Oct 1864
  - d 6 Nov 1946, WRC
Dora L, d 3 Dec 1962, ae

KAMER (continued)
9y, LNC
KARZUTSKI, Dorthy, b 26 Dec
  1885 - d 1 Apr 1959, DRL
Edmond, b 26 Oct 1866 - d
  1 Jan 1959, DRL
Theresa, b 16 Oct 1857 - d
  9 Sept 1939, DRL
KAUFMAN, Anna Mae, b 17
  March 1930 - d 25 June
  1935, WRC
David L, d 7 July 1973, ae
  77y, WRC
David L Sr, d 7 July 1973,
  ae 77y, WMG
J L, b 23 Oct 1867 - d 29
  Apr 1947, WRC
Matilda, b 24 Sept 1873 -
  d 10 Sept 1925, MNT
Raymond, b 14 Dec 1925 - d
  6 June 1928, WRC
KEATHLEY, Boyd, b 2 June
  1908 - no death date,
  EST
Flower, b 10 Oct 1916 - d
  19 July 1967, EST
KEENEY, Arietta, b 1919 - d
  1951, LBR
Janette, b&d 12 Aug 1958,
  CRO
KEETON, Annie, b 8 March
  1878 - d 16 July 1947,
  CRO
Cora, b 30 May 1888 - d 3
  March 1952, LNE
H Clay, b 29 May 1940 - d
  20 Jan 1942, MNT
Julian F, b 6 Oct 1936 - d
  14 July 1960, MNT
Mary Carter, b 12 Oct 1866
  - d 18 Sept 1940, WRC
Patrick, b 27 July 1900 -
  d 10 July 1940, WRC
William S, b 18 Apr 1875 -
  d 3 Dec 1941, MNT
KEILB, Anna, b 10 Feb 1885
  - d 5 June 1960, DRL
John A, b 10 July 1884 - d

KEILB (continued)
24 Apr 1964, DRL
KEITH, Cecil, no dates, MNT
G W, Capt 2nd TN Inf, b
1814 - d 21 May 1886,
LBR
Garrett, no dates, MNT
George L, no dates, MNT
Hulda D, b 25 Sept 1850 -
d 27 Dec 1862, MNT
James, b 18 Jan 1844 - d 1
Oct 1959, MNT
John, b 11 Nov 1854 - d 22
Aug 1856, MNT
Killey, d 2 Sept 1973, ae
63y, MNT
Lonnie, b 17 Oct 1905 - d
19 Sept 1965, CLC
Mary E, b 28 July 1849 - d
9 Aug 1868, MNT
Omer Jr, b 27 Oct 1925 - d
31 March 1926, MNT
Ruth, b 1822 - d 6 Jan
1906, MNT
Sarah J Ray, b 1842 - d 11
March 1913, MNT
W J, Sgt Co B 2nd TN Inf,
b 1846 - d 8 Dec 1870,
LBR
KELLEY, Anna Lee, b 21 Nov
1922 - d 10 Feb 1924,
UNN
Barbara Robinson, b 18 Feb
1857 - d 5 Aug 1924, UNN
Bertha Ann, b 4 Jan 1877 -
d 16 Aug 1877, UNN
Claude Henry, b 28 Nov
1900 - d 1 Jan 1903, UNN
D M, b 8 March 1826 - d 24
June 1905, UNN
David W, b 18 March 1906 -
d 20 Feb 1907, UNN
Delia P, b 11 Aug 1882 - d
10 Jan 1969, UNN
Douglas, b 9 Aug 1884 - d ,
12 Jan 1964, UNN
Eliza F, d 21 June 1978,
ae 98y, UNN

KELLEY (continued)
Ethel, b 22 May 1890 - d
22 June 1912, UNN
Fay, b 1 Dec 1883 - d 23
Aug 1941, WRC
Hilda Smith, b 31 Oct 1895
- d 17 Oct 1971, UNN
James B, b 19 March 1850 -
d 22 Jun 1903, UNN
Jessie Barton, b 2 Nov
1884 - d 26 Aug 1967,
WRC
John H, b 24 Aug 1886 - d
10 Nov 1958, UNN
Joseph, b 11 Sept 1875 - d
16 Nov 1895, UNN
Julia Ann, b 1 Apr 1855 -
d 15 Oct 1943, UNN
Lee Roy, b 28 July 1930 -
d 6 Nov 1931, UNN
Lloyd Edward Jr, b&d 3 Aug
1973, DRL
Martha A, b 8 March 1854 -
d 5 Sept 1906, UNN
Mary Jones, b 8 Apr 1822 -
d 7 Dec 1877, UNN
Nancy, b 30 July 1895 - d
4 Nov 1965, UNN
Ray S, b 13 Sept 1881 - d
24 Apr 1928, UNN
Ruth Wilson, b 1854 - d
1933, UNN
S Y, b 1 Apr 1894 - d 11
Jan 1895, UNN
Samuel W, b 15 Feb 1857 -
d 13 June 1922, UNN
Telma, b 16 Aug 1909 - d
16 Jan 1910, UNN
W Church, b 6 Nov 1854 - d
17 Feb 1917, UNN
Wade Hampton, b 20 Apr
1877 - d 9 July 1901,
UNN
Wm Cecil, b 17 Apr 1899 -
d 30 Aug 1900, UNN
KELLOGG, Ida Mae, b 1856 -
d 1945, RGB
Nelson H, b 1850 - d 1925,

KELLOGG (continued)
RGB
KELLY, A D, d 20 May ----,
DDN
Mary E, b 26 Oct 1879 - d
1 Jan 1957, UNN
Ralph C, b 1909 - d 1953,
WRC
Sherman, b 16 Sept 1895 -
d 11 Nov 1919, DVS
Will Rubyn, b 1905 - d
1955, WRC
KEMPER, G W, b 6 Aug 1849 -
d 3 Feb 1903, DRL
KENNEDY, Allen, b 1956 - d
1963, NWP
Cary Grant, b 12 Oct 1943
- d 4 Aug 1975, SNB
Casonet, b 1888 - d 3 May
1974, LBR
Charles V, b 1887 - d
1959, FLR
Darleen, d 29 March 1960,
ae 2y 10mo, NWP
Delphia, d 9 Dec 1976, ae
60y, EST
Francis Hurst, b 9 Sept
1875 - d 22 Jan 1945,
DRL
Harry T, b 17 July 1893 -
d 28 Oct 1918, BRR
Hershel, d 24 March 1979,
ae 70y, DRL
Inf Boy, d 9 July 1969, ae
1da, PTC
Inf Son, no dates, SNB
Inf Son, no dates, SNB
J Bradford, b 1860 - d
1887, UNN
Jeff, b 1964 - d 1965, SNB
Jewel Charline, b 1 May
1938 - d 24 Nov 1938,
FLR
Louverna, b 1923 - d 1966,
SNB
Marine, b 9 Jan 1944 - no
death date, SNB
Marion, b 25 Dec 1884 - d

KENNEDY (continued)
24 Feb 1956, NWP
Michael Anthony, b 30 July
1965 - d 6 Dec 1965, DRL
Orene, b 1895 - d 1969,
NWP
Rayburn, b 1917 - d 20 Oct
1974, SNB
Rose M, b 1890 - d 1969,
FLR
Sadie, b 1891 - no death
date, LBR
W R, b 17 Sept 1909 - d 29
March 1946, LBR
KENNINGTON, M A, b 1860 - d
1950, RGB
M D, b 1845 - d 1929, RGB
KERNEY, Tommie Clinton, b 1
Sept 1930 - d 13 June
193, SNB
KESSLER, Darrell Glen, b 3
Oct 1956 - d 19 Nov
1977, LBR
KESTERSON, Aless Z, Sgt Co
A 825 TD BN, WWII, b 7
Jan 1916 - d 12 March
1964, LNE
J Roland, b 1 Aug 1893 - d
29 May 1967, WRC
James Samuel, b 13 Jan
1927 - d 29 June 1938,
WRC
Katherine J, b 3 Feb 1870
- d 21 Oct 1912, MLC
Margaret Cath, d 9 Dec
1960, ae 77y 3mo, LNE
Nell Lester, d 17 Nov
1975, ae 64y, LST
Samuel P, b 23 Apr 1919 -
d 28 Sept 1958, LNE
Samuel P Sr, b 12 June
1868 - d 3 Aug 1950, WRC
Tilda S, b 14 Nov 1914 -
no death date, WRC
Wm Riley, b 22 Sept 1926 -
d 24 July 1942, PLR
KESTON, Julian F, Co 2C
USAF, Korea, b 6 Oct

KESTON (continued)
1936 – d 14 July 1960, OOO

KETCHERSON, William, d 19 June 1890, ae 1y 9mo, CHN

KETCHUM, Mary U, b 30 July 1878 – d 8 Aug 1878, STP

KETERSON, Hazel Goad, b 29 Apr 1929 – no death date, LNE

KEY, Sam, Pvt Co C 165 Inf WWI, b 28 Feb 1894 – d 15 Oct 1918, PTC

KIDD, Linville Ray, d 19 July 1975, ae 34y, WRC

KIETON, Pa, b 18 July 19--- – d 8 July 1971, WMG

KILEY, Georgette, b 9 May 1939 – d 22 Aug 1939, CRO

KINCANNON, Dorothy Ruffner, b 22 Feb 1917 – no death date, EST

KINDRED, Millard G, b 1911 – d 22 Aug 1974, DRL

KINDRICK, Sharon K, 1971, UNG

KING, Albert S, b 16 July 1894 – d 30 Nov 1956, PLR

Bertha McDonald, d 26 Apr 1927, CRO

Flora M, b 12 Oct 1897 – no death date, CRO

Fannie, b 3 Jan 1888 – 13 May 1952, DVS

Harry C, b 8 Nov 1886 – d 1 Jan 1950, CRO

James, b 2 March 1865 – d 4 Feb 1943, PTC

John Lee, WWII Vet, d 6 Sept 1978, ARM

Lee B, b 11 Aug 1903 – d 2 May 1955, DVS

Mary, b 1878 – d 1970, ARM

Mary J, b 1833 – d 1909, RGB

KING (continued)
Porter, Pvt USA WWI, b 2 Oct 1894 – d 24 Jan 1958, PTC

Rosa E, b 18 March 1892 – no death date, PLR

Shirley Jean, d 15 July 1980, ae 24y, BRR

William R, b 19 Oct 1866 – d 24 Apr 1952, ARM

KINSER, George W, b 27 March ---- – d 1886 (stone broken), LNE

Josie M, b 5 Feb 1885 – d 22 Apr 1885, LNE

KIRKHAM, Minnie, no dates, DRL

Walter, b 1881 – d 1948, DRL

KIRKLAND, Charlie, b 1907 – d 1959, EST

Isabelle L, b 29 Dec 1896 – d 11 March 1968, EST

KISER, Elmer D, b 26 March 1942 – d 3 June 1970, BRN

Elmer D, b 26 May 1947 – d 3 June 1970, BRN

KITCHEN, Amos, b 31 Aug 1920 – d 28 March 1924, FLF

Matilda, b 12 March 1832 – d 9 Sept 1893, DRL

KITTRELL, Charles L, b 10 Sept 1892 – d 6 Dec 1972, CRO

Clarence C, b 1915 – d 1934, CRO

Donal George, b 12 Nov 1930 – d 22 June 1954, CRO

Edna Potts, b 17 Feb 1905 – no death date, CRO

Ella E, b 25 Jan 1872 – d 1 Dec 1938, CRO

Emma, b 1895 – no death date, CRO

Francis, b -- Jan 1805 – d

KITTRELL (continued)
12 Feb 1867, CRO
Francis Marion, b 2 Apr 1863 - d 21 Dec 1906, CRO
Grover C, d 19 Apr 1976, ae 83y, CRO
Gusta C, b 22 June 1876 - no death date, CRO
John C, b 4 Dec 1924 - d 14 Sept 1974, CRO
John W, b 1858 - d 1939, CRO
Laura Webb, b 9 July 1888 - d 12 Dec 1939, WBB
Lawrence A, b 1895 - d 1938, CRO
Louis M, b 30 Apr 1917 - d 17 Jan 1964, CRO
Maggie Bingham, b 14 Sept 1896 - d 3 March 1976, ae 79y, CRO
Malinda, b 26 Sept 1834 - d 26 Feb 1887, CRO
Mary Goldston, b 1863 - d 1939, CRO
Philip E, b 27 Nov 1912 - d 7 Nov 1950, CRO
Robert T, b 21 Aug 1865 - d 6 Jan 1945, CRO
Roland, b 3 Aug 1803 - d 1 March 1871, CRO
Willard W Sr, d 18 Aug 1977, ae 76y, CRO
KNAPP, Georgia A, b 4 July 1907 - no death date, BRR
William H, Pfc 4 Co 158 Depot Brig WWI, b 27 May 1899 - d 14 Feb 1964, BRR
KNEPP, Frank E, b 1877 - d 1952, SHD
Julia C, b 1881 - d 1971, SHD
KNIGHT, Anna Jones, b 29 June 1884 - d 25 March 1935, UNN

KNIGHT (continued)
Eliza F, b 4 Feb 1884 - d 19 Jan 1980, UNN
Harmon T, b 3 Dec 1871 - d 27 May 1954, BRR
James S, b 18 June 1882 - d 8 Apr 1904, LBR
Marion Carr, Cpl 5 Ord Korea, b 30 Oct 1928 - d 6 Aug 1972, LBR
Mattie T, b 25 Dec 1873 - no death date, BRR
Raymond, d 2 May 1978, ae 62y, LBR
S J, b 31 Jan 1861 - d 25 March 1920, LBR
KNOWLING, Hattie, b 5 Apr 1872 - d 5 Dec 1923, LBR
J S, b 24 May 1867 - d 19 Feb 1943, LBR
Johnie G, b 17 Sept 1925 - d 20 Sept 1925, LBR
KOLB, Rev Charles B, b 1868 - d 1935, RGB
Francis S, b 1870 - no death date, RGB
KON, Barbara B, b 20 Apr 1885 - d 10 Dec 1970, DRL
John Joseph, b 22 May 1874 - d 27 Sept 1964, DRL
KOONTZ, Flora Langley, b 10 July 1886 - d 13 Feb 1967, NWP
George M, b 28 July 1883 - d 21 March 1932, OLP
Leona Elizabeth, b 14 Nov 1863 - d 30 Aug 1941, OLP
Richard Arnold, b 31 July 1908 - d 27 Aug 1953, NWP
W C, b 8 Dec 1859 - d 31 Dec 1919, OLP
KREIS, Augusta Gsch, b 22 Aug 1853 - d 9 Feb 1921, WRC
Bertha Ann, b 11 Sept 1894

KREIS (continued)
- d 20 July 1947, WRC
Billy Jean, b 23 June 1920
- d 25 Feb 1923, WRC
Carl L, b 25 Aug 1893 - d
21 Oct 1961, WRC
Carl L, b 22 Sept 1890 - d
17 Aug 1940, WRC
Charles D, b 13 Dec 1859 -
d 6 Nov 1892, WRC
Christian Hendrick, b 27
Feb 1863 - d 3 May 1863,
WRC
Cynthia Jones, b 27 Oct
1858 - d 10 Nov 1942,
WRC
D, b 14 Feb 1928 (?) - d
20 Oct 1893 (?), WRC
Daniel L, b 20 Sept 1869 -
d 22 Nov 1955, WRC
David Joe, b 25 Feb 1883 -
d 15 Feb 1884, WRC
Deadrick, b 11 Aug 1780 -
d 1858, WRC
Dorothy B, b 23 Oct 1890 -
d 26 Jan 1969, WRC
Edith A, b 16 Oct 1902 - d
1 March 1964, WRC
Elizabeth K, b 16 Aug 1824
- d 1 May 1904, WRC
Fred A, b 5 Feb 1890 - d
19 March 1961, WRC
Fred Morris, b 5 June 1916
- d 5 June 1916, WRC
Gertrude Hall, b 9 Sept
1892 - d 4 Feb 1963, WRC
Henry Ernest, b 24 Feb
1887 - d 20 June 1896,
WRC
J J, b 28 Jan 1874 - d 2
March 1954, WRC
Jacob J, b 21 May 1815 - d
15 Nov 1859, WRC
Jester L, b 28 Sept 1892 -
no death date, WRC
Johann, b 16 Aug 1820 - d
24 Jan 1892, WRC
John A, b 20 June 1879 - d

KREIS (continued)
24 July 1969, WRC
John Dedrick, b 19 Apr
1848 - d 10 Oct 1933,
WRC
John Jacob, b 9 Sept 1878
- d 25 Sept 1879, WRC
Leonard, b 17 Jan 1851 - d
10 June 1918, WRC
Louis D, b 7 Oct 1900 - d
22 May 1960, WRC
Lucy Gadner, b 11 May 1783
- d 1856, WRC
Maria Anna, d/o L & M, no
dates, WRC
Mary A, b 18 Oct 1884 - d
7 Feb 1885, WRC
Mary Gschwind, b 2 May
1857 - d 24 Apr 1937,
WRC
Mary Z, b 25 Jan 1834 - d
22 Dec 1928, WRC
Ruby Lee, b 31 July 1922 -
d 16 July 1924, WRC
Sarah L, b 5 Feb 1920 - d
10 March 1920, WRC
Walter Bernard, b 21 Jan
1896 - d 24 Apr 1955,
WRC
Willard C, b 7 Apr 1915 -
d 24 Dec 1935, WRC
William L, b 14 Oct 1885 -
d 4 Dec 1964, WRC
Wm Harry, Pfc, b 26 Jan
1912 - d 13 Apr 1945,
WRC
KRING, Alice, d 5 March
1980, ae 91y, CLH
Bettie, b 5 June 1889 - d
12 Oct 1922, BRR
Lester, d 2 Jan 1980, ae
67y, CLH
KRON, Andarias, b 1802 - d
7 July 1873, WRC
Ursula, b 25 Dec 1798 - d
11 Sept 1880, WRC
KRUPA, Josephine E, b 19
March 1879 - d 12 Oct

KRUPA (continued)
1956, UNG
Walter F, b 27 June 1862 -
d 29 July 1928, UNG
KUHN, David, b 20 Feb 1803
- d 13 Apr 1874, WRC
Rosina, b 1820 - d 20 Sept
1890, WRC
L, H M, foot stone, SNB
L, W H, foot stone, SNB
LACY, Eliza S, b 23 Dec
1857 - no death date,
SNB
Walter Herbert, b 8 Dec
1845 - d 28 June 1900,
SNB
LAIRD, Helen, b 1838 - d
1911, SNB
LAMANCE, Dave P, b 5 Jan
1897 - d 29 Jan 1925,
LBR
David J, b 16 Aug 1855 - d
11 Feb 1931, LBR
David R, b&d 16 Sept 1939,
WMG
Eugene A, Sgt, b 20 Sept
1920 - d 9 July 1944,
LBR
Everett, b 5 Feb 1891 - d
7 Jan 1957, LBR
Gilbert W, b 13 Feb 1894 -
d 25 May 1971, LBR
Hugh G, b 9 July 1885 - d
22 Aug 1963, LBR
Ira L, b 11 June 1901 - d
3 July 1966, LBR
Rachel J, b 25 Sept 1898 -
no death date, LBR
Ray H, Cpl 40th Air Sqdn,
b 13 Sept 1926 - d 2 Jan
1947, LBR
Raymond Carl, b 13 Apr
1929 - d 25 May 1951,
WRC
Rebecca M, b 2 March 1904
- no death date, LBR
LANCE, ----, b 18 March
1922 - d 24 Dec 1925,

LANCE (continued)
ELZ
LAND, Gilbert, b 5 July
1884 - d 6 June 1914,
CLC
Jerry, b 1858 - d 1912,
CLC
Keith, b 1862 - d 1954,
CLC
Rose, b 12 Dec 1903 - d 11
Feb 1970, CRO
LANDERS, Reba McCormack, d
16 Aug 1975, ae 47y, LNC
LANDFORD, Albert E, b 10
May 1909 - d 8 Dec 1936,
BRR
LANDRUM, Abb R, d 18 Oct
1974, ae 80y, ELZ
Alpha, b 14 Feb 1907 - d 4
May 1948, ELZ
Amanda Gale, b&d 1 Aug
1980, LNE
Autha, b 23 Feb 1910 - d
14 Aug 1933, ELZ
Billie Jean, d 6 Sept
1976, ae 3mo, MLC
Elda June, b 15 May 1941 -
no death date, LNE
Geraldine, b 1937 - d
1971, ELZ
Haley Lee, b 8 May 1933 -
d 15 June 1972, LNE
Harry Lee, b 27 Feb 1903 -
d 11 Dec 1932, ELZ
Hollie M, b 25 May 1927 -
d 21 Aug 1928, LNE
Isaac, b 11 July 1860 - d
13 Oct 1903, ELZ
Isiah, b 1889 - d 1967,
ELZ
Lauvernia, d 11 Sept 1978,
ae 64y, ELZ
Leany G, b 31 Oct 1893 -
no death date, LNE
Lewis S, b 8 March 1883 -
d 13 Aug 1955, LNE
Lilly Meleany, b 14 March
1930 - d 6 Nov 1934, ELZ

LANDRUM (continued)

Martin, d 4 July 1967, WRC

Martin Tom, d 5 Apr 1980, ae 90y, LNE

Mary W, b 27 Sept 1901 - d 23 Dec 1968, LNE

Ruby, b 27 Dec 1841 - d 17 Dec 1945, ELZ

Thomas Scott, d 11 Apr 1979, ae 47y, LNE

Winnie Maden, d 4 Aug 1975, ae 57y, LBR

LANE, Esther D, b 12 Aug 1947 - d 7 Feb 1964, PNY

John B, b 14 May 1880 - d 15 June 1959, LNE

Mary, b 6 Oct 1890 - d 17 March 1894, WRC

W C, b 6 Dec 1876 - d 13 Nov 1903, LNE

William S, b 18 Apr 1885 - d 24 Oct 1918, WRC

William Sebuin, b 26 Sept 1910 - d 17 Sept 1938, WRC

LANGLEY, A J, b 1 Aug 1857 - d 26 Dec 1896, LNG

Albert M, b 1869 - d 1875, LBR

Anna May, b 12 Jan 1897 - d 16 March 1898, WRC

Arthur, b 18 Nov 1884 - d 10 March 1954, WRC

Baalam J, d 31 Oct 1979, ae 88y, CLC

Bertha L, b 31 Dec 1923 - no death date, CRO

C M, b 15 May 1874 - d 29 Nov 1899, LNG

Cecil, b&d 29 Nov 1923, PNY

Cecil M, b 29 Nov 1899 - d 19 March 1963, PNY

Claud D Jack, b 14 Dec 1919 - d 12 Nov 1975, CRO

Daniel C, b 30 June 1869 - d 9 Oct 1951, UNN

LANGLEY (continued)

David O, b 3 Feb 1856 - d 18 Jan 1908, CLC

Dora E, b 1894 - d 1944, PNY

E, b 27 Apr ---- - d 27 Aug 197-, WRC

Earl, b -- Oct 1907 - d 20 Oct ----, CLC

Eliza, b 27 Dec 1845 - d 16 Aug 1919, LNG

Ella, b 11 Aug 1893 - d 11 Jan 1969, CBJ

Ellen S Goddard, b 28 Sept 1871 - d 27 Feb 1953, PNY

Ephriam, b 27 July 1857 - d 21 July 1921, LBR

Ethel D, b 27 May 1890 - d 7 Jan 1975, CRO

Everett, b 3 May 1897 - no death date, PNY

Fred E Jr, b 1937 - d 3 Apr 1977, JCJ

Fred E Sr, d 3 Dec 1974, ae 86y, JCJ

George F, b 2 Dec 1878 - d 5 July 1959, CLC

Gilbert, b 14 Aug 1898 - d 6 Apr 1928, CLC

Gracie, b 17 Feb 1832 - d 17 June 1895, LNG

Hopey C, b 20 Nov 1860 - d 22 Nov 1919, CLC

Hugh E, d -- Nov 1914, CLC

J M, b 16 July 1859 - d 29 Sept 1933, WRC

J Paul, d 21 Sept 1979, ae 46y, WRC

James, b 16 Jan 1842 - d 28 July 1917, LNG

James Floyd, d 25 May 1975, ae 69y, NWP

James Huston, b 10 Apr 1929 - d 30 Sept 1935, JCJ

James W, b 26 July 1854 - d 23 Apr 1923, DVS

LANGLEY (continued)
John, b 15 June 1833 - d 1
  Aug 1921, LNG
John H, b 7 Apr 1895 (?) -
  d 20 Oct 1884 (?), DVS
Joseph W, b 21 Oct 1887 -
  d 5 May 1964, CRO
Josie, b 29 Jan 1896 - d
  31 July 1897, UNN
Julia A, b&d 25 May 1883,
  LNG
Katherine M, b 22 March
  1884 - no death date,
  MSG
L M, b 15 March 1825 - d
  19 Jan 1892, LNG
Lillard, b 1934 - d 1949,
  CLC
Luther H, d 20 Nov 1973,
  ae 85y, CBJ
Lydia F, b 1846 - d 2 Jan
  1886, LBR
M Henry R, d 27 May 1893,
  ae 29y 9mo, LNG
M M, b 1803 (1828) - d 6
  Jan 1904, DRM
Maggie E, b 11 July 1892 -
  d 3 Oct 1902, DVS
Malinda, b 24 Dec 1846 - d
  15 June 1916, LNG
Margaret, b 1 Jan 1810 - d
  23 Oct 1887, LNG
Margaret Ellen, b 1877 - d
  1977, CLC
Martha, b 28 July 1870 - d
  11 Oct 1926, LBR
Mary B, b 1 May 1852 - d
  10 Apr 1912, LNG
Mary J, b 1873 - d 1880,
  LBR
Matilda, b 26 Oct 1869 - d
  9 Sept 1963, UNN
Minnie, b 14 Oct 1963 - d
  3 June 1968, PNY
Rachel Matilda, b 25 Dec
  1859 - d 18 Nov 1928,
  WRC
Ray Hooner, b 12 Apr 1907

LANGLEY (continued)
- no death date, WRC
Ray Hooper, b 6 Jan 1910 -
  d 22 Nov 1912, WRC
Ray Spurgeon, b 19 July
  1902 - d 26 July 1947,
  PNY
Rosa E, b 24 Sept 1900 -
  no death date, PNY
Sadie, d 5 Dec 1978, ae
  96y, WMG
Sarah, b 19 May 1956 - d
  19 July 1922, DVS
Susan, b 16 Oct 1886 - d 1
  Feb 1974, WMG
Susan Byrd, b 16 Oct 1886
  - d 1 Feb 1974, WRC
W B, Pvt Co F 1st TN Inf,
  b 16 Dec 1841 - d 1933,
  LBR
W M, b 13 May 1875 - d 31
  Oct 1961, LNG
W O, b 30 Nov 1808 - d 3
  June 1894, LNG
W T, b 18 Jan 1856 - d 11
  June 1933, LNG
Welda E Sr, b 10 July 1892
  - d 25 Oct 1959, WRC
William H, b 27 May 1882 -
  d 19 Nov 1970, MSG
William M, b 21 Jan 1867 -
  d 23 Feb 1937, PNY
Wm, b 13 Apr 1932 - d 14
  Apr 1932, PNY
LANKFORD, A J, b 6 Sept
  1874 - d 22 Aug 1925,
  SHD
Carson Loyd, b 22 July
  1911 - no death date,
  BRR
Cinth, b 16 Aug 1922 - d 4
  Sept 1923, SHD
Ednie, b 10 Dec 1903 - d
  18 Dec 1903, SHD
Gladys, b 16 June 1920 - d
  14 June 1923, SHD
Infant, b 11 Feb 1899 - d
  12 Feb 1899, SHD

LANKFORD (continued)
Infant, b 10 Aug 1913 - d 6 Oct 1913, SHD
J H, b 29 Dec 1847 - d 6 July 1910, SHD
Johnnie W, b 28 Jan 1864 - d 28 July 1951, BRR
Josie E, b 2 March 1886 - d 22 Sept 1931, BRR
Julia, b 1 Dec 1880 - d 2 Feb 1915, SHD
Mary Ann, b 13 July 1847 - d 1894, SHD
Neva, b 22 Aug 1924 - d 4 June 1925, SHD
Paresona, b 12 May 1865 - d 8 Oct 1894, SHD
Vergil, b 3 Nov 1907 - d 8 Jan 1916, SHD
Walter, b 11 Sept 1896 - d 1 Dec 1896, SHD
LANSTEN, Marjorie L, d 11 Nov 1975, ae 72y, PTC
LARICK, G W, b 2 Jan 1862 - d 24 Jan 1884, DVS
LAUGHTER, Furman, b 22 June 1918 - d 27 Nov 1939, MSG
Tommy Kinae, b 13 May 1963 - d 28 Oct 1963, MSG
Zeb, no birth date - d 13 June 1944, MSG
LAVENDER, Amanda, b 20 Sept 1871 - d 24 Sept 1961, DRL
Austin, b 12 Feb 1868 - d 6 Apr 1951, DRL
Basine I, b 18 Sept 1874 - d 25 Sept 1889, CLC
Jane, b 1867 - d 1945, CLC
Jennie M, b 28 June 1902 - d 17 June 1968, BRN
Jessie C, b 8 Sept 1896 - d 19 June 1979, BRN
John, d 5 March 1897, ae 55y, CLC
Leonard C, b 14 May 1902 - d 1 Dec 1909, BRN

LAVENDER (continued)
Lucinda, b 1 Jan 1879 - d 6 May 1971, BRN
Mr, d 19 June 1974, ae 82y, BRN
Nero, b 1 Jan 1870 - d 5 Aug 1954, BRN
Rena Myatt, b 10 Oct 1887 - d 25 Oct 1977, DRL
Samuel, b 1868 - d 1933, CLC
Tilden, b 15 Sept 1876 - d 11 Nov 1961, BRN
Warren, b 26 March 1882 - no death date, DRL
LAWHORN, Hiram, b 21 Jan 1917 - d 16 Nov 1930, RGB
LAWRENCE, Raymond Cal, Pfc 23 Inf 2 Div WWII/Korea, b 13 Apr 1929 - d 25 May 1951, OOO
LAWSON, Ethel, no dates, OLP
Kathlyn Goldbert, d 10 Apr 1978, ae 56y, LBR
Mahaley, b 2 March 1830 - d 12 Nov 1912, WRJ
LAYMANCE, Archie W, b 14 Apr 1908 - d 15 Feb 1968, LBR
Charles, Pfc USA, b 26 June 1932 - d 12 March 1975, LBR
Chesley, b 1856 - d 1926, LBR
Chester, b 26 Nov 1912 - d 24 March 1936, WRC
Clarence, b 1935 - d 1972, LBR
Edna T, b 26 Oct 1910 - no death date, LBR
Edward, d -- Nov 1974, ae 44y, MSG
Elizabeth A, b 1845 - d 1977, LBR
Emma, b 13 July 1889 - d 1 July 1890, LBR

LAYMANCE (continued)

H E, b 22 Apr 1886 - d 10 Dec 1951, UNN

Ida May, b 28 Feb 1888 - d 11 June 1895, LBR

J L, 1956, LBR

J L, b 21 Jan 1850 - d 18 Sept 1918, CRO

Jacob A, b 12 Oct 1875 - d 5 May 1959, LBR

James L, b 20 July 1901 - d 28 Dec 1955, LBR

Jennie L, (no notation), LBR

Joe, b 1878 - d 1962, MSG

John H, no dates, LBR

Kizzie, d 20 May 1980, ae 82y, MSG

Laura B, b 24 Aug 1891 - no death date, LBR

Luvernia, b 9 Dec 1889 - d 10 Apr 1965, UNN

Mary Ellen, b 11 Apr 1871 - d 25 Jan 1934, LBR

N O, b 7 Mar 1893 - d 13 June 1950, WRC

Ola, b 22 June 1903 - d 17 March 1920, LBR

Ray, b 22 Feb 1921 - d 27 Aug 1963, MSG

Sam Carson, b 29 Jan 1864 - d 13 Dec 1949, LBR

Vance, b 12 Aug 1881 - d 26 Aug 1960, UNN

Vane, d 3 May 1978, ae 70y, LBR

Viola M, b 10 Sept 1904 - d 26 July 1969, LBR

William Jr, b 1919 - d 1951, WRC

LAYNE, Claude Allen, GM 3 USNR WWII, b 7 June 1922 - d 22 Apr 1968, LBR

LE COULTRU, Eugene A, b 3 Nov 1840 - d 27 Jan 1960, WRC

Laura H, b 19 July 1879 - d 21 Feb 1975, WRC

LEACH, Marlina, b 26 Oct 1938 - d 7 Aug 1939, WRC

Wayne Benny, b 24 Sept 1935 - d 7 Dec 1935, WRC

LEDFORD, Johnson, b 15 July 1891 - d 4 Feb 1940, DVS

Maggie E, b 12 July 1927 - no death date, LNE

Roxie, b 9 Jan 1905 - d 6 Jan 1925, WRJ

Truman W, b 4 Sept 1927 - d 29 Apr 1965, LNE

LEE, Arnie, b 9 Aug 1898 - d -- May 1901, PTC

Arthur W, b 13 Oct 1894 - d 11 Aug 1920, PTC

Barbara, b 5 Jan 1801 - d -- Jan 1879, PTC

Bertha, b 19 Feb 1885 - d 13 Aug 1917, HWN

Bertha M, b 4 Sept 1888 - d 6 May 1970, MSG

Bonie, b 2 June 1895 - d 19 Jan 1896, PTC

Clifford, d 29 Nov 1974, ae 61y, WMG

Dennis, Sgt Stu Sq AF, b 2 March 1945 - d 10 July 1968, DRL

Harry, b 8 May 1933 - d 15 June 1972, LNE

J W, b 8 March 1833 - d 14 Nov 1903, PTC

James L, b 26 Feb 1877 - d 25 Jan 1962, CRO

June Elda, b 15 May 1941 - no death date, LNE

Laura, b 1880 - d 1942, DRL

Lissa, b 2 March 1894 - d 22 Feb 1966, PTC

N J Potter, b 15 Oct 1869 - d 30 Dec 1888, PTC

Sam A, b 12 May 1874 - d 5 Jan 1929, PTC

Violet M, b 4 Aug 1898 - d 4 Oct 1917, PTC

W Austin, b 7 July 1888 -

LEE (continued)
d 14 Nov 1965, MSG
William J, b 30 Sept 1869
- d 20 July 1918, PTC
LEHMAN, Anna P, b 13 Nov
1893 - no death date,
DRM
Catherine C, b&d 30 Dec
1897, DRM
Charity Carolyn, b 4 May
1886 - d 14 Feb 1953,
CRO
Earl J, b 12 Oct 1909 - d
28 Jan 1968, CRO
Emma Rogers, b 1886 - d
1972, WRC
Frank E, b 25 Sept 1902 -
d 14 Aug 1968, CRO
Frederick W, b 12 Jan 1896
- d 12 Aug 1897, DRM
Henry Lawrence, b 14 Nov
1908 - d 15 Feb 1941,
DRM
J F W, b 23 Sept 1838 - d
19 March 1915, WRC
John T, b 25 March 1881 -
d 23 July 1971, CRO
Mary, b 19 May 1873 - d 23
Dec 1934, DRM
Toney, b 18 May 1872 - d
21 Oct 1876, WRC
Velma Rose, d 24 Aug 1980,
ae 65y, CRO
W C, b 27 June 1866 - d 17
June 1956, DRM
Walter C, b 12 May 1911 -
d 12 Jue 1911, DRM
William O, b&d 31 Oct
1893, WRC
Woodrow C, b 31 Dec 1916 -
d 18 Oct 1970, DRM
LENDER, Barbara, b 1818 - d
1905, RGB
LENTER, Charles A, b 12
June 1948 - d 15 Sept
1948, BRN
LEOPPER, Anna P, b 12 July
1884 - d 7 Apr 965, WRC

LEOPPER (continued)
Annie Christine, d 15 July
1901, ae 1y 16da, WRC
Charles, b 26 May 1879 - d
4 Apr 1967, PNY
Christiane W, b 26 Oct
1845 - d 24 Aug 1943,
WRC
Ed, b 6 Sept 1881 - d 14
May 1974, CRO
Edith, b 22 Jan 1926 - d
15 Jan 1928, WRC
Emma, b 23 Dec 1884 - d 26
Feb 1969, PNY
Fritz, b 1871 - d 1955,
WRC
George H, b 7 Apr 1849 - d
17 Feb 1933, WRC
Glen, b 3 Nov 1911 - d 20
June 1930, PNY
Henry G, b 29 May 1877 - d
25 March 1968, WRC
Ida F, b 29 Dec 189- - d
27 Apr 1981, CRO
Mary, b 1879 - d 1966, WRC
Otto Edward, b 28 Nov 1943
- d 27 Dec 1945, CRO
Otto G, b 4 March 1886 - d
14 Feb 1964, WRC
Ralph, d 14 July 1980, ae
71y, CRO
Ruth, b 22 June 1881 - d
24 July 1924, WRC
LESTER, Grace, b 1904 - d
1972, LST
James Henry, Co E 16 Reg
VA Cav, 25 Sept 1935 -
no other date, LST
James R, b 10 Oct 1900 - d
17 Oct 1958, LST
James R Jr, 19 Feb 1951 -
no other date, LST
LETNER, David W, b 23 May
1961 - d 2 March 1968,
RGB
Trenna G, b 28 Apr 1967 -
d 2 March 1968, RGB
LETORY, Honorine Thersa, b

LETORY (continued)
5 June 1878 - d 3 May
1892, WRC
Pauline V, b 4 Jan 1847 -
d 7 Aug 1897, WRC
Victor, b 21 Dec 1839 - d
5 Mar 1910, WRC
Victor A, b 27 March 1873
- d 19 May 1949, WRC
LEVY, Robert P Jr, b 4 May
1940 - d 14 March 1970,
LNC
Thomas E, b 28 Aug 1942 -
d 27 Feb 1943, LNC
LEWALLEN, Andrew, b 7 Oct
1793 - d 30 Nov 1873,
NDK
Arole D, Pvt Co B 8 Armd
WWII, b 7 May 1925 - d 7
Aug 1969, UNH
C K Sr, b 12 March 1879 -
d 10 Oct 1971, WBB
Donald A, b 1925 - d 1929,
UNH
Eunice F, b 24 Jan 1869 -
d 23 March 1932, BRR
Henry Clay, Pvt 311 Inf
WWI, b 22 March 1894 - d
18 Oct 1953, UNH
Horace Allen, b 22 Jan
1871 - d 9 June 1938,
BRR
Malinda, b 1 Apr 1792 - d
11 Apr 1876, NDK
Margaret Webb, b 1878 - d
1930, WBB
Mary Emaline, d -- Sept
1961, UNH
Rhoda, b 28 Oct 1899 - d
22 July 1916, WBB
LEWELLEN, Anderson, b 20
May 1834 - d 18 Sept
1855, MNT
Charles H, b 12 May 1845 -
d 25 March 1872, MNT
David T, b 8 Feb 1868 - d
23 Dec 1890, MNT
LEWIS, William T, Pvt 11

LEWIS (continued)
Inf, b 27 July 1867 - d
3 May 1948, CRO
LILES, Anna M, b 1907 - d
1970, NWP
Audie M, b 1904 - d 1960,
CBJ
Charles C, b 1878 - d
1952, NWP
Charles L, BM2 USNR WWII,
b 6 Oct 1901 - d 23 Oct
1967, NWP
Effie W, b 6 July 1906 - d
8 Oct 1979, NWP
Evie, b 15 Sept 1899 - d
16 Nov 1918, OLP
H W, b 18 Nov 1859 - d 21
Apr 1913, UNG
James Thomas, b 12 July
1869 - d 4 Oct 1943, WRJ
John, no dates, CBJ
L, Co E 1st TN Inf, no
dates, 000
Millard E, b 22 May 1886 -
d 25 Apr 1951, EST
Minnie J, b 1878 - no
death date, NWP
Susan L, b 14 Aug 1881 - d
6 Jan 1936, CBJ
W Tom, b 9 July 1879 - d
15 March 1963, CBJ
Walter, b 31 March 1906 -
d 30 Aug 1968, NWP
Wm H, b 24 March 1909 - d
22 March 1978, NWP
LILIES, Cynthia Ann, b 16
Nov 1869 - d 8 Dec 1941,
WRJ
LINDSAY, Alex, b 1882 - d
1956, MLC
Joseph W, b 6 Sept 1880 -
d 27 Aug 1916, MLC
Martha Eliz, b 11 Jan 1851
- d 15 March 1921, MLC
Minor K, b 7 Oct 1894 - d
19 Jan 1952, MLC
Samuel W, b 31 Jan 1845 -
24 July 1927, MLC

LINDSTEN, Elmer T, d 7 Dec 1979, ae 80y, PTC
LITTLE, Joseph Odel, b&d 1 March 1978, BRD
LITTON, Allard L, b 2 July 1889 - d 26 March 1927, CRO
Amy, b 2 Jan 1893 - d 2 May 1961, LBR
Anna Louise, b 15 May 1892 - d 22 March 1975, CRO
Freeman A, b 6 July 1916 - d 11 Aug 1917, PLR
James T, 1Sgt Bt B 321 FA WWI, b 5 June 1889 - d 8 June 1964, LBR
LIVELY, Louis, b 23 May 1897 - d 30 July 1940, UNN
Serinda Ann, b 3 Feb 1962 - d 5 Feb 1962, NWP
Shella Ruth, d 7 Feb 1978, ae 18y, NWP
LLEWELLEN, Infant, b&d 10 Jan 1899, WRC
LLOYD, Claiburn, no birth date - d 10 March 1950, ELZ
Mrs Paul, d 13 July 1978, WRC
LOCKETT, Julia, b 20 Sept 1882 - d -- Feb 1974, WMG
Julia B Joyner, b 20 Sept 1882 - d 1 Feb 1974, UNN
LOCKHART, Wm Bedford, b 11 July 1918 - d 27 Oct 1918, OLP
LONG, ----, stone eroded, LBR
Albert, b 20 June 1891 - d 30 Jan 1915, LNC
Arthur, b 5 Feb 1894 - d 27 Jan 1959, WRC
Betty, b 1865 - d 1937, LNC
Elizabeth, b 28 Sept 1850 - d 20 --- 1852, LBR

LONG (continued)
Gregory, b 3 Jan 1953 - d 31 July 1953, DVS
John, b 9 Jan 1832 - d 2 Oct 1880, WRC
John M, b 29 Jan 1849 - d 11 Aug ----, LBR
Mary A, b 10 Aug 1836 - d 28 Oct 1889, WRC
Mary Lizzie, b 24 Feb 1899 - d 1 Nov 1918, LNC
LONGMERE, Adeline, b 27 Sept 1872 - d 11 Jan 1953, UNN
Annie, b 11 May 1904 - d 4 Sept 1952, UNN
Daniel M, b 29 March 1871 - d 6 March 1949, UNN
Edith Anita, b 1960 - d 1974, UNN
Mathew, b 4 Aug 1913 - d 6 Jan 1937, UNN
Edith Anita, d 25 July 1974, ae 14y, LBR
LOURIE, Helen B, d 9 Nov 1981, ae 74y, RGB
LOVE, Avalene, b 21 July 1854 - d 1 June 1914, MSG
C R, b 19 June 1881 - d 8 Oct 1962, MSG
Cordelia, b 9 Sept 1891 - d 2 Aug 1973, MSG
Dora E, b 3 Sept 1871 - d 2 Jan 1947, MSG
Flora, b 1 Sept 1904 - d 8 Sept 1904, MSG
Henry E, b 15 May 1887 - d 10 Dec 1973, MSG
Inf s/o W W & Dora, no dates, MSG
Inf son, 4 Sept 1910 - no other dates, MSG
Jacob O, b 6 June 1883 - d 5 Aug 1884, LBR
John F MD, b 11 Dec 1879 - d 3 Oct 1951, WRC
Mrs John F, b 23 Apr 1877

LOVE (continued)
- d 24 Dec 1960, WRC
John, TN Coast Art Corps,
d 11 Dec 1933, DVS
Lucy, b 11 Dec 1885 - d 4
Jan 1914, MSG
Martha F, b 5 Nov 1824 - d
12 Apr 1902, LBR
Mary Elizabeth, b 17 June
1861 - d 13 June 1906,
MSG
Robert E C, b 20 Dec 1903
- d 2 Oct 1973, WRC
Robert E C, d 2 Oct 1973,
ae --, WMG
Thomas L, b -- March 1856
- d 6 May 1929, MSG
W W, b 6 July 1854 - d 2
June 1939, MSG
William M, b 11 March 1828
- d 5 July 1884, LBR
LOVELACE, Edith Scott, b 4
Apr 1903 - d 3 May 1935,
WRC
Lolita G, b 27 Oct 1924 -
d 19 Jan 1973, WRC
Robert A, Sgt Co B 12 Inf
Korea/Vietnam, b 23 Aug
1930 - d 14 Nov 1967,
WRC
LOW, Lucian B, Pvt 36 Fld
Art, 8 Aug 1936, MNT
LOWE, Doris, b 1958 - d
1975, UNN
Farris Ray, b 22 Dec 1945
- d 9 Jan 1952, STP
Herbert, b 12 Dec 1898 - d
22 May 1970, NWP
Johnnie B, b 6 June 1904 -
d 8 March 1973, NWP
Lewis M, b 15 Aug 1920 - d
29 Oct 1944, UNN
Turney, b 1897 - d 1975,
UNN
Turney, d 1 Jan 1975, ae
75y, NWP
Willie, b 1 Feb 1909 - d
30 July 1966, STP

LOWERY, Burl Jr, b 10 June
1945 - d 13 Aug 1963,
UNG
Hugh W, b 13 Sept 1907 - d
10 Oct 1964, BRN
Jerry William, b 26 Sept
1955 - d 10 Sept 1970,
UNG
Mary A, b -- Aug 1906 - d
19 Jan 1961, NWP
Mildean M, b 25 Oct 1922 -
no death date, BRN
Rodney, b 14 Jan 1961 - d
15 Jan 1961, BRN
LUCHIN, Micael, b 28 July
1887 - d 25 Feb 1967,
DRL
Paraskieva, b 28 Oct 1886
- no death date, DRL
LUMPKIN, Laura, b 1899 - d
1936, BRR
LUNN, Andrew, b 30 Oct 1880
- d 6 June 1908, DRL
LYKE, William E Jr, d 21
Aug 1940, ae 2y 9mo, PLR
LYLES, Elizabeth Allen, no
dates, WRJ
Ida Bell, b 2 March 1883 -
d 26 Nov 1955, WRJ
James A, Pvt 3 TN Inf
Sp/Am War, b 16 Sept
1871 - d 23 Jan 1950,
WRJ
Maj L, no dates - military
stone, WRJ
Mabel Lillian, d 21 Oct
1966, ae 58y 6mo, CRO
Marion L, d 25 Oct 1886,
ae 19y, WRJ
Nancy A Davis, b 14 Sept
1842 - d 3 Aug 1890, WRJ
Oscar B, b 3 July 1908 - d
30 July 1908, WRJ
Shirley V, b 17 July 1926
- no death date, WRJ
LYNCH, Eugene, b 25 Sept
1825 - d 1 Dec 1900, DRL
Fred E, b 19 July 1901 - d

LYNCH (continued)
20 Oct 1901, SNB
Glenice Miller, d 23 Oct 1977, ae 54y, SNB
John, b 13 June 1883 - d 1 Sept 1902, DRL
John P, b 14 Feb 1888 - d 9 Sept 1941, SNB
Lizzie, b 20 May 1884 - d 8 Apr 1908, SNB
LYON, Rachel N, b 12 Apr 1867 - d 19 Jan 1897, BRR
LYONS, Clyde Jr, b 20 Apr 1925 - d -- Aug 1973, UNG
Dernon Gene, b&d 21 Sept 1950, PLR
Ethel, d 20 June 1981l, ae 75y, DRL
Ethel Ritter, b 1887 - d 1940, DRL
Hattie J, b 2 March 1968 (?) - d 31 March 1901 (?), DRL
Irene E, b 2 June 1925 - d 27 Sept 1966, UNG
John E, b 23 Feb 1878 - no death date, DRL
Malinda Davidson, b 15 Oct 1842 - d 30 Apr 1923, DVD
Margaret Jett, b 15 June 1850 - d 14 Oct 1950, DRL
Martin, b 14 July 1836 - d 10 Oct 1921, DVD
Mattie C, b 24 Dec 1891 - d 30 Sept 1927, DVD
Minnie Lee, b 11 Aug 1882 - d 19 Oct 1930, SNB
P C, b 9 July 1848 - d 8 Oct 1922, DRL
Regina E, b 11 Oct 1881 - d 26 Oct 1965, DRL
Rhoda, b 22 Oct 1877 - d 26 Nov 1953, DRL
Robert, d 4 Sept 1976, ae

LYONS (continued)
72y, DRL
Robert M, b 25 Aug 1879 - d 19 June 1963, DRL
LYTLE, Clifford, b 4 June 1877 - d 22 Aug 1902, DRL
Nina W, b 16 Sept 1866 - d 30 July 1901, DRL
MABE, Maude, b 1892 - d 1935, LNC
MABREY, Allen, b 9 Aug 1882 - d 19 May 1978, FLR
Bruce A, b 16 Apr 1963 - d 20 Apr 1963, FLR
Esta Ellen, b 4 Dec 1904 - d 8 Dec 1960, FLR
Ettie, b 30 May 1887 - d 2 Feb 1959, FLR
Lem G, b 1 Nov 1884 - d 25 Apr 1954, FLR
McALLISTER, Margaret, b 12 Dec 1842 - d 4 Jan 1908, SHD
Dr R C, b 3 May 1830 - d 24 Nov 1909, SHD
McCABE, Kathryn, b 7 Dec 1919 - d 7 Dec 1922, WRC
Herbert E, b 11 Sept 1916 - d 15 Nov 1918, WRC
McCANN, Benj Harrison, d 23 March 1974, ae 84y, SHD
Donald Ray, d 12 Nov 1979, ae 45y, WRC
Edd, b 16 Nov 1886 - d 20 July 1955, WRC
Ephrian, b 1885 - d 1967, BRR
H Clark, b 7 Feb 1885 - d 23 Feb 1939, WRC
Myrtle, b 31 July 1891 - d 26 Nov 1970, WRC
Sarah, b 1900 - d 1969, SNB
Thelma A, b 16 Jan 1921 - d 12 Dec 1922, SHD
McCART, Annie Ruth, b&d 9 July 1923, DVS

McCART (continued)
John c, d 1 Aug 1960, ae 75y, DVS
Josiepaine M, b 6 March 1873 - d 21 Apr 1945, DVS
McCARTT, Alice M, b 12 July 1876 - d 18 Feb 1958, LNE
Alice Forstner, b 14 May 1859 - d 27 May 1892, WRC
Alta Dixon, d 11 Oct 1975, ae 68y, DRL
Annie, d 22 Feb 1975, ae 62y, MCR
Barney, b 8 Apr 1910 - d 11 Feb 1935, LNE
Bessie Thomas, b 6 July 1915 - d 23 Feb 1971, FRV
Bill, b 1 June 1897 - no death date, DVS
Carrie E, b 21 Oct 1882 - d 6 Dec 1882, ELZ
Cindy, d 13 Dec 1979, ae 63y, SNB
Dan, b 1871 - d 1942, ELZ
Delilia Dyer, d 3 June 1979, ae 88y, MCR
George W Sr, b 17 July 1890 - d 31 Jan 1973, FRV
Rev H A, b 12 Feb 1844 - d 28 Jan 1921, WRC
Homer H, b 26 Sept 1889 - d 17 Nov 1960, ELZ
Ida M, b 12 Feb 1908 - d 12 Aug 1957, LNE
Infant, b&d 22 Feb 1920, OLP
James A, b 31 May 1851 - d 7 Aug 1923, SNB
James Harris, b 29 May 1887 - d 27 Nov 1923, ELZ
John, b 8 Aug 1891 - d 11 Oct 1961, NWP

McCARTT (continued)
John F, b 16 Jan 1887 - d 20 March 1961, CLC
John F, b 2 Dec 1868 - d 21 Nov 1948, LNE
John H, b 1827 - d 31 Jan 1908, WRC
Juan F, b 6 March 1864 - d -- May 1940, MNT
Julia A, b 2 Aug 1892 - d 24 Feb 1971, FRV
Louise Catherine, b 1868 - d 1929, ELZ
Lucille, b 27 Feb 1881 - d 6 Aug 1920, MLC
Lucille, baby, no dates, MLC
Luther C, b 9 Sept 1900 - d 28 Dec 1969, LNE
Mae, b 17 Dec 1899 - no death date, DVS
Margaret, b 1 May 1830 - d 10 Dec 1904, WRC
Marion W, b 31 May 1910 - d 28 May 1933, SNB
Mary E, b 8 Sept 1879 - d 3 Oct 1910, MNT
Mary Elizabeth, b 28 March 1861 - d 24 Dec 1940, SNB
Maude, d 8 Nov 1973, ae 80y, ELZ
Millie H, b 22 Oct 1850 - d 19 Dec 1930, WRC
Missouri, b 28 Jan 1850 - d 28 Apr 1931, MNT
Myra Della, d 22 Feb 1952, ae 6mo, LNE
Nora Robbins, d 26 Feb 1969, ae 82y, BRZ
Sam E, b 1933 - d 8 May 1973, SNB
Samuel A, b 14 Jan 1875 - d 28 Oct 1884, MNT
Stanley, b 19 March 1906 - d 10 May 1938, LNE
Tunal Beene, d 22 June 1973, ae 78y, OLP

McCARTT (continued)

Turrah, b 13 Feb 1895 - no death date, NWP

Wm R, b 14 Aug 1848 - d 11 Jan 1924, MNT

McCARTY, Della Robbins, b 5 March 1897 - d 26 Dec 1975, CRO

Stanley K, S2 USN WWI, b 25 Apr 1893 - d 20 Dec 1966, CRO

McCOLLISTER, ----, b 25 June 1925 - d 25 Sept 1933, LNC

Wm Samuel, b 23 Sept 1871 - d 10 June 1951, LNC

McCORMACK, Inf s/o R & Myrtle, 2 Sept 1929, ELZ

McCORMICK, Andrew J, b 6 May 1896 - d 23 Sept 1952, LNC

Arline, b 3 Apr 1906 - d 27 Oct 1913, LNC

David A, b -- Feb 1832 - d 4 May 1880, BRR

David Lindsey, b 10 Feb 1861 - d 6 Aug 1923, BRR

Edley Walker, b 10 Jan 1881 - d 25 Jan 1928, BRD

Edna C, b 1921 - d 1952, DRM

Grace Edith, d 25 Oct 1981, ae 79y, PTC

Harold, b 10 Feb 1888 - d 12 Apr 1908, BRR

Infant, b&d 28 Dec 1918, BRR

King D, b 14 Dec 1879 - d 24 Jan 1931, BRD

Lennie, b 1883 - d 1965, LNC

Mary, b 19 Nov 1958 - d 20 Nov 1958, PTC

Mary L Byrd, b 12 Feb 1861 - d 20 Nov 1947, BRD

Nancy A, b 14 Apr 1882 - d 23 Jan 1931, BRD

McCORMICK (continued)

Orlena G, b 9 Feb 1856 - d 8 March 1948, BRR

Sarah A, b 28 Feb 1831 - d 23 Feb 1892, BRR

Sarah Luverna, d 5 June 1979, ae 79y, LNC

Tom, b 16 Apr 1854 - d 8 Nov 1928, BRD

Walter, b 1900 - d 1968, LNC

Mrs Walter, b 26 Feb 1909 - d 14 Jan 1935, LNC

Willie Henry, b 8 Dec 1856 - d 6 June 1933, BRD

McCOWAN, Christine, b 28 Oct 1922 - d 5 Sept 1937, ELZ

Rebecca Mae, b 16 Dec 1896 - d 14 Nov 1973, SNB

William J, b 24 June 1889 - d 23 Apr 1961, SNB

McCOY, A J, b 1847 - d 1920, LNE

Arley, b 10 Feb 1915 - d 22 July 1964, NWP

Boyd, b 25 March 1908 - no death date, NWP

Carolyn Lois, d 5 Feb 1967, ae 16y 2mo, NWP

Carrie W, b 1887 - d 1962, NWP

Clara, b 30 May 1890 - d 20 Sept 1920, MRR

Della Mae, b 9 May 1900 - d 20 Dec 1976, CRO

Della Rose, b 9 May 1900 - d 24 Dec 1976, CRO

E Layne, b 9 July 1913 - d 8 March 1965, NWP

Edna, b 3 Nov 1906 - no death date, CRO

Florence W, b 24 July 1903 - no death date, LNE

H E, b 19 Nov 1846 - d 1 March 1873, ELZ

Helen, d 17 Nov 1980, ae 57y, CLC

McCOY (continued)

Jack Franklin, b 7 July 1928 - d 19 Jan 1929, LNE

James Lawrence, b 20 Apr 1898 - d 28 Sept 1960, CRO

James M, b 8 Apr 1897 - d 17 Sept 1977, LNE

John Henry, b 18 Jan 1903 - d 19 May 1917, OLP

Joseph W, b 1881 - d 1957, NWP

Julia Anne, b 1858 - d 1940, LNE

Laura W, b 13 March 1911 - no death date, NWP

Lillian L V, b 27 Oct 1916 - d 12 May 1937, NWP

Luada, b 21 Sept 1915 - d 8 Oct 1918, OLP

Maggie, b 27 July 1914 - d 17 Aug 1914, OLP

Magline, b&d 30 Aug 1927, LNE

Margaret, b 1877 - d 1966, CRO

Mary Jane, b 9 Apr 1884 - d 17 Jan 1968, NWP

Oather, b 11 Apr 1914 - d 9 June 1917, OLP

Pat Edward, b 19 Dec 1934 - d 6 Oct 1956, NWP

Ralph , b 24 Nov 1911 - d 20 Aug 1961, NWP

Richard, b 1 March 1906 - d 21 Sept 1924, OLP

Robert, b 22 Apr 1909 - d 8 Jan 1960, NWP

Robert Ransom, b 25 March 1887 - d 8 Aug 1946, MRR

Rosetta, b 23 Oct 1886 - d 11 Sept 1943, OLP

Roy, b 8 July 1909 - d 8 Oct 1910, OLP

Ruby, b 1855 - d 1939, ELZ

Sam D, b 17 Feb 1884 - d 13 Jan 1959, NWP

McCOY (continued)

Ted, b 22 Aug 1905 - d 25 June 1974, CRO

William B, Co L 1st Rgt TN Inf Sp/Am War, b 26 Jan 1879 - d 2 Apr 1954, NWP

William Burlow, d 6 Aug 1975, ae 65y, CRO

William Chester, b 6 Apr 1917 - d 3 May 1917, OLP

McCURRY, Dewey, b 20 Jan 1900 - d 3 Feb 1978, BRR

Nola M, b 14 March 1909 - d 11 Nov 1965, BRR

McDANIEL, Faye, b 23 Apr 1934 - d 10 Oct 1967, DRL

Funstal I, Pvt Co F 4 Rgt Sp/Am War, b 28 Nov 1874 - d 4 May 1956, WRC

William R, d 1 March 1942, WRC

McDOWELL, Funstal Q, Pvt Co L 4 Rgt KY Inf Sp/Am War, b 28 Nov 1874 - d 4 May 1956, OOO

Lee, d 5 Jan 1979, ae 67y, WRC

Verna Hamby, b 9 March 1879 - d 2 July 1975, WRC

McELHANEY, Tina, b 11 Nov 1876 - d 21 Aug 1907, WRC

McGEE, Leslie, b 18 Jan 1912 - d 8 March 1912, SNB

Topay, b 10 Aug 1909 - d 28 June 1910, SNB

McGHEE, Allen J, b 6 June 1895 - d 9 Jan 1947, NWP

Brass T, b 19 March 1883 - d 18 July 1961, EST

Cordelia, b 1852 - d 1971, WMG

Elizabeth G, b 29 Aug 1874 - d 10 Feb 1958, WRC

Emily A, b 18 July 1888 -

McGHEE (continued)
d 18 May 1969, PTC
Garfield, b 1881 - d 1965, WMG
Hannah J, b 29 June 1892 - d 13 Aug 1948, WRC
Laura L, b 28 Sept 1912 - no death date, PNY
Lonnie, b 16 Apr 1905 - d 1 Aug 1963, PNY
Margaret, b 28 Jan 1895 - d 6 Aug 1974, EST
Minnie, no birth date - d 2 Jan 1962, ELZ
Vester, b 23 Nov 1889 - d 6 Aug 1952, WRC
McGILL, Charlie, b 21 May 1893 - d 7 June 1948, CRO
E J, b 11 July 1869 - d 26 Apr 1943, CRO
E J Jr, b 5 July 1919 - d 26 Nov 1950, CRO
Eller C, b 27 Nov 1882 - d 1 May 1899, CRO
Ernest A, b 21 May 1905 - d 18 Apr 1926, PNY
Ethel, b 17 Oct 1885 - d 16 Feb 1946, CRO
Harriet, b 3 Nov 1857 - d 2 July 1914, CRO
Infant c/o J H, no dates, CRO
James E, b 3 Jan 1901 - d 19 June 1903, CRO
Leslie, b 17 July 1916 - d 19 Apr 1960, CRO
Lou, b 31 Aug 1864 - d 1 Jan 1901, CRO
Lucinda, b 1881 - d 1967, CRO
Martha (Phillips), b 5 Oct 1836 - d 19 Dec 1920, CRO
Martha V, b 21 Aug 1893 - d 23 May 1903, CRO
Mary A Goddard, b 17 Dec 1867 - d 3 Feb 1955, PNY

McGILL (continued)
Patsy Ann, b 24 July 1935 - d 26 Dec 1939, CRO
Robert H Jr, b 19 July 1913 - d 25 July 1944, CRO
Robert Harvey, b 23 May 1888 - d 30 June 1946, CRO
W M, b 15 Sept 1841 - d 11 Nov 1907, CRO
William Isiah, b 21 Sept 1866 - d 16 Dec 1926, PNY
Willie, b 15 March 1915 - d 18 Oct 1919, CRO
McGLOTHEN, Rev David, b 16 Jan 1900 - d 16 Nov 1955, DVS
McGLOTHIN, Alzie Lee, b 1891 - d 1964, DVS
Benton Alfred, Pvt USA WWII, b 10 Aug 1928 - d 24 Sept 1976, DVS
Bessie Gough, b 17 Feb 1894 - d 15 Nov 1951, DVS
Cassie, d -- Nov 1953, ae 56y, JCJ
Cena, b 3 Apr 1966, ae 78y, JCJ
Dennie, d 19 Aug 1963, ae 76y, DVS
Effie, d 6 Nov 1948, ae 69y, JCJ
Elijah, d 22 Apr 1976, ae 82y, JCJ
Ezra, b 10 Nov 1891 - d 14 Nov 1936, DVS
Gertrude Mae, b 1893 - d 1941, DVS
James L, b 2 Oct 1863 - d 29 Dec 1946, JCJ
Jas Clarence, b 28 Jan 1896 - d 15 Oct 1945, JCJ
Jewel, b 4 May 1935 - d 5 May 1935, DVS

McGLOTHIN (continued)

John, d 11 March 1960, ae 76y, JCJ

Lewis, d 6 Dec 1936, ae 27y, JCJ

Martha Jane, b 4 March 1858 - d 22 July 1955, DVS

Mary Jackson, b 11 Dec 1865 - d 23 Oct 1918, JCJ

Maud Hinds, b 9 Sept 1906 - d 19 Sept 1923, DVS

Meredith, d 27 Feb 1980, ae 66y, JCJ

Myrtle Belle, b 12 Sept 1896 - d 18 Oct 1918, DVS

Otto, d 7 Feb 1978, ae 60y, DVS

Richard, b 29 Jan 1868 - d 30 Nov 1916, DVS

Susan, b 16 Jan 1870 - d 29 Apr 1940, DVS

W Wesley, d 18 Sept 1894, ae c 50y, DVS

Willard Rich, b&d 11 Nov 1921, DVS

Wilma Jean, b 5 Aug 1924 - d 13 July 1925, DVS

McGLOVE, Nancy, b 22 March 1899 - no death date, LNE

Shirley, b 4 May 1904 - d 28 July 1967, LNE

McGRATH, George, b 28 Dec 1871 - d 26 Apr 1954, BRR

Lula, b 20 July 1881 - d 29 July 1946, BRR

McGUFFEY, ----, b 3 March 1885 - d 28 Oct 1915, DRM

Amy Z, b 7 Jan 1886 - d 2 Nov 1950, WRC

Annia Peters, b 6 Apr 1873 - d 26 Oct 1905, BRR

John C, b 16 May 1872 - d

McGUFFEY (continued)

5 Nov 1963, WRC

McHAHON, Irene Triplett, b 31 July 1902 - d 9 Jan 1971, CRO

McHUGH, Catherine, b 8 July 1885 - d 11 Feb 1962, CRO

McKEE, Brenda Lou, b 3 Apr 1949 - d 13 July 1956, WRC

McKEEHAN, Carl F, b 16 May 1913 - d 4 Nov 1968, LNE

Maggie B, b 18 July 1911 - no death date, LNE

Timothy A, b 23 Sept 1969 - d 24 Sept 1969, LNE

McKEETHAN, Ann Elizabeth, b 13 Aug 1840 - d 5 Jan 1941, SNB

Emmett, b 20 Feb 1884 - d 7 Nov 1957, PLR

Ethel Marie, b 10 Sept 1902 - d 16 Feb 1908, SNB

Eugene J, b 1 June 1892 - d 4 July 1961, SNB

Freeman E, b 22 June 1913 - d 10 Sept 1913, SNB

H H, b 15 Feb 1843 - d 27 Nov 1921, SNB

Jack D, b 25 Feb 1922 - d 3 Nov 1945, PLR

Larry, b&d 1941, PLR

Lucinda, b 8 July 1893 - d 28 Dec 1910, SNB

Mattye L, b 13 Jan 1893 - no death date, SNB

Millie M, b 22 June 1871 - d 1 Nov 1905, SNB

Thomas M, b 23 Oct 1876 - d 10 March 1900, SNB

McKENZIE, Florence, b 1882 - no death date, CRO

Henry M, b 26 Feb 1902 - d 2 Sept 1962, CRO

Rae, b 1879 - d 1926, CRO

McKINEY, Rankins, b 11 May

McKINEY (continued)
1844 - d 8 Sept 1922,
BRD
McKINNEY, ----, b 13 May
1872 - d 2 Nov 1880, CLC
Allen James, b 16 Apr 1908
- d 26 July 1975, LBR
Arthur R, b 5 July 1910 -
d 12 Dec 1960, NWP
Geneva M, b 27 Sept 1912 -
no death date, NWP
Jane E, b 23 Dec 1877 - d
5 May 1954, CRO
McKINNY, William A, b 14
July 1881 - no death
date, CRO
McLAUGHIN, John, no dates,
DVS
McMAHON, Bessie M, b 31
March 1893 - d 26 Feb
1963, CRO
Eva, b 1901 - d 1953, CRO
James S, b 17 Sept 1885 -
d 30 Oct 1961, CRO
Mollie, b 1883 - d 1963,
CRO
Ruth, b 1892 - d 1931, CRO
Venatia Grace, b 5 Nov
1925 - d 11 Jan 1929,
CRO
McNEAL, James L, b 9 Sept
1897 - d 14 May 1973,
LBR
John L, b 26 June 1852 - d
26 Aug 1904, LBR
Martha Jackson, b 30 March
1866 - d 14 Jan 1954,
LBR
Ruby E Kenwick, b 3 Oct
1901 - d 24 July 1966,
LBR
McNEELY, Peggy, d 21 Jan
1979, ae 43y, NWP
McNISH, Wiley L, b -- Apr
1901 - d -- Feb 1972,
WRJ
McPETERS, Ailcy, b 12 Dec
1933 - d 1 Jan 1907, FLF

McPETERS (continued)
Beuna, b 15 Feb 1885 - d
14 Oct 1914, FLF
Conrad, d 1 Dec 1977, ae
57y, FLF
Gilbert, d 1 March 1980,
ae 61y, LBR
Harriet, b 31 March 1859 -
d 13 June 1859, UNN
Inman, b 4 May 1866 - d 7
June 1935, LBR
Jane, b 4 Feb 1855 - d 10
March 1919, FLF
John, b 10 June 1830 - d
11 Nov 1882, FLF
John, b 4 May 1866 - d 12
Jan 1957, LBR
John H, b 24 Dec 1880 - d
17 March 1918, FLF
Joyce, b 7 Oct 1910 - d 8
June 1911, FLF
Leroy, b 1826 - d 30 June
1901, UNN
Letitia Hall, b 1861 - d
27 Apr 1911, LBR
Malinda, b 24 Dec 1851 - d
8 June 1926, UNN
Manda, b 11 May 1884 - d
20 Oct 1896, FLF
Margaret, b 15 Nov 1857 -
14 June 1941, FLF
Martha A, b 15 July 11866
- no death date, UNN
Nancy, b 31 March 1834 - d
23 June 1917, UNN
Naomi, b 5 Aug 1908 - no
death date, LBR
Riley, b 18 Dec 1888 - d
15 Apr 1963, LBR
Rosey, b 12 Aug 1893 - d
15 June 1894, FLF
Rufus, b 3 Feb 1838 - d 19
May 1885, UNN
Saloma Ann, b 23 May 1831
- d 18 May 1888, UNN
Samson S, b 1 Aug 1856 - d
30 Apr 1891, UNN
Susan F, b 5 Oct 1884 - d

McPETERS (continued)
10 May 1960, LBR
Terry Lynn, b 14 Oct 1951
- d 19 July 1968, LBR
Vernia, b 14 Dec 1876 - d
23 Dec 1876, FLF
William Arthur, b 22 Nov
1866 - d 13 Aug 1967,
FLF
William Clyde, b 1 March
1914 - d 14 Nov 1916,
FLF
William E, b 13 Dec 1858 -
d 11 July 1886, UNN
Wm Jennings, d 19 June
1973, ae 33y, FLF
MACKS, Ella R, b 22 Oct
1922 - d 7 Apr 1981, FLR
Harry Jr, b 31 Oct 1912 -
d 26 June 1972, FLR
Harry Sr, b 28 Jan 1891 -
d 13 Feb 1964, DRL
Helen, b 18 March 1893 - d
1 March 1973, DRL
MADEN, Arthur F, d 19 Aug
1979, ae 86y, ELZ
Augusta, b 18 Aug 1875 - d
12 June 1961, ELZ
David Ray, b&d 28 Nov
1942, ELZ
Floyd, twin s/o Wm &
Augusta (see Loyd), 19
Dec ----, ELZ
Geneva, b 1 July 1919 - d
17 May 1949, ELZ
Infant s/o Wm & Augusta,
no dates, ELZ
James Franklin, b 5 March
1877 - d 27 Oct 1966,
ELZ
John, b 27 March 1874 - d
6 March 1927, ELZ
John M, b 4 Nov 1835 - d 9
Oct 1904, ELZ
Juanita Webb, d 24 Dec
1978, ae 52y, ELZ
Julia, d 9 May 1977, ae
71y, ELZ

MADEN (continued)
Loyd, twin s/o Wm &
Augusta (see Floyd), 19
Dec ----, ELZ
Margaret Garrett, b 9 Feb
1868 - d 6 June 1959,
ELZ
Mary, b 1839 - d 22 Nov
1918, ELZ
Rufus H, b 5 Aug 1866 - d
15 Jan 1927, ELZ
Savannah McCartt, b 16
March 1895 - d 20 May
1961, ELZ
Will C, b 29 July 1868 - d
31 March 1959, ELZ
William, b 19 Dec 1868 - d
8 May 1914, ELZ
MAHAN, Ohmer Otto, b 3 June
1896 (?) - d 26 Aug 1893
(?), DRL
MAISEMAN, C R, b 9 June
1923 - d 19 Oct 1900,
DRL
MALONE, Cora L, b 30 Nov
1902 - d 13 Aug 1976,
WRC
Otis, b 6 Dec 1902 - d 15
March 1969, WRC
MALTHON, Larry Gene, b 5
Nov 1953 - d 26 Feb
1977, FRC
MANI, Inf, no dates, MSG
MANTEL, Sarah C, d 1 March
1979, ae 73y, MST
MARKLEY, Helen Aleta, b 6
Feb 1886 - no death
date, SNB
John S, b 31 Jan 1877 - d
26 Dec 1934, SNB
MARLOW, Beechem, b 2 June
1915 - d 2 Dec 1973, LBR
Lillie, no birth date - d
1893, NWP
Sarah, b 22 June 1921 - no
death date, LBR
Virgie, b 1898 - d 1963,
NWP

MARSH, James Orville, b 7 June 1898 - d 22 Feb 1967, DRL
MARSHALL, Augusta Jane, b 3 Nov 1866 - d 23 Nov 1943, SNB
MARTIN, Mr, no dates, MSG
A J, b 14 Jan 1834 - d 11 Aug 1896, WRC
Miss Anita, b 1903 - d 2 Aug 1978, MST
Arthur, b 6 Aug 1884 - d 19 Nov 1931, DVS
Claudette, b 24 Feb 1941 - d 17 Jan 1950, DVS
Fred, d 24 Apr ----, ae 32y, DVS
James L, b 22 July 1893 - d 20 Aug 1954, CBJ
Mary L, b 27 May 1886 - d 22 Feb 1918, DVS
Oscar, b 19 Jan 1896 - d 6 Feb 1913, CBJ
Ruth, d 23 Nov 1970, ae 64y, CBJ
MARTZ, Louis A, b 18 Apr 1856 - d 26 Aug 1889, WRC
MASHBURN, William S, d 12 Dec 1974, ae 84y, PTC
MASLIGER, Julia Hall, b 22 Feb 1912 - d 2 May 1969, WRC
MASON, C L, b 28 Feb 1880 - d 7 Feb 1900, DRL
Charles, no dates, DRL
Edith M, no dates, DRL
Edith M, b 19 Oct 1874 - d 10 Sept 1901, DRL
Henry F, b 22 March 1840 - d 4 Feb 1904, SNB
Joe H, b 26 Nov 1880 - d 13 Oct 1944, PLR
Maggie L, b 8 Apr 1881 - d 18 June 1952, PLR
Mary J, b 26 Jan 1837 - d 4 March 1914, SNB
MASSENGALE, Dicie, d 26 May

MASSENGALE (continued) 1978, ae 64y, NWP
Ernest S, b 1901 - d 1957, WRC
Larry T, d 14 Aug 1979, ae 21y, UNN
MASSENGILL, Bobbie Dean, d 27 June 1937, ae 3y 17da, NWP
Carrie Lou, b 3 March 1945 - d 18 March 1946, OLP
Clarence D, b 27 Apr 1942 - d 11 Jan 1961, NWP
Clifford, b 9 Aug 1949 - d 10 Feb 1950, STP
Franklin C, b 23 March 1941 - d 7 Oct 1963, NWP
George Billy, b 23 June 1933 - d 3 Sept 1933, OLP
Jimmie Ray, b&d 22 Aug 1939, NWP
Mary E McCoy, b 14 Jan 1887 - d 23 July 1963, NWP
Mollie K, b 15 June 1915 - d 3 Apr 1952, NWP
Peggy Joe, b 13 May 1942 - d 19 Dec 1958, NWP
Raymond, b 13 Dec 1944 - d 16 Sept 1947, NWP
Roger Lee, b 12 Jan 1941 - d 15 March 1941, NWP
Scott Edward, d 26 Dec 1963, ae 1mo, NWP
Thomas, b 9 Jan 1903 - d 10 Nov 1963, NWP
William, b 12 March 1870 - d 12 Aug 1942, NWP
MASSEY, Daisy, b 5 Apr 1890 - d 11 June 1891, SNB
Willie L, b 8 July 1886 - d 19 May 1887, SNB
Zina, b&d 19 May 1888, SNB
MATHESON, Cassie, d 12 Oct 1978, ae 86y, ELZ
Ruby Jackline, b 9 Feb 1926 - d 6 Jan 1928, ELZ

MATHEWS, Jack, d 10 June
1976, ae 56y, BRR
Minnie Young, b 15 May
1889 - no death date,
BRR
Rebecca Mc, b 4 March 1867
- no death date, BRR
W M, b 10 Sept 1860 - d 17
Aug 1933, BRR
William H, b 14 Apr 1889 -
d 17 Oct 1945, BRR
MATHIS, Aaron Randolph, b 7
Sept 1914 - d 21 July
1958, WRC
Brenda, b 1960 - d 1971,
CRO
Dalton, d 15 Jan 1975, ae
57y, MSG
Donald R (Buzz), b 15 Feb
1950 - d 18 May 1971,
MSG
Dorothy Collins, b 26 May
1920 - no death date,
WRC
Florence Langley, b 21 Jan
1879 - d 19 Dec 1963,
MSG
Jake L, b 21 Oct 1868 - d
13 May 1958, MSG
Jessie Lee, b 22 Aug 1905
- d 26 Apr 1971, WRC
John Leonard, b 1900 - d
1970, MSG
John M, b 17 Feb 1878 - d
22 Sept 1901, MSG
John M, b 5 Nov 1901 - d
24 May 1973, WRC
Karen, b 13 May 1954 - d
13 May 1954, WRC
Louisa A, b 27 June 1839 -
d 1 Apr 1921, MSG
Luther, b 23 Jan 1899 - d
14 Apr 1970, CRO
Lydia Williams, b 5 Apr
1874 - d 17 Feb 1946,
MSG
Marshal O, b 4 Dec 1870 -
d 31 Jan 1954, MSG

MATHIS (continued)
Peter, d 9 Dec 1973, ae
74y, WMG
Peter L, b 21 Oct 1838 - d
24 Aug 1902, MSG
Sallie Honeycutt, b 3 Oct
1872 - d 13 Sept 1900,
LBR
Stepen Warren, d 2 June
1955, ae 3mo 29da, CRO
Thelma V, b 5 Aug 1904 -
no death date, CRO
Thos A, b 24 Dec 1905 - d
21 Aug 1975, LBR
V, b 1 Oct 1855 - d 21
March 1890, WRC
Wanda Jones, b 24 Apr 1952
- no death date, MSG
MATTI, Sharon J, b 25 Sept
1943 - d 9 Feb 1974, DRL
MAXWELL, Joseph Callier, d
7 June 1968, ae 4y 11mo,
LBR
MAY, Charlie, b 8 June 1897
- d 26 Aug 1929, DVS
Dollie, b&d 16 July 1918,
CBJ
Jack, b 11 Apr 1901 - d 16
Oct 1918, CBJ
Sarah, b 1880 - d 1951,
CBJ
Sinah, b 20 Dec 1812 - d
19 Aug 1883, WRC
Verdie J, b 23 Aug 1899 -
d 29 Jan 1900, OLP
Vidie E, b 20 March 1901 -
d 19 Sept 1902, OLP
William, d 6 Dec 1959, ae
84y, CBJ
MAYS, Erwin Lavender, b 8
Aug 1888 - no death
date, LNE
James J, b 13 Oct 1888 - d
6 March 1960, LNE
Jimmy Leon, b 20 June 1955
- d 13 Nov 1974, LNE
MAYTON, Harve, b 9 June
1890 - d 18 Feb 1942,

MAYTON (continued)
CBJ
Oril Sr, b 15 June 1904 -
d 5 March 1973, DVS
Ruby A, b 1 Aug 1922 - no
death date, DVS
MEERS, Zennery Ernest, b&d
15 July 1929, PNY
MEISTER, Adam, b 1860 - d
1953, DRL
Annie, b 1863 - d 1928,
DRL
Harold, d 4 Dec 1979, ae
77y, MST
MELHORN, Alex F, b 16 Apr
1882 - d 20 March 1919,
WRC
Anna Emila, b 2 Aug 1879 -
d 29 Dec 1907, WRC
Anna Heidel, b 10 Dec 1861
- d 25 May 1935, WRC
Anna Maria, b 24 Oct 1882
- d 7 Nov 1935, WRC
Arthur Roger, d 14 May
1981, ae 46y, WRC
Benjamin A, b 25 Aug 1891
- d 1 March 1911, DRM
Benjamin Otto, b 22 June
1892 - d 4 Apr 1971, WRC
Bobby K, b 21 Sept 1931 -
d 13 July 1932, WRC
C F, b 22 Aug 1843 - d 12
Dec 1901, WRC
Christian Fred, b 6 May
1820 - d 3 May 1884, DRM
Dorathea, b 12 Oct 1886 -
no death date, WRC
Edward V, b 4 July 1895 -
d 7 Sept 1955, WRC
Elsie S, b 23 Dec 1912 -
no death date, WRC
Emma, b 13 Aug 1860 - d 14
Feb 1935, DRM
Emma Estella, d 28 Sept
1981, ae 84y, WRC
Fred O, d 12 Jan 1979, ae
94y, DRM
Frederick Edmon, d 9 July

MELHORN (continued)
1979, ae 69y, DRM
Frederick O Jr, b 19 Sept
1922 - d 17 Apr 1945,
DRM
Henry G, b 1886 - d 1929,
WRC
Human F, b 20 Aug 1850 - d
12 Dec 1912, WRC
Infant, b&d -- June 1880,
DRM
Infant, 5 March 1943, DRM
James Michael, b 17 Aug
1956 - d 9 June 1959,
WRC
John F, b 28 Feb 1884 - d
13 Oct 1955, DRM
John T, b 10 July 1874 - d
17 Nov 1919, WRC
Josephine, b 22 Jan 1900 -
d 9 Nov 1940, DRM
K W, b 22 Apr 1902 - d 29
Apr 1902, DRM
Marcella, b 2 Dec 1914 - d
4 May 1918, DRM
Margaret, b 3 Feb 1848 - d
17 Dec 1910, WRC
Mary A, b 1889 - d 1972,
WRC
Robert Lee, b 10 Sept 1923
- d 6 Nov 1926, DRM
Ruby Redmon, d 9 Feb 1980,
ae 62y, WRC
Rudolph F, b 8 March 1879
- d 10 Dec 1879, DRM
Mrs Russia, d 23 May 1979,
ae 75y, UNN
Steve, 13 Jan 1950, DRM
Vesta Arlena, b 26 Oct
1892 - d 18 May 1953,
WRC
Walter T, b 4 Dec 1905 - d
15 Feb 1970 , WRC
Willimina, b 4 July 1819 -
d 20 Nov 1899, DRM
MELTON, Alpha L, b 17 Nov
1904 - d 6 Oct 1967, CLC
Amanda L, b 29 July 1860 -

MELTON (continued)
d 9 March 1934, CLC
Annie, b 1902 - d 1948,
CLC
Annie, b 1886 - d 1927,
CLC
Artie E, b 1864 - d 1965,
CLC
Boyd, b 30 May 1905 - d 1
Jan 1911, CLC
Charles Futi (or Foote),
Pvt 3 Co WWI, b 1 Oct
1893 - d 1 June 1958,
WRC
Charlie, b 1892 - d 1964,
CLC
Christine, b 13 Jan 1930 -
d 10 July 1934, CLC
Clayton, b 23 Jan 1915 - d
19 Aug 1919, CLC
Columbia Ann, b 18 May
1877 - d 29 Nov 1945,
EST
Columbus, b 15 Aug 1868 -
d 17 Oct 1948, CLC
David Elmer, b 10 Aug 1902
- d 15 Apr 1956, CLC
Ed, b 24 Oct 1872 - d 10
Sept 1934, EST
Miss Edna, d 25 June 1980,
ae 71y, CLC
Edwin R, b 21 Jan 1929 - d
19 March 1929, CLC
Emons, b 20 March 1895 - d
18 Aug 1898, CLC
Ermadian, b 9 Sept 1938 -
d 16 Jan 1939, CLC
Eugene, b 29 Jan 1933 - d
22 July 1934, CLC
Eveline Hatfield, b 24 May
1834 - d 10 Nov 1887,
CLC
Freeman, d 27 Nov 1980, ae
52y, WRC
G Finley, b 30 Jan 1887 -
d 6 June 1921, CLC
Geneviene E, b 23 Aug 1920
- d 16 Jan 1936, WRC

MELTON (continued)
George, b 1845 - d 1895,
PTC
Gertrude Mae, b 10 Aug
1903 - d 21 Oct 1964,
CLC
Grady V, b 7 June 1918 - d
7 Aug 1918, CLC
H Baalam, b 20 Feb 1874 -
d 23 Jan 1967, CLC
Henry, b 18 Oct 1818 - d
21 June 1882, CLC
Henry E, b 15 Dec 1895 - d
4 Aug 1968, CLC
Hugh G, b 13 June 1911 - d
1 June 1939, CLC
Ida, b 25 Aug 1888 - d 1
Dec 1911, EST
Infant Son, b&d 7 Oct
1911, EST
Infant, s/o Elmer, no
dates, CLC
Isom, b 15 June 1797 - d 5
Dec 1880, UNN
James H, b 11 Nov 1883 - d
30 Aug 1966, NWP
James W, b 1849 - d 1927,
CLC
James W, b 24 Feb 1831 - d
7 Aug 1908, CLC
Jewel, b 29 Sept 1907 - d
19 Nov 1918, CLC
Kenneth R, d 26 July 1981,
ae 31y, CLC
L C Hank, b 13 Apr 1884 -
d 30 Jan 1954, CLC
Laura Etta, b 12 Dec 1869
- d 10 Nov 1923, CLC
Lou, b 30 Aug 1873 - d 30
Oct 1961, CLC
Lucy, b 15 March 1793 - d
1858, UNN
Luther J, b 4 Oct 1905 - d
21 Apr 1935, CLC
Margaret A, b 25 Dec 1876
- d 24 Oct 1959, CLC
Mary E, b 22 Sept 1929 - d
10 July 1903, CLC

MELTON (continued)

Mary Jane, b 1852 - d 1923, CLC

Minerva, b 18 May 1903 - no death date, CLC

N B, b 14 Feb 1860 - d 5 May 1924, CLC

Nancy, b 1850 - d 1930, PTC

Orpha J, b 16 Nov 1893 - d 23 July 1903, CLC

Patricia, b&d 1927, CLC

Royal Freedom, b 28 March 1930 - d 5 Sept 1931, WRC

Russell H, d 19 July 1981, ae 45y, CLC

Wilburn C, b 16 Oct 1878 - d 18 May 1931, CLC

William H, b 16 Jan 1938 - d 2 Dec 1938, CLC

MENDELL, Nova Lee, b 18 March 1918 - no death date, EST

William H, b 6 Apr 1912 - d 3 Dec 1968, EST

MEREDITH, June Carson, b 26 May 1925 - d 16 Sept 1957, WRC

Laurence Dinton, b 30 Dec 1924 - no death date, WRC

Beeler B, b 7 Dec 1901 - no death date, DVS

Ruby, b 16 Dec 1921 - d 5 Apr 1970, DVS

MERONEY, Rev U S, b 22 May 1865 - d 10 Jan 1962, EST

METCALF, Frank, b 11 Oct 1865 - d 6 Jan 1938, OLP

Frank Jr, b 27 Sept 1905 - d 14 Nov 1917, OLP

Infant, b 9 May 1904 - d 12 May 1904, OLP

Lula, b 1 Apr 1871 - d 15 Dec 1932, OLP

Maggie L, b 17 May 1902 -

METCALF (continued)

d 26 Feb 1915, OLP

MILAS, Lena Kelley, b 12 Jan 1887 - d 2 Jan 1956, DVS

MILHORN, Durart T, d 15 Apr 1979, ae 42y, WMG

Joseph, 8 July 1968 - no other date, LNC

Walter Ray, b 30 May ---- - d 14 July ----, LNC

MILLER, Alex, d 2 Apr 1942, ae 72y, LNC

Anna Pagel, b 8 June 1849 - d 26 Dec 1938, DRL

August, b 10 Aug 1852 - d 14 July 1921, DRL

Calvin N, b 29 Dec 1896 - d 22 Jan 1960, BRR

Charley, b 11 Apr 1861 - d 6 Sept 1926, CRO

Clara, b 25 May 1903 - d 14 Aug 1978, JCJ

Edna M, b 15 May 1907 - d 10 Sept 1967, WMG

F S, b 18 March 1848 - d 10 March 1908, SNB

Gideon, d 3 Jan 1981, ae 84y, WMG

Harriett, b 10 July 1887 - d 22 Dec 1954, DVS

Harry, d 9 Apr 1942, ae 47y, CRO

Rev Hobert, b 1900 - d 21 March 1975, JCJ

Infant, b 14 Dec 1918 - d 26 March 19--, MLC

James M, b 26 Sept 1886 - d 19 Feb 1966, WMG

Jerry A, b 23 Sept 1944 - d 7 May 1954, LBR

John Henry, d 8 Apr 1977, ae 70y, BRR

John R, d 28 May 1979, ae 59y, WMG

Julia, b 21 July 1901 - d 30 Nov 1965, WRC

June, b 10 Jan 1935 - d 5

MILLER (continued)
Jan 1943, WRC
Junior, b 27 Feb 1926 - d
21 Jan 1944, WRC
Lewis, b 15 Sept 1867 - d
9 Feb 1923, CRO
Lizzie, b 13 Feb 1861 - d
6 July 1926, CRO
Maynard, b 7 Apr 1908 - d
3 Sept 1947, WRC
Minnie S, b 3 Apr 1879 -
no death date, CRO
Otis D, d 16 Dec 1979, ae
58y, WMG
Pauline, d 2 June 1974, ae
78y, WMG
Pearl, d 13 Feb 1971, ae
84y, CBJ
Pearlie, d 12 May 1980, ae
67y, DRL
Reba, b 30 Dec 1929 - d 4
Sept 1936, ELZ
Roscoe C, b 30 Apr 1916 -
d 30 Apr 1949, DVS
Ruth J, b 2 Dec 1901 - d
28 July 1973, BRR
Vera, b 1877 - d 1965, LNC
MILLS, Lou C, b 23 May 1907
- no death date, CRO
Louis T, Pfc Co C 88 Co
Mtr Bat WWII, b 30 Jan
1907 - d 10 Oct 1965,
CRO
MINEY, John D, b 18 May
1884 - d 28 March 1964,
EST
Virginia W, b 5 Apr 1894 -
d 2 Aug 1967, EST
MINNS, Alfred George, b 17
Nov 1890 - d 5 Jan 1901,
OLP
MINTON, Ruth Ann, b 22 Feb
1898 - d 24 May 1943,
CBJ
MITCHELL, Maude, b 15 Sept
1890 - d 27 Oct 1890,
SNB
MITEMAN, Marie Morris, b 20

MITEMAN (continued)
Apr 1876 - d 4 May 1955,
PLR
MITTS, Ben, b 15 Dec 1888 -
d 6 May 1956, DVS
Mary Ines, d 3 March 1966,
ae 72y, DVS
MOATES, Edith, b 19 Sept
1915 - d 12 Feb 1919,
LVN
Everett, b 23 Feb 1917 - d
28 Jan 1919, LVN
Kenneth, b 25 Nov 1927 - d
1 Sept 1929, CRO
L C, b 8 Dec 1884 - d 22
Jan 1929, CRO
Marie, b 26 Aug 1914 - d 5
Nov 1914, LVN
MOHN, Dr R P, b 26 Sept
1866 - d 29 Jan 1898,
WRC
MOLTHEN, Larry Gene, d 26
Feb 1979, ae 23y, MST
MOLYNEUX, John, b 18 May
1882 - d 20 March 1885,
RGB
Richard, b 3 Apr 1885 - d
16 July 1885, RGB
MONDAY, Audrey L, b 7 Aug
1928 - d 1 May 1938, BRW
Byrd, Pfc Co G 6 Inf WWI,
b 28 Dec 1894 - d 13 Oct
1965, BRW
Clifford, b 10 June 1908 -
d 21 Aug 1953, PNY
Dean, b 3 Jan 1927 - d 17
Aug 1932, PNY
John, b 1872 - d 1924, PNY
Josie Cooper, b 18 June
1902 - d 10 May 1953,
PNY
Ollie, b 26 July 1903 - no
death date, BRW
Versa E, b 21 March 1894 -
d 13 Sept 1932, PNY
MONG, Bess C, b 22 Aug 1871
- d 29 Jan 1957, WRC
Joe I, b 27 July 1871 - d

MONG (continued)
13 Jan 1951, WRC
Mary P, b 31 Aug 1896 - d
15 Jan 1963, WRC
Myrtle May Neely, b 20 May
1903 - d 22 May 1940,
UNH
Ralph L, b 14 July 1896 -
d 13 Dec 1961, WRC
Wilhorn Benton, b 18 Aug
1922 - d 13 March 1949,
WRC
MONHALLEN, Norris Wendell,
d 14 Apr 1974, ae 36y,
WMG
MONROE, Ruth Louise, b 10
March 1923 - d 2 July
----, WRC
MOODY, Marion, b 1882 - d
1921, DRL
MOORE, Arthur M, b 11 Aug
1896 - 29 Jan 1962, EST
Carolin Augusta, b 14 July
1886 - d 28 June 1940,
WRC
Charles b, b 17 Dec 1889 -
d 9 Apr 1923, PNY
Emmaline, b 19 Aug 1885 -
d 23 Apr 1941, LNE
Miss Ida Mae, d 21 Aug
1978, ae 66y, WRC
J C, b 1 June 1853 - d 18
Oct 1922, LNG
J E, b 7 Jan 1878 - d 8 Feb
1946, WRC
J W, b 1853 - d 27 March
1907, PNY
Jane, b 25 Nov 1882 - d 15
Dec 1962, CRO
Jim, b 1911 - d 1950, NWP
Joe M, b 10 May 1853 - d
20 May 1941, PNY
John Fred, b 19 Sept 1905
- d 21 May 1971, WRC
Mary Jane, b 30 Sept 1858
- d 10 Dec 1912, LNG
Millie, b 22 May 1847 - d
16 Dec 1932, PNY

MOORE (continued)
Nena L, b 31 Jan 1907 - d
17 July 1951, CRO
Miss Rubenia, d 17 Sept
1978, ae 71y, WRC
Sarah, b 12 May 1865 - d 6
Feb 1924, LBR
Sylvester, b 24 Sept 1879
- d 4 June 1945, LNE
Viola, b&d 14 Aug 1909,
PNY
Virginia, d 1951, CRO
William H, b 14 Dec 1905 -
8 Sept 1953, CRO
William Robert, b 7 Dec
1907 - d 2 Aug 1970, WRC
MORGAN, Albert, b 10 May
1873 - d 31 July 1951,
LBR
Alex, b 1887 - d 6 June
1938, MNT
Alexander, b 11 Dec 1870 -
d 6 June 1937, MNT
Alfred W, b 5 May 1876 - d
14 July 1946, BRR
Artemia, b 11 Feb 1897 -
no death date, PLR
Augmon, d 10 Jan 1978, ae
56y, UNG
B M, b 7 July 1861 - d 25
July 1930, RTT
Badie, b 27 May 1886 - d 8
June 1952, LBR
Belle Lyons, b 1872 - d
1961, DRL
Bertha Osborne, b 7 Jan
1888 - d 14 June 1951,
LBR
Bessie B, b 1908 - no
death date, WRC
Bessie Malone, b 9 Feb
1907 - d 14 May 1941,
PNY
Bill, d 7 March 1976, ae
89y, WRJ
Bobby Jean, b 25 June 1928
- d 13 Dec 1931, UNN
Brenda Carol, b 5 Jan 1948

MORGAN (continued)
- d 11 Feb 1948, PNY
Carl, b 3 Aug 1953 - d 3
Dec 1953, LBR
Charles, b 16 Jan 1920 - d
18 June 1976, LBR
Charles V, d 16 June 1970,
ae 56y, LBR
Charley W, b 26 Apr 1888 -
d 16 Oct 1907, UNN
Clara, b 1898 - d 1957,
SHD
Cleo Henry, d 23 Apr 1978,
ae 60y, UNG
Clifford, b 15 Apr 1901 -
d 24 Aug 1931, LBR
Della, b 19 May 1862 - d
22 March 1934, RTT
Delmer, b 19 March 1914 -
d 6 July 1914, PNY
Dillie J, b 15 Nov 1880 -
d 13 Dec 1966, BRR
Donald Ray, b 7 Jan 1949 -
d 18 Jan 1949, NWP
Donnie Earl, b 14 Feb 1949
- d 21 March 1949, PNY
Rev Edd, d 1 March 1974,
ae 56y, LBR
Elmer, b 19 March 1914 - d
6 July 1914, PNY
Ethel S, b 14 June 1891 -
d 23 Oct 1971, UNG
Eva Jane, b 1 Feb 1920 - d
17 May 1936, MNT
George, b 1894 - d 1968,
SHD
George C, b 28 May 1902 -
d 10 Feb 1968, NWP
George Carson, b 25 Apr
1939 - d 23 Aug 1939,
PLR
George W, b 1882 - d 1958,
DRL
Gilmer Elmer, b 15 Oct
1906 - d 10 Jan 1965,
UNN
Haywood, no dates, UNN
Horace F, b 14 Oct 1895 -

MORGAN (continued)
d 5 Apr 1969, PLR
Infant, b&d 15 Aug 1950,
NWP
J H, no birth date - d 19
June 1924, PNY
James Arthur, b 8 Nov 1911
- d 20 July 1912, SNB
James V, b 23 June 1923 -
d 23 May 1962, UNG
Jennie, b 14 Oct 1884 - d
22 July 1898, RTT
Jessie J, d 6 June 1975,
ae 59y, LNE
John, b 8 Aug 1835 - d 16
May 1866, UNN
John F, b 20 Oct 1890 - d
2 March 1961, UNN
John G, b 19 Jan 1877 - d
20 July 1919, LBR
John Sr, d 11 May 1976, ae
52y, LBR
John T, b 12 July 1838 - d
21 Feb 1891, UNN
Johnnie F, Cpl Co A 163
Eng WWII, b 24 July 1908
(1909?) - d 1 (7?) June
1964, WRC
Juanita, b 9 Dec 1917 - d
3 Nov 1941, PNY
Julia, b 3 Aug 1880 - d 30
June 1928, ELZ
Kathy Mae, d 2 June 1960,
ARM
Kenneth Cair, b 7 Apr 1935
- d 28 Apr 1974, LBR
L B, b 29 Aug 1920 - d 5
Oct 1920, LBR
L D, dates illegible, LBR
Lawrence, b 1921 - d 5 Nov
1974, CRO
Lisa Rene, b 1 Apr 1960 -
d 16 June 1960, NWP
Lora Alice, b 1 May 1844 -
d 28 Oct 1940, LBR
Louise Buxton, b 25 Sept
1910 - d 17 July 1968,
DRL

MORGAN (continued)

Loyed David, b 26 Jan 1938 - d 9 Sept 1938, LBR

Lucile Bodine, b 6 June 1929 - d 13 March 1949, WRC

Lucy F, b 5 Oct 1886 - d 23 Sept 1883, UNN

Luther E, USN WWII, b 26 Oct 1917 - d 1 March 1974, LBR

Mae, b 2 Feb 1920 - d 11 Aug 1945, PLR

Maggie, b 23 Dec 1891 - d 19 Nov 1933, WRJ

Mahala Jane, b 26 Jan 1849 - d 15 May 1915, MNT

Marlene G, b 29 May 1906 - no death date, NWP

Martha, b 10 Oct 1874 - d 21 May 1894, MNT

Mary Jane, b 27 Apr 1887 - d 13 Feb 1967, MNT

Mathew Allen, b 26 March 1972 - d 5 Apr 1972, BRN

Minnie, b 10 Nov 1889 - d 19 July 1899, RTT

Myrtle R, b 20 May 1917 - no death date, UNN

Nancy J, b 21 July 1852 - d 26 Aug 1940, LBR

Nellie Carroll, b 25 March 1918 - no death date, LBR

Oather A, b 3 Oct 1921 - d 4 March 1960, MNT

Ollie Dyer, b 30 Sept 1904 - d 1 June 1954, ELZ

Pat, b 25 Jan 1907 - d 19 July 1968, DRL

Paul, b 25 June 1955 - d 27 Dec 1959, UNN

Paul Richard, b 1 Nov 1953 - d 11 Nov 1976, LBR

Polly Ann Foster, b 3 Nov 1881 - d 10 Sept 1960, PNY

Robert, b 18 Apr 1895 - d

MORGAN (continued)

21 July 1923, UNN

Roma Lee, 1 Jan 1967, UNN

Samuel, b 2 May 1880 - d 14 Dec 1963, UNG

Vance, b 7 June 1880 - d 28 Nov 1929, LBR

Violet S, b 29 June 1929 - d 2 Nov 1932, MNT

Virgil, b 30 Sept 1911 - d 27 Feb 1915, PNY

Virginia Mae, b 31 Jan 1916 - d 18 Nov 1919, WRJ

W F, b 27 March 1884 - d 28 July 1918, LBR

Wade Dean, d 14 Mar 1962, ARM

William E, b 8 Oct 1910 - d 26 May 1974, UNN

Woodrow, no dates, UNN

MORRIS, Arvil A, b 1913 - d 1956, UNG

Charles W, b 19 Dec 1872 - d 21 Dec 1930, PLR

Cornelia F, b 1849 - d 1942, DRL

Dora Kries, b 15 Dec 1880 - d 26 July 1952, WRC

Edwin Oscar, b 11 Aug 1879 - d 13 Aug 1880, MRR

Miss Fay, d 16 Aug 1981, ARM

George, b 12 Dec 1976 - d 1 Dec 1955, UNG

George Balan, b 29 Apr 1883 - d 19 May 1891, MRR

Hattie, b 30 March 1895 - d 19 Feb 1964, WRC

Lloyd, b 22 Apr 1916 - d 5 Sept 1937, UNG

Margaret V, b 20 March 1880 - d 2 March 1932, UNG

Mary J, b 31 Aug 1852 - d 12 July 1901, MRR

Mary S, b 25 Jan 1874 - d

MORRIS (continued)
14 March 1951, PLR
Nancy Hanks, b 31 Dec 1814
- d 17 March 1901, MRR
Thomas Asbury, b 30 Nov
1852 - d 1 Jan 1941, WRC
Thomas O, b 7 Oct 1888 - d
1 March 1952, WRC
Vane B, b 17 Nov 1875 - d
30 Mar 1949, WRC
William Fay, b 15 March
1904 - d 12 Apr 1966,
EST
Willis, b 14 July 1805 - d
7 Oct 1870, MRR
MORRISON, J John, b 15 Aug
1868 - d 24 March 1965,
WRJ
James D, b 1 Nov 1900 - d
30 Dec 1975, CRO
Ona Jackson, b 3 Nov 1880
- d 13 Jan 1947, WRJ
MORTON, A Hix, b 9 June
1904 - d 29 May 1967,
EST
Gardina Payne, d 29 March
1979, ae 44y, UNG
Nancy C, b 2 March 1866 -
d 30 May 1903, DVS
Ruby J, b 10 Sept 1909 -
no death date, EST
MOSIER, Delia, b 11 July
1865 - d 20 March 1937,
MLC
Dorcas E, b 1791 - d 20
Sept 1886, ELZ
Elizabeth, b 15 Dec 1832 -
d 17 May 1907, SNB
James A, b 17 Nov 1864 - d
25 Nov 1936, SNB
Jim, d 30 Oct 1978, ae
67y, SNB
John W, b 23 Feb 1862 - d
20 March 1935, MLC
Lewis Henry, b 3 March
1876 - d 2 Nov 1880, SNB
Louis H, b 3 Oct 1825 - d
13 Feb 1897, SNB

MOSIER (continued)
Miella Magnolia, b 31 Dec
1866 - d 15 Sept 1882,
SNB
Sam E, b 22 Sept 1900 - d
15 July 1939, SNB
MOSS, Duke M, b 1 Jan 1898
- d 9 May 1960, BRZ
MOZER, Carl August, b 1 Jan
1802 - d 5 Jan 1851, WRC
MULLINS, Allen Keith, b 19
Nov 1962 - d 20 Nov
1962, EST
Bessie, b 11 June 1902 - d
7 May 1926, OLP
Ernest, b 7 Jan 1924 - d
24 Jan 1926, OLP
Johie C, b 11 Apr 1949 - d
7 March 1966, EST
John, b 1862 - d 1934, NWP
Kate, b 1867 - d 1937, NWP
Larry Leon, d 4 Sept 1953,
ae 2y 7mo, NWP
Nannie, b 15 Feb 1882 - d
13 July 1916, OLP
Nellie B, b 3 July 1916 -
d 3 Oct 1916, OLP
MURPHY, Mary K, b 16 Nov
1922 - d 21 Nov 1974,
CRO
MURRAY, Ben S, d 21 June
1974, ae 54y, BRR
Jane, b 29 June 1847 - d 3
July 1925, BRR
W A, b 25 Jan 1849 - d 23
Sept 1903, BRR
MUSE, Pascal, b 17 Jan 1909
- d 21 July 1968, CRO
MUSGROVE, Wilda L, b 1904 -
d 1969, CRO
NABORS, Clarence Allen, b
1933 - d 1964, WMG
NANCE, Carl Edwin, b&d 3
Apr 1941, LNC
Douglas, d 10 Dec 1974, ae
31y, LBR
Gordon, d 22 May 1975, ae
19y, LBR

NANCE (continued)
Harold, b&d -- Nov 1928, CBJ
Joe, 12 Sept 1918 - no other date, LNC
Lois Ralston, b 1880 - d 1948, CBJ
Mary J, b 1 Aug 1871 - d 25 Sept 1954, LNC
Orvel Arthur, b 30 July 1915 - d 18 Aug 1915, CBJ
Roberta Jean, b 10 July 1939 - d 29 Dec 1939, LNC
Wade, b 23 Nov 1879 - d 18 Feb 1956, CBJ
Wade Jr, b&d -- Dec 1924, CBJ
William B, b 25 Dec 1856 - d 8 March 1940, LNC
William H, b 19 Feb 1937 - d 27 Jan 1970, LBR
William Ray, Cpl USA Korea, d 27 Aug 1976, ae 50y, EST
Winifred, b&d -- Jan 1924, CBJ
NARRIMORE, J S, Co D 2nd MN Cav, no dates, DRL
Marietta A, b 31 Jan 1830 - d 18 May 1911, DRL
NASH, Albert, b 30 Oct 1875 - d 14 Sept 1945, DRL
Dennis Terry, 1950, DRL
Jean Irene, b 8 May 1927 - d 30 July 1928, BRN
Minnie Branstetter, b 26 Feb 1901 - d 16 May 1923, BRN
Zera J, b 25 June 1880 - d 6 Jan 1913, DRL
NEAL, Emma Jae, b 20 Jan 1935 - d 3 June 1965, CRO
I Euge, b 6 Sep 1929 - no death date, CRO
James Bertes, b 10 Apr

NEAL (continued)
1953 - d 9 May 1956, ELZ
NEARHOOD, Floyd H Pap, d 6 Feb 1978, ae 70y, WMG
NEEDHAM, Nellie G, d 4 Apr 1900, ae 26da, DRL
NEEL, Leon Thomas, b 15 Jan 1904 - d 9 Nov 1974, SNB
Rheba Norris, b 1 Nov 1901 - d 26 May 1971, SNB
NEELY, Ben J, b 15 July 1866 - d 12 Nov 1945, UNH
Benjamin, 1913, UNH
Charley E, b 8 Aug 1886 - d 24 Jan 1915, CBJ
Edith, b 29 June 1897 - no death date, UNH
Frank A, b 15 Oct 1920 - d 15 May 1944, UNH
Fred, b 19 Apr 1891 - d 11 June 1959, UNH
Joyce Cochran, d 9 July 1981, ae 55y, UNH
L C, b 2 June 1880 - d 9 June 1942, UNH
Lorene, b 1915 - d 1953, UNH
Mack Allen, b 1957 - d 18 Aug 1973, UNH
Marie, b 5 Feb 1918 - d 11 Feb 1918, UNH
Texan, b 5 Jan 1870 - d 5 July 1899, UNH
Von, b 12 May 1920 - d 12 March 1972, UNH
NEFF, Julia Ann, b 29 Apr 1891 - d 13 June 1961, DVS
NEIL, A J, b 1861 - d 1946, WRC
Clyde S, b 15 Oct 1897 - d 25 June 1921, SNB
Isa J, b 1848 - d 1939, SNB
Leo A, b 9 Jan 1892 - d 6 June 1892, SNB
Mabel, b 16 Nov 1903 - d 2

NEIL (continued)
May 1904, WRC
Mary Doyle, b 6 Oct 1876 -
d 3 March 1972, SNB
P J, b 1848 - d 1914, SNB
Ruth M, b 1941 (?) - d
1908 (?), WRC
Sarah A, b 1866 - d 1938,
WRC
William M, b 13 Oct 1873 -
d 13 July 1955, SNB
William S, b 1856 - d
1935, WRC
NELSON, Alta L, b 11 July
1912 - no death date,
CLC
Ben G, b 14 Apr 1906 - d
13 March 1970, CLC
Bessie Human, b 7 Aug 1900
- d 8 Aug 1971, SNB
Carl E, b 1 Aug 1886 - d
23 May 1968, PLR
Charles J, d 21 March
1978, ae 82y, CLC
Elmer D, b 29 Oct 1918 - d
7 Apr 1924, DRL
Forrest A, d 25 Jan 1979,
ae 80y, CLC
Georginia L, b 23 Apr 1935
- d 27 Oct 1976, BRN
Gloria, b&d 1953, PLR
H Conrad, b 23 May 1895 -
no death date, SNB
Haley Brown, b 30 Oct 1868
- d 12 May 1962, PLR
Harold Edward, b 29 Jan
1923 - d 28 Jan 1944,
PLR
Infant, b 19 May 1908 - d
30 June 1908, CLC
Irene, b 24 May 1924 - d
28 July 1925, CLC
Jack, b 5 Feb 1908 - d 14
July 1908, UNN
James Thomas, b -- March
1889 - d 2 March 1923,
DVS
Lee Hatcher, Pfc Co H 13

NELSON (continued)
Inf WWI, b 26 March
1896 - d 22 Sept 1954,
CRO
Lewis B, b 24 Oct 1887 - d
8 Feb 1892, CLC
Mattie C, b 4 Nov 1886 - d
7 Apr 1943, CLC
Nancy Thornton, b 25 Dec
1858 - d -- March 1932,
DVS
Orval E, b 27 Nov 1920 - d
12 July 1971, PLR
Romea, b 10 Oct 1866 - d
14 Oct 1944, CLC
Sewell W, d 2 July 1975,
ae 74y, CLC
Sylvia, b 23 Dec 1906 - d
17 Nov 1917, CLC
Thomas, b 1850 - d 1913,
DVS
Valera Marie, b 20 Jan
1919 - d 26 Oct 1929,
SNB
William P, b 4 July 1861 -
d 21 Dec 1936, CLC
Wilma, b 24 Oct 1925 - d
14 Oct 1945, CLC
NERENBERG, F A, b 7 Oct
1900 - d 29 Jan 1936,
PLR
NESKAUG, Andreas S, b 17
Sept 1851 - d 12 Apr
1934, DRL
Anna, b 13 June 1909 - d
11 Oct 1909, DRL
Gertrude Lovick, b 185- -
d 1897, DRL
Minnie Lund, b 14 Oct 1865
- d 1 Dec 1949, DRL
NEW, Louann, b 9 Apr 1916 -
d 1 June 1961, PTC
NEWBERRY, Alfred, b 1904 -
d 1921, WRC
Albie, b 7 May 1887 - d 11
March 1909, MNT
Archie P, b 6 March 1912 -
no death date, FLF

NEWBERRY (continued)
Bennie, b 1931 - d 1953, WRC
Charlie, b 1902 - no death date, WMG
Ella Mae, d 2 May 1973, ae 70y, ARM
Ethel, d 15 Jan 1977, ae 70y, WMG
Frankie, b&d 23 Aug 1960, ARM
Harney, b 2 Aug 1901 - d 25 Nov 1962, WRC
Harry L, d 18 Aug 1977, ae 77y, WMG
Jackie, b 1929 - no death date, WRC
Jacob, b 25 Dec 1847 - d 25 Aug 1911, MNT
John C, b 25 June 1937 - d 28 March 1941, FLF
June A, b 9 Apr 1914 - d 31 Aug 1966, FLF
Leatha, d 27 May 1978, ae 44y, FLF
Mary I, b 1904 - d 1972, WMG
Mary Lee, b 1879 - no death date, WRC
Matilda, b 12 Dec 1867 - d 2 Apr 1936, WRC
S B (Boss), b 1874 - d 1941, WRC
Samuel, b 25 Dec 1865 - d 8 Nov 1938, WRC
Samuel O, b 3 Feb 1911 - d 18 July 1922, LBR
Sharon A, Pfc USA Korea, b 23 Dec 1932 - d 31 Jan 1958, WRC
NEWBROUGH, Elsie, b 1927 - d 1969, LST
NEWCOMB, Della C, b 22 March 1869 - d 18 Feb 1905, CBJ
NEWPORT, Addie Carter, d 24 Aug 1975, ae 61y, DRM
Ann Hicks, b 3 March 1912

NEWPORT (continued)
- no death date, RGB
Arthur D, b 18 Aug 1911 - d 24 Nov 1969, RGB
Barney, b 1885 - d 1969, MCD
E Carson, b 1880 - d 1941, SNB
Edith L, b 22 Sept 1903 - no death date, MLC
Freeman J, b 13 Sept 1905 - d 24 Aug 1951, MLC
Idle, b 26 June 190- - d 10 May 1980, SNB
John T, b 10 Sept 1936 - d 8 Dec 1972, DRL
Lillie, b 1887 - d 1968, MCD
Linda, b 29 June 1896 - d 5 Feb 1976, SNB
Mary, b 13 July 1914 - d 13 Apr 1976, SNB
Mayagele, b 16 July 1937 - no death date, DRL
Nathaniel, d 14 Dec 1980, ae 52y, WHO
Oscar, b 28 Aug 1908 - d 16 Nov 1937, WRC
Tony N, b&d 1952, STC
William M, b 16 Sept 1900 - no death date, SNB
Zina, b 1925 - d 1968, LNE
NICHOLS, Josephine J, d 10 Jan 1977, WRC
NITZSCHKE, Harriet, b 1861 - d 1939, BRR
NITZSCHKE, Jennie, b 3 Dec 1929 - d 26 Jan 1958, BRR
Julius J, b 1855 - d 1934, BRR
Roland, b 11 Dec 1920 - d 24 July 1932, BRR
NIZSCHKE, Mark Allen, d 14 Oct 1977, SNB
NOLDER, Cora, b 10 Aug 1902 - no death date, NWP
Leo, b 2 Oct 1889 - d 28

NOLDER (continued)
March 1967, NWP
NORMAN, Berry, b 24 Oct
1896 - d 11 Dec 1955,
WRC
Delores, b 12 Mar 1930 - d
27 March 1930, WRC
Francis C, b 20 Apr 1910 -
d 13 July 1971, NWP
James H, b 1887 - d 1957,
WRC
James W, b 18 Nov 1896 - d
16 Jan 1895, CRO
Josephine, b 3 Apr 1921 -
d 16 June 1923, WRC
Love, b&d 9 Aug 1934, WRC
Luther, b 1902 - d 1967,
WMG
Michael D, b&d 13 Feb
1950, WRC
Mildred, b&d 15 Oct 1937,
WRC
Nannie, b 1903 - d 25 Feb
1973, WMG
Virginia D, b 3 June 1918
- no death date, NWP
NORRIS, Anna, b 14 Nov 1869
- d 29 Oct 1933, WRC
Bennie Arnold, d 11 Apr
1977, ae 49y, PLR
Curtis Dale, b 3 June 1955
- d 23 June 1973, DRL
E M, b 15 July 1863 - d 24
Sept 1951, WRC
Edward R, Pvt Co A 79 Rgt
WWII, b 16 June 1898 - d
21 June 1960, WRC
Ella Jones, b 20 March
1874 - d 7 March 1964,
SNB
Gladys, b 1925 - d 1966,
DRL
J C, b 29 March 1869 - d 5
May 1934, DRL
John B, d 30 May 1980, ae
58y, PLR
Lyman, b 18 Apr 1905 - d
21 March 1963, WRC

NORRIS (continued)
Nancy, b 23 Dec 1833 - d
27 Oct 1892, RGB
Samuel H, d 5 Nov 1980, ae
62y, DRL
Samuel Jacob, b 29 Feb
1872 - d 10 May 1967,
SNB
Sarah, b 1901 - d 1966,
DRL
Sonny Allen, d 10 Apr
1978, ae 20y, PLR
T C, b 1 Sept 1878 - d 3
July 1968, DRL
NORTHERN, Betty J Rogers,
no dates, CRO
NORTHRUP, Billy, b 14 Aug
1927 - d 18 Feb 1930,
PLR
Clifford W, b 25 Oct 1934
- d 28 Nov 1971, PLR
Doris L, b 28 Feb 1938 -
no death date, PLR
Grasie, d 2 Dec 1978, ae
66y, PLR
Gregory Allen, b 19 March
1969 - d 11 Apr 1969,
PLR
Inman, b 1924 - d 1966,
PLR
Iva, b 20 July 1936 - d 9
Feb 1941, PLR
Mazie, b 1900 - d 1964,
PLR
Samuel Lee, d 22 Feb 1981,
ae 62y, PLR
Sylvia F, b 1882 - d 1954,
PLR
Virgil C, b 12 Jan 1891 -
d 14 Aug 1945, PLR
NORTHRUP, Walter N, b 1870
- d 1957, PLR
NUNLEY, Eva, d 11 March
1978, ae 65y, NWP
OAKLEY, Laura Holladay, b
1887 - d 7 March 1972,
SNB
Samuel N, b 1886 - d 1961,

OAKLEY (continued)
SNB
William H, Cpl Bty C 316
Fld Art WWII, b 25 Jan
1920 - d 5 Apr 1967,
SNBO
OBERHEW, Emma Linda, b 1839
- d 1910, RGB
Louis C, b 1830 - d 1910,
RGB
OFFERLE, Frank Brooks, b&d
17 Apr 1936, PLR
OGLE, Carrie S, b 22 Oct
1892 - d 6 May 1947, WRC
Cora Jane, b 31 July 1896
- d 28 Jan 1939, CBJ
OLLIS, Catherine, b 8 Jan
1919 - d 10 Jan 1919,
ADC
George, b 15 March 1894 -
no death date, DVS
Jennie, b 3 Oct 1880 - d
31 March 1970, DVS
OLMSTEAD, C, b 5 June 1893
- no death date, DRL
James H, d 16 June 1905,
ae 6wk, CLC
L, b 17 July 1891 - no
death date, DRL
Mary Alice, b 20 Aug 1870
- d 21 March 1935, DRL
Mildred, b 25 July 1912 -
d 25 Aug 1912, LVN
Richard, b 27 Oct 1864 - d
4 Dec 1937, DRL
Richard Carl, b 1896 - d
11 Nov 1973, DRL
Rosetia, b 19 Feb 1894 - d
16 Jan 1977, UNG
Terry Lynn, d 9 June 1976,
ae 17y, DRL
Tilda, b 8 Dec 1883 - d 23
Apr 1918, LVN
Tommy Keith, d 26 May
1976, ae 13y, DRL
William, b 28 Sept 1884 -
d 21 Feb 1962, UNG
OLSEN, Menford, d 13 Aug

OLSEN (continued)
1975, ae 76y, ALB
ONEY, Charles Oscar, b 30
Jan 1976, ae 78y, WMG
OOATEN, Altha J, b 7 Jan
1909 - d 7 July 1967,
DRL
Clyde E, b 18 Nov 1899 - d
29 Apr 1973, DRL
OOTEN, Alta M, b 21 May
1886 - d 6 Jan 1888, SHD
Blanch, b 21 Dec 1909 - d
2 May 1912, CRO
Charles, d 4 Apr 1879, ae
66y, LVN
Darlene, b 1955 - d 1960,
DRM
Doris Phillips, b 1906 - d
21 Aug 1978, UNG
Dortha E, b 13 March 1921
- d 22 Oct 1922, SHD
Edith, b 3 Oct 1901 - d 26
Oct 1910, CRO
Edith Jossie, b 26 Feb
1928 - d 4 March 1924,
UNG
Elizabeth M, b 1875 - d
1944, PNY
Elmer Lee, d 7 Oct 1951,
ae 9y 1mo, DRM
Erna Lehman, b 1906 - d
1956, PNY
Genera Bell, d 20 Nov
1979, ae 78y, LNE
Hobert, d 10 Oct 1977, ae
78y, DRM
Imogen, b 1928 - d 1966,
PLR
J P, b 19 Apr 1856 - d 2
Oct 1924, SHD
Joan, d 17 March 19--, ae
?, PLR
John L, b 1868 - d 1945,
PNY
LeRoy, d 16 Sept 1974, ae
25y, LNE
Leonard W, b 6 Sept 1916 -
d 7 March 1946, PLR

OOTEN (continued)
Margaret B, b 4 Nov 1933 -
d 27 Nov 1969, DRM
Melvin, b 30 March 1931 -
d 1 Apr 1931, SHD
Mindian, b 16 Aug 1875 - d
28 May 1942, LVN
Nancy Jane, b 17 May 1857
- d 25 Feb 1929, SHD
Porker, b 1898 - d 1963,
UNG
Richard, b 1903 - no death
date, PNY
Rita Eileen, d 26 Aug
1961, DRM
Robert Glenn, b 20 June
1946 - d 25 Apr 1947,
PLR
Robert Lee, d 24 Dec 1973,
ae 58y, ARM
Sarah Ellen, d 16 Oct
1973, ae 93y, PLR
Theodore Roosevelt, d 14
July 1974, ae 62y, MRR
Walter C, b 14 Feb 1915 -
d 18 Aug 1923, SHD
Webley C, b 18 Feb 1888 -
no death date, SHD
Willis M, b 18 Sept 1881 -
d 20 June 1882, SHD
OSBORN, William L, b 22 Apr
1876 - d 25 Nov 1949,
CRO
Betty Lee, d 1 Oct 1838,
ae 1y 2mo, CRO
Gertie S, d 17 July 1980,
ae 87y, FLR
John F, b 1891 - d 1969,
FLR
Ray B, b 19 Apr 1909 - d 6
Nov 1968, LBR
Thomas, d 25 Sept 195-, ae
82y, FLR
William L, Co H 2 Reg VA
Inf Sp/Am War, b 22 Apr
1876 - d 25 Nov 1949,
000
OSTROWSKI, Dr L M, d 15

OSTROWSKI (continued)
March 1918, ae 59y, DRL
OTT, Cora Ellen, b 21 Aug
1894 - d 8 May 1896, WRC
Glena K, d 20 Sept 1977,
ae 84y, WMG
Glenn D Kreis, b 17 Dec
1892 - d 20 Sept 1977,
WRC
Katie Redmon, b 22 Apr
1876 - d 1 May 1924, WRC
Milo Tygen J, b 26 Feb
1926 - d 26 Feb 1926,
WRC
Shirley Dewey, b 7 Aug
1898 - d 28 Nov 1899,
WRC
Tiffin, b 26 Dec 1867 - d
28 Oct 1932, WRC
Winnie May, b 16 July 1902
- d 31 Aug 1905, WRC
OTTO, Marilyn Kelly, b 1929
- d 1971, WRC
OVERSTREET, Charley, b 24
Apr 1908 - d 25 June
1908, LNC
Emily Cordeli, d 20 Nov
1974, ae 84y, SHD
John L, b 28 Jan 1856 - d
14 June 1925, MRR
Minerva, b 24 Feb 1832 - d
19 May 1891, MRR
OVERTON, Minnie, b 28 Aug
1894 - no death date,
NWP
OWENS, Bertha Sands, b 11
Aug 1888 - d 15 May
1911, DVS
Beulah A, b 25 Feb 1925 -
no death date, DRL
Catherine, b 28 March 1928
- d 22 Sept 1928, DVS
Curtis, d 9 Dec 1872, ae
54y, DRL
Harold T, b 19 Oct 1919 -
d 12 May 1923, WRC
Ina Gibson, b 19 June 1890
- d 15 Dec 1967, DRL

OWENS (continued)

J Cornelius, b 26 Aug 1906 - d 5 Oct 1909, DVS

J F, b 15 March 1906 - d 23 Apr 1946, WRC

J H, b 20 May 1879 - d 13 Dec 1953, WRC

Rev J L, b 13 June 1882 - no death date, DVS

James F, b 18 Feb 1888 - d 28 Jan 1959, DRL

Johnny I, d 9 Nov 1977, ae 69y, DVS

Margaret Maggie, d 23 Jan 1981, ae 88y, DVS

Margaret Paul, b 17 Jan 1842 - d 11 Sept 1915, PLR

Marl L, b 28 Nov 1888 - d 28 Dec 1959, DVS

Porter, b 1 Nov 1869 - d 24 Nov 1952, DVD

Rachel, b 23 Sept 1879 - d 24 July 1967, DVD

Rachel B, b 8 May 1923 - d 7 Feb 1924, DVS

Ruth C, b&d 27 Oct 1915, DVS

Veldia Collien, b 27 Feb 1929 - d 13 July 1929, DVD

Winford C, Tc 5 SVC B7 KY 178 FA BLN, b 30 June 1918 - d 12 Dec 1972, DRL

PACE, George W, b 3 Aug 1856 - d 20 Jan 1957, PTC

PACK, John, b 28 Sept 1871 - d 22 Aug 1936, SNB

Roberta, b 1 March 1878 - d 31 July 1946, SNB

PAGE, Cleveland D Sr, Pfc Bat D WWI/WWII, b 1 Apr 1893 - d 12 Sept 1965, LBR

Hilda Schubert, d 19 Apr 1973, ae 89y, WRC

PALMER, Carl Lee, b 15 Jan 1879 - d 7 Oct 1949, RTT

Nora Mae, b 20 May 1881 - d 24 Oct 1957, RTT

PARIS, Robert, b 1958 - d 1959, MSG

PARKE, m/o Ranser, d 9 Sept ----, RGB

PARKER, John B Sr, b 29 July 1907 - no death date, SNB

John Bryant Jr, b 10 Sept 1939 - d 10 Dec 1950, SNB

Judith Jane, b 31 Aug 1940 - d 9 Dec 1950, SNB

Laura Mae, b 4 Jan 1898 - d 27 Sept 1898, UNN

Martha L, b 20 Nov 1853 - d 21 July 1897, PTC

Mary F, b 23 Feb 1871 - d 3 June 1890, LBR

Mary Rubry (?), b 17 June 1905 - d 9 Dec 1950, SNB

Thomas Avery, b 26 July 1943 - d 9 Dec 1950, SNB

PARKS, Chester M, b 14 Jan 1920 - d 9 Aug 1973, LNE

Chester R, d 9 July 1973, ae 53y, LNE

Gary Lyons, b -- July 1959 - d -- Nov 1959, LST

Ione, b 24 Feb 1921 - no death date, LNE

PARRIS, Lillie S, b 11 Feb 1889 - no death date, EST

PARRIS, William Joseph, b 14 Sept 1882 - d 9 Nov 1963, ae 81y, EST

PARSONS, J C, b 16 March 1860 - d 20 Dec 1925, CRO

PARTIN, Andrew Jr, b&d 10 Aug 1958, BRR

Infant, no dates, BRR

PASEY, Theresa Lynn, 1954 - no other date, BRW

PASS, Claud W, b 22 Apr 1907 - d 15 July 1967, LNE
Geneva, b 27 March 1917 - no death date, LNE
Levi T, b 28 June 1875 - d 20 Nov 1944, LNE
Mary, b 19 Feb 1878 - d 17 Aug 1952, LNE
Vester, b 7 Oct 1904 - d 5 Sept 1962, LNE
Vola E, b 2 March 1912 - d 26 July 1973, LNE
PATCHING, Amanda Stevenson, b 1889 - d 1961, WRC
Baby B, b&d 13 June 1893, BRR
Elizabeth, b 16 Apr 1848 - d 17 Jan 1932, BRR
Everett, b 13 June 1882 - d 1 July 1927, PNY
George, b 21 Aug 1845 - d 21 Oct 1936, BRR
Inez J, b 17 July 1889 - d 13 Sept 1889, BRR
James Edward, b 1880 - d 1956, WRC
Jennie M, b 24 July 1877 - d 10 Oct 1884, BRR
Stella, b 21 Apr 1890 - no death date, WRC
Walt, b 6 Dec 1890 - d 4 Aug 1977, WRC
PATRICK, Ancil, b 30 March 1883 - d 1 March 1954, NWP
Dessie, d -- Sept 1981, ae 67y, NWP
Elijah, Sgt, b 28 May 1917 - d 17 Nov 1947, NWP
Eliza, b 22 Feb 1892 - d 27 Oct 1954, NWP
Lawrence, d 19 Jan 1980, ae 71y, NWP
Linda Sue, b 27 Dec 1950 - d 23 Dec 1959, NWP
Paul F, b 17 Apr 1895 - d 15 Nov 1970, NWP

PATTEN, Columbus L, b 17 Feb 1883 - d 9 May 1945, DVS
William Andrew, d 29 Apr 1973, ae 90y, PTC
PATTERSON, Adah D, b 1888 - d 27 Apr 1974, NWP
Alex, b 1908 - d 1947, UNN
Arlena, b 15 Sept 1905 - d 6 Nov 1918, OLP
Artinee, b 26 Aug 1909 - d 10 Nov 1918, OLP
Bertha, d 5 Feb 1975, ae 81y, NWP
Beulah E, d 14 May 1974, ae 69y, NWP
Beulah Lee, d 14 May 1964, ae 69y, NWP
Cynthia, b 21 Nov 1883 - d 7 Aug 1955, UNN
Delbert W, b 12 May 1913 - d 30 Apr 1976, UNN
F B, b 15 Nov 1903 - d 14 Feb 1946, NWP
Guy M, b 1909 - d 1970, NWP
Hazel, no dates, UNN
Helen, d 20 Sept 1981, ae 70y, UNN
Hinson, b 11 March 1911 - d 9 Apr 1968, STP
Homer, b 5 March 1901 - d 14 Apr 1904, OLP
James M, b 1883 - d 1938, NWP
James W, b 16 March 1926 - d 19 March 1961, DVS
Kelsey, b&d 17 March 1919, UNN
L R, b 21 Dec 1856 - d 19 Dec 1938, NWP
Lucinda, b 1859 - d 1934, UNN
Martha, b 5 Nov 1822 - d 14 Jan 1911, OLP
Mary Jones, b 27 Nov 1893 - d 14 Apr 1926, UNN
Oscar, WT USN WWI, b 4 Aug

PATTERSON (continued)
1890 - d 13 Feb 1957, NWP
Rev R B, b 17 Jan 1862 - d 9 Sept 1910, OLP
Sally, d 27 Jan 1979, ae 70y, STP
Sally A, b 1887 - d 1957, NWP
Samuel, b 1858 - d 1936, UNN
Srelda, b 27 Oct 1870 - d 20 Feb 1942, NWP
Talbert, b 8 July 1912 - d 21 Jan 1915, OLP
Urbau B, b 20 May 1894 - d 16 June 1947, NWP
Velmer, b 24 Nov 1916 - d 10 Nov 1918, OLP
Vesta, d -- Sept 1972, ae 80y, NWP
Will M, b 16 Sept 1879 - d 2 Apr 1955, UNN
Z, Cpl USA WWI, b 14 Apr 1893 - d 22 Dec 1957, NWP
PATTON, Christine, d 28 May 1977, ae 65y, CLC
Dora, b 24 July 1912 - d 23 July 1935, MNT
Elmer, d 19 Nov 1976, ae 72y, ARM
Mary Ellen, d 4 Jan 1974, ae 95y, HWN
Winnie K, b 20 Sept 1882 - d 10 Aug 1959, DVS
PAUL, A F, b 18 May 1879 - d 23 Oct 1961, PLR
Arthur, d 9 Jan 1979, ae 73y, PLR
Catherine B, b 11 Sept 1836 - d 19 Apr 1896, NDK
Clara, b 17 June 1886 - d 22 Aug 1959, PLR
Dixie Jewel, b 21 Feb 1930 - d 10 July 1930, PLR
George Mae, b 22 Feb 1914

PAUL (continued)
- d 27 Oct 1914, BRR
Ida Reba, b&d 5 Jan 1919, BRR
Infant, b&d 1937, MSG
James Alvin, b 31 July 1876 - d 21 June 1952, PLR
Mary M, b 16 Aug 1825 - d 19 Nov 1874, NDK
Sarah A C Wright, b 9 Sept 1840 - d 12 Jan 1915, PLR
Timothy Daily, d 2 Feb 1957, ae 75y 11mo, BRR
Walker B, b 4 June 1833 - d 22 Dec 1908, PLR
PAXTON, Katherine, b 6 Nov 1958 - d 31 March 1961, LNC
Mrs Lona, d 9 Feb 1980, ae 82y, LNC
William R, b 20 Apr 1894 - d 16 March 1963, LNC
PAYNE, Arnold E, b 31 July 1935 - d 17 Oct 1936, UNG
Betty Catherine, b&d 19 Jan 1938, DRL
Bobbie Jean, b 30 July 1930 - d 28 Nov 1932, DRL
Eddie E, b 29 May 1892 - d 28 Dec 1943, UNG
Emma G, b 1898 - no death date, DRL
Georgia A, b 8 Apr 1896 - d 11 Dec 1930, UNG
James, b 29 May 1872 - d 14 Jan 1898, UNG
James A, b 1897 - d 1954, DRL
John J, b 16 May 1875 - d 15 Aug 1897, UNG
Lewis P, b 26 Jan 1842 - d 1 Jan 1923, UNG
Lora, b 18 Oct 1925 - d 20 Oct 1937, UNG

PAYNE (continued)
Maggie L, b 31 Oct 1897 - d 1 June 1898, UNG
Margaret T, b&d 1915, UNG
Mary C, b 5 Oct 1856 - d 21 July 1917, UNG
Mary J, b 22 June 1899 - d 24 Jan 1900, UNG
Nancy Jane, b 10 Aug 1846 - d 10 July 1889, UNG
Ora M, b 2 May 1900 - d 22 May 1927, UNG
Theodore A, b 18 Sept 1891 - d 24 Nov 1897, UNG
William A, d 20 June 1981, ae 87y, UNG
PEARSON, Adeline, b 16 Dec 1859 - d 1 May 1936, CRO
Albert F, b 23 Apr 1882 - no death date, PNY
Charles, Bugler Co M 1st NH Art, no dates, NDK
Cleane M, b 19 March 1936 - d 14 Apr 1961, PNY
Edna Julie, d 11 Apr 1979, ae 56y, WRC
Evelyn L, b 19 Oct 1907 - d 13 July 1958, PNY
Harvey B, b 2 Aug 1882 - d 9 Nov 1941, ELZ
Hazel, d 30 Dec 1978, ae 70y, RGB
Jenia Wilson, b 20 May 1890 - d 25 June 1929, UNN
Maggie Sexton, b 11 March 1884 - d 23 June 1943, ELZ
Walter R, b 2 Jan 1887 - d 4 May 1957, CRO
PEIFER, Amanda G, b 7 Nov 1839 - d -- Nov 1891, SNB
PEMBERTON, Archie E, b 6 June 1919 - d 30 Oct 1920, UNH
Archie M, b 11 Feb 1891 - d 19 March 1967, UNH

PEMBERTON (continued)
Arthur W, b 1 Feb 1916 - d 2 Apr 1916, UNH
Benton, b 5 Feb 1929 - d 4 Apr 1957, UNH
Carbin, b 21 Dec 1903 - d 3 Nov 1910, UNH
Clarence, b 28 May 1923 - d 21 Sept 1935, UNH
Clinton, b 23 Dec 1929 - d 10 Aug 1969, UNH
Coy Floyd, b 26 Aug 1931 - d 11 Sept 1932, UNH
David W, b 6 June 1952 - d 23 Sept 1952, SNB
E, b 188- - d 19---, WBB
Elihue, d 29 Feb 1980, ae 82y, WBB
Flora, b 1934 - d 1963, UNH
Franklin Haywood, b 9 Sept 1882 - d 3 Feb 1977, WBB
J Defoe, Sgt USAAF, b 10 Nov 1905 - d 4 Oct 1974, SNB
Jas Cummings, b 28 Dec 1856 - d 9 June 1928, UNH
John Dean, b 25 Jan 1872 - d 13 Dec 1943, WRC
Joseph L, d 4 Mar 1977, ae 75y, WRC
Lawrence C, b 29 July 1924 - d 26 Jan 1952, UNH
Leon, b 18 Jan 1900 - d 31 Dec 1954, WRC
Lionel C, b 20 Oct 1908 - d 19 March 1932, UNH
Mrs. Luola, d 11 Nov 1980, ae 67y, WRC
Martha Joyner, b 17 Dec 1882 - d 2 Apr 1949, WRC
Myntha B, b 31 March 189- - d 11 Sept 1964, UNH
Myrtle N, b 21 Aug 1889 - d 8 Apr 1965, WBB
Ralph J, d 20 Jan 1978, ae 73y, WRC

PEMBERTON (continued)
Robert, b 5 Sept 1944 - d
13 Dec 1945, UNH
Rosa, b 1888 - d 20 Dec
1973, WBB
Ruby P, d 16 March 1980,
ae 78y, UNH
PENNELS, Lou, b 12 Oct 1859
- d 6 March 1943, WRC
PENNINGTON, Florence, b 10
Nov 1890 - no death
date, NWP
George W, b 8 Apr 1887 - d
15 June 1970, NWP
George W, Co G 320 Inf, b
3 Jan 1925 - d 17 Aug
1944, NWP
John R, b 8 Aug 1883 - d
14 Feb 1968, NWP
Myrtle B, b 15 Apr 1895 -
no death date, NWP
Vernon D, b 2 Dec 1931 - d
23 Dec 1937, NWP
Wanda Mathis, d 16 June
1977, ae 49y, WMG
PERKINS, Belvia S, b 18 Jan
1890 - d 11 June 1969,
WRC
James M, b 30 March 1859 -
d 17 Dec 1888, PTC
Orelia W, b 1898 - d 1963,
DRL
Parthenia E, b 21 May 1877
- d 3 Dec 1958, DRL
Samuel Edward, b 7 June
1871 - d 16 June 1939,
WRC
PERRIGO, Ora, b 2 March
1856 - d 29 Dec 1903,
RGB
PERRY, Eston Lee, b 12 Oct
1911 - d 25 May 1960,
LBR
Willie Mae, b 1 May 1910 -
no death date, LBR
PETERS, A B, Corp Co G 1st
TN Inf Sp/Am War, b 31
July 1871 - d 15 July

PETERS (continued)
1923, BRR
Rev A C, b 6 Nov 1843 - d
31 May 1917, BRR
Arthur C, b&d -- Apr 1891,
NDK
Bertha Edith, b 25 July
1911 - d 25 July 1937,
EST
C C, b 8 May 1879 - d 24
July 1879, BRR
Charley D, Pvt 71 Inf WWI,
b 9 March 1898 - d 20
Jan 1943, JCJ
Charlie Allen, b 29 Aug
1878 - d 13 Sept 1955,
EST
Clarence H, b&d -- Apr
1891, NDK
Earl Cranston, b 7 July
1901 - d 11 July 1901,
BRR
Elbert H, Pfc 317 Fld Art
81 Div WWI, b 17 Sept
1895 - d 9 May 1952, JCJ
Elijah, b 23 Apr 1837 - d
26 Sept 1926, BRR
Elijah, Corp 1st TN Inf
Civ War, b 8 May 1879 -
d 26 Sept 1926, OOO
Ella W, b 28 Aug 1916 - d
22 Feb 1969, NWP
Eugene Ken, d 30 Dec 1979,
ae 56y, JCJ
Garfield, d 31 March 1952,
ae 66y 6mo, EST
Henry F, b 13 Sept 1839 -
d 2 July 1908, BRR
Ida M, b 25 Sept 1882 - d
12 Oct 1886, BRR
J O, b 16 March 1875 - d
30 Oct 1896, BRR
James, b 25 Aug 1798 - d 8
Feb 1874, BRR
James H, d 28 Oct 1888, ae
16y 9da, BRR
James T, b 22 Sept 1901 -
d 18 June 1933, BRR

PETERS (continued)

Jessie Love, b 8 Aug 1877 - d 20 Jan 1968, BRR

John, b&d 1913, BRR

John Boyd, Pvt Co K 1st Rgt TN Sp/Am War, b 9 Oct 1874 - d 8 July 1958, BRR

John Thomas, b 1881 - d 1905, EST

Johnnie, b 1954 - d 1974, NWP

Kesiah, b 25 Dec 1865 - d 25 Feb 1949, BRR

Laura T, b 3 Apr 1888 - d 24 Feb 1971, EST

Linnie, b 1872 - d 1925, BRR

Linnie J, b 26 Oct 1906 - no death date, EST

Lizzie, b 29 Aug 1876 - no death date, EST

Lizzie M, b 15 Aug 1920 - d 12 Sept 1920, EST

Lottie, b 1845 - d 1926, EST

Mahala, b 17 Jan 1869 - d 25 March 1903, JCJ

Margaret Jackson, b 4 Dec 1944 - d 25 Apr 1972, EST

Martha, b 22 June 1833 - d 8 June 1909, BRR

Martha L, b&d 29 Feb 1882, NDK

Mary Jane, d 13 Aug 1917, ae 66y 11mo, BRR

Mary S York, b 24 Sept 1862 - d 8 Feb 1896, NDK

Maud, b 1898 - d 1914, BRR

Nina, d 27 Dec 1897, ae 46y 6mo, BRR

Oscar O, b 10 Aug 1894 - d 19 Apr 1919, JCJ

R H, no dates, BRR

Rachel, b 1805 - d 8 Apr 1889, BRR

Sarah Elizabeth, b 12 Nov

PETERS (continued)

1878 - d 19 Nov 196-, BRR

Sherman R, b 1 Feb 1897 - d 1 Apr 1897, NDK

Thomas J, b 1853 - d 1881, EST

Tobias, b 27 May 1835 - d 27 Sept 1901, BRR

Wesley C, b 9 May 1861 - d 21 Feb 1906, NDK

Wesley Iridell, b 26 July 1866 - d 3 Feb 1941, JCJ

William W, b 10 Sept 1876 - d 14 Nov 1955, EST

Worcester O, b 1870 - d 1939, BRR

PETIT, Gilbert R, b 18 Oct 1882 - d 2 July 1883, LBR

PETITT, Annie E, b 6 May 1840 - d 7 Apr 1865, LBR

Dove Morris, b 4 Aug 1877 - d 15 June 1954, WRC

Flora Ann, b 15 Oct 1878 - d 31 Aug 1902, LBR

Gustavis S, b 10 Sept 1846 - d 31 May 1885, LBR

James M, b 26 Sept 1873 - d 26 Feb 1955, WRC

John B, b 10 Sept 1846 - d 11 Sept 1924, LBR

John R Jr, b 1 March 1875 - d 8 Aug 1897, LBR

Lonnie, b 13 Aug 1884 - d 25 May 1969, WRC

Malinda, b 1849 - d 1938, LBR

Molino J Williams, b 14 Dec 1850 - d 15 Dec 1900, LBR

Nancy, b 9 Feb 1848 - d 13 Apr 1904, LBR

Ollie, b 30 June 1880 - no death date, WRC

PETTY, Bridget, d 5 May 1981, ae 82y, DRL

PHILLIPS, Amanda, b 15 Feb

PHILLIPS (continued)
1883 - d 6 Feb 1940, WRC
Arlie, b 12 Sept 1904 - d 27 July 1970, ARM
Barbara Ann, b 24 Sept 1948 - d 20 Dec 1952, WRC
Benjamin F, b 8 Feb 1873 - d 17 Feb 1935, UNG
Bessie Mae, b 1904 - d 1972, UNH
Cardilie, b 11 Apr 1868 - d 13 Apr 1936, UNH
Charlie W, b 3 Dec 1889 - d 29 June 1972, DRL
Clay H, Co A 124 Inf 31 Div b 17 Oct 1911 - d 6 May 1945 (killed/Phillippines),DRL
Clifford S, b 19 March 1910 - no death date, DRL
David Ray, b 31 March 1949 - d 22 Feb 1951, NWP
Debbie, b 1955 - d 1978, SNB
Earl, b 14 June 1892 - no death date, DRL
Earl, d 13 Aug 1976, ae 84y, DRL
Edna, b 14 Apr 1909 - d 2 Dec 1913, UNG
Edward Gateway, b 27 Feb 1873 - d 13 March 1955, WRC
Eliza Bass, b 20 May 1901 - no death date, WRC
Elizabeth, b 15 Sept 1891 - d 9 Jan 1977, UNN
Elzwig S, Co E 3 Rgt Sp/Am War, b 6 Dec 1866 - d 27 Oct 1954, UNH
Ethel, b 1892 - d 1947, UNH
Everett, b 8 Oct 1915 - d 5 May 1946, CRO
Florence, b 1864 - d 1965, SNB

PHILLIPS (continued)
Francis A, d 24 Dec 1922, DRL
Fred J, b 13 Feb 1873 - d 9 July 1960, DRL
Geo W, b 3 May 1835 - d 30 Oct 1963, DRL
Harry R, b 29 Apr 1866 - d 29 July 1928, DRL
Harvy, b 9 Feb 1924 - d 27 July 1924, DVS
Infant, b 6 Sept 1931 - d 29 May 1933, DRL
Infant, b&d 26 Sept 1943, DRL
Infant, b&d 11 Oct 1945, DRL
Isaac S, b 2 Oct 1890 - d 31 Jan 1970, UNN
James Deriton, d 15 Nov 1978, ae 53y, UNG
Jane, b 1898 - d 1972, UNG
Joice, d 6 June 1959, NWP
Joseph L, b 17 Apr 1898 - d 22 Sept 1964, UNH
Josie, b 24 Aug 1901 - d 4 Feb 1940, WRC
Josie Dixie, b 22 Feb 1919 - d 18 Aug 1922, WRC
Juanita, b 18 Sept 1917 - d 29 Apr 1920, WRC
Kathy, b&d 1955, MNT
Kenneth, b 27 Oct 1931 - d 19 Dec 1931, WRC
Kenneth Vincent, d 26 Sept 1974, ae 51y, UNG
Kizzie A, b 17 Sep 1877 - d 10 Sept 1969, DRL
Lewis Bucky, d 10 Dec 1977, ae 88y, LBR
Lois, b 3 March 1929 - d 18 Jan 1948, DVS
Louise d/o J A, no dates, RTT
Lyndon R, d 30 March 1976, ae 70y, DRL
Mabel M, b 3 Dec 1889 - d 29 June 1972, DRL

PHILLIPS (continued)
Madge, b 20 Oct 1874 - d
23 Sept 1942, WRC
Mary Bell, b 1 March 1887
- d 11 May 1974, CRO
Mary F, b 11 Oct 1869 - d
29 Dec 1928, UNG
Mary Howard, b 22 March
1882 - d 21 Nov 199-,
DRL
Mary Louise, b 1 Jan 1933
- d 18 June 1966, LBR
Mary R, b 9 Dec 1889 - d 3
March 1981, WRC
Matthew, b 27 Dec 1927 -
no death date, LBR
Maude, b 30 March 1906 -
no death date, ARM
Mr, no dates, MSG
Nola Hurst, b 22 May 1895
- no death date, DRL
Rachel B, 24 Aug 1919 - d
27 May 1972, DRL
Sherman P, b 19 Jan 1892 -
d 2 March 1969, WRC
Terry, b 1952 - d 22 Feb
1976, NWP
William O, b 1 May 1897 -
d 18 Jan 1967, WRC
Willie Edna, b 3 March
1910 - d 27 Jan 1954,
WRC
Zona, b 1895 - d 1970, LBR
PHIPPS, Herbert Lee, d 4
Feb 1981, ae 74y, SNB
Pearl C, d 14 Apr 1976, ae
57y, SNB
PICKETT, George William, d
24 Aug 1952, ae 67y 5mo,
CRO
PIERCE, Flora M, b 18 Aug
1860 - d 13 Aug 1942,
SNB
Glen, 1936 (?), MLC
Manley A, b 25 Oct 1856 -
d 14 Jan 1937, SNB
Mary L, b 14 Dec 1890 - d
21 Nov 1943, SNB

PILON, Williard, b&d 1 Jan
1908, PNY
Willie, b&d 1 Jan 1908,
PNY
PIPER, Arthur, b 1889 - d
1966, WMG
Virgie, b 1889 - d 26 Sept
1975, WMG
PITMAN, Daniel, b 1 Jan
1890 - d 9 Dec 1918
(Camp Meade MD), LNG
PITT, Bessie M, b 24 Apr
1901 - d 7 June 1964,
DRL
Harry S, b 4 July 1880 - d
27 Feb 1964, DRL
PITTMAN, Alonzo, b 23 June
1873 - d 23 March 1959,
UNG
B, 15 July 1904, UNG
Bertie D, b 1889 - d 1941,
MRR
Bessie G, b 7 Dec 1920 - d
20 Dec 1923, SHD
Bettie England, b 7 Aug
1874 - d 8 Feb 1936, SNB
Clemmie, b 19 March 1867 -
d 18 March 1915, UNG
Daniel, b 24 Sept 1832 - d
2 Sept 1890, BRR
Earl W, b 11 Oct 1894 - d
18 Apr 1897, UNG
Edna, b 28 Feb 1911 - no
death date, UNG
Frances M, b 4 July 1861 -
d 15 Dec 1905, SHD
Frank E, b 1882 - d 1948,
MRR
George, b 9 March 1908 -
no death date, UNG
Gladys Marie, b 10 Feb
1913 - d 23 Dec 1913,
SHD
Hillman, b 11 Nov 1864 - d
27 Sept 1935, UNG
Ibbie A, b 24 June 1905 -
no death date, DRL
Jane A, b 1866 - d 1941,

PITTMAN (continued)
UNG
John O, b 18 June 1879 - d
13 Dec 1959, UNG
Leslie, 1902, UNG
Margaret, b 2 Nov 1840 - d
19 Feb 1882, BRR
Mary S, b 4 Oct 1887 - d
24 Feb 1936, UNG
Myra Jane, b 18 Feb 1868 -
d 21 Jan 1953, SHD
Myrtle, b 30 June 1908 -
no death date, UNG
Myrtle F, b 6 March 1902 -
d 1 Feb 1951, RGB
Ova Ann, b 18 June 1877 -
d 23 Dec 1955, UNG
Richard C, b 1854 - d
1925, UNG
S E, no dates, SHD
Wilburn R, b 15 June 1900
- d 28 June 1950, DRL
PLESSINGER, Sarah O, b 1894
- d 1920, BRR
POLLARD, Charles Willard, b
27 June 1917 - d 4 July
1917, CRO
Grace Bell, b 4 March 1894
- d 27 June 1917, CRO
Grace Mildred, b 27 June
1917 - d 4 July 1917,
CRO
James, d 22 March 1979, ae
27y, ARM
Margeurete, b 28 Apr 1914
- d 3 Aug 1914, CRO
POLSON, Infant, b 20 Aug
1892 - d 10 Oct 1895,
MRR
Maggie S, b 12 July 1891 -
d 8 Apr 1893, MRR
POLSTON, Amanda, b 8 Sept
1862 - d 29 Feb 1929,
PNY
Amanda L, b 8 Apr 1894 - d
10 March 1945, PNY
John W, b 7 Aug 1884 - d
17 Apr 1961, PNY

POORE, Margaret, b&d 9 Oct
1959, MSG
PORTER, Freeman L, b&d 14
June 1914, MNT
John, b 1864 - d 1935, MNT
Johnnie D, b 14 March 1914
- d 4 May 1967, MNT
Patchens, b 1881 - d 1932,
MNT
Roy, d 31 Jan 1955, ae 49y
10mo, DRM
PORTWOOD, Alice, b 13 March
1897 - d 28 July 1973,
UNN
Alice, b 27 July 1878 - d
15 Aug 1950, OLP
David C, b 9 March 1890 -
d 16 Oct 1920, UNN
Dorothy, b 19 Dec 1909 - d
30 Oct 1979, OLP
Flora, b 10 Dec 1901 - no
death date, UNN
Gaoner L, b 10 Jan 1914 -
no death date, UNN
Martin L, b 17 Nov 1876 -
d 30 March 1957, OLP
Omah B, b 17 Feb 1894 - d
14 March 1963, OLP
Rev Owen C, b 20 June 1908
- d 12 May 1957, OLP
Spurgeon C, b 10 June 1887
- d 30 May 1951, OLP
POTTER, ----, no dates, PTC
Abbie E, b 11 Apr 1858 - d
25 July 1939, MSG
Absalom, b 23 Aug 1822 - d
19 Apr 1873, CLC
Alice, b 3 Apr 1910 - d 17
Apr 1910, WRC
Annie (inf), d 1853 (old-
est grave), CLC
Annie A, b 10 Apr 1882 - d
4 Aug 1970, WRC
Arnold Jr, b 25 Feb 1928 -
d 1 March 1965, PTC
Avery B, b 18 May 1885 - d
6 Feb 1904, PTC
Barbara R, b 1968 - d

POTTER (continued)
1971, PTC
Benjamin H, Pvt 159 Dpt
Brig, 18 Feb 1942 - no
other date, PTC
Bertha Mary, b 2 Aug 1904
- d 12 Dec 1909, LNC
Bertie, b 11 Feb 1963 - d
11 Apr 1922, PTC
Bessie Mabee, b 9 May 1884
- d 20 Oct 1887, PTC
C W, b 18 Jan 1825 - d 4
Nov 1968, WRC
Catherine Ann, b 27 Dec
1944 - d 11 Apr 1945,
CRO
Chester, 37 AAA Gun Bat
Korea, b 12 Nov 1931 - d
16 Oct 1958, PTC
Christine, b 1923 - d
1967, DRL
Clarence, b 11 July 1895 -
d 23 June 1919, PTC
Clarence M, d 23 March
1978, ae 52y, PTC
Cora P, b 11 Aug 1886 - d
7 Apr 1943, LNC
Curtie, b 19 Aug 1911 - d
11 Aug 1924, PTC
Donna Rose Ann, b 23 May
1973 - d 18 Feb 1974,
FRN
Dorothy, 16 Feb 1923 - no
other date, PTC
Eliza E, b 30 March 1882 -
d 9 Jan 1922, PTC
Elizabeth, b 12 Oct 1845 -
d 19 Jan 1916, WRC
Elmer, b 1887 - d 19 Sept
1976, WMG
Elsie Ruth, b 4 Sept 1926
- d 18 Sept 1926, PTC
Emma Dora, b 12 Sept 1894
- d 4 Apr 1980, PTC
Essie, b 1892 - d 1969,
WMG
Florence, b 27 March 1878
- d 4 May 1951, PTC

POTTER (continued)
Flossie, b 13 Aug 1911 - d
6 Jan 1912, WRC
Francis E, b 1 Sept 1913 -
no death date, DRL
Frankie, b 1843 - d 29 Apr
1905, PTC
Fred, d 10 Feb 1937, ae
26y, NWP
G A, b 18 March 1872 - d 4
May 1931, PTC
G W, b 16 March 1875 -
death date illegible,
CLC
George, b 1891 - d 1961,
PTC
Gordon B, b 30 June 1912 -
d 28 Dec 1973, DRL
Gregory Paul, b 26 Apr
1964 - d -- Nov 1964,
PTC
Henry J, dates illegible,
CLC
Infant, b 8 Oct 1910 - d
10 Nov 1910, PTC
Infant, b 12 Aug 1883, PTC
J R, b 16 May 1856 - d 21
Nov 1943, MSG
James, b 25 Aug 1876 - d
12 Feb 1892, PTC
James K, b 25 Dec 1840 - d
2 Aug 1916, PTC
James L, b 19 Oct 1904 - d
29 June 1932, HWN
James Ronald, b 6 June
1943 - d 12 June 1943,
FLR
Rev John I, b 11 Aug 1873
- d 1 Sept 1946, PTC
John Ray, b&d 25 Feb 1956,
RGB
Johnnie Darrell, d 26 Aug
1978, ae 7y, PTC
Mrs Josie L, d 10 Dec
1979, ae 71y, PTC
Lelin, d 13 Aug 1975, ae
70y, PTC
Leona Rebecca, b 12 Aug

POTTER (continued)
1874 - d 2 Nov 1947, PTC
Lewis Houston, b 20 Apr 1854 - d 16 Dec 1941, PTC
Lilley M, b 28 Apr 1891 - d 1 June 1896, PTC
Lois Irene, b 15 Jan 1919 - d 11 Oct 1922, PTC
Luther A, d 29 Oct 1979, ae 85y, PTC
Martha Honeycutt, d 20 Feb 1974, CLC
Martha R, b 1896 - d 1974, FST
Mary, 16 Feb 1923 - no other date, PTC
Mary Ann, d 14 June 1976, ae 75y, PTC
Mary E, b 8 March 1853 - d 21 March 1921, PTC
Mary F, b 15 Aug 1898 - no death date, PTC
Mildred, b 1920 - d 1932, PTC
Minnie M, d 28 Oct 1978, ae 76y, DRL
Nancy, b 8 Sept 1815 - d 26 Apr 1894, CLC
Noah Arthur, d 3 Nov 1975, ae 84y, DRL
Oliver, no dates, PTC
Onsa Columbia, b 5 Dec 1863 - d 14 Oct 1913, PTC
Panny, b 31 Aug 1865 - d 12 Feb 1947, WRC
Pearl M, d 19 June 1981, ae 88y, DRL
Rachel, b 1870 - d 1896, DRL
Reed, b 1914 - d 1970, DRL
Robert Clinton, b 10 May 1921 - d 26 Feb 1926, WRC
Robert P, b 1 Aug 1891 - d 27 July 1955, PTC
S M, b 30 Dec 1870 - d 25

POTTER (continued)
Dec 1934, PTC
Sarah, b 19 June 1882 - d 18 Aug 1911, PTC
Sarah C, b 12 Aug 1883 - d 27 Sept 1886, PTC
Solomon N, b 11 Sept 1879 - d 16 Aug 1943, LNC
Solomon S, b 10 Apr 1853 - d 10 May 1913, PTC
Stanley, d 18 Aug 1978, ae 54y, PTC
W James, b 1 Jan 1873 - d 14 Nov 1887, CLC
Walter Dale, b 22 March 1930 - d 24 June 1930, LNC
William T, b 5 Sept 1858 - d 29 Jan 1930, PTC
POTTS, Fred C, d 20 Apr 1975, ae 76y, CRO
POWELL, Mrs Ernest, b 5 Apr 1886 - no death date, CRO
Joseph Barton, b 1871 - d 1955, WRC
Velea M Blake, b 1878 - d 4 Apr 1969, WRC
POWERS, Mrs J Bardill, b 9 March 1943 - d 1 July 1974, CRO
John Thomas, d 19 March 1971, ae 81y, CRO
Joyce Bardill, b 9 March 1943 - d 9 July 1974, CRO
Mrs Sarah, d 15 July 1950, ae 82y, CRO
Wayne Luther, b 17 Sept 1938 - no death date, CRO
POYNTER, Ceph E, b 27 July 1880 - no death date, DRL
Infant, d 5 Aug 1906, BRR
Jennie Chaney, b 21 Sept 1888 - d 4 Apr 1945, MLC
Minnie, b 11 July 1893 -

POYNTER (continued)
no death date, DRL
PRATER, Nola, b 16 Oct 1893
- d 19 July 1915, BRR
PRESSLEY, Jimmy Ray Jr, b 7
Nov 1966 - d 8 Nov 1966,
ADC
Mrs, 1926, MSG
PRESSWOOD, C E, b 1882 - d
1949, LNC
Mary, b 16 March 1891 - d
16 Feb 1913, LNC
Wallace C, b 31 Dec 1912 -
d 7 May 1964, LNC
PRICE, Cyntha, d 10 Dec
1971, ae 2mo 12da, RTT
Fannie, b 2 March 1882 - d
-- March 1921, OLP
Icey, b 1892 - d 1968, NWP
Margaret, w/o Wm, b 1837 -
d 1897, WRC
Mary E, d 12 June 1913, ae
55y 5mo, LNC
PRIGMORE, Edwin Shelton, b
27 Oct 1898 - d 22 Dec
1941, FGN
Essie Fagan, b 11 Sept
1902 - d 29 June 1932,
FGN
PRIVETT, Ella M, b 1 Nov
1930 - no death date,
DRL
Mary E, b 6 Feb 1880 - d 8
June 1901, DVS
PRIVETTE, Elizabeth, b 1
Dec 1880 - d 1 Oct 1959,
DVS
Robert B, b 20 Feb 1882 -
d 24 Dec 1957, DVS
PROPES, Alma Eastridge, b 9
March 1922 - d 25 May
1976, EST
PROXMIRE, C Tom, b 1875 - d
1933, LNE
Infant, b 13 Oct 1913 - d
7 Nov 1913, LNE
Theodore, b 17 Aug 1903 -
d 12 Nov 1909, MRR

PUCKETT, Walter, b 21 Apr
1881 - d 16 Sept 1939,
RGB
PURVIS, Joseph, b 17 Dec
1878 - no death date,
DRL
Robert T, b 8 Dec 1875 -
no death date, DRL
QUALLS, Joe A, b 30 Apr
1872 - d 29 Sept 1941,
FRV
John H, b 3 Aug 1869 - d
18 Sept 1905, PTC
Minnie M, b 25 May 1872 -
d 28 Apr 1947, EST
Salina A, b 28 Nov 1875 -
d 18 June 1954, FRV
W A, b 4 March 1862 - d 21
Dec 1918, PTC
Mrs Wyllodean, d 10 July
1978, ae 79y, WRC
QUILLEN, Eunice, b 12 Jan
1888 - d 2 June 1891,
CRO
QUINN, Charles A, b 1861 -
d 1917, DVD
Gerrie S, b 1941 - d 1973,
LST
Loraine Davis, b 11 Oct
1906 - d 25 Nov 1975,
WRC
Rachel A, b 1874 - d 1941,
DVD
Ray B, b 1893 - d 1965,
WRC
QUINSENBERRY, Emma Ruth, b
2 Oct 1876 - d 24 May
1942, NWP
Leonard L, b 13 Oct 1879 -
d 25 Oct 1961, NWP
RABY, Annie E, b 22 Oct
1837 - d 12 Aug 1889,
DVS
RAINEY, Mrs Jessie Pittman,
d 1 May 1981, ae 65y,
NWP
Ralph, d 5 May 1981, ae
47y, NWP

RAMEY, Florence, b 1885 - d 1957, NWP

Jessee, b 1876 - d 1936, NWP

RANCY, Charles, 1950, MLC

RANGE, M H, b 7 Jan 1884 - no death date, BRR

RANKIN, Henry V, b 24 Apr 1884 - d 28 Nov 1951, NWP

RANKINS, Crystal Beene, d 12 July 1981, ae 72y, NWP

Patsy Lou, b 27 Nov 1936 - d 17 Jan 1937, NWP

RARDEN, Alice M, b 8 Sept 1880 - d 20 Dec 1963, WRC

Frank M, b 4 Oct 1875 - d 1 May 1959, WRC

RATLIFF, Dennis Owen, Pvt USA, b 1955 - d 2 Jan 1975, DRM

RAYDER, Heirstle, b 8 March 1934 - d 2 Sept 1968, NWP

Karen James, d 3 July 1979, ae 23y, WRC

REAGAN, W J, b 26 Jan 1882 - d 13 Apr 1950, RGB

REDMON, Anna M, b 22 Dec 1902 - no death date, WRC

Annie Beatrice, b 17 Aug 1903 - d 25 Jan 1907, WRC

Beatrice, b 28 May 1920 - d 28 June 1920, WRC

Betty June, b 1 June 1939 - d 17 Sept 1960, WRC

Charlotte, b 19 Dec 1877 - d 11 Nov 1907, WRC

Dave, b 28 Jue 1887 - d 20 Sept 1967, WRC

Dollie A, b 8 Dec 1896 - no death date, WRC

Elles J, d 2 March 1956, ae 77y, WRC

REDMON (continued)

Eugene K, d 25 Jan 1975, ae 56y, WRC

Frieda Heidel, b 31 Aug 1881 - d 23 Apr 1967, WRC

James Sr, b 8 Jan 1872 - d 22 Feb 1958, WRC

James T, d 4 Sept 1977, ae 73y, WRC

Jannis, b -- July 1921 - d 28 Feb 1942, WRC

John, b 12 Aug 1836 - d 4 July 1908, WRC

John, b 14 Oct 1879 - d 1 Feb 1936, WRC

John Jr, b 16 Aug 1910 - d 25 July 1941, WRC

Julia Ann, b 11 May 1882 - d 12 Jan 1967, CRO

Landa Jean, b 26 May 1941 - d -- July 1941, WRC

Larry, b 27 March 1855 - 8 Dec 1906, WRC

Lillie Emory, b 28 Dec 1892 - d 2 Dec 1931, WRC

Little Mae, b 23 June 1895 - d 8 June 1907, WRC

Lizzie Mae, b 11 Oct 1903 - d 16 Nov 1975, WRC

M, b 1909 - d 1963, WRC

Martin, b 16 May 1895 - d 16 Nov 1925, WRC

Mary Baxter, b 12 June 1850 - d 9 March 1922, WRC

Murrell Jr, b 21 Jan 1931 - d 7 March 1931, WRC

Murrell R, b 23 Aug 1878 - no death date, WRC

Oretta, b 9 Oct 1924 - d 26 Jan 1940, WRC

Patrick, b 17 Sept 1917 - d 10 Oct 1918, WRC

Samuel L, b&d 12 Nov 1907, WRC

Sybil Taylor, b 21 Apr 1920 - d 16 Jan 1943

REDMON (continued)
WRC
Terry Lynn, d 17 June 1974, ae 24y, WMG
Thelma L, b 1912 - d 24 Sept 1976, WRC
Viola Potter, b 3 Oct 1875 - d 21 Feb 1967, WRC
William, b 4 March 1888 - d 13 Oct 1959, CRO
REED, L, b 1874 - d 1938, CRO
R, b 1882 - d 1939, CRO
REEVES, Gertie, d 9 July 1976, ae 62y, PLR
RESEDEN, J Wiley, b 1886 - d 1932, WRC
Labrm, b 25 May 1854 - d 1923, WRC
Lou, b 1855 - d 1929, WRC
REW, Mary Florence, b 4 Nov 1878 - d 29 Dec 1945, PNY
Sarah C, b 19 Feb 1831 - d 31 July 1890, CRO
W W, b 1827 - d 1899, CRO
REYNOLDS, Adeline W, b 1859 - d 1933, WBB
Andrew J, b 24 Aug 1867 - d 27 Sept 1960, PNY
Eliza Ann, b 28 Apr 1872 - d 29 Nov 1948, PNY
Francis, b 1941 - d 1945, PNY
Maxine, b 29 Nov 1926 - d 2 Aug 1934, PNY
Thomas, b 1849 - d 1920, WBB
Tina Renee, b 19 Nov 1967 - d 21 Nov 1967, PNY
Valeria Ann, b 8 Oct 1951 - d 8 Oct 1959, PNY
RHODCHAMEL, Sarah, b 1891 - d 1947, PNY
RICH, Calvin C, d 28 July -----, ae 65y, ARM
Elmira Griffith, b 25 Dec 1884 - d 3 Nov 1948, LNE

RHODCHAMEL (continued)
Ervin, b 29 June 1889 - d 4 Feb 1958, LNE
J E (Shug), b 1894 - d 1961, ARM
Jacob I, b 31 Sept 1808 - d -- March 1886, WRC
James Frank, b 22 Sept 1883 - d 12 Nov 1979, LNE
Lamoyine, b 1910 - d 1969, ARM
Larry C, b 26 Jan 1950 - d 20 Nov 1975, LNE
Lois M, b 1955 - no death date, LNE
Ola Mae, b 1905 - no death date, ARM
Rufus, b 9 Dec 1882 - no death date, LNE
Timothy Gale, b 6 June 1958 - d 25 July 1977, LBR
RICHARDSON, Albert C, b 10 Oct 1910 - d 23 Dec 1961, NWP
RIDDELL, Bench, b 26 Dec 1847 - d 11 Aug 1897, RGB
Mary J, b 20 May 1838 - d 23 Sept 1913, RGB
RIDINGS, Lee Ellen Carson, b 16 Aug 1878 - d 19 Apr 1944, DVS
RIGHT, George Washington, b 16 Aug 1863 - d 17 Oct 1863, DVS
Lizy Caldona, b 5 July 1861 - d 17 Oct 1863, DVS
RING, Melba, b 17 Aug 1910 - d 10 Oct 1910, SNB
RITTER, Angeline T, b 18 Nov 1859 - d 3 June 1949, DRL
Edward, b 19 Aug 1893 - d 11 July 1894, EST
Herman, b 27 June 1939 - d

RITTER (continued)
28 June 1939, NWP
Howard, b 1856 - d 1929, DRL
J B, b 26 Feb 1858 - d 25 Jan 1920, EST
James D, b 14 May 1908 - d 10 July 1972, NWP
Lillie G, b 2 Sept 1895 - no death date, EST
Liza, b 20 July 1823 - d 31 Dec 1866, DVS
Manus R, b 16 Feb 1888 - d 22 Sept 1962, EST
Mary L, b 22 Nov 1862 - d 13 Apr 1930, RTT
Monroe C, b 1854 - d 1931, RTT
Samuel, b 1834 - d 1913, DRL

RIVER, Ellen C, b 19 Sept 1914 - no death date, DVS

RIVERS, John W Sr, b 15 June 1914 - d 24 Dec 1973, DVS

ROACH, Berry, b 30 Aug 1842 - d -- Feb 1902, WRC

ROAT, Regrand G, b 1909 - d 1910, CRO

ROBBINS, Albert, b 1905 - d 1970, FLR
Clyde, b 2 Apr 1907 - d 2 Aug 1958, CRO
Hilaey, d 26 March 1964, ae 79y, CRO
James A, b 5 May 1901 - d 11 July 1902, CRO
Lizzie, b 1900 - d 1964, FLR
Lydia Alley, b 11 Oct 1876 - d 12 Feb 1946, CRO
Marshall E, b 28 Jan 1895 - d 3 Dec 1898, CRO
Mary C, b 1860 - d 1933, BRZ
Melvin C, b 1861 - d 1932, BRZ

ROBBINS (continued)
Walter, b 20 March 1899 - d 21 Apr 1899, CRO

ROBERTS, Charles Edwin, b 15 Jan 1943 - d 22 March 1967, EST
Francis A, b 24 Feb 1989 - d 18 Nov 1967, EST
Hugh, b 1881 - d 19 Jan 1921, CBJ
Lawrence T, b 30 Apr 1894 - d 4 Oct 1970, EST
Lucille, d 10 July 1972, ae 66y 9mo, CBJ
Mary H J, b 28 Oct 1842 - d 5 Apr 1896, WRC
Mollie M, b 1881 - d 1937, CBJ
Ostus C, b 21 Oct 1880 - d 6 Aug 1953, WRC
Wanda, d 10 March 1979, ae 32y, NWP

ROBINSON, Amanda Lee, b&d 24 Dec ----, ae 1da, WMG
Arthur E, Sgt Co I 407 Inf WWII, b 3 May 1919 - d 29 Dec 1958, PTC
Mrs. Augusta, d 11 Jan 1975, ae 83y, DRL
Celia, b 10 May 1825 - d 16 March 1908, LBR
Dewey, b 7 Jan 1899 - d 19 Oct 1975, LBR
Elvira, b 1856 - d 1927, WRC
Francis E, b 10 Feb 1852 - d 29 Apr 1908, LBR
Frank, b 3 Jan 1882 - d 27 Feb 1973, DRL
Frank R, b 19 July 1853 - d 21 Apr 1923, CRO
Gupsie D, b 15 Dec 1903 - d 11 March 1970, UNN
Infant, b&d 12 Apr 1926, LBR
James G, b -- Aug 1845 - d -- July 1919, UNN
Jessie D, b 29 Aug 1901 -

ROBINSON (continued)
d 7 Sept 1971, UNN
Joe, b 1 June 1854 - d 5 July 1928, ELZ
John J, b 1854 - d 1929, WRC
Johnson, b 1863 - d 12 Jan 1926, LBR
Joseph A, b 24 Sept 1880 - d 27 May 1973, CRO
Lawrence L, b 1915 - d 1935, CRO
Martha Ann, d 23 Nov 1954, ae 90y, HCK
Mary, b -- Dec 1847 - d -- Dec 1918, UNN
Mary E, b 27 May 1890 - d 18 Aug 1890, LBR
Mildred, b 18 Apr 1854 - d 15 Jan 1933, CRO
Nancy C, b 15 Nov 1815 - d 13 Jan 1900, UNN
Nellie F, b 19 Feb 1917 - d 30 Oct 1917, LBR
Pamela Dean, d 13 Apr 1969, ae 2da, NWP
Pearl Taylor, b 29 Jan 1889 - d 16 Apr 1960, PNY
Roy L, b 11 Nov 1925 - d 27 Sept 1947, UNN
Sarah E, b 8 Nov 1887 - d 23 Sept 1970, CRO
Sarah Matilda, b 10 Oct 1858 - d 24 July 1950, LBR
Sarah Tenn Garrett, b 11 July 1859 - d 26 June 1936, ELZ
Taylor S, b 19 July 1882 - d 21 July 1941, PNY
W L, b 1888 - d 1923, WRC
RODDY, Baby, b&d 1928, DVS
ROGERS, Beacher W, b 1 Nov 1907 - d 19 Dec 1959, CRO
Bessie P, b 1 May 1917 - no death date, CRO

ROGERS (continued)
Dorsie M, b 16 Feb 1891 - d 16 Sept 1928, OLP
Earl, Pvt USA WWI, b 22 May 1896 - d 9 Feb 1973, CRO
Kate A, b 31 Jan 1899 - no death date, CRO
Lorene, b 19 July 1940 - d 31 Jan 1960, UNN
Mary C, d 31 Dec 1980, ae 68y, WRC
Minnie M, b 26 Nov 1888 - d 6 May 1928, OLP
Niva Portwood, b 6 Sept 1914 - d 1 Jan 1942, WRC
William P, b 1865 - d 1962, WRC
ROLAND, Betty Elizabeth, b 16 May 1849 - d 7 June 1924, MLC
ROSE, Cynthia W, d 29 Jan 1892, ae c 23y, NDK
Franklin, b 6 May 1868 - d 17 July 1895, NDK
Rev J H, b 13 Feb 1873 - d 19 March 1951, MSG
Jennifer, 6 May 1969, WBB
Martha J, b 18 Dec 1873 - d 9 July 1952, MSG
W Joe, b 1894 - d 1969, MSG
ROSENBAUM, Bessie M, b 7 Oct 1901 - no death date, WBB
Edward, b 1895 - d 1933, BRR
Frank, b 31 May 1901 - d 26 Aug 1902, PLR
Joe B, b 17 March 1897 - d 11 Aug 1965, WBB
Nina, b 12 Aug 1860 - d 16 Apr 1930, BRR
ROSS, Archie, b 22 Nov 1901 - d 1 Dec 1903, OLP
Nellie, b 15 July 1904 - d 12 Dec 1905, OLP
W R, b 5 June 1842 - d 9

ROSS (continued)
Nov 1890, DRL

ROWE, Joe Stacy, b 17 Aug 1888 - d 2 Feb 1972, WRC

ROYSDEN, George W, b 24 Feb 1896 - d 13 Aug 1971, EST

RUFFNER, Albert T, no dates, DVS

Alice, b 1895 - d 1920, EST

Alvia, b 15 May 1894 - d 17 June 1894, EST

Bertha Walls, b 1881 - d 1966, DVS

Bessie R, b 1883 - d 1971, RTT

C J, b 30 Oct 1945 - d 15 Jan 1929, DVS

Christian, b 1834 - d 1897, DVS

Clifton L, b 7 Nov 1914 - d 5 March 1917, DVS

Dave M, b 1878 - d 1964, DVS

E, d 9 Feb 1957, ae 51y, DVS

Ellen, b 7 Feb 1882 - d 31 Dec 1944, DVS

Eva, b 10 May 1890 - d 26 Feb 1892, EST

Floyd, b 6 Apr 1901 - no death date, EST

Franklin, b 2 Apr 1935 - d 2 Nov 1937, DVS

Fred, b 3 Sept 1880 - d 9 Oct 1964, DVS

Gerald H, b 22 June 1904 - d 11 Apr 1978, ae 73y, DVS

Grace Hinds, b 23 Jan 1980, ae 82y, DVS

Harry Glen, b 29 Dec 1908 - d 14 July 1916, RTT

Harvey H, b 1883 - d 1965, RTT

Itress, b 29 June 1906 - d 6 Dec 1964, DVS

RUFFNER (continued)
James F, d 20 Apr 1980, ae 79y, EST

James W, b 31 Oct 1867 - d 1943, EST

John H, b 1877 - d 1943, DVS

John W, b 12 March 1851 - d 4 Feb 1916, DVS

Joseph Daniel, d 11 Apr 1966, DVS

Leater Guy, Sgt 112 AAGS Sq USAAF WWII, b 6 Apr 1915 - d 5 May 1946, DVS

Leonard, b 17 Jan 1900 - d 29 Nov 1946, DVS

Linda, b 1858 - d 1945, DVS

Loyd Dean, b 14 Sept 1933 - d 15 Sept 1933, DVS

Lula M, b 1882 - d 1962, DVS

Maggie A, b 1 July 1882 - d 31 July 1882, DVS

Mamie, b 1896 - no death date, EST

Margrette Langley, b 18 Feb 1865 - d 21 May 1944, DVS

Nancy Ann, d 17 Apr 1888, ae 22y 5mo, DVS

Nancy J, b 9 Sept 1861 - d 10 June 1963, DVS

Peter, Cpl Co C 1st TN Inf, b 9 June 1839 - d 17 June 1892, DVS

Peter A, b 10 Nov 1858 - d 7 July 1923, DVS

Rosetta, b 28 March 1903 - d 4 Apr 1964, EST

S M, b 1891 - d 1962, EST

Sim V, b 1879 - d 1968, WRC

Susie May, b 1885 - d 1930, WRC

Teha A, b 1866 - d 1953, EST

Tuddie, b 9 Nov 1887 - d 6

RUFFNER (continued)
Apr 1938, DVS
William C, b 2 March 1861
- d 14 June 1944, DVS
RUNION, Della, b 3 March
1896 - d 30 Dec 1900,
CRO
RUPPE, Augusta E, b 4 Jun
1855 - d 16 Dec 1895,
DRM
Ben F, b 25 July 1890 - d
30 Aug 1955, DRM
Christina, b 11 Nov 1821 -
d 31 March 1895, DRM
Edward W, b 26 June 1890 -
d 23 June 1965, DRM
Miss Esther M, b 1905 - d
11 Aug 1974, DRM
Frederick, b 4 Feb 1825 -
d 25 June 1906, DRM
Frederick L, b 21 Jan 1862
- d 12 May 1936, DRM
Gertie Davis, d 21 June
1979, ae 75y, DRM
Gustavis A, b 31 May 1891
- d 8 Jan 1923, DRM
Henry T, b 11 June 1860 -
d 22 May 1952, DRM
Herman, b 4 Apr 1856 - d
18 Sept 1903, DRM
Ida, b 4 Feb 1851 - d 25
Oct 1905, DRM
Infant, d 28 Apr 1888, ae
3da, DRM
Infant, b&d 18 Feb 1911,
DRM
J C Fred, b 23 March 1882
- d 16 Sept 1886, DRM
John F, b 22 Dec 1886 - d
20 Dec 1887, DRM
Rosa P, b 28 Apr 1899 - d
1905, DRM
Wilhemina P (arrived USA
1885), b Langen Back,
Germany 27 Dec 1865 - d
25 March 1949, DRM
RUSSELL, Carleton, b 17 Aug
1924 - d 7 Nov 1943, CRO

RUSSELL (continued)
Clifford C (or J), 236
Engineer WWII, b 12 July
1912 - d 25 June 1953,
EST
Cordelia, b 3 Aug 1880 - d
17 Nov 1964, WRC
Eilen, b 10 Nov 1857 - d
10 Sept 1935, DVS
Elizabeth Jane, b 28 July
1889 - d 10 Feb 1963,
WRJ
Gorman, no dates, SNB
Jane, d 6 Oct 1892, DVS
John W, b 1898 - d 1962,
EST
Liola, b 11 Aug 1902 - no
death date, EST
Martha, b 23 March 1869 -
d 10 Jan 1963, EST
Mary Josephine, b 4 Dec
1923 - d 21 Nov 1925,
EST
Ollie, b&d 30 Apr 1974,
EST
Robert M, 4 Nov 1898 - d
24 Dec 1916, CLP
S M, b 23 Jan 1851 - d 4
July 1922, DVS
Sim Lee, b 4 July 1890 - d
28 Jan 1964, EST
Susan O, b 12 Nov 1874 -
no death date, EST
Rev T M, d 12 Apr 1902, ae
74y, SNB
Terry Douglas, b 1 June
1948 - d 29 March 1951,
EST
Thomas C, b 29 Apr 1877 -
d 10 Feb 1942, WRJ
Thomas J, b 25 May 1875 -
d 14 June 1955, EST
Walter, Pvt 813th WWII, b
6 Oct 1910 - d 2 Sept
1954, EST
William R, b 1 May 1892 -
d 24 Dec 1913, CLP
William, WWII, b 9 May

RUSSELL (continued)
1922 - d 23 July 1944, EST
Wm Madison, b 31 March 1859 - d 15 March 1939, EST
Wm Morgan, b -- Jan 1868 - d 23 Nov 1942, WRC
RUSTICK, Hannah Smarsh, d 29 Sept 1975, ae 58y, DRL
RUTH, Woodrow, d 4 March 1976, ae 62y, PLR
RUTHERFORD, Bobby Wayne, d 7 Feb 1969, ae 1mo, NWP
RYAN, Audrey M, b 1921 - d 1972, BRR
Herbert, d 15 July 1974, ae 60y, WMG
Luther R, d 7 Jan 1869, ae 58y, BRR
Mary E, b -- Aug ---- - d 12 March 1898, UNG
RYDER, Cora, b 28 Oct 1878 - d 7 Apr 1973, WRC
Fred, b 6 Aug 1906 - d 21 Nov 1960, WRC
RYE, Lola Hooks, b 17 July 1902 - no death date, LNE
Thomas H, b 29 Oct 1901 - d 1 March 1963, LNE
RYON, Abner, b 21 Sept 1886 - d 20 Sept 1956, DRL
Addie, b 22 June 1912 - no death date, DRL
Agnes M, b 16 Oct 1914 - d 4 Nov 1914, DRL
Albert R, b&d 1947, DRL
Arlo M, b 2 Oct 1892 - d 11 Feb 1922, DRL
Charles, b 3 Oct 1941 - d 8 March 1966, DRL
Christopher C, b 1888 - d 1953, DRL
Cora Ethel, b 16 Oct 1916 - no death date, DRL
Drucilla, b 1892 - d 19

RYON (continued)
Sept 1978, DRL
Herbert E, b 25 Dec 1913 - d 8 March 1966, DRL
Inf son, b 10 March 1917 - d 11 March 1917, DRL
J C, b&d 10 Aug 1943, DRL
Jake, b 8 Jan 1851 - d 4 March 1907, DRL
Joseph C, b 3 Nov 1857 - d 17 July 1919, DRL
Joseph Ernest, b 19 March 1913 - d 17 Sept 1967, DRL
Joseph H, b 13 May 1963 - d 24 Dec 1970, DRL
Lydia Scott, b 7 Dec 1863 - d 23 Nov 1943, DRL
Martha Elizabeth, b 29 March 1861 - d 10 Jan 1908, DRL
Pearl A Ernest, b 1 Feb 1892 - d 21 Apr 1925, DRL
Phillis June, b&d 2 Sept 1948, DRL
R L, b 11 July 1941 - d 11 Aug 1941, DRL
W C, b 5 Jan 1936 - d 11 March 1938, DRL
W S, b 1 Jan 1824 - d 27 July 1893, DRL
W S, b 13 Jan 1930 - d 4 Sept 1939, DRL
Willis, d 28 Dec 1900, ae 1mo 23da, DRL
Winston Francis, b 2 Sept 1938 - d 23 Nov 1938, DRL
SAFFELL, C H, Lt Adjt 11 TN Cav Civ War Vet/ Union, no dates, LBR
SAFFILL, Fred R, b 13 Oct 1869 - d 8 Feb 1946, WRC
Mary S, b 9 Nov 1873 - d 28 July 1964, WRC
SALOCK, Annie Stranka, b 11 Feb 1893 - d 10 Apr

SALOCK (continued)
1945, DRL
Mike, b 10 Oct 1881 - no
death date, DRL
Pete, b 5 June 1919 - d 15
Oct 1945, DRL
SAMPSEL, Sadie, b 1897 - d
7 Nov 1974, WRJ
Walter, b 1897 - d 21 Nov
1968, WRJ
SAMPSELL, Charles A, b 10
March 1897 - d 17 Aug
1971, EST
Cleophas, b 1867 - d 1953,
DVS
Fannie, b 1866 - d 1937,
DVS
Mary L, b 21 July 1901 -
no death date, EST
Mary Lou, d 20 Oct 1979,
ae 78y, EST
SAMPSON, Ezra, Pvt USA WWI,
b 1 Aug 1896 - d 20 Dec
1974, SNB
SAMSEL, Claudie C, b 30 Dec
1894 - d 30 Aug 1903,
ELZ
Saleya, b 22 Nov 1879 - d
10 Aug 1900, WRJ
Samuel R, b 10 Sept 1875 -
d 12 Oct 1903, WRJ
SANDERS, Laura Justice, b
1891 - d 1967, FLF
SANDS, Aurther B, b 5 Sept
1892 - d 22 Jan 1964,
WRC
SANFORD, Mary H, b 1 March
1888 - d 18 Nov 1888,
LBR
Sarah Ann, b 14 May 1886 -
d 4 Aug 1887, LBR
SARTIN, Lillian, b 13 June
1915 - d 17 Apr 1944,
CRO
SATTERFIELD, Winnerd, b 5
Dec 1904 - d 1 Nov 1906,
WRC
SATTERTHWAITE, Herbert, b

SATTERTHWAITE (continued)
20 Nov 1888 - d 6 March
1964, BRR
SAVAGE, Lena B, b 13 June
1913 - no death date,
SNB
Stirley, b 8 Dec 1901 - d
22 Dec 1906, SNB
SCANDLYN, Clyde V, b 6 June
1901 - d 6 May 1962, FGN
Ethel M, b 17 May 1904 - d
20 Nov 1976, FGN
Wayne Roger, b 6 March
1931 - d 12 May 1937,
FGN
SCARBOROUGH, Lora R, d 29
July 1979, ae 69y, DVS
SCARBRO, Clifford, d 16 Oct
1978, ae 75y, WRC
Dorsey, b 5 May 1919 - d 4
Feb 1968, NWP
J Frank, b 26 Feb 1885 - d
13 May 1938, NWP
Mary Jane, b 28 May 1893 -
d 20 June 1955, NWP
SCARBROUGH, Kenneth, d 6
Feb 1981, ae 67y, DVS
Stella, b 1896 - d 1903,
CLC
Teresa Gale, b&d 7 Sept
1952, PNY
SCATES, Claude J, d 31 May
1979, ae ?, PLR
Louisa, b 1870 - d 1947,
PLR
Ottie, b 28 Aug 1897 - d
22 Oct 1977, PLR
Thomas N, b 1865 - d 1927,
PLR
SCHICK, Carrie E R, b 18
Aug 1861 - d 4 Apr 1946,
BRR
Elsie, d 26 May 1966, ae
84y 4mo, BRR
George, b 16 Feb 1850 - d
5 May 1928, BRR
SCHOOLER, Dorotha S, b 11
May 1788 - d 24 Feb

SCHOOLER (continued)
1859, LBR
Infant, d 28 Oct 1858, ae
14h, LBR
Joseph H Jr, b 6 Aug 1820
- d 1 Sept 1839, LBR
Joseph Sr, b 15 Nov 1777 -
d 6 Aug 1844, LBR
SCHUBERT, Anita M, no
dates, LBR
Archer, b 1928 - d 1950,
NWP
Arthur H, d 23 May 1974,
ae 83y, LBR
Bill, b 15 Jan 1888 - d 28
Dec 1941, WRC
Bruno, b 1869 - d 1946,
WRC
Carl F, b 16 Aug 1895 - d
26 Dec 1976, WRC
Carl F, d 26 Dec 1976, ae
--, WMG
Cora Hornsby, b 1896 - d
1953, WRC
Emma Trail, d 4 March
1981, ae 83y, NWP
Ernest, b 1897 - d 1957,
NWP
Ethel Russell, b 1894 - d
1923, WRC
Frank, b 7 June 1849 - d
10 Dec 1935, WRC
Rev Frank P, d 11 Sept
1975, ae 75y, LBR
Hugo B, b 24 May 1879 - d
13 Sept 1971, WRC
Jacke N, b 1937 - d 1972,
LBR
Jacob G, b 17 July 1872 -
d 4 March 1958, WRC
Joe G, Pvt Co C 4 Reg
Sp/Am War, b 17 July
1872 - d 4 March 1958,
000
John H, Tech 5 61st Armed
Inf WWII, b 13 Oct 1919
- d 12 June 1967, NWP
Lillian Miller, b 18 Dec

SCHUBERT (continued)
1879 - d 5 June 1956,
WRC
Lorena M, b 7 May 1915 - d
9 Dec 1970, LBR
Lou Della, b 10 May 1882 -
d 19 Sept 1973, WRC
Louis Sr, b 1905 - d 1973,
WRC
Louisa, b 1870 - d 1915,
WRC
Minnie, b 7 June 1851 - d
4 Feb 1930, WRC
Ott, b 1890 - d 1974, LBR
Otto, b 1897 - d 1973, WRC
Otto P, d 7 Feb 1973, ae
75y, WMG
Paul C, b 2 Oct 1874 - d 6
Jan 1951, WRC
R Clark, b 6 Aug 1939 - d
24 Feb 1940, LBR
Rachel Hall, d 6 Apr 1981,
ae 91y, FLF
Rita Sue, b&d 24 May 1944,
NWP
Roger (inf), b&d 1935, WRC
Sarah Byrd, b 29 July 1879
- d 13 Nov 1918, WRC
Sarah Maud, b 31 Aug 1943
- d 4 Dec 1943, WRC
William T, b 30 Oct 1933 -
d 27 Feb 1953, LBR
Woody E, b 4 June 1946 - d
11 Dec 1965, LBR
SCHULTZ, Janice, b&d 9 May
1941, ADC
SCHWENDT, Dr F A, b 1 Feb
184- - d 16 July 1883,
WRC
SCOTT, Allie M, b 18 March
1868 - d 15 Dec 1929,
UNG
Alta Clark, b 1889 - d 15
Sept 1979, WRC
Arnietta J, b 20 Nov 1846
- d 30 March 1906, ELZ
Ben J, b 27 March 1861 - d
2 Sept 1917, DRL

SCOTT (continued)

Bertie O, b 23 Apr 1903 - d 21 Oct 1969, DRM

Billie G, b 8 Aug 1859 - d 24 Nov 1881, WRC

Billy Earl Jr, b 31 Dec 1955 - d 29 March 1969, DRM

Blanch P, b 28 March 1900 - d 17 June 1965, WRC

Caroline M, b 21 Apr 1912 - d 16 Nov 1970, WRC

Della Griffith, d 31 May 1981, ae 71y, WMG

Emma C, b 20 Oct 1884 - d 2 Apr 1927, DRL

Ervin E, b 22 Nov 1903 - d 18 Feb 1953, DRL

Everett, d 17 Oct 1978, ae 62y, DRL

Hazel, b 1908 - d 1929, DRL

J C, b 15 Aug 1939 - d 9 Feb 1940, ELZ

Jena, b 4 March 1890 - d 14 June 1891, WRC

Jimmie, b&d 1931, DRL

Joe, b 4 Oct 1867 - d 31 Oct 1932, WRC

John H, b 2 Nov 1881 - d 24 Dec 1881, WRC

John L, b 1832 - d 1908, WRC

John L, b 21 Apr 1873 - d 20 Oct 1934, WRC

John Long, b 1882 - d 24 May 1948, WRC

L K, b 11 Apr 1880 - d 30 June 1928, WRC

Lida C, b 18 Dec 1838 - d 30 Apr 1884, MNT

Luther, b 1932 - d 1968, DRL

Lydia, b 13 Dec 1777 - d 21 Sept 1870, MNT

Mae E, b 16 Aug 1910 - no death date, DRL

Maggie C, b 20 March 1892

SCOTT (continued)

- d 27 March 1939, UNG

Mamie I, b 6 Sept 1884 - d 24 March 1958, UNG

Martha A, b 1 Dec 1812 - d 18 Jan 1855, MNT

Mary, b 2 May 1871 - d 30 May 1959, WRC

Mary, b 1811 - d 11 Aug 1854, ELZ

Mary P, b 18 Aug 1856 - d 18 July 1937, PLR

Mary T, b 11 March 1848, MNT

Minnie Chaney, d 23 July 1979, ae 81y, MLC

Oliver E, b 12 Aug 1903 - d 25 March 1965, DRM

Pearlina Ann, b 1834 - d 1921, WRC

Rachel R, b 1 June 1884 - d 26 May 1964, WRC

Robert M, b 7 July 1893 - d 24 Dec 1966, WRC

Robert T, b 5 Jan 1848 - d 2 Feb 1924, UNG

Rupert L, b 2 Oct 1872 - d 5 Nov 1947, DRL

Rusell Sr, b 19 Aug 1808 - d 23 Feb 1896, HLL

Russell E, b 24 Jan 1873 - d 26 Dec 1904, WRC

Samuel, b 19 June 1777 - d 25 May 1841 (oldest), MNT

Samuel F, b 23 Feb 1844 - d 25 Jan 1883, MNT

Samuel H, b 6 Feb 1867 - d 20 Apr 1896, WRC

Seril C, b 30 March 1877 - d 31 Oct 1956, UNG

W A, b 19 Dec 1897 - d 16 March 1914, WRC

W R, b 7 July 1872 - d 13 Apr 1917, HLL

William D, d 24 March 1968, ae 59y, WRC

William J, b 16 Dec 1876 -

SCOTT (continued)
d 21 Jan 1962, WRC
William J, Lt 3 Reg TN Vol Inf, b 20 Feb 1835 - d 14 Feb 1903, WRC
Wilthia, b 1 Oct 1906 - d 12 Aug 1961, DRL
Zachery T, b 28 Feb 1849 - d 4 Oct 1931, PLR
SCROGGINS, Lisa Ann, b 12 July 1968 - d 12 Dec 1968, SNB
SEABOLT, Clyde, b 29 Feb 1924 - d 8 Nov 1944, SNB
Ealire, d 24 Dec 1949, ae 33y, MRR
Grace, d 5 Jan 1977, ae 67y, RGB
Henry C, Pvt Co D 46 Inf WWI, b 11 Apr 1895 - d 1 Aug 1960, RGB
Holley Earl, d 7 Aug 1974, ae 55y, RGB
Linda C Byrd, b 18 Sept 1881 - d 29 Nov 1948, RGB
Lula, b 10 Sept 1892 - d 17 Dec 1964, SNB
William M, b 1 May 1871 - d 27 Oct 1948, RGB
SEARS, Keavin Lee, b&d 16 July 1965, WRJ
SEDGEWICH, Ella, no dates, DRL
SEDMAN, E W, b 16 Aug 1866 - d 12 May 1946, WRC
SEIBER, Addie, b 3 Jan 1889 - no death date, DVS
Albert, b 2 Feb 1916 - no death date, NWP
Andy, b 24 March 1921 - d 17 Apr 1958, NWP
Daniel R, b 26 July 1953 - d 27 March 1974, EST
Elizabeth, b 22 March 1881 - d 21 May 1957, NWP
Ezekiel, Tech 5 2229 AAA SLT BN CAC WWII, b 18

SEIBER (continued)
Sept 1920 - d 19 Jan 1962, DVS
Fred, b 8 March 1892 - d 14 March 1954, DVS
George, b 1 May 1895 - no death date, DVS
Homer, d 8 Sept 1967, ae 30y 5mo, NWP
Laura, b 17 Apr 1905 - d 28 June 1963, NWP
Maggie, b 15 June 1912 - d 18 Sept 1971, NWP
Myrtle Carson, d 4 July 1973, ae 81y, DVS
Nancy Elizabeth, b 15 June 1889 - d 12 Oct 1958, NWP
Rev Oliver, b 14 Dec 1889 - d 1 Jan 1968, NWP
Pless W, b 6 June 1891 - d 23 Jan 1974, NWP
Polly, b 12 March 1848 - d 12 July 1914, OLP
Rena S, b 26 Oct 1892 - no death date, DVS
Rosana, b 8 Sept 1866 - d 2 July 1959, DVS
Rossie, b 2 Apr 1903 - no death date, NWP
Sallie A, b 1 Oct 1899 - d 20 Feb 1968, NWP
SELLS, Gertie L, b 25 Nov 1899 - no death date, WBB
Laudon M, b 24 May 1896 - d 15 Apr 1971, WBB
SETTLES, J Logan, b 1888 - d 1953, UNN
Logan, b 4 June 1896 - d 8 Sept 1953, UNN
Nealie Longmear, b 1906 - d 9 Oct 1974, UNN
SEXTON, ------, b&d 10 Aug 1944, CRO
Bart, b 15 July 1860 - d 19 Dec 1926, WRC
Berry F, b 30 May 1895 - d

17 Oct 1951, LBR

Bessie T, b 14 Nov 1890 -
d 22 Sept 1977, LNE

Bettie Ann, b 1929 - d
1975, WRC

Betty Ann, d 13 Feb 1975,
WRC

Billie Joe, b 31 Aug 1925
- d 5 March 1968, LNE

Calvin, b 3 July 1939 - d
4 July 1939, PNY

Carl F, b 16 Aug 1895 - d
16 Dec 1976, WRC

Carson S, WWII, b 12 Jan
1903 - d 11 Nov 1958,
ELZ

Charity, b 26 March 1902 -
d 1936, MCD

Debbie Kay, b 9 Dec 1957 -
d 23 July 1958, WRC

Dora Shannon, b 11 Sept
1902 - d 3 March 1958,
ELZ

Ellen M, b 6 Apr 1894 - no
death date, PNY

Essie, b 1893 - d 1963,
NWP

Estille, b 15 July 1937 -
d 23 March 1939, ELZ

Feral, b 27 Nov 1901 - no
death date, LNE

Flonnie M, b 26 June 1891
- d 4 Jan 1913, BRD

Harold, b 1945 - d 1968,
LNE

Isa D, b 13 Oct 1873 - d
21 Dec 1964, LNE

Isa Hamby, d 4 Apr 1975,
ae 98y, ELZ

J C, b 2 Dec 1926 - d 28
March 1973, LNE

James R, b 1892 - d 1962,
NWP

Joe F, b 11 Feb 1894 - d
23 June 1972, MCD

John Freeman, b 7 Oct 1893
- d 17 May 1941, NWP

John P, b 1 Sept 1857 - d
10 Feb 1942, LBR

Joseph J, Pvt Co D 101 Inf
WWI, b 28 Feb 1894 - d
27 July 1956, LNE

Julia, b 1906 - d 1971,
LNE

Julie, no dates, MLC

Julie E, b 11 June 1865 -
d 6 June 1948, LBR

Kermet, b 30 Oct 1915 - d
10 Dec 1918, ELZ

Leamon, b 26 March 1892 -
d 18 Jan 1959, ELZ

Leonard F, b 11 June 1893
- d 26 July 1966, PNY

Leslie, d 8 March 1976, ae
65y, LNE

Mable, b 3 Oct 1897 - d 28
Dec 1921, ELZ

Mable, b 16 Jan 1907 - d
17 July 1936, WHO

Maggie, b 4 Aug 1892 - d 3
July 1916, LBR

Margaret Ann, b 5 July
1936 - d 15 March 1939,
NWP

Marshall, b 25 Oct 1884 -
d 5 Dec 1970, LNE

Mary, b 7 July 1875 - d 30
Jan 1968, LNE

Mary Scott, b 6 Apr 1883 -
d 23 March 1923, WRC

Mount, b 1868 - d 1949,
MLC

Ollie Garrett, b 30 May
1895 - d 25 Jan 1956,
ELZ

Rebecca, b 4 Sept 1898 - d
1 Apr 1969, NWP

Rebecca H, b 7 Oct 1880 -
d 17 July 1938, PLR

Reldia, b 1 Jan 1859 - d 9
Jan 1929, MCD

Robert G, b 1920 - d 1928,
PNY

Roy, b 7 Apr 1890 - d 26

SEXTON (continued)
Jan 1930, LBR
Roy Arnold s/o Reld &
Annie, 14 May 1943, ELZ
Sallie, b 4 July 1901 - d
4 Apr 1934, MCD
Sarah, b 22 Sept 1872 - d
8 Dec 1929, MCD
Moselle, Sgt, b 1921 - d
1946, WRC
Sonia (Sissy), d 28 Apr
1978, LNE
Ted, b 31 Dec 1935 - d 13
July 1973, LNE
Vestie Shannon, b 14 Jan
1911 - d 29 Apr 1964,
LNE
Violet E, b 1920 - d 1969,
LNE
W M (Bill), b 26 Sept 1866
- d 14 July 1958, LNE
William L, b 29 Nov 1900 -
d 9 Feb 1964, LNE
William, Pvt USA, b 1 May
1880 - d 10 Aug 1955,
PLR
William R, b 11 Jan 1884 -
d 16 May 1966, LNE
Willis (Red), b 3 June
1914 - d 30 June 1958,
NWP
Wright, b 13 Feb 1899 - d
2 Jan 1978, LNE
SHADDEN, Thomas A, d 5 Jan
1978, ae 93y, WRC
SHADOW, Austin, b 1871 - d
1943, WRC
Betty M, b 1875 - no death
date, WRC
SHANNON, ----, b 14 May
1909 - d 10 Dec 1914,
ELZ
Ada May, b 31 Oct 1886 - d
19 Feb 1973, SNB
Alfred L, b 13 Nov 1904 -
d 19 Oct 1970, MLC
Andy M, b 14 May 1835 - d
16 May 1875, MCD

SHANNON (continued)
Annie Louise, d 7 Nov
1979, ae 95y, SNB
Charles H, b 22 Dec 1901 -
d 31 Dec 1927, WRC
Clara, b 30 May 1833 - d
11 Jan 1888, MCD
Dilia, b 14 July 1876 - d
11 Nov 1922, ELZ
Earl Preston, b 7 Nov 1912
- d 6 June 1965, SNB
Eldridge, b 9 June 1876 -
d 23 Sept 1888, MCD
Elizabeth H, b 12 Sept
1875 - d 12 Nov 1974,
LNE
Elmer K, b 29 March 1937 -
d 4 June 1946, WRC
F A, b 14 Nov 1908 - d 6
Jan 1977, SNB
Mrs Frank, b -- Aug 1878 -
d 21 Apr 1904, LBR
Frankie, b 17 June 1906 -
no death date, MLC
G T, b 22 Nov 1856 - d 23
Nov 1926, SNB
George, b 10 Apr 1913 - d
23 Dec 1973, SNB
Harold E, b 27 Apr 1903 -
d 22 June 1960, SNB
Hezekiah, b 1870 - d 1953,
WRC
Houston M Sr, b 1902 - d
1945, LBR
Hubert I, b 17 June 1892 -
d 31 Oct 1894, LBR
Isadora, b 10 Oct 1882 - d
20 June 1913, LBR
J F, b 13 May 1874 - d 12
Feb 1953, LBR
James M, b 18 Aug 1881 - d
4 Nov 1964, SNB
James R, b 16 Nov 1867 - d
18 May 1882, MCD
Joe, b 28 Dec 1876 - d 15
Feb 1952, LNE
June, 1911, MLC
Laura H, b 1886 - no death

SHANNON (continued)
date, WRC
Lee, b 10 July 1897 - d 4
Apr 1922, BRZ
Levi Marie, d 14 Sept
1978, ae 7mo, LBR
Lydia F, b 9 Sept 1865 - d
29 Jan 1891, LBR
Matilda, b 25 May 1889 - d
4 June 1947, ELZ
Maud I, b 3 Aug 1890 - d
14 March 1892, LBR
Orville B, d 17 Oct 1974,
UNH
P R, b 17 July 1846 - d 12
Apr 1924, SNB
Reba, 1909, MLC
Right, b 9 Nov 1869 - d 19
Oct 1891, SNB
Sabert R, b 25 Apr 1865 -
d 10 Feb 1941, EST
Sarah E, b 13 May 1868 - d
25 Jan 1938, EST
Stella May, d 25 Feb 1899,
FLF
Tedmore, b 1886 - d 1958,
WRC
Terisa, b 1870 - d 1960,
WRC
Victor Edward, b 8 Nov
1952 - d 24 May 1973,
UNH
Virgie A, b 3 Sept 1989 -
d 12 Apr 1957, WHO
W M, b 16 Sept 1895 - d 12
Apr 1900, LBR
Winnie E, b 29 Sept 1886 -
no death date, LBR
SHARP, ----, d 13 June
1901, OLP
Beulah Mae, b 10 Aug 1899
- d 7 May 1967, CRO
Charles, b 5 Jan 1905 - d
13 Oct 1957, CRO
Clifford, d 22 July 1980,
ae 59y, UNG
Delila w/o W E, MNT
James E Jr, b 18 May 1925

SHARP (continued)
- d 16 Feb 1931, CRO
Jerry D, b 5 Nov 1940 - d
3 March 1958, CRO
Lester Bunch, d 8 Oct
1975, ae 73y, UNN
Maude, b 1896 - d 1970,
UNG
Nona Lanella, b 4 Sept
1924 - d 24 Dec 1927,
ELZ
Ora L Sr, b 9 Jan 1900 - d
10 May 1971, CRO
Ronald C, b 19 June 1945 -
d 23 March 1946 CRO
Rudy Joe, b 28 Nov 1957 -
d 13 Dec 1957, LNE
Vena (or Vina), b 20 Aug
1903 - d 14 Mar 1975,
CRO
SHAVER, Emmet F, b 18 Oct
1883 - d 9 Sept 1912,
DRL
Horatio, Pvt Co L 311 Inf
78 Div, b 3 Aug 1889 - d
25 Dec 1970, FST
Mabel Gertrude, b 23 July
1902 - d 18 Aug 1905,
PTC
Oscar E, b 11 June 1887 -
d 16 Dec 1970, DRL
Rachel M, b 30 Sept 1888 -
d 26 Oct 1973, DRL
SHEIHAN, Tim, d 18 Sept
1897, ae about 45y, MNT
SHELDON, Charles Alvin, d
24 Apr 1978, ae 22y, RTT
Dale Monroe, d 11 Aug
1968, ae 18y, RTT
Sandra Sue, b 5 Oct 1959 -
d 8 Jan 1960, RTT
Willa Ritter, b 28 Feb
1896 - no death date,
RTT
Wm Joseph, b 18 Feb 1894 -
d 1 Aug 1935, RTT
SHELLY, Betty Lou, d 12 Aug
1980, ae 42y, BRR

SHELTON, Bertha Headrick, b
1883 - d 1951, CRO
D L, b 1881 - d 1953, CRO
Elbert L, b 8 March 1910 -
d 22 Feb 1967, DRM
Harry, b 20 Jan 1903 - d
14 Feb 1929, CRO
Infant, b 9 Jan 1923 - d
28 Jan 1923, CRO
Laura, b 15 Sept 1900 - d
24 Oct 1923, CRO
Ralph E, b 13 March 1922 -
d 18 Dec 1933, CRO
SHEPHARD, Brenda Jean, b 9
June 1964 - d 6 Sept
1964, SNB
Maurice G, b 1901 - d
1967, SNB
Norma J, 1963, EST
SHEPHERD, Kenny Lynn, b&d
1957, DVS
SHIELDS, Bertha, b 6 July
1883 - d 6 June 1939,
WRC
James R, b 1908 - d 1970,
WMG
Johanne C, b 12 Feb 1922 -
d 26 June 1937, WRC
W M, b 27 Apr 1882 - d 13
Oct 1952, WRC
Willard, b&d 16 March
1981, LNE
SHILLING, Shirley, b 5 Dec
1912 - d 3 June 1913,
SNB
Willie R, b 21 Apr 1886 -
d 10 March 1918, SNB
SHILLINGS, Dollie, b 12
Sept 1879 - d 21 Feb
1925, PLR
Mary C, b&d 16 Oct 1939,
PLR
Vilia, d 17 Jan 1977, ae
61y, PLR
SHIPWASH, Allie Belle, b 21
July 1882 - d 28 Apr
1963, WRJ
Clara M, d 10 Oct 1981, ae

SHIPWASH (continued)
88y, EST
Dallas, b 10 Oct 1897 - d
12 March 1912, WRJ
Gearaldine, b 6 Apr 1921 -
d 5 Dec 1921, RTT
Infant Son, 1908, WRJ
James T, b 12 March 1893 -
d 26 Nov 1934, WRJ
M L, d 9 March 1975, ae
83y, EST
Martha, b 18 Oct 1873 - d
20 Dec 1947, WRJ
SHIRKS, Lummie, b 8 Aug
1888 - d 30 Dec 1967,
NWP
Michelle Denise, b 8 Apr
1964 - d 11 Oct 1964,
NWP
Robert Hobart, d 1 Nov
1981, ae 55y, NWP
Sam, b 15 Nov 1880 - d 18
July 1936, NWP
SHORT, Bonnie, b 15 March
1900 - no death date,
PNY
Cleola F, b 7 Feb 1907 - d
25 March 1965, CRO
Clola T, b 7 Feb 1907 - d
25 March 1965, CRO
Francis, b 29 Aug 1876 - d
24 Jan 1928, PNY
Lavinnah Alley, b 7 June
1914 - d 18 Apr 1937,
CRO
Rebecca M, b 1890 - d
1971, WRC
William G, b 1871 - d
1951, WRC
Wm Harry, b 11 June 1897 -
d 22 Apr 1974, CRO
SIEBER, Donald Ray, b 26
Aug 1959 - d 11 Nov
1974, WRJ
SILCOX, Arthur, b 15 Apr
1893 - d 6 July 1896,
WRC
Billie V, b 13 Jan 1926 -

173

SILCOX (continued)
d 11 Dec 1939, WBB
Loney, b 13 Oct 1884 - d
24 Nov 1892, WRC
Mary, b 25 Oct 1863 - d 2
Apr 1921, WRC
Shirley Fay, b 21 Jan 1939
- d 2 July 1941, WBB
Thomas, b 25 July 1852 - d
13 Dec 1913, WRC
SILVEY, Anna A, b 27 June
1913 - d 8 Nov 1946, CRO
Artia, b 22 July 1911 - d
29 June 1912, CRO
Daniel Lyons, b 6 Aug 1944
- d 8 Aug 1944, CRO
Hazel West, b 27 March
1923 - d 24 Oct 1942,
CRO
Tilton, b 17 Sept 1877 - d
11 May 1915, CRO
Vigil, b 15 Dec 1907 - d
19 Nov 1961, CRO
SIMERVIS, Bartervis (na-
tive/Italy), d 5 June
1875 on section 149
CSRR, HLL
SIMPSON, Adam Monroe, b 9
Sept 1849 - d 18 Apr
1923, PTC
Alma Creekmore, d 3 Oct
1980, ae 78y, WMG
Everett, Sgt Co E 113 Ammo
WWI, b 21 July 1892 - d
6 Sept 1966, WMG
Florence, d 5 Oct 1976, ae
72y, SNB
Hattie Huskins, b 1889 - d
6 Sept 1978, NWP
Jessie F, b 1876 - d 1960,
NWP
McGhee, b 26 Aug 1910 - d
6 Aug 1946, WRC
Nattie b, b 1889 - no
death date, NWP
SIMS, Amanda, b 10 March
1880 - d 19 Apr 1910,
MLC

SIMS (continued)
Edith, b 27 July 1904 - no
death date, MSG
George, b 10 Jan 1893 - d
8 March 1962, MSG
Goldie May, d 2 Jan 1956,
ae 61y, NWP
Kenneth, b f6 Apr 1910 - d
12 July 1910, MLC
Lonnie C, d 29 Sept 1973,
ae 40y, MSG
Ollie, b 29 Sept 1910 - d
19 July 1911, MLC
SISSON, Albert J, b 30 Dec
1893 - d 12 Dec 1958,
EST
Beulah Marie, b 30 June
1907 - no death date,
EST
C Luffman, b 13 Feb 1871 -
d 5 Jan 1896, EST
Helen, b 26 Feb 1908 - no
death date, EST
Ronnie Lynn, b 12 June
1945 - d 7 June 1962,
EST
Wm David, b 14 Nov 1900 -
d 24 July 1974, EST
SIVILS, Mary Ruth, b 12 Dec
1921 - d 20 Dec 1921,
SNB
SKAGGS, Laura Mae, b 12 Nov
1943 - d 11 Nov 1963,
BRN
SKILES, James Leslie, b 7
Apr 1913 - d 14 Jan
1949, EST
James Leslie Jr, b 23 Apr
1949 - d 24 Apr 1949,
EST
SLIGER, Rosalee, b 28 Aug
1877 - d 2 July 1927,
DVS
SLOAN, James, b 18 Feb 1894
- d 27 Nov 1953, PNY
SMARSH, John, b 12 March
1914 - d 18 May 1950,
DRL

SMARSH (continued)
Pete P, b 4 Aug 1922 — d
21 Dec 1964, DRL
SMEAT, Dalphus, b 7 Arp
1915 — d 17 Apr 1969,
LNE
Joyce Fay, b 7 Arp 1949 —
d 17 Feb 1964, LNE
SMITH, A A, b 8 Nov 1891 —
d 18 Nov 1969, FLR
Agnes, d 15 May 1974, ae
59y, UNG
Alberta Rose, b 17 May
1947 — d 28 Oct 1948,
RGB
Alex G, b 19 May 1899 — d
1 May 1962, PNY
Alice, b 13 Sept 1872 — d
4 July 1947, PNY
Anna, b 29 June 1864 — d
18 June 1949, PNY
Bennie (or Bettie) Carol,
d 9 Nov 1973, ae 26y,
DVS
Betty Lou, b 31 Aug 1951 —
d 5 Aug 1969, EST
Bobby Ann, b 22 March 1931
— d 24 June 1933, RTT
C P, b 13 May 1888 — d 11
March 1905, OLP
Charles, b 24 Nov 1903 — d
3 May 1939, CRO
Charles, Co A 2nd US Vol,
b 6 Jan 1841 — d 29 Dec
1912, PTC
Charles H Jr, d 4 Oct
1976, ae 56y, MLC
Charlie R, d 11 May 1979,
ae 52y, FLR
Cheryl Lynn, b 24 July
1947 — d 5 Aug 1969, EST
Clay Evans, d 6 July 1973,
ae 65y, FLR
Cora Louise, b 21 March
1892 — d 4 Sept 1892,
DRL
Dewey Joe, b 1899 — d
1968, UNN

SMITH (continued)
Donna Gail, b 29 May 1946
— d 31 May 1963, EST
Elizabeth, b 20 Sept 1875
— no death date, EST
Ella Cain, b 11 Nov 1900 —
d 30 Oct 1967, UNG
Elmer J, b 14 Aug 1912 — d
4 Aug 1980, EST
Estella, b 12 Nov 1928 — d
7Jan 1969, WRC
Fane B, b 20 Apr 1906 — d
19 June 1968, NWP
Fannie B, b 9 Feb 1906 —
no death date, PNY
Garland W, Tech 4 Bty B
WWII, b 18 Aug 1921 — d
29 Dec 1959, WRC
George, b 17 March 1858 —
d 3 Aug 1930, PLR
George D, b 1872 — d 1934,
DRL
George H, b 30 May 1872 —
d 8 Feb 1932, CRO
Georgia, b 2 Feb 1875 — d
10 Oct 1960, UNN
Harwell M, Co H 3 KY Inf,
mil stone, no dates, LNC
Hazel Lyons, b 14 Feb 1911
— d 1 Nov 1943, DRL
Ida, b 14 Jan 1913 — no
death date, EST
Jack, b 9 Dec 1925 — d 20
Sept 1928, WRC
Jane, b 30 March 192- — d
31 May 196-, FLR
Jane E, b 1872 — d 1889,
RGB
Jesse, b 9 Sept 1948 — d
31 Oct 1948, WRC
John H, b 20 Feb 1866 — d
27 Sept 1957, PNY
Junius S, Cpl 22 MI Inf, b
30 May 1843 — d 18 Sept
1924, BRR
Justin, b 15 Sept 1872 — d
10 Apr 1945, PNY
Lawrence, b 1880 — d 1964,

SMITH (continued)
WRC
Lena A, b 1893 - d 1962,
WRC
Lewis, b 11 Dec 1919 (?) -
d 5 Jan 1916 (?), CRO
Lewis S, b 1 Aug 1871 - d
24 Nov 1946, EST
Lola Irene, b 10 Jan 1886
- d 29 March 1940, BRR
Lycie Marie, b 4 May 1957
- d 6 May 1957, LNC
Margaret, d 14 Apr 1860,
ae 61y 11mo, NDK
Margaret L, b 12 Apr 1886
- d 3 May 1955, CRO
Maria, b 31 May 1845 - d
18 Feb 1926, DRL
Mary E, b 2 Sept 1878 - d
9 Nov 1944, UNH
Mary E Dougherty, b 5 Dec
1870 - d 6 Feb 1940, PNY
Mary Rose, d 10 March
1973, ae 6da, BRR
Mirtha Lilie, b 10 March
1882 - d 9 May 1932, DVS
Nona Evelyn, b 12 Feb 1878
- d 25 Dec 1948, BRR
Pamela Sue, b 26 Oct 1953
- d 28 Oct 1953, WRC
Patricia Ann, b 4 July
1919 - d 5 Aug 1969, EST
Rachel E, b 5 Feb 1848 - d
14 Jan 1931, BRR
Richard, b 22 Feb 1863 - d
17 Jan 1935, UNN
Roy, b 1 May 1914 - d 26
July 1914, PNY
Roy V, b 26 Jan 1909 - d 3
March 1912, PLR
Samuel W, b 2 Nov 1869 - d
14 Jan 1948, PNY
Steve, d 24 Nov 1979, ae
15y, MCR
Stobert A, d 12 Aug 1978,
ae 72y, LNC
Thomas Andrew, Pvt Co L
1st Rgt TN Inf Sp/Am

SMITH (continued)
War, b 31 March 1881 - d
8 Nov 1965, OOO
Thurmond H, d 25 Dec 1979,
ae 53y, FLR
Tommie, b 28 Sept 1905 - d
17 Jan 1913, PNY
Veria, b 4 Dec 1895 - d 12
Jan 1977, FLR
Virgil E, b 30 Aug 1909 -
no death date, DRL
W A, b 1846 - d 1929, DRL
Willard, b 31 Dec 1909 - d
5 Apr 1965, LNC
William Albert, b 6 Nov
1900 - d 3 Oct 1921, PNY
William H, b 4 March 1894
- d 8 May 1964, UNG
Winnie, b 14 Aug 1890 - d
20 Jan 1891, DRL
Wm Perry, b 30 May 1866 -
d 2 Jan 1927, PNY
SMITHERS, Dennis J, b 1889
- d 1963, SNB
Emma, b 1907 - d 1961, LNE
John F, b 2 Dec 1882 - d 5
Aug 1966, LNE
SNIPER, Victoria, b 23 Apr
1906 - d 26 June 1950,
UNN
SNIPES, Victoria Fair, b
1927 - d 1968, UNN
SNOW, Alphia Carpenter, d
12 Apr 1978, ae 96y, CRO
Charlie, d 3 Feb 1979, ae
79y, CRO
Larkin, b 26 May 1813 - d
7 Dec 1881, CRO
Martha, b 1881 - d 1966,
CRO
Mildred Irene, b 19 Jan
1924 - d 25 Jan 1924,
CRO
Rita Pearson, b 25 June
1915 - 1 May 1935, UNN
Stanley J, Pfc Coast Art
Corps WWII, b 10 June
1908 - d 13 Apr 1943,

SNOW (continued)
CRO
William Bearl, d 16 July
1979, ae 63y, CRO
SNYDER, Charles Blake, b 19
Feb 1911 - d 9 July
1935, CRO
Charles P, b 7 July 1879 -
d 3 Sept 1966, CRO
Maggie B, b 26 Nov 1889 -
no death date, CRO
Margaret Ray, b 23 Jan
1937 - d 11 Oct 1937,
CRO
SOLOMON, Harriet, b 2 March
1858 - d 10 Apr 1939,
HCK
James D, b 29 Nov 1914 - d
18 Jan 1953, LNE
Jesse B, b 29 Nov 1895 - d
15 Nov 1956, LNE
Jessie B Jr, b 1917 - d 12
Oct 1873, LNE
John W, b 23 Sept 1854 - d
11 March 1951, HCK
Josie Freels, d 10 Jan
1979, ae 82y, LNE
Mames, b 3 Dec 1899 - no
death date, EST
Mattie, b 8 Sept 1889 - d
1 March 1962, EST
SOLONE, Baby, no dates, MLC
SPAGLER, Hester, b 1879 - d
1963, WRC
SPAINHOUR, Bunch Mary, b 21
Sept 1921 - d 11 Oct
1958, DVS
SPEECH, Anna, b 15 May 1853
- no death date, WRC
Sebastian, b 4 July 1855 -
d -- Aug 1890, WRC
SPRADLIN, Glen, b 25 July
1912 - d 27 March 1915,
SNB
SPURLING, A A, b 21 Sept
1904 - d 29 July 1924,
UNG
Alfred F, b 12 June 1874 -

SPURLING (continued)
d 9 March 1956, UNG
Bobby Lee Jr, b 15 May
1966 - d 30 Jan 1970,
UNG
Commodore L, b 14 Aug 1887
- d 29 June 1969, UNG
Cora L, b 25 March 1896 -
d 29 Apr 1963, UNG
Daniel W, Pvt 114 Inf 29
Div WWI, b 29 July 1893
- d 18 Dec 1927, LBR
Dicie J, b 21 Aug 1879 - d
5 Apr 1932, UNG
Ethel L, b 27 Apr 1895 -
no death date, UNG
Henry, b 2 Dec 1930 - d 24
Sept 1939, UNG
Hiram, b 23 Feb 1849 - d
30 March 1922, DVD
Jacob M, b 12 Apr 1892 - d
22 March 1963, UNG
Mark Anthony, b 11 Aug
1969 - d 5 Sept 1969,
UNG
Martha E, b 4 March 1852 -
d 12 Dec 1921, UNG
R A, b 2 Feb 1857 - d 13
Jan 1923, UNG
Robert R, d 30 Oct 1973,
ae 57y, UNG
Sarah Thornton, b 14 Dec
1885 - d 2 Feb 1964, LBR
Shirley, d 19 Jan 1979, ae
64y, UNG
William A, Co H 10 TN Inf
Civil War, b 24 Nov 1844
- d 24 Nov 1904, UNG
STAFFORD, Rebecca S, b 1809
- 1892, RGB
STAGG, Ted S, b 16 May 1910
- d 19 May 1971, DRL
STAGOSTI, A P, b 1866 - d
1947, DRL
STAHL, Charlotte B, b 8
July 1881 - d 2 Aug
1971, UNN
Frederick, b 4 March 1845

STAHL (continued)
- no death date, LNC
L M, b 14 Aug 1871 - d 22
June 1961, UNN
Lucinda Dunn, b 30 Dec
1831 - d 28 March 1930,
LNC
Milda Jones, b 16 Dec 1869
- d 27 March 1947, UNN
STANCIL, Major, d 21 May
1975, ae 90y, MRR
Vesta P, b 25 Oct 1893 - d
21 Nov 1943, MRR
STANFIELD, Anna Melhorn, d
3 May 1981, ae 60y, WRC
STANFORD, M T, b 25 Feb
1896 - d 16 March 1949,
UNH
Mary, b 17 July 1862 - d 7
Jan 1935, UNH
STANGEL, Della, b 23 Nov
1877 - d 5 Aug 1967, BRD
STANLEY, W M, b 25 June
1878 - d 20 June 1914,
PNY
STANSBURY, Earl, b 25 Aug
1911 - d 28 Aug 1911,
CRO
Edward, b&d 8 Apr 1913,
CRO
Elizabeth, b 29 Nov 1852 -
d 23 Oct 1910, CRO
James T, b 8 Sept 1885 - d
3 June 1966, CRO
STAPLES, ----, no dates,
SNB
Benjamin, b 24 Dec 1817 -
d 22 March 1863, LBR
Delila C, b 10 Nov 1890 -
d 16 June 1891, SNB
John M, b 8 Oct 1825 - d
22 Oct 1852, LBR
Joseph S, b 5 Sept 1849 -
d 6 March 1907, LBR
Leota, b 10 June 1892 - d
26 Jun 1894, SNB
Llion, no dates, SNB
Samuel H, b 1844 - d 1913,

STAPLES (continued)
WRC
Samuel Jr, b 1874 - d
1912, WRC
W R Jr, b 6 Oct 1867 - d
15 Aug 1898, DRL
STAPLETON, Melton, b 1883 -
d 1931, MLC
Wheeler, d 9 Sept 1970, ae
42y, DVS
STARK, Raymond O, b 24 Dec
1896 - d 6 Jan 1930, EST
STEELE, Elsie Reece, d 8
Dec 1970, ae 62y 7mo,
NWP
Silas O, d 8 Sept 1978, ae
77y, LBR
STEELMAN, Carl Edward s/o E
H, 27 Jan 1946, MSG
Edna Lee, b 7 Aug 1902 -
no death date, PLR
Jesse R, b 1910 - d 1934,
MSG
Jewel, b 1933 - d 1963,
PLR
Marvin W, b 4 Sept 1908 -
d 20 Sept 1974, PLR
Matilda, b 1867 - d 1940,
PLR
STEPHENS, Banner O, d 16
Sept 1981, ae 81y, WRC
Charles S, b 29 March 1821
- d 15 Dec 1858, STP
Eldridge H, b 20 Apr 1917
- d 2 Nov 1917, SNB
Jackie, b 14 May 1927 - d
30 June 1929, WBB
James, b 3 June 1857 - d
10 Apr 1940, LBR
James E, b 27 Apr 1906 - d
13 June 1977, DRL
James E Jr, b 28 Apr 1940
- d 19 Aug 1966, DRL
John, b 10 May 1826 - d 27
Dec 1848, STP
John Turman, Fireman 3
Class WWI, b 27 June
1889 - d 18 July 1946,

178

STEPHENS (continued)
OOO
Kenneth Ott, b 28 Oct 1892
- d 1 March 1922, LBR
M L, b 10 Sept 1879 - d 21
Feb 1962, PLR
Mary, b 3 March 1861 - d
25 Feb 1928, LBR
Mary J, b 7 March 1882 -
no death date, PLR
Meshack, Maj USA, b 16 Jan
1828 - d 25 Jan 1910,
STP
Millie, b 4 Aug 1824 - d
12 March 1858, STP
N R, b 18 Aug 1859 - d 12
Aug 1893, LBR
Ova, b 1911 - d 2 Dec
1963, DRL
Robert K, b 9 Sept 1925 -
d 20 June 1957, WBB
Shadrack, b -- Feb 1791 -
d 6 Dec 1856, STP
Susannah, b 4 Feb 1802 - d
6 Oct 1887, STP
W K, b 18 Aug 1859 - d 12
Aug 1893, LBR
Walton L, b 1906 - d 1971,
PTC
STEPP, Bertie Mae C, b 4
Dec 1893 - d 3 June
1937, UNG
Robert A, d 17 June 1975,
ae 77y, DRL
S T, b 11 March 1900 - d
28 Sept 1927, DRL
S W, b 12 May 1902 - d 26
July 1928, DRL
STEVENS, Isabel Cooper, b
1891 - d 1956, LVN
Millie A, b 23 Dec 1865 -
d 14 Sept 1927, LBR
STEWARD, Bertha, b 27 Feb
1908 - d 29 Sept 1947,
LNE
Mrs, d 4 Apr 1977, ae
------, CRO
William A, b 26 June 1897

STEWARD (continued)
- d 16 Aug 1917, BRR
STEWART, A L, no dates, CLC
Albert William, b 4 Nov
1874 - d 14 Apr 1950,
LBR
Anna B, b 20 Aug 1899 - d
17 March 1963, NWP
Annie Jones, b 26 Aug 1883
- d 3 Jan 1968, LNC
C R (Brownie), d 11 Aug
1981, ae 69y, MRR
Charles, d 25 Aug 1977, ae
66y, CRO
Cinda, b 12 Jan 1896 - d 9
March 1908, MCD
Cleates, d 14 Nov 1979, ae
61y, SNB
Dave, b 5 March 1894 - d
26 Nov 1941, NWP
Della, b 2 Oct 1896 - no
death date, NWP
Edna Maden, b 26 March
1871 - d 16 March 1912,
ELZ
Ella, b 29 Apr 1909 - no
death date, MCD
Elsie Potter, d 17 Dec
1973, ae 35y, PTC
Ethel L, b 1887 - no death
date, SNB
Floyd, dates illegible,
LBR
Garlan J, b 12 Apr 1906 -
d 20 Feb 1969, MCD
George, b 18 June 1848 - d
29 Feb 1916, BRR
Grace, b 18 Oct 1907 - d
20 March 1908, PLR
Harold F, b 15 Jan 1916 -
d 2 July 1931, PLR
Haskel, b 5 Dec 1911 - d
30 Dec 1911, MCD
Henry C, d 14 May 1977, ae
68y, PLR
J F, dates illegible, LBR
James, b 13 Feb 1896 - d 7
Sept 1964, NWP

STEWART (continued)
Jess J, b 21 Oct 1906 - d
  18 Aug 1951, PLR
Jessie Ellen, b 14 Jan
  1943 - d 9 Apr 1943, PLR
Joe, b 14 Feb 1882 - d 5
  Nov 1935, LNC
John, b 11 Feb 1848 - d 8
  Nov 1919, LBR
John Cooper, b 29 July
  1912 - d 22 July 1971,
  PLR
John Frederick, b 20 May
  1885 - d 8 Nov 1961, LBR
John M, b 2 Feb 1879 - d
  28 May 1967, PLR
Kenneth, b 1924 - d 1927,
  LBR
Larry Ralph, b 1 June 1941
  - d 4 Apr 1977, CRO
Leroy, b 25 Jan 1901 - d 4
  Apr 1904, MCD
Linda A, b 21 March 1899 -
  d 8 Apr 1908, MCD
Madelyn Human, b 21 Aug
  1924 - no death date,
  PLR
Margaret J, b 26 June 1882
  - no death date, PLR
Martha, b 30 Jan 1879 - d
  14 May 1980, LBR
Martha D w/o John, (no
  dates), LBR
Mary, d 31 Jan 1951, MCD
Minda M Hall, b 30 Apr
  1893 - d 1 June 1962,
  LBR
Ralph, b 10 Sept 1904 - d
  19 Sept 1905, OLP
Robbie Nell, b 17 Nov 1928
  - d 8 Nov 1931, PLR
Robert L, b 1885 - d 1954,
  SNB
Rosie w/o J F, (no dates),
  LBR
Sallie A, b 27 Dec 1896 -
  d 4 Jan 1897, MCD
Sarah, b 10 Dec 1854 - d

STEWART (continued)
  24 March 1905, BRR
Sarah -, b 16 Dec 1845 -
  no death date, DRL
Savannah C, b 12 March
  1935 - d 19 March 1935,
  PLR
Tami Elaine, b&d 1957, SNB
STOFA, M, b 18 Apr 1897 - d
  14 Nov 1926, DRL
Michael J Sr, b 23 Sept
  1863 - d 11 Feb 1939,
  DRL
Susan Grecula, b 4 June
  1876 - d 11 Nov 1955,
  DRL
STONE, Edna A, b 5 March
  1876 - d 16 Sept 1942,
  DRL
Fred, d 27 Jan 1979, ae
  60y, DRL
John W, b 7 July 1874 - d
  20 June 1953, DRL
Laura S, b 5 Dec 1842 - d
  3 Sept 1914, DRL
Ray P, b 22 May 188- - d
  11 Sept 1973, CRO
Vivan, b 22 Aug 18-- - d
  July 16, 19--, CRO
STONECIPHER, A Y, b 22 May
  1894 - d 23 Mar 1974,
  BRR
Andrew J, b 31 Jan 1857 -
  d 19 May 1915, UNN
Annis Lee, b 26 Dec 1894 -
  d 28 Apr 1976, UNN
Beatrice S, b 19 June 1923
  - d 12 Feb 1972, BRR
Calvin, b 11 Apr 1825 - d
  14 Jan 1894, UNN
Carrie T, b 1 Sept 1900 -
  d 23 Mar 1974, BRR
Desma, b 23 Feb 1933 - d
  15 Feb 1936, UNN
Edd, b 19 Feb 1915 - d 25
  Apr 1937, UNN
Elender, b 9 March 1808 -
  d 1890, PLR

STONECIPHER (continued)

Elizabeth, b c1837 - d 11 Sept 1907, DVS

Elizabeth, b 13 Dec 1830 - d -- May 1899, UNN

Emily Wilson, b 15 June 1860 - d 27 Nov 1934, UNN

Ezra, b 15 Dec 1841 - d 17 Dec 1910, DVS

Francis Ann, b 31 Oct 1932 - d 23 Dec 1932, UNN

Joe, b&d 1 Nov 1921, UNN

John Hiram, b 22 July 1856 - d 2 June 1885, UNN

John L, b 3 Feb 1892 - d 19 Dec 1910, UNN

Joseph M, b 16 Apr 1858 - d 1 Aug 1943, UNN

Joseph O, b 5 Feb 1896 - d 30 Oct 1944, UNN

Julia S, b 10 Feb 1868 - d 10 Dec 1888, DVS

Kyle, b 23 March 1914 - d 8 Apr 1914, UNN

Lorene, b 19 Oct 1912 - d 21 Oct 1912, DVS

Louisa, b 1871 - no death date, DVS

Lucy Irene, b 22 March 1911 - d 19 March 1914, DVS

Luther, b 23 Apr 1909 - d 15 July 1912, UNN

Martin, b 15 Jan 1832 - d 12 Jan 1909, UNN

Martin Luther, b 23 Feb 1895 - d 9 Dec 1898, UNN

Mary D, b 19 Dec 1807 - d 7 Dec 1888, DVS

Mary Patt, b 21 Aug 1921 - d 9 Nov 1959, UNN

N Jasper, b 23 June 1874 - d 18 Apr 1939, DVS

Nancy Milton, b 6 Dec 1835 - d 6 Feb 1897, UNN

Nathan J, b 2 Sept 1866 - d 11 Nov 1934, UNN

STONECIPHER (continued)

Noah, b 26 Feb 1804 - d 8 July 1875, DVS

Nora Wilson, b 9 July 1899 - no death date, UNN

Perry, b 9 Nov 1882 - d 9 Dec 1888, UNN

Robert N, b 1 Apr 1901 - d 13 Sept 1902, UNN

Rollin J, b 16 Apr 1884 - d 16 Oct 1887, UNN

Sallie, b&d 15 Oct 1919, UNN

Samuel, b 11 Oct 1783 - d 26 Aug 1879, BCF

Samuel W, b 31 Jan 1887 - d 24 Sept 1937, UNN

Sarah B, b 3 Nov 1871 - d 26 Dec 1944, UNN

Susan C, b 23 Aug 1870 - d 5 May 1903, UNN

Thomas, b 12 March 1809 - d 13 Feb 1885, PLR

Vard L, b 22 July 1859 - d 20 Sept 1920, UNN

William M, b 1865 - d 1918, DVS

Wm Martin, b 29 Dec 1898 - d 18 Dec 1972, UNN

Woodrow, b 1 Aug 1912 - d 2 Oct 1914, UNN

STOWERS, Adra E, b 11 March 1911 - d 9 Feb 1929, SHD

STRAND, Alfred G, d 11 Jan 1980, ae 81y, DRL

Alma, b 29 Oct 1899 - no death date, DRL

Anna, b 1903 - d 1910, DRL

Malla, b 7 Sept 1888 - d 7 Jan 1965, DRL

Marie, b 1864 - d 1910, DRL

Peter H, b 1864 - d 1922, DRL

Terval, b 23 Feb 1893 - no death date, DRL

STRICKLEN, May R, d ca 1963, WRC

STRICKLEN (continued)
W J, b 1869 - d 1938, WRC
STRICKLIN, Cora J, b 21 Jan 1874 - d 16 Feb 1941, EST
Mae Riseden, d 1963, ae 86y, WMG
STRINGER, Alana, b 16 March 1918 - no death date, NWP
Noble, b 17 Apr 1909 - d 25 Feb 1974, NWP
STRINGFIELD, Albert W, b 23 Aug 1900 - d 26 Aug 1963, LNE
Alex, b 20 March 1872 - d 22 Feb 1946, ELZ
Alex Sr, b 1 March 1898 - d 6 Sept 1933, MCD
Angela M, b 2 July 1972 - d 3 July 1972, LNE
Baby, no dates, MLC
Brenda Sue, 9 Aug 1948, MLC
C S, b 7 March 1873 - d 8 Feb 1945, SNB
Cloah, b 1860 - d 19--, ELZ
Mrs Columbia, d 9 May 1951, ae 76y, SNB
Cordie, no dates, MLC
Daniel, 1867, LBR
Delila, b 1879 - d 1943, LNE
Earl L, b 1 May 1904 - d 8 Nov 1971, SNB
Elizabeth, b 18 Nov 1897 - d 18 Sept 1898, SNB
Emma Chaney, b 9 Dec 1890 - d 15 Feb 1933, MLC
Enas, b 11 Jan 1905 - d 14 Sept 1906, SNB
Erel Lawrence, d 24 Aug 1978, ae 46y, LNE
Florence, b 28 May 1887 - d 23 Sept 1922, ELZ
Frazier J, b 28 Feb 1883 - d 8 Dec 1964, ELZ

STRINGFIELD (continued)
Gaither, d 8 Sept 1977, ae 66y, STC
Guy T, b 30 Sept 1909 - no death date, LNE
J C, no dates, ELZ
Rev J W, d 5 Dec 1981, ae 82y, LNE
James, b 15 May 1842 - d 22 Sept 1912, ELZ
James T, b 7 Oct 1872 - d 17 June 1943, ELZ
Jefferson, b 20 March 1850 - d 9 Dec 1918, WRC
Jettie B, b 3 Jan 1882 - no death date, ELZ
Rev John, b 29 Sept 1898 - no death date, LNE
John, b 27 Sept 1881 - d 7 Nov 1926, WRC
John A, b 29 March 1864 - d 25 Jan 1931, PNY
John Clinton, b 5 June 1914 - d 10 May 1962, LNE
John W, b 18 Dec 1882 - d 29 Apr 1972, LNE
Julia, b 5 Feb 1880 - d 13 Jan 1950, ELZ
Julia A, b 27 Oct 1892 - d 16 June 1972, LNE
Julian, b 1866 - d 1939, ELZ
Laura O, b 31 Aug 1910 - d 7 Sept 1970, LNE
Lielie Mae, b 30 Oct 1915 - d 14 Oct 1918, ELZ
Lydia D, b 1 Oct 1847 - d 16 Apr 1900, HLL
M, b 29 Sept 1940 - d 5 July 1941, WRC
Martha, b 1826 - no death date, ELZ
Mary, b 29 July 1869 - d 14 June 1944, ELZ
Mary, b 1916 - d 1962, PNY
Meda, b 10 Dec 1900 - d 30 Jan 1953, LNE

STRINGFIELD (continued)

Millard, b 1877 - d 1951, LNE

Minney, b 20 Apr 1873 - d 30 Oct 1953, STC

Nancy M, b 15 Feb 1863 - d 28 May 1966, PNY

Oma, b 27 May 1904 - no death date, LNE

Opal Human, b 7 Aug 1906 - d 11 Apr 1980, SNB

Oscar s/o James & Julia, 3 Nov 18--, ELZ

Sam, b 18 June 1875 - d 11 Nov 1955, STC

Thomas, b 1963 - d 1963, WRC

Virgil Bud, d 22 July 1977, ae 23y, ELZ

Wesley, b 19 Aug 1900 - d 10 Aug 1912, ELZ

Wilham A, d 29 May 1977, ae 58y, SNB

William, b 1820 - no death date, ELZ

STRUNK, Billie Mae, b&d 1923, CRO

Carl L, b 2 Nov 1906 - d 1 Feb 1908, WBB

Elizabeth N, b 1845 - d 1923, UNH

Hortio G, b 1847 - d 1928, UNH

James Ray, b 30 May 1905 - d 14 July 1956, CRO

Marion E, b 28 Apr 1877 - d 26 May 1948, CRO

Mary Stewart, b 1885 - d 1951, CRO

Paul, d 15 Dec 1979, ae 55y, WRC

Ralph, Sgt 3502 Base Unit WWII, b 31 Dec 1915 - d 12 May 1956, CRO

Thomas, d 13 Apr 1981, ae 65y, MNT

STRUTTON, ----, b&d 29 July 1931, WRC

STRUTTON (continued)

Harry L, b 18 May 1890 - d 21 Jan 1946, WRC

John, b 1894 - d 1966, WRC

Lonzo B, d 14 Feb 1976, ae 63y, WRC

Odie Ray, d June 1965, WRC

Wanda Faye, b 29 May 1954 - d 18 Jan 1958, WRC

STUBBS, Charles S, b 6 Sept 1899 - d 21 March 1965, EST

Kate I, b 10 May 1906 - no death date, EST

Robert Eugene, b 3 Jan 1925 - d 4 Jan 1925, EST

SUDDATH, Linda Blake, 2 Dec 1874 - no other dates, CRO

SULLIVAN, V, b 17 Jan 1862 - d 3 May 1944, WRC

W N, b 1842 - d 31 Aug 1928, WRC

SUMMER, Charles T, b 7 Aug 1876 - d 20 Feb 1944, SNB

Leona Galloway, b 11 Sept 1879 - no death date, SNB

SUMMERS, Albert H, b 14 Aug 1901 - d 1 March 1952, LBR

Ben T, b 19 Sept 1874 - d 14 June 1955, LBR

Boyle Cullen, b 1 Dec 1908 - d 20 June 1953, SNB

Charles W, b 16 Oct 1870 - d 24 July 1922, LBR

Cornelius Doug, b 22 Feb 1912 - d 10 Feb 1966, WRC

D R, b 20 Jan 1866 - d 16 July 1932, UNN

David, b 2 Jan 1849 - d -- March 1940, WRC

Elizabeth, b 22 Aug 1841 - d 25 Apr 1883, LBR

Ellen, d 26 Apr 1889, ae

SUMMERS (continued)
80y, LBR
Mrs F C, b 16 Apr 1853 - d
29 July 1937, WRC
Fred A, b 14 Apr 1898 - d
13 Jan 1971, WRC
Harry O, b 16 Oct 1897 - d
4 Nov 1970, LBR
Henry, b 17 March 1878 - d
1 June 1943, WRC
Henry, b 1882 - d 1966,
LBR
Horace Greely, b 30 May
1881 - d 15 June 1914,
CRO
Infant, b 25 June 1928 - d
20 July 1928, MLC
J Callen, b 22 Feb 1871 -
d 20 June 1970, SNB
Jack, b 14 Apr 1900 - d 12
Jan 1967, SNB
John M, b 16 Sept 1869 - d
20 Jan 1942, LBR
Juliau B, b 25 Jan 1911 -
d 12 March 1913, SNB
Kiley W, b 20 May 1828 - d
4 Feb 1909, LBR
Leurmie L, b 1918 - d 11
Feb 1975, WRC
Lillian A, b 30 Aug 1902 -
no death date, WRC
Lillian Mae, b 18 Oct 1921
- d 25 Sept 1922, MLC
Lonnie, b 17 July 1902 - d
14 Sept 1924, LBR
Lula Higgin, b 2 Nov 1898
- d 14 Feb 1957, SNB
M C Liles, b 11 June 1878
- d 9 Sept 1959, UNN
Martha Ann, b 25 Nov 1830
- d 1 Dec 1909, LBR
Martha C, b 10 Sept 1872 -
d 4 June 1947, LBR
Mary Ada, b 25 June 1874 -
d 22 Oct 1956, SNB
Matilda, b 10 June 1872 -
d 1 Jan 1956, LBR
Mercy A, b 14 Nov 1885 - d

SUMMERS (continued)
2 May 1942, WRC
Millie B, b 1 Dec 1879 - d
18 Nov 1952, WRC
Minnie Ann, b 6 May 1883 -
d 13 Feb 1958, LBR
Nellie Walker, d 28 Feb
1979, ae 53y, BRD
Polly England, b 24 May
1883 - d 24 May 1945,
WRC
Sam H, b 30 Aug 1903 - d 8
Dec 1949, LBR
Samuel H, b 13 July 1872 -
d 17 July 1909, FLF
Vera C, b 23 Feb 1919 - no
death date, WRC
W R Bill, b 12 Jan 1903 -
no death date, SNB
William J, b 29 Oct 1876 -
d 30 Nov 1951, WRC
Wilson, d 20 Feb 1891, ae
80y, LBR
Winnie Matilda, b 30 May
1902 - d 6 Aug 1902, LBR
SUMNER, Anna M, b 25 Apr
1892 - d 16 June 1958,
WRC
Eliza A, d 15 July 1980,
ae 92y, WRC
Ellis A, b 12 Dec 1886 - d
15 July 1979, WRC
Fred E, b 3 Sept 1892 - d
31 March 1954, WRC
Harvey, b 26 Nov 1883 - d
5 Nov 1950, WRC
Infant Son, 13 Aug 1937 -
no other date, PLR
Infant Son, d 5 July 1938,
PLR
Laura J, b 6 June 1888 - d
14 July 1964, WRC
Lawrence, b 1910 - d 1962,
PLR
Minerva H, b 7 Oct 1880 -
d 29 Jan 1959, WRC
Stanton Allen, b 28 Sept
1924 - d 25 Aug 1931,

184

SUMNER (continued)
UNH
SUPECK, Caroline, b 18 Oct
1880 - no death date,
DRL
John, b 20 Oct 1878 - no
death date, DRL
SUSACK, Andrew, b 17 Nov
1865 - d 2 Jan 1937, DRL
Joseph Pete, b 17 March
1894 - d 5 Jan 1978, DRL
Thomas S, b 11 Dec 1899 -
d 25 May 1968, DRL
SWEET, Don E, d 9 Dec 1976,
ae 74y, WMG
SWEETEN, Dora, d 26 Apr
1975, ae 71y, PLR
SWINT, Michael Vaughn, b 23
Sept 1958 - d 14 Feb
1973, ELZ
TAKACS, Mary, b 1874 - no
death date, DRL
Dr Steve, b 1893 - d 1926,
DRL
Stine, b 1869 - d 1929,
DRL
TALLMAN, Cloice D, b 20 Apr
1905 - d 28 July 1928,
PLR
Lueman, b 15 Sept 1877 - d
31 Aug 1961, PLR
William H, b 11 Dec 1868 -
d 10 July 1954, PLR
TANNER, John E, b 1886 - d
1936, WRC
Karen Elaine, b&d 18 Apr
1901, WRC
Maude W, b 22 May 1889 - d
27 Dec 1968, WRC
William Herbert, b 15 Jan
1922 - d 16 July 1937,
WRC
TARUS, Albert, b 1876 - d
1949, DVS
TATE, Dallas M, b 16 Sept
1893 - d 8 Nov 1967, LNE
TAYLOR, A J, b 5 May 1853 -
d 16 Jan 1936, PTC

TAYLOR (continued)
Addie, b 9 Jan 1911 - d 18
Sept 1916, PTC
Alex, no dates, MLC
Amanda, b 18 Oct 1858 - d
18 Apr 1908, WRC
Amos, b 30 March 1812 - d
3 Jan 1891, LBR
Amos A, b 18 Dec 1873 - d
5 May 1902, PNY
Amos D, b 1868 - d 1943,
PNY
Anida, b 1956 - d 1958,
NWP
Anna Mae, d 18 July 1973,
ae 79y, PTC
Annie, b 17 Jan 1897 - no
death date, MLC
Annie Potter, b 20 June
1883 - d 3 March 1942,
PTC
Archie, b 14 June 1897 - d
30 Oct 1957, PNY
Archie, ae 72y 11mo, WBB
Billie Joe, d 19 March
1980, ae 45y, LBR
Bobby J, b 3 Nov 1933 - d
10 July 1953, PNY
Caroline E, b 8 June 1871
- d 28 March 1919, LBR
Carrie S, b 12 June 1912 -
d 8 Feb 1971, LNE
Charlie I, b 29 June ----
- d 31 Dec ----, LNE
China, b 20 March 1884 - d
14 Sept 1964, PTC
Clara E, b 3 Dec 1892 - d
5 July 1911, PNY
Cledys, b 8 May 1919 - d
16 Jan 1936, PTC
Cora C, b 1 Aug 1847 - d
14 May 1898, PTC
Cora Z, b 1880 - d 1929,
LBR
Cornelia, b 26 Nov 1911 -
d 10 July 1947, PTC
Rev D H, b 1869 - d 28
March 1943, LBR

TAYLOR (continued)
Dianna, b 19 Jan 1835 - d
  19 Aug 1899, LBR
Dorothy Lucile,   22 Aug
  1942, PTC
Drew Gillar, b 1844 - d
  1934, DVS
Earl, b 1950 - d 1958, MLC
Edward H, b 30 Jan 1922 -
  d 20 Nov 1939, PNY
Elias, b 1889 - d 1967,
  PTC
Elizabeth, b 30 March 1843
  - d 14 June 1901, CRO
Elizabeth, b 5 May 1911 -
  d 24 Oct 1917, MLC
Etta, d 27 March 1930, ae
  8y 10mo, MLC
Evelyn, b 22 March 1925 -
  d 12 Aug 1955, WBB
Florence, b 7 March 1900 -
  no death date, PNY
Floyd, b 12 May 1913 - d 4
  June 1913, PTC
Francis, d 20 June 1921,
  ae 3y 11mo, MLC
Glen, b 17 Dec 1925 - d 3
  May 1930, PTC
H A, b 15 Aug 1877 - d 12
  July 1920, PTC
Hazel R, b 1 Apr 1906 - d
  26 March 1968, WRC
Hobart M, b 23 July 1896 -
  d 27 Oct 1967, LBR
Homer D, b 1896 - d 1906,
  PNY
Hubert H, Pfc 18 Inf WWII,
  b 25 July 1923 - d 2 Jan
  1953, MLC
Infant Son, no dates, OLP
James P, b 9 Jan 1837 - d
  25 Apr 1885, CRO
Jay, b 8 Sept 1927 - d 28
  Dec 1972, NWP
John, no dates, MLC
John L, b 6 Sept 1887 - d
  2 Apr 1960, CLC
John P, b 9 Aug 1866 - d 5

TAYLOR (continued)
  Dec 1918, PNY
Joseph A, b 20 Jan 1885 -
  d 12 Sept 1927, LBR
Judy Ann, b 30 Sept 1946 -
  d 21 May 1954, ELZ
Julia A, b 20 May 1851 - d
  12 Apr 1900, LBR
Julia Elizabeth, b 1864 -
  d 1906, PTC
Karleen, b 27 Aug 1908 -
  no death date, LBR
Kelley, d 5 Sept 1920, ae
  1y 1mo, MLC
Lawrence, b&d 1906, PTC
Lonnie, b&d 1906, PTC
Louise, b 25 Oct 1885 - d
  6 Aug 1887, LBR
Lula Hickman, d 3 Nov
  1980, ae 89y, CLC
Lula M, b 31 Dec 1890 - d
  3 Nov 1980, CLC
Mahala, b 20 Jan 1831 - d
  16 Feb 1895, PTC
Martha H Engert, b 4 Aug
  1879 - d 12 May 1953,
  WRC
Mary, b 30 Nov 1897 - d 14
  Dec 1951, PNY
Mary, no dates, MLC
Mary Arnfield, b 22 Sept
  1840 - d 12 Dec 1918,
  RGB
Mary E Niel, b 1851 - no
  death date, WRC
Mary Goldie, b 1905 - d
  1940, PNY
Mary M, b 22 May 1871 - d
  8 Apr 1873, LBR
Millie, 1973, UNN
Minnie, b 1886 - d 1893,
  PTC
Nadine, b 1939 - d 1955,
  MLC
Nina M, b 1898 - d 1906,
  PNY
Omar, d 21 Nov 1940, ae 2y
  16da, MLC

TAYLOR (continued)

Pauline, d 5 Aug 1937, ae 1y 4mo, MLC

Rev R O, b 16 Oct 1835 - d 4 July 1908, PNY

R S, b 11 Jan 1868 - d 23 Apr 1889, CRO

Ramsy, b 30 Nov 1888 - d 16 Dec 1969, MLC

Ray L Jr, d 9 May 1973, ae 25y, DRL

Rebecca, b 21 Oct 1872 - d 17 Apr 1962, PNY

Rhoda Francis, b 1873 - d 1940, PNY

Richard, b 11 Jan 1883 - d 12 July 1925, OLP

Richard R, b 15 June 1883 - d 16 Dec 1884, LBR

Roy, b 1 Dec 1888 - no death date, WRC

Sarah A, b 27 Nov 1877 - d 27 Apr 1879, LBR

Sarah Potter, b 8 July 1853 - d 4 March 1949, PTC

Sharon Sally, b 28 June 1814 - d 8 Sept 1876, LBR

Sidney, b 14 Apr 1894 - d 9 Aug 1960, WHO

Theodore, b 18 Jan 1904 - d 4 July 1959, LBR

Thomas, b 28 Apr 1840 - d 16 Oct 1905, RGB

Tressie, d 9 Nov 1932, ae 1y 2mo, MLC

Violet L, b 1902 - d 1905, PNY

W H H, b 8 Oct 1841 - d 22 Jan 1922, LBR

W M, b 30 March 1872 - d 25 July 1874, LBR

Walter, b 1 Feb 1904 - d 25 July 1904, CLC

Walter W, b 28 July 1881 - d 16 Sept 1936, CLC

William, b 5 Oct 1878 - d

TAYLOR (continued)

24 Oct 1962, MLC

William A, b 16 May 1882 - d 12 Jan 1962, PTC

William E, b 21 May 1893 - d 8 Aug 1976, PNY

Willie, d 11 Oct 1934, ae 26y 7mo, MLC

Wm Riley, Pvt Co C 4 Reg TN Vol Sp/Am War, b 27 June 1870 - d 14 Dec 1962, WRC

TERRELL, Wanda Mae, b 13 May 1938 - d 16 June 1938, LNE

TERRY, Anna May, b 10 May 1891 - no death date, WRC

Bertha S, b 3 Oct 1891 - d 4 Nov 1964, WRC

Carl, b 7 Jan 1900 - d 7 Dec 1965, LBR

Ella, b 8 Sept 1900 - no death date, LBR

Inman, b 19 Jan 1885 - d 16 June 1961, WRC

John Wesley, b 15 July 1896 - d 21 May 1969, LBR

Manda, b 4 Feb 1897 - no death date, LBR

Roy, b 1941 - d 1967, LBR

Ruby, b 9 Jan 1923 - no death date, LBR

Thomas A, b 16 Aug 1920 - d 27 Feb 1960, LBR

THOMAS, Andy J, b 2 Feb 1877 - d 7 Apr 1952, PNY

Mrs Demple, d 16 Jan 1978, ae 69y, CRO

Emmett, d 20 Feb 1977, ae 71y, WRC

Floyd, b&d 26 June 1905, PNY

George Franklin, b 13 July 1873 - d 31 Oct 1961, WRC

Gus, b 21 May 1887 - d 28

THOMAS (continued)
Nov 1940, EST
Harry G, b 4 June 1892 - d
20 May 1935, CRO
Hubert Lee, Cpl 16 Inf HQ
Co, b 18 Dec 1928 - d 5
Jan 1952, WRC
Inez M, b 3 Jan 1872 - d
14 Feb 1944, CRO
Laurine, b 23 Apr 1899 - d
29 Jan 1961, EST
Linda, b 17 Nov 1877 - d
29 Nov 1953, PNY
Mrs Lula, d 4 Aug 1979, ae
74y, WMG
Nora H, b 3 March 1889 - d
3 May 1965, WRC
Robert Mason, b 29 Aug
1894 - d 13 Oct 1897,
SNB
Shirley W, b 23 Aug 1902 -
d 23 July 1958, CRO
THOMPSON, Apylona F, b 10
Sept 1879 - d 4 Jan
1902, FLF
Carnin Goldston, b 1 June
1904 - d 10 July 1960,
CRO
Charlotte C, b 20 Jan 1892
- d 13 Sept 1904, FLF
Deborah Faye, b 9 Apr 1956
- d 9 Apr 1956, WRC
George M, b 4 Aug 1852 - d
1 Aug 1905, FLF
Hattie E, b 22 Aug 1899 -
d stone broken, BRD
Lawrence, b 20 Dec 1895 -
d 23 Apr 1896, FLF
Ora E Peters, b 31 Jan
1901 - d 14 June 1925,
BRR
Ray F, d 18 March 1978, ae
74y, WMG
THORNTON, Addie Young, b 13
June 1897 - d 7 March
1920, LBR
Alia, b 25 May 1815 - d 4
July 1888, LBR

THORNTON (continued)
Charles, b 1871 - d 1927,
LBR
Charlie, b 1 Jan 1870 - d
12 Feb 1931, THR
Chloe Ethel, d 9 Jan 1980,
ae 85y, EST
Church, b 7 Apr 1878 - d
22 March 1961, THR
Clarence Archie, inf, 9
March 1920, LBR
Claud, b 5 Sept 1906 - d
11 March 1967, THR
Clifford, no dates, THR
Daisy, b 19 Sept 1880 - d
18 March 1966, THR
Donna Lynn, d 16 Nov 1956,
ae 6y 19da, THR
Edward, b 22 Sept 1812 - d
14 Feb 1885, LBR
Frank, b 23 Aug 1883 - d
11 May 1946, LBR
Fred, b 6 June 1887 - d 31
Dec 1947, LBR
Infant, 1927, LBR
John, no dates, THR
John Alvin, b 27 Apr 1889
- d 12 March 1920, LBR
John C, b 22 Feb 1862 - d
25 Oct 1889, LBR
John G, no dates, THR
Joseph, b 6 Jan 1848 - d 8
Oct 1916, LBR
Kenneth, b 12 Aug 1917 - d
10 Jan 1954, EST
Lewis, d 2 Oct 1964, ae
74y, EST
Louiseiana H, b 9 Oct 1861
- d 26 Dec 1947, LBR
Mae, no dates, THR
Marcella H, b 29 June 1929
- no death date, EST
Marshall, b 3 Apr 1892 - d
3 Dec 1908, LBR
Martha, b 1888 - d 1942,
LBR
Sally Viola, b 25 Oct 1882
- d 10 Apr 1962, THR

THORNTON (continued)
W M, b 25 Dec 1854 - d 1
Apr 1908, LBR
Wade H Jr, b 28 Dec 1926 -
d 7 Sept 1976, EST
Wade H Jr, d 7 Sept 1976,
ae 49y, THR
William S, b 20 June 1904
- d 17 Oct 1946, THR
TIDWELL, Aud 'J, d 1 Aug
1974, ae 88y, LBR
Aust J, b 10 Oct 1885 - d
1 Aug 1974, LBR
Henrietta, b 5 June 1893 -
d 4 Sept 1933, DVS
Homer L, Sgt USAF, b 16
July 1925 - d 26 June
1974, LBR
James Riley, b 11 May 1885
- d 6 Feb 1972, DVS
James W, Cpl USA WWII, b
11 Oct 1918 - d 20 June
1973, DVS
Rex L, b 2 Oct 1938 - d 17
Jan 1956, LBR
Rose (Francis), 10 Sept
1895, LBR
TILSON, Eva M, b 1890 - d
18 Dec 1972, CRO
Fay, b 29 March 1899 - d 1
May 1970, ELZ
Gerald Wayne, b 21 Dec
1942 - d 2 Aug 1943, ELZ
Mealey E, b 1884 - d 1972,
CRO
TINCH, Andrew, b 21 Apr
1888 - d 6 Apr 1937, PLR
Flossie I, b 17 Apr 1890 -
d 3 July 1978, PLR
Jewel, b 26 Feb 1923 - d
19 July 1923, PLR
TINSLEY, Mary F, b 27 Feb
1884 - d 15 Nov 1965,
PLR
Oliver N, b 1877 - d 7
March 1929, PLR
TIPPS, Nannie E, b 10 Aug
1886 - d 17 Nov 1963,

TIPPS (continued)
WRC
William J, b 6 March 1883
- d 28 Jan 1967, WRC
TIPTON, Joseph, b 3 March
1857 - d 1 July 1930,
UNG
Martha, b 6 May 1812 - d
22 Oct 1884, UNG
TODD, C C, b 6 June 1845 -
d 5 Sept 1933, CRO
J M, b 21 Aug 1853 - d 5
Jan 1890, WRC
James Monroe, b 29 July
1880 - d 4 Dec 1935, CRO
Joe W, b 6 June 1885 - d
20 March 1926, CRO
Tempie Rich, b 7 May 1842
- d 2 June 1933, CRO
TOMPKINS, Carrie Iona, b
1871 - d 1950, BRR
Ellsworth, b 1867 - d
1935, BRR
Eva, b 1903 - d 1932, BRR
Marlyn Ruth, d 13 Nov
1955, ae 3y 5mo, BRR
Paul L, Sgt USA, b 11 May
1930 - d 19 Apr 1964,
BRR
Ralph, b 29 June 1891 - d
14 Dec 1895, BRR
Raymond C, d 18 March
1975, ae 68y, BRR
Ruby D, b 31 Aug 1924 - d
25 June 1964, DRL
Virgie, dates illegible,
RGB
TONDENBERGER, J A, b 4 Dec
1825 - d 14 May 1895,
RGB
TONEY, Clifford, b 14 Apr
1916, MNT
Clifton Viviace, b 27 Apr
1903 - d 11 Aug 1910,
WRC
John, b 21 Jan 1842 - d 7
Jan 1926, WRC
Julia Ann, b 1 May 1858 -

TONEY (continued)
d 7 Feb 1925, WRC
Julian F, Pvt 45 US Vol
Inf, 15 Aug 1936, 000
Minnie Lee, b 19 Aug 1880
- d 16 Aug 1919, MNT
Wilburn, b 6 Feb 1876 - d
16 March 1936, WRC
TONG, Elza, b 1874 - d
1969, LNC
Julian F, 15 Aug 1936 - no
other date, LNC
TONY, Burl, d 16 Apr 1980,
ae 72y, MLC
TOOMEY, Dan, b 1868 - d
1946, WRC
Ella, b 1854 - d 1944, WRC
Fred Barthell, b 19 July
1900 - d 11 March 1922,
SNB
John, b 1820 - d 4 July
1904, WRC
John Samuel, b 4 March
1926 - d 21 Jan 1975,
SNB
Mona Anna Norris, b 11 May
1900 - d 14 March 1930,
SNB
TOPER, Catherine, b 1899 -
d 1972, DRL
Frank, b 1877 - d 1949,
DRL
Infant, b&d 1 Nov 1924,
DRL
TRACY, Henry, b 18 Dec 1837
- d 27 Aug 1913, MRR
Hitter, b 18 May 1858 - d
19 Feb 1912, MRR
TRAIL, Adriene, b 2 March
1930 - d 6 June 1974,
NWP
Archie, b 9 Oct 1917 - d
12 Dec 1921, OLP
Frank, Pfc 135 Med WWII, b
24 Jan 1922 - d 13 Oct
1967, NWP
Georgia, d 12 Dec 1970 -
ae 45da, NWP

TRAIL (continued)
Houck, b 16 Feb 1891 - d
16 Oct 1921, OLP
Irona, b 5 July 1894 - d
19 Jan 1970, NWP
W M, b 28 March 1880 - d
20 Nov 1907, OLP
TRESP, Virginia, b 15 March
1875 - d 12 May 1912,
SNB
TREW, Charles William, b 12
July 1920 - d 3 Dec
1922, PLR
Florence J, b 17 July 1904
- d 27 May 1906, PLR
Isham S, b 15 Oct 1909 - d
22 Aug 1910, PLR
Preston J, b 17 July 1904
- d 27 May 1906, PLR
Virginia Kathaleen, b 28
July 1922 - d 16 Nov
1922, PLR
TRIPLETT, Dixie M Voyles, b
8 March 1864 - d 24 Aug
1944, CRO
Jessie, b 10 Jan 1858 - d
11 Feb 1936, CRO
TROUT, John C, b 16 Oct
1878 - d 19 Oct 1952,
PNY
Mary A, b -- Aug ---- - no
death date, PNY
Reba H, b 3 Dec 1911 - no
death date, PNY
William B, b 3 May 1910 -
d 2 Aug 1961, PNY
TRUIX, Jeanie R, b 2 Jan
1932 - no death date,
UNN
Marion H, b 9 Oct 1902 - d
3 June 1971, UNN
TUCKER, A J (Jack), b 4
March 1878 - d 9 March
1943, NWP
Delia, b 1882 - d 1902,
UNN
Edward J, Pvt USA WWI, b
19 Aug 1899 - d 20 Oct

TUCKER (continued)
1970, NWP
Etler, b 3 May 1892 - d 27
March 1914, CRO
Harold, inf s/o H E, 1937,
NWP
Henry Lee, d 16 Apr 1954,
ae 18y, CRO
Irene Delaney, d 14 June
1978, ae 57y, NWP
J K (Polk), b 14 March
1878 - d 24 Dec 1941,
NWP
Jasper B, b 2 July 1902 -
d 7 Oct 1967, UNN
June Myrl, b 23 June 1947
- d 27 June 1947, UNN
Lola M, b 2 May 1865 - d
12 March 1875, NWP
Mae, d 18 Feb 1978, ae
73y, NWP
Paralee, b 19 Nov 1882 - d
19 Oct 1962, NWP
William C, b 8 May 1939 -
d 28 July 1967, CRO
Willie Lee, b 25 Dec 1927
- d 16 Sept 1928, UNN
Wilma J, b 3 June 1927 - d
17 Dec 1949, NWP
TURNER, Doyle Stanton, Sgt
Fld Art WWII, b 5 Sept
1912 - d 24 July 1963,
WHO
Freddie Clarence, b 6 June
1907 - d 10 March 1974,
STC
James Frank, b 15 July
1874 - d 15 Jan 1947,
STC
Rodney K, d 10 Nov 1949,
ae 2y 11mo, BRR
Sarah Belle, b 29 Feb 1876
- d 8 July 1948, STC
TURPIN, James, b 1 Apr 1910
- d 8 June 1973, EST
Jimmie R, d 9 July 1957,
ae 10mo, DVS
Lucille, b 22 May 1918 - d

TURPIN (continued)
15 June 1981, EST
UNDERWOOD, Billie, b 17
March 1927 - d 9 Aug
1929, LNE
Charlie, b 15 March 1875 -
d 8 March 1940, LNE
Edward, b 7 Feb 1886 - d 5
Oct 1890, LNE
Elizabeth, b 30 Apr 1858 -
d 13 Jan 1883, LNE
Elizabeth Peters, b 13 Feb
1871 - d 22 May 1887,
LNE
Estel W E, d 7 Aug 1981,
ae 84y, LNE
Ettie, d 9 Feb 1901, ae
1da, LNE
Father, no dates, PLR
Florence, no dates, PLR
Franklin, no dates, PLR
George, b 1842 - d 1915,
DRL
Infant, d 19 May 1894, LNE
James, b 3 July 1865 - d 2
June 1940, LNE
James Lloyd, d 20 Sept
1976, ae 67y, LNE
Jane Rich, b 28 May 1858 -
d 28 May 1928, LNE
Julyan, b 1 March 1876 - d
10 Feb 1878, LNE
Lee, b 10 Sept 1898 - d 21
Feb 1966, LNE
Leonard T, b 17 Jan 1905 -
d 29 Dec 1947, LNE
Lizzie, b 24 May 1864 - d
27 Sept 1939, CRO
Lonous, Sgt 400 Bat Co I
MC WWI, b 1 May 1893 - d
1 Aug 1970, LNE
Lula dau/o ?, no dates,
PLR
Luther C, b 7 Dec 1901 - d
8 July 1964, CRO
Maggie, b 4 Apr 1870 - d 9
March 1893, LNE
Minnie Brock, b 1875 - d

UNDERWOOD (continued)
1962, LNE
Mother, no dates, PLR
Polly, b 14 June 1812 - d
29 March 1867, LNE
Ralph F, d 29 Apr 1978, ae
70y, LNE
Reed R, d 22 Aug 1898, ae
3mo 22da, LNE
Virgie, b 14 Oct 1903 - no
death date, LNE
Virgie Stringfield, d 29
Nov 1977, ae 74y, LNE
W M, b 1872 - d 1911, LNE
Wanda, b 29 March 1932 - d
5 Sept 1947, LNE
William H, b 15 Feb 1865 -
d 17 March 1885, LNE
UNGER, Arlevia M, b 1883 -
d 1960, DRM
Curt, b 1879 - d 1955, DRM
Emma Elizabeth, b 23 Feb
1916 - d 15 March 1918,
DRM
Rose Mae, b 4 Jan 1922 - d
6 Jan 1922, DRM
UNSER, Joe, b 8 March 1863
- d 3 Aug 1941, PNY
Julia Parker, b 19 May
1859 - d 30 March 1927,
PNY
VADEN, Berdie, b 3 June
1940 - d 5 Aug 1965, MLC
VAILES, John H, b 26 Oct
1884 - d 12 Oct 1918,
WRC
Louis, b 4 March 1888 - d
1976, WRC
Louise (Laud), b 24 Feb
1890 - d 25 Jan 1974,
WRC
Phillip Frank, b 12 July
1904 - d 19 March 1905,
WRC
VALENTINE, Aletha A, b 25
July 1926 - d 29 Nov
1965, ALB
VAN FORSTNER, Julie F, b 2

VAN FORSTNER (continued)
Nov 1811 - d 20 Oct
1891, WRC
Karl, b 1800 - d 11 Apr
1860, WRC
VANDERGUFF, Bobbie, b 9
March 1929 - d 16 Jan
1931, DVS
VANN, Dennis, Pvt 54 Rgt
Coast Art, d 10 March
1934, ae 40y, CRO
Jackie Wayne Jr, d 26 Dec
1975, ae 14mo, NWP
James Thomas, d 28 Nov
1970, ae 27y, BRZ
Maggie, b 1888 - d 1977,
CRO
VANNORSTRAN, Clara Belle
d/o ----, d 1925, WRC
Clem E, b 17 Feb 1897 - d
4 Sept 1967, WRC
Parlia H w/o Clem, b 1902
- d 1926, WRC
Ruth Jeanette, b 9 Sept
1861 - d 27 Feb 1946,
WRC
VANNOSTRAN, Fred, b 23 Nov
1889 - d 4 Sept 1967,
MSG
Gladys d/o Fred, 29 Aug
1940 , MSG
Grace, b 22 March 1902 - d
23 Dec 1902, DRL
Herbert E, b 25 July 1851
- d 12 Oct 1909, DRL
Mae Nelson, d 8 Nov 1980,
ae 90y, WMG
Stella S, b 5 June 1900 -
d 20 Sept 1980, MSG
Virginia B, b 21 Sept 1894
- no death date, DRL
VANNOUTRAN, Lora Hooks, d
19 Oct 1977, ae 75y, LNE
VARGA, Esther, b 18 July
1886 - no death date,
DRL
Samuel, b 11 May 1885 - d
19 Nov 1970, DRL

VAUGHN, Dennis Wayne, Cpl
Co C 20 Inf VN, b 31 Oct
1948 - d 27 Sept 1968,
WMG
VERTNER, Dean Wayne, b 27
Jan 1922 - d 5 Nov 1961,
LNE
Fred, d 28 Dec 1978, ae
71y, LNE
George W, d 25 Aug 1975,
ae 74y, LNE
John, d 19 March 1940, ae
74y, LNE
Roy, b 1911 - d 1976, LNE
VESPEE, Eva, d 30 Oct 1981,
ae 72y, LNC
VESPIE, Boyd Ernest, d 7
Apr 1975, ae 63y, FST
Catherine Haag, b 20 Jun
1846 - d 25 Aug 1928,
WRC
Cecil A, b 10 Apr 1918 - d
28 Apr 1962, WRC
Charles, b 1880 - d 1944,
WRC
Daisy L Augusta, b 2 May
1882 - d 18 March 1912,
WRC
Elizabeth B, b 19 Dec 1885
- d 16 Sep 1945, WRC
Gus H, Pvt I Eng WWI, b 21
Oct 1871 - d 23 Oct
1971, WMG
Harl B, d 7 Nov 1978, WRC
Jacob J, b 1 Apr 1875 - d
12 Oct 1966, WRC
John Jacob, b 25 July 1847
- d 7 Feb 1918, WRC
John L, b 2 Aug 1884 - d
14 Dec 1935, WRC
Louise K, b 1880 - d 1963,
WRC
Maggie M, b 20 Dec 1905 -
d 14 May 1955, LNC
Martin C, b 26 May 1905 -
d 24 March 1965, LNC
Nina Kreis, b 1897 - d
1932, WRC

VESPIE (continued)
Orlando, b 1919 - d 1926,
WRC
Otto W, b 1888 - d 1960,
WRC
VESTNER, Dean Wayne, Sgt
USAF WWII, b 27 Jan 1922
- d 5 Nov 1961, 000
VINCENT, Alvin Burton, d --
June 1973, ae 50y, WMG
Cora V, b 1894 - no death
date, MSG
Harold J, b 4 July 1924 -
d 26 Sept 1975, MSG
Lola J, b 7 June 1924 - no
death date, MSG
Sid, b 1892 - d 1934, MSG
VINEYARD, Brejettie Ally, b
22 July 1891 - d 5 Jan
1944, WRJ
Ira H, b 8 May 1891 - d 27
May 1967, WRJ
Ruby Mae, b 14 March 1927
- d 9 March 1955, WRJ
VITATOE, Charles W, b 16
Sept 1906 - d 6 Aug
1972, NWP
VITTATOE, John W, b 4 Sept
1882 - d 17 Sept 1957,
NWP
Sallie M Justice, b 6 June
1885 - d 13 March 1963,
NWP
VOSS, Louis Worth, b 11 Aug
1870 - d 17 Aug 1886,
LNC
VOYLES, Clara A, b 13 July
1903 - no death date,
CRO
Enoch, b 5 July 1890 - d
23 June 1955, CRO
Gladys Kittrell, b 13 June
1899 - d 15 Apr 1924,
CRO
Jess T, b 1887 - d 1949,
CRO
John Arthur, b 12 Oct 1897
- d 22 Oct 1943, CRO

VOYLES (continued)
John Arthur Jr, b 4 Oct
1926 - d 1 May 1946 ,
CRO
Rebecca J, b 1868 - d
1907, CRO
Theodore, b 14 July 1903 -
d 3 March 1965, CRO
W M, b 12 Apr 1857 - d 11
March 1928, CRO
WADDELL, Alva I, no dates,
WRC
Mary W, b 7 Sept 1894 - d
8 Aug 1916, DRL
WAITS, Emma, b 20 Dec 1895
- d 24 Nov 1937, LNC
J F M, b 6 Oct 1860 - d 12
March 1936, LNC
John T, b 15 June 1925 - d
3 Oct 1926, LNC
Margaret, b 31 Dec 1862 -
d 23 Jan 1925, LNC
Rachel A, b 27 July 1883 -
d 4 June 1922, LNC
Thomas J, Pvt 324 Inf 81
Div WWI, b 12 Nov 1888 -
d 16 Sept 1948, LNC
WALDRIP, Leslie, b 27 Oct
1882 - d 25 Oct 1937,
CRO
WALDRUP, Martha, b 3 Aug
1879 - d 3 Sept 1879,
CRO
WALKER, Burnes, b 14 Apr
1919 - d 27 May 1919,
MRR
Clinton Hubert, b 1928 - d
1930, BRD
Drucilla, b 11 Jan 1864 -
d 11 March 1953, BRD
E H, Co A 11th TN Cav, b
12 Sept 1837 - d 7 Sept
1899, MRR
Ernest M, d 21 June 1952,
ae 1y, PLR
Esther Smith, b 1 Nov 1921
- no death date, BRD
Eva Lena, b 16 July 1896 -

WALKER (continued)
d 21 March ----, PNY
George E, b 8 Aug 1893 - d
1 Nov 1918, MRR
Harriet, b 3 Oct 1829 - d
16 Nov 1916, OLP
James F, b 2 July 1904 - d
6 June 1968, PLR
James H, b 17 Sept 1869 -
d 17 Sept 1923, MRR
James Lee, b 7 Aug 1929 -
d 5 May 1951, BRD
James P, b 1826 - d 1861,
NDK
John Franklin, b 13 July
1929 - d 12 June 1971,
PLR
Lewis, b 28 May 1925 - d
25 Aug 1925, BRD
Martha A, b 11 Dec 1857 -
d 17 June 1926, MRR
Milton Joseph, b 26 March
1879 - d 28 Dec 1953,
PNY
Naomi, d 1935, BRD
Rebecca, no dates, MRR
William Lee, d 29 Jan
1973, ae 74y, BRD
Willis W, b 2 Oct 1872 - d
17 Sept 1946, BRD
Wm Harvey, b 10 July 1892
- d 29 March 1971, BRD
Zella Dean, d 28 Apr 1981,
ae 49y, PLR
WALL, Annie, d 16 Sept
1875, ae 76y, RTT
Infant Dau, d 5 Dec 1866,
ae 14da, RTT
John, d 22 Apr 1866, ae
71y, RTT
Louisa, b 12 Apr 1896 - d
4 Jan 1904, ELZ
WALLACE, Bonnie B, b 10 Oct
1914 - d 31 July 1963,
WRC
Clara Engert, b 1 May 1887
- no death date, WRC
Ethel M, b 2 May 1919 - d

WALLACE (continued)
14 June 1919, OLP
Homer, d 7 Aug 1977, ae 67y, ADM
Jim (Sneid), b 26 March 1881 - d 10 Oct 1956, NWP
Mollie, b 17 Aug 1886 - d 28 Sept 1904, OLP
Robert W, b 11 Oct 1911 - no death date, WRC
T D, b 2 May 1876 - d 10 Oct 1957, WRC
WALLEN, H M, b 17 Jan 1924 - d 15 March 1924, UNH
WALLS, -----, d 1947, EST
Alex J, b 11 Aug 1888 - d 26 Apr 1968, DVS
Andy, b 19 July 187- - d 1 July 194-, EST
Beatrice J, b 10 Sept 1912 - no death date, EST
Clarence, b 20 May 1911 - d 16 Feb 1914, DVS
Daisy, b 2 Dec 1902 - d 4 March 1922, DVS
David Raymond, b 20 Feb 1908 - d 12 May 1976, EST
Eda A, b 14 Sept 1830 - d 1 March 1912, DVS
George C, 19th Inf Korea, b 1933 - d 1955, DVS
Infant dau, d ae 3mo 15da, DVS
Irene, b 5 June 1916 - d 22 May 1918, DVS
James Daniel, Pfc USAAF WWII, b 2 Oct 1920 - d 21 Nov 1951, DVS
James Samuel, b 17 Feb 1865 - d 7 March 1929, DVS
Joseph H, b 1 Aug 1860 - d 29 May 1913, DVS
Maggie, b 29 May 1896 - no death date, DVS
Mamie E, b 21 May 1893 -

WALLS (continued)
no death date, DVS
Marie, b 25 Sept 18-- - d 8 Feb 195-, EST
Mary A, d 25 Dec 1882, ae 5da, UNN
Mary Alley, b 1883 - d 1914, CRO
Mary E, b 28 May 1884 - d 13 March 1905, DVS
Mary F Hudson, b 7 Feb 1863 - d 27 Aug 1910, DVS
Philibenia Gisi, b 1 May 1856 - d 24 July 1921, DVS
Robert C, b 30 Aug 1891 - d 2 March 1966, DVS
Samuel Alexander, b 8 July 1897 - d 20 Sept 1961, EST
Shirley, b 20 Nov 1936 - d 24 Dec 1936, DVS
Walter L, b 1900 - d 1924, BRR
William C, b 5 July 1878 - d 21 July 1907, DVS
William E Dude, d 31 March 1979, ae 60y, DVS
William G, d 29 July 1887, ae 57y, DVS
William Wesley, b 7 March 1896 - d 25 Dec 1946, EST
WALT, E B, b 28 Apr 1843 - d 27 Dec 1886, ELZ
Frederick, b 21 Jan 1846 - d 28 July 1887, WRC
WALTER, Thomas, d 2 Nov 1978, ae 68y, WMG
WALTON, -----, no dates, RGB
Anna J, b 1890 - d 1892, RGB
Elizabeth T, b 1849 - d 1947, RGB
George T, b 1885 - d 1912, RGB
J Kimber, b 1883 - d 1933,

WALTON (continued)
RGB
Robert, b 1841 - d 1947,
RGB
WANKLEY, J S, d 23 May
1882, ae 43y, RGB
WARD, ----, no dates, RGB
Anna E, b 13 Aug 1910 - d
14 Oct 1912, DRL
Cynthia R, b 1 Oct 1841 -
d 2 March 1920, DRL
Dassie D, Pvt TN 29 Inf,
22 July 1927, OOO
David Fletcher, b 12 Sept
1875 - d 16 Dec 1952,
DRL
Dean C, b 13 Aug 1911 - d
8 July 1965, EST
Donnie R, b 1881 - d 1965,
DRL
Ed, b 1909 - d 1971, MNT
Edith Pallard, b 3 Nov
1884 - d 12 Jan 1975,
DRL
Ernest M, d 20 Feb 1981,
ae 23y, WBB
Grace, b 2 Feb 1880 - no
death date, DRL
Herbert, b 19 Feb 1898 - d
21 March 1954, WRJ
Ida Florence, b 1 May 1878
- d 22 July 1927, WRJ
Isabella, b 8 May 1890 -
no death date, DVS
James, b 17 Dec 1843 - d
14 Aug 1928, DRL
Jessie L, d 16 Dec 1960,
ae 21y 11mo, MSG
John, b 1855 - d 1938, DRL
John Douglas, b 16 Aug
1947 - d 31 Jan 1968,
DRL
Juanita, no dates, RGB
Lawrence, no dates, MSG
Lee Jr, d 19 Sept 1981, ae
54y, SNB
Lester J, b 6 June 1932 -
d 1 Aug 1952 (in Korea),

WARD (continued)
NWP
Mary Headrick, b 1899 - d
1929, DRM
Mrs, 3 Feb 1965 - no other
date, MSG
Ora Lou, d 31 Dec 1979, ae
77y, NWP
Phebe A Stone, b 1852 - d
1929, DRL
Roland G, b 21 Dec 1942 -
d 24 June 1965, NWP
Susan Ann, d 29 June 1979,
ae 48y, DVS
Waymond R, b 9 May 1907 -
d 4 Feb 1952, WRJ
William Horace, b 15 Apr
1875 - d 16 Feb 1958,
DVS
WATERS, Howard, d 2 May
1980, ae 69y, NWP
Roger Dale, b&d 15 Jan
1961, PTC
WATKINS, Edward S, b 28 Apr
1917 - d 14 Feb 1941,
WRC
Hassie M, b 25 July 1897 -
d 5 July 1976, WRC
WATSON, Bessie M, b 1895 -
d 1965, CLC
Cornelia, b 28 Dec 1890 -
no death date, CRO
Frank, Pfc BN 7 Mar 1,
Korea, b 1 Nov 1933 - d
13 July 1953, NWP
Harriet F, b 7 Apr 1924 -
d 10 July 1925, CRO
James C, b 13 Nov 1861 - d
19 Feb 1952, WRC
James H, b 13 July 1891 -
d 20 Oct 1940, CRO
John A, b&d 4 Oct 1931,
CRO
Labau Jack, b 23 Apr 1896
- d 5 Nov 1957, CLC
Margaret, b 3 Nov 1886 - d
13 June 1973, DRL
Margaret Howard, d 13 June

WATSON (continued)
1973, ae 86y, DRL
Mary, b 31 March 1913 - no
death date, ARM
Sarah B, b 23 Sept 1861 -
d 1 June 1952, WRC
Vivian Strong, d 15 Aug
1979, ae 64y, DRL
William, b 30 March 1910 -
d 1 Aug 1968, ARM
William A, b 14 Apr 1887 -
d 20 Feb 1972, DRL
Woodrow J, b 1 May 1925 -
d 9 May 1934, CRO
WATT, Margaret M, b 24 Aug
1891 - d 14 Dec 1891,
NDK
WATTS, F Toney, b 30 Oct
1885 - d 20 June 1970,
WMG
WEAVER, Archie H, b 1896 -
d 1963, LNC
Frank, 31 Aug 1936 - no
other date, NWP
Julian, d 24 June 1918, ae
3y 7mo, DVD
Martha, b 6 Apr 1885 - no
death date, DVD
P H MD, b 1827 - d 1909,
DRL
Timothy, b 10 Dec 1864 - d
23 Feb 1927, DVD
V, no birth date - d 1913,
DRL
WEBB, Andy, Cpl USAAF WWII,
b 11 Nov 1911 - d 27 Apr
1964, LNE
Anna Sue, b 14 Apr 1940 -
d 19 Feb 1941, CRO
Beatrice J, b 1913 - d 23
Aug 1947, PNY
Bennie F, b 23 Sept 1904 -
d 8 March 1928, WBB
Charles, 1967, DRL
Daisy A, b 8 July 1890 -
no death date, CRO
David, b 7 June 1877 - d
11 Jan 1880, ELZ

WEBB (continued)
Donnie M, b 2 Nov 1970 - d
22 May 1971, WBB
Elizabeth A, b 21 May 1880
- d 21 Apr 1949, ELZ
Ernest, b 28 Nov 1892 - d
4 Oct 1951, CRO
H C, b 26 Oct 1856 - d 4
March 1912, WBB
Hannah McCoy, b 19 Nov
1844 - d 1 March 1873,
ELZ
Hiram H, b 15 March 1846 -
d 22 Aug 1855, NDK
Isham, b 1884 - d 1962,
SNB
James, b 15 Nov 1847 - d
14 Nov 1862, NDK
James, b 20 Sept 1875 - d
12 Apr 1896, PLR
James C, d 16 Dec 1974, ae
82y, LNE
Jess, d 20 Jan 1978, ae
64y, FST
John, b 10 Sept 1813 - d
26 July 1863, ELZ
John C, b 1 Jan 1892 - d
1974, LNE
John H, b 4 May 1866 - d
27 Nov 1941, WBB
Rev John T, b 26 Feb 1854
- d 21 Dec 1925, WBB
Johnnie, b 9 Apr 1923 - d
6 Nov 1938, MLC
Johnnie Ray, b 8 Dec 1964
- d 28 Jan 1972, SNB
Josiah, b 17 Nov 1812 - d
9 Feb 1887, MNT
Josie Todd, b 15 Jan 1885
- d 30 Sept 1933, WBB
Julia Ann, b 12 Apr 1906 -
d 24 March 1971, LNE
L Wayne, b 16 Dec 1950 - d
22 May 1971, WBB
L Y, b 24 Apr 1851 - d 15
Jan 1948, WBB
Lebert, b 1954 - d 1974,
WBB

WEBB (continued)

Lewis, b 11 Nov 1811 - d 19 May 1890, ELZ

Lloyd L, b 20 March 1927 - d 19 Jan 1969, WBB

Louisa, b 25 March 1813 - d 16 Aug 1878, ELZ

Louisa, b 25 March 1817 - d 18 Oct 1873, ELZ

Luiza, b 22 Apr 1903 - d 3 May 1907, ELZ

Mrs Lynde, d 24 Oct 1981, ae 87y, LNE

Martha, b 15 Jan 1931 - d 17 Jan 1931, MLC

Martha A, b 10 March 1845 - d 14 Nov 1876, NDK

Martin, b 24 Feb 1852 - d 22 Sept 1862, NDK

Mary E, b 1890 - d 1971, SNB

Maureen Sue, b 7 Dec 1946 - d 19 Jan 1951, LNE

Nancy, b 12 Nov 1861 - d 18 Dec 1927, ELZ

Nancy, b 9 May 1849 - d 13 Sept 1862, NDK

Nora Honeycutt, b 7 Dec 1883 - d 26 Apr 1958, PNY

Othenia, b 29 Jan 1883 - d 20 July 1952, LNE

Preston F, b 2 June 1865 - d 14 Apr 1932, ELZ

R B, b 17 March 1852 - d 18 March 1897, ELZ

Ralph, Pvt 34 AA Rep TNG WWII, b 1 Feb 1898 - d 30 March 1952, LNE

Richard Allen, d 14 July 1980, ae infant, FST

Robert, b 24 Nov 1916 - d 28 July 1966, ELZ

Robert A, d 23 Apr 1977, ae 70y, WRC

Rose, b 1914 - d 1967, LNE

Sadie, b 13 July 1916 - d 9 Apr 1976, ae 59y, LNE

WEBB (continued)

Sam, b 12 July 1862 - d 25 Sept 1926, LNE

Sam H, b 14 Jan 1898 - d 11 Aug 1976, LNE

Samuel, b 4 Sept 1842 - d 8 Sept 1862, NDK

Samuel Willis, b 1 Feb 1884 - d 29 July 1959, WBB

Sarah Ann, b 13 Dec 1867 - d 12 March 1936, WBB

Sarah T, b 19 Feb 1879 - d 1 Apr 1956, LNE

Susie E, b 7 May 1887 - d 31 Dec 1907, WBB

Sylvania Taylor, d 30 Jan 1977, ae 86y, MLC

Ullery, b 2 July 1902 - d 25 Dec 1956, PNY

W D, b 22 Jan 1858 - d 12 Jan 1938, WBB

Welcom, b 13 Jan 1841 - d 10 Feb 1922, ELZ

William, b 1935 - d 1969, LNE

William E, b 14 May 1883 - d 5 July 1953, PNY

William N, b 16 Nov 1935 - d 23 Apr 1969, LNE

William R, b 16 March 1887 - d 3 Nov 1971, LNE

Willis, b 1890 - d 1930, WBB

Wm R, b 1918 - d 1944, SNB

WEBSTER, Addie, b 1 June 1889 - d 13 Oct 1918, DVS

Amanda, b 29 March 1890 - d 21 Jan 1913, DVS

C R, b 5 July 1857 - d 5 June 1884, DVS

Clarence Dilos, b 9 June 1891 - d 20 Sept 1934, RTT

Claude, b 1911 - d 1912, DVS

Cordie, b 1869 - d 1912,

WEBSTER (continued)
DVS
Dale, b&d 28 Sept 1959, DVS
Eva B, b 27 Nov 1894 - d 3 June 1896, DVS
Everett W, b 1 Feb 1884 - d 28 Aug 1965, DVS
Harvey L, b 26 Apr 1905 - d 15 July 1957, DVS
Hugh L, b 30 Nov 1853 - d 29 Jan 1903, RTT
Infant s/o J W & M J, no dates, DVS
John B, b 24 Sept 1867 - d 29 Oct 1960, DVS
John C, b 22 July 1862 - d 21 Jan 1919, DVS
John Carl, b 7 Feb 1934 - d 11 Feb 1934, RTT
John W, b 1 Dec 1832 - d 17 Dec 1901, DVS
Lania, b 20 Oct 1879 - d 20 June 1951, DVS
Lawrence, b 28 Dec 1893 - d 23 Jan 1899, RTT
Mary A, b 3 June 1868 - d 12 Feb 1941, RTT
Naoma, b 6 June 1890 - d 18 June 1890, RTT
Nellie C, b 4 Dec 1900 - no death date, DVS
Orville, d 14 June 1980, ae 71y, RTT
Oswell, b 7 Nov 1896 - d 28 Dec 1898, RTT
Paris, d 22 March 1966, ae 75y, DVS
Riley G, b 15 July 1881 - d -- ---- 1885, DVS
Sarah M, b 5 Sept 1829 - d 6 Dec 1884, DVS
Susan F, b 27 Nov 1887 - d 12 May 1890, DVS
Willburn, b&d 12 Oct 1918, DVS
William, b 25 Dec 1829 - d 6 May 1909, DVS

WEDGEWORTH, David Johnnie, d 8 Nov 1974, ae 32y, FLF
WEIDMANN, Jenne L, b 24 June 1885 - d 10 Oct 1942, DRL
Thorwald, b 28 July 1875 - d 7 March 1955, DRL
WEIFORD, Bessie Armes, d 21 March 1973, ae 79y, NWP
WEINIMAN, A, d 7 Aug 1905, ae 78y, PTC
WELCH, Amanda, b 1 July 1893 - d 11 Dec 1897, PLR
Mrs Elzana McK, d 4 Aug 1978, ae 72y, LBR
John R, b 24 June 1873 - d 20 Aug 1906, PLR
Maggie, b 1872 - d 1958, CRO
Melvin, b 3 Aug 1918 - d 8 Feb 1975, CRO
Oda G, b 1895 - d 1930, CRO
Sarah, b 17 Oct 1867 - d 24 Aug 1914, PLR
WELLENSICK, William, b 22 Oct 1864 - d 18 Aug 1892, WRC
WELLS, Edward Burton, b 30 March 1886 - d 28 May 1971, WRC
Gerald W, d 27 Oct 1974, ae 65y, WRC
Paul Leroy, b 21 July 1916 - d 13 Feb 1965, WRC
Stella Waldrip, b 11 Oct 1886 - d 9 March 1965, WRC
William O, d 17 Jan 1981, WRC
WENDT, William R, b 31 Dec 1906 - d 14 Aug 1960, EST
WENTON, John Lenoir, b 3 Dec 1878 - d 24 Feb 1919, BRZ

WEST, Charley, b 24 July 1901 - d 24 Nov 1920, JCJ

Charlie Sr, b 26 Sept 1904 - d 6 Dec 1972, THR

Cleophus, b 13 June 1905 - d 5 Apr 1908, OLP

G B, b 1 Apr 1859 (or 1849) - d 6 Oct 1936, JCJ

Harvey, b 9 Sept 1893 - d 13 Feb 1950, DVS

J W, b 7 Apr 1872 - d 8 Apr 1948, JCJ

Jerry, b 17 Nov 1880 - 21 Oct 1947, DVS

Joyce, d 14 Dec 1958, ae 1da, DVS

Letha R, b 3 Oct 1888 - d 12 Nov 1959, WRC

Marjorie, b 7 June 1914 - no death date, WRC

Mastie, d 10 March 1972, ae 71y, DVS

Oscar, d 12 Jan 1977, ae 71y, CBJ

Oscar, b 19 March 1905 - no death date, CBJ

Owen F, b 30 Oct 1906 - 28 Oct 1918, CBJ

Randall L, d 3 Oct 1981, ae 37y, JCJ

Ray, b 1 Sept 1911 - d 2 Apr 1968, WRC

Raymond Edgar, d 8 Jan 1975, ae 77y, JCJ

Ruben T, b 26 Jan 1889 - d 22 Sept 1963, WRC

Sarah, b 25 July 1865 - d 9 July 1959, UNN

Savannah, b 11 Sept 1907 - no death date, THR

Tammie, d 6 Jan 1965, ae 4y, THR

Viola Mayton, b 1 Aug 1906 - d 16 Jan 1971, CBJ

WHALEN, Maggie M, b 10 Feb 1899 - d 27 March 1899,

WHALEN (continued) LNC

WHALEY, Bessie E, b 29 Dec 1908 - no death date, PNY

Carlos W, b 22 Aug 1902 - d 13 Feb 1957, PNY

Rev Isaac C, b 28 Feb 1880 - d 20 July 1933, LBR

Infant, 1936, LBR

M Tranner Kennedy, b 2 May 1884 - d 25 Sept 1970, LBR

WHEELER, Donnie, d 27 May 1955, ae 74y, LNC

Lorine, d 8 Apr 1959, ae 80y, DVD

Mannie E, b 13 Feb 1879 - d 27 May 1953, LNC

Thomas, b 21 June 1811 - d Thanksgiving Day, 1897, DRL

WHIPPLE, Kenneth, b 18 Feb 1895 - d 14 Oct 1901, DRL

WHITE, Alice, b 1 Jan 1875 - d 1 Dec 1899, UNN

Christine, no dates, MNT

Claude T, b 1898 - d 1972, WMG

David C, b 22 July 1838 - d 16 Feb 1892, ELZ

Ella Mae, b 18 Aug 1898 - d 19 Dec 1950, NWP

Emma Ruth, b 11 June 1919 - d 25 Aug 1973, NWP

Ethel E, b 17 Nov 1895 - no death date, NWP

Fred, b 1890 - d 1935, CLC

Ida Bell, b 31 Aug 1893 - d 28 May 1917, OLP

John, b 31 Aug 1863 - d 26 Nov 1926, OLP

John, b 1806 - d 16 Feb 1887, FST

John William, d 7 May 1975, ae 67y, WMG

Pearl, b 27 March 1897 - d

WHITE (continued)
12 Jan 1898, UNN
Rachel, b 23 June 1877 - d
26 Apr 1878, ELZ
Rachel, b 1 July 1815 - d
10 May 1879, ELZ
Sally, b 1877 - d 1953,
NWP
Sarah W, b 7 May 1853 - d
2 Aug 1903, LBR
Susana, b 1 Aug 1864 - d
19 May 1921, OLP
Yoonne, b 10 Sept 1922 -
no death date, DRL
WHITTAKER, Clay, b 14 Dec
1905 - d 16 March 1937,
NWP
WHITUS, Cora M, b 26 Oct
1886 - d 1 Feb 1958, NWP
Eddie H, b 19 Jan 1884 - d
29 Apr 1936, NWP
Mary, b 11 Nov 1898 - d 4
Jan 1949, NWP
William G, b 10 May 1891 -
d 5 Dec 1968, NWP
WICHMAN, Patricia, d 14 Feb
1979, ae 86y, RGB
WICKS, Jewel, b 24 Sept
1917 - d 30 Oct 1952,
WRC
John D, b 20 Nov 1913 - d
31 Jan 1970, WRC
WIEDMANN, Victoria, d 11
July 1904, ae 24y, BRR
WIGGINS, Ed, d 8 Sept 1974,
ae 77y, CBJ
John F, Pvt US Inf 30 Div
WWI, b 9 June 1891 - d
14 May 1950, CBJ
Lillian A, b 26 Aug 1901 -
d 15 July 1943, EST
Polk Alvin, d 16 Nov 1969,
ae 45y, ADC
Scott, Pvt Co E 120 Inf 30
Div, b 26 May 1894 - d 7
July 1955, EST
WILDER, Carl H, b 10 Jan
1922 - d 6 May 1954, CRO

WILDER (continued)
Carson Clay, d 19 Oct
1958, ae 60y, CRO
Infant, c/o C H Wilder, no
dates, CRO
WILDS, Anna B Sams, b 27
June 1886 - d 17 Feb
1925, CRO
J B, b 17 Feb 1925 - d 20
June 1925, CRO
J Robert, b 7 Apr 1879 - d
25 Apr 1967, CRO
WILEY, C D, b 24 Oct 1872 -
d 21 Apr 1949, WRC
Mary Jane, b 1 March 1858
- d 21 Jan 1921, WRC
WILL, Elizabeth, b 9 Feb
1908 - d 4 Feb 1969, LBR
John M, b 5 May 1909 - d 3
Feb 1961, LBR
WILLIAMS, A D, b 1855 - d
1922, WRC
Albert, b 1865 - d 1939,
SNB
Aldine, b 15 June 1915 - d
27 Apr 1921, UNN
Alma Mae, no dates, MNT
Amanda, b 22 March 1882 -
d 6 Aug 1959, WRC
Amy I, b 6 Nov 1892 - d 16
Oct 1960, CLH
Audrey, d 31 Jan 1977, ae
34y, PTC
Audrey Lee, b 31 Aug 1933
- d 12 March 1939, WRC
Benj Franklin, d 4 Sept
1965, ae 77y 6mo, PLR
Benton, b 20 Nov 1898 - d
11 Dec 1900, CLC
Bertha Ann, b 23 Feb 1904
- d 1 Apr 1938, WRC
C H, b 6 Jan 1898 - d 7
Oct 1898, OLP
Clifford M, b 20 Nov 1920
- no death date, FST
Clinton Parker, b 18 Oct
1884 - d 23 Jan 1969,
WRC

WILLIAMS (continued)
Camily, b 4 Sept 1919 - d 22 Dec 1943, LBR
Charles V Sr, b 1871 - d 1944, NWP
Christine, b 1883 - d 1960, LBR
Clemmie, b 1909 - d 1960, LBR
Dudley W, b 23 July 1925 - d 22 Oct 1953, CLC
Earl, b 1 Jan 1899 - d 4 Jan 1956, NWP
Earl W, b 1894 - d 1973, WRC
Eliza, d 16 Jan 1886, ae 53y 7mo, WRC
Miss Eliza, d 31 Jan 1976, ae 90y, WRC
Eliza R, b 17 Oct 1825 - d 22 Dec 1905, CLC
Ellen, b 5 Apr 1880 - d 11 Sept 1912, LBR
Ellen C, b 1866 - d 1922, WRC
Ellis M, b 1863 - d 1936, WRC
Elsie Ott, b 28 Apr 1896 - d 14 July 1948, WRC
Emma O, b 22 March 1912 - no death date, WRC
Emma T, d 19 Apr 1977, ae 87y, WRC
Eugene, b 14 Oct 1891 - d 2 Jun 1896, WRC
Eugene H, b 7 Dec 1860 - d 17 Feb 1946, WRC
Evangeline, b 15 May 1924 - d 3 Jan 1973, FST
Evelyn Goans, b 22 Nov 1893 - d 22 June 1950, CRO
Florence V, b 3 Oct 1895 - d 15 Sept 1963, WBB
Frank, b 8 May 1883 - d 10 Sept 1977, UNN
Fred W, d 20 Dec 1958, NWP
Geo W, b 1 Dec 1872 - d 30

WILLIAMS (continued)
Dec 1906, UNN
Grace F, 7 June 1899, PLR
Gus C, b 1854 - d 1919, WRC
Harrison, b 15 March 1888 - d 16 July 1932, UNN
Helen, b 7 March 1918 - d 7 May 1921, UNN
Irene, b 8 Apr 1905 - d 5 June 1907, WRC
J, b 3 June 1890 - d 20 July 1964, FLR
J B, b 11 Aug 1943 - d 17 Oct 1943, LBR
J Winford, b 5 Nov 1916 - d 6 May 1913, CLH
Jack, b 3 June 1896 - d 15 July 1897, WRC
James L, b 6 Aug 1882 - d 21 Aug 1961, CLH
John, b 6 Feb 1819 - d 21 March 1921, WRC
John, d 27 Apr 1865, ae 72y, CLC
John B, b 2 July 1852 - d 15 Sept 1932, WRC
Johnny, d 22 May 1976, ae 58y, ALB
Kenneth Ray, b 20 March 193-- - d 6 Feb 1964, LNE
Lenora Sue d/o Jack & Mildred, d 20 Jan 1939, WRC
Leonard, d 30 Oct 1976, ae 59y, LBR
Lige, b 5 Dec 1881 - no death date, PLR
Lillie, b 1887 - d 1950, MSG
Logan, b 13 July 1914 - no death date, NWP
Lora, b 7 Feb 1902 - d 29 Nov 19--, PTC
Lora Mae Kreis, b 13 July 1920 - d 9 Sept 1974, NWP
Louise Toomey, b 1861 - d

WILLIAMS (continued)
    1937, WRC
    Luan, b 16 Dec 1880 - d 15
      Jan 1964, PLR
    Lucinda, b 28 May 1865 - d
      29 Aug 1880, UNN
    Lummie, b 5 Sept 1876 - d
      17 Jan 1903, UNN
    Lydia, b 26 June 1916 - no
      death date, PLR
    Malinda, b 12 Nov 1838 - d
      10 Aug 1897, UNN
    Marion M, b 1 Apr 1865 - d
      23 June 1889, WRC
    Martha Ross, b 22 June
      1833 - d 6 March 1898,
      DRL
    Mary, b 1843 - d 15 July
      1895, UNN
    Mary A, b -- June 1818 - d
      7 May 1867, UNN
    Mary E, b 18 May 1882 - d
      25 Sept 1958, UNN
    Mary J, b 15 Jan 1849 - d
      18 May 1939, DRL
    Minerva, b 1870 - d 1935,
      WRC
    Mrs. Rutha, d 15 March
      1976, ae 90y, LBR
    N A, b 15 March 1859 - d
      17 June 1932, CLC
    Nannie, b 16 May 1884 - d
      3 March 1949, UNN
    Omer Willis, b 1919 - d 19
      March 1974, PLR
    Otto R, b 17 Jan 1901 - d
      15 June 1963, CLC
    Paul Gene Jr, b 24 Dec
      1972 - d 25 Jan 1973,
      NWP
    Paul M, b 1859 - d 6 July
      1900, CRO
    Pearl, b 30 Jan 1888 - d 5
      Aug 1888, WRC
    Mrs R H, b 15 Oct 1862 - d
      17 June 1900, OLP
    R T, Co F 5th TN Inf, d 16
      Aug 1875, DVS

WILLIAMS (continued)
    R Theodore, b 3 June 1914
      - d 25 Oct 1919, CLH
    Raymond, b 8 Dec 1909 - d
      5 May 1971, WRC
    Robert Leon, b 1965 - d
      1966, FLR
    Robert T, b 16 Feb 1896 -
      d 1 May 1969, NWP
    Ross H Sr, d 31 Jan 1973,
      ae 81y, WMG
    Ross Hope, WWI, b 28 Nov
      1891 - d 31 Jan 1973,
      WRC
    Ruben, b 3 June 1896 - d
      20 June 1896, WRC
    Russel Clyde, b 31 Oct
      1923 - d 13 July 1970,
      CLH
    S H, b 18 Jan 1900 - d 14
      June 1900, OLP
    Sain, 1884, LBR
    Sam W, b 10 Nov 1875 - d
      26 Jan 1976, UNN
    Scott, b 16 March 1928 - d
      26 June 1940, MNT
    Susan F, b 6 Jan 1888 - d
      30 Feb 1916, UNN
    Susan Honeycutt, b 5 Sept
      1882 - d 20 Oct 1946,
      CRO
    T J, b 6 Apr 1853 - d 29
      March 1906, PTC
    Thelma I, b&d 15 May 1926,
      CLH
    Virginia D, b 5 May 1858 -
      d 27 May 1940, WRC
    W R, b 22 May 1824 - d 12
      March 1886, CLC
    Walter N, b 1 June 1896 -
      d 27 Jan 1962, PTC
    Wilburn G, b 27 Feb 1862 -
      d 1888, CLC
    Wilhemina B, b 17 Aug 1878
      - d 14 Dec 1934, RGB
    William, b 28 July 1879 -
      d 3 Nov 1936, CRO
    William, b 10 March 1803 -

WILLIAMS (continued)
d 1 May 1881, UNN
William, Co L 3 Rgt TN Inf
Sp/Am War, b 7 Dec 1873
- d 4 Oct 1961, LBR
William H, Civil War Vet,
b 15 June 1835 - d 13
July 1910, UNN
WILLIS, Arthur, b 14 Nov
1914 - no death date,
BRR
Cora Lee, b 15 Jan 1887 -
d 16 July 1952, CRO
James Gilbert, b 25 July
1947 - d 13 Jan 1948,
CRO
John W, b 14 Apr 1888 - d
24 Jan 1971, CRO
WILLMAN, Sarah Worthington,
b 1840 - d 1902, RGB
WILLMORE, Charles, b 1 July
1853 - d 21 July 1903,
PLR
WILLOUGHBY, Granville, b 20
Jan 1913 - d 13 May
1939, OLP
Joseph Henry, b 29 Jan
1881 - d 3 Jan 1955, OLP
Katy, no dates on stone,
PLR
Mosell, b 13 Apr 1918 - d
12 March 1919, OLP
Press, b 2 Feb 1858 - d 20
Aug 1932, OLP
Rose Trail, d 26 Aug 1977,
ae 86y, OLP
Walter, b 18 Oct 1889 - d
15 Feb 1912, OLP
WILSON, Abba N, b 6 Dec
1831 - d 1 Jan 1902, BCF
Ann Goldberg, b 22 Aug
1879 - d 9 Apr 1969, UNN
Anna, b 20 Aug 1906 - no
death date, UNN
Bill, b 24 June 1927 - d 1
Aug 1975, ae 46y, NWP
Bonnie, b 4 June 1912 - d
9 June 1912, UNN

WILSON (continued)
Boyd L, b 4 June 1914 - no
death date, WRC
California, b 1882 - d
1946, EST
Charles, d 30 July 1891,
ae 63y 9mo, BCF
Charles H, b 19 Nov 1883 -
d 1 Dec 1966, UNN
Charles H, b 14 Aug 1858 -
d 16 March 1944, UNN
Clarence, b 18 June 1903 -
d 12 July 1903, UNN
Pvt David, b 25 Feb 1897 -
d 15 Oct 1919, UNN
David M, b 21 June 1884 -
d 25 Aug 1967, UNN
Earl, b 18 June 1902 - d 9
July 1902, UNN
Eliza J, b 25 Dec 1878 - d
13 Oct 1967, UNN
Elizabeth, b 14 Dec 1894 -
d 14 July 1970, UNN
Elizabeth P, d -- Oct
1977, ae 52y, WMG
Ellen R, b 26 March 1892 -
d 23 Oct 1918, UNN
Elmer R, b 10 Jan 1919 - d
13 Feb 1970, UNN
Eltha Clay, b 9 Oct 1899 -
d 17 Apr 1922, UNN
Dr F G, b 2 Aug 1845 - d
14 Feb 1909, RGB
Esther, b 27 Sept 1872 - d
4 Feb 1968, UNN
Grace, b 19 Dec 1911 - d
29 Oct 1969, EST
Granville E, b 1909 - d
1941, EST
Harold E, b 11 Nov 1923 -
d 21 June 1925, UNN
Harold L, b 6 May 1924 - d
3 Oct 1975, LBR
Harold L, Sgt USA WWII, b
6 May 1924 - d 3 Oct
1975, LBR
Harriet C, b 12 March 1867
- no death date, UNN

WILSON (continued)

Ivan Kenneth, b 28 Sept 1919 - d 14 Jan 1923, EST

Jackie Lenton, b 28 Aug 1910 - d 8 Sept 1911, UNN

James H, b 29 Jan 1917 - no death date, UNN

James R, b 1874 - d 1943, EST

Jane Brasel, b 6 Dec 1865 - d 7 June 1945, BRZ

Jessie M, b 2 Nov 1871 - d 16 June 1936, UNN

John C, b 6 June 1856 - d 1 Feb 1932, UNN

John F, d 3 May 1974, ae 85y, DVS

Joseph H, b 27 March 1893 - d 6 May 1954, UNN

Laura Anne, b 11 Aug 1865 - d 10 May 1913, BRZ

Leiton, b 1901 - d 1960, LBR

Leslie, b 21 Oct 1899 - d 9 Feb 1974, UNN

Linda Darline, d 9 Nov 1955, ae 7y, WRJ

Lizza, b 24 March 1884 - d 1906, UNN

Lydia Jones, b 1858 - d 1895, UNN

Mae F, b 6 May 1896 - no death date, LBR

Malinda J, d 25 Aug 1883, ae 53y, BCF

Mamie A, d 21 July 1979, ae 70y, UNN

Mary Duncan, b 19 Aug 1865 - d 13 Oct 1909, UNN

Mary J, b 6 Nov 1841 - d 2 Feb 1911, RGB

Maude, b 1908 - d 1966, PLR

Melvin E, b 1 July 1910 - d 10 Apr 1934, UNN

Minnie Lee, b 15 July 1887

WILSON (continued)

- d 14 Apr 1975, UNN

Nellie B, b 17 Nov 1900 - d 12 Oct 1978, EST

Obaman, b 2 May 1896 - d 30 March 1905, ELZ

Obedience, b 6 June 1860 - d 30 Oct 1940, UNN

Peter A, b 20 March 1866 - d 4 Apr 1940, UNN

Ray M, b 16 Feb 1901 - d 29 July 1902, UNN

Reed M, b 13 Apr 1925 - d 10 Aug 1957, LBR

Robert Lee Jr, d 21 July 1980, ae 25y, UNN

Rufus A, b 23 July 1863 - d 14 Apr 1910, UNN

Ruth D, b 16 Feb 1894 - d 27 Jan 1931, UNN

Ruth Griffith, d 25 July 1976, ae 87y, PLR

S G, b 29 March 1860 - d 23 Aug 1936, RGB

Sallie Jones, b 6 Jan 1894 - d 20 Feb 1916, UNN

Sarah J, b 1865 - d 1959, ELZ

Thelma O, b 24 Dec 1917 - d 15 March 1970, WRC

Vada G, b 7 Jan 1925 - no death date, UNN

W Worth, b 21 Feb 1858 - d 21 Sept 1943, UNN

Wagner Marton, d 27 March 1966, ae 71y, EST

William, Co K 1 TN Inf, b 1835 - d 10 Feb 1862, RTT

William Harry, b 13 Aug 1917 - d 17 March 1933, EST

William W, b 4 Nov 1895 - d 12 Sept 1972, LBR

Willie R, b 15 Apr 1907 - d 23 Dec 1940, UNN

Wm Howard, b 2 Dec 1886 - d 8 July 1961, UNN

WILSON (continued)
Wm Howard Jr, b 6 Dec 1920
  - d 2 Sept 1968, UNN
WILTER, Marcia Blair, d 13
  March 1978, ae 38y, UNH
WILTSIE, Jason, b 30 Dec
  1876 - d 12 Nov 1900,
  CLC
Mary, d/o Hardee, d ae
  14da, CLC
WINNIE, Allen Gene, USA VN,
  b 17 May 1945 - d 8 Oct
  1976, LBR
John F, b 14 Feb 1888 - d
  30 Apr 1933, LBR
Ruby Z, b 19 Nov 1919 - d
  15 June 1923, LBR
Tennie V, b 19 Oct 1890 -
  d 3 Dec 1923, LBR
WINTON, Dora Brasel, b 10
  Apr 1877 - d 7 Apr 1955,
  BRZ
WIRT, Mrs Jonnie Woolum, b
  23 Sept 1905 - d 16 June
  1974, LBR
WISENHUNT, Emma, b 1902 - d
  1968, CRO
WOOD, James Thomas, b 8
  Sept 1905 - d 25 Feb
  1964, EST
John William, b 25 Aug
  1874 - d 10 June 1965,
  EST
Mamie E, b 4 Feb 1902 - d
  9 March 1973, EST
Rebecca Hammond, b 7 Oct
  1879 - d 20 Aug 1956,
  EST
Ruth Elizabeth, b 1911 - d
  23 May 1963, EST
Sarah E, b 15 Nov 1856 - d
  30 Nov 1949, EST
WOODALL, George Doug, d 29
  Oct 1978, ae 36y, PTC
WOODS, Allen, b 1838 - d
  1913, UNN
Allen Jerome, 1941 - no
  other date, UNN

WOODS (continued)
Beatrice L, b 25 Nov 1911
  - no death date, EST
Campbell, ae 40y, UNN
Freddie R, b 6 July 1914 -
  d 12 July 1915, UNN
Gladys, b 15 June 1908 - d
  11 July 1926, UNN
Glen Allen, b 2 Jan 1915 -
  d 2 Oct 1917, UNN
Gypsy Jackson, b 1 Dec
  1891 - d 30 Oct 1945,
  UNN
James W, b 27 Apr 1885 - d
  31 March 1962, UNN
Joe W, b 1 June 1907 - d 8
  May 1972, EST
John T, b 21 Dec 1882 - d
  6 July 1916, UNN
Kisiah Adcock, b 20 Oct
  1829 - d 25 May 1894,
  UNN
L, d 2 Feb 1941, NWP
Lacey A, b 7 Apr 1882 - d
  27 Aug 1948, UNN
Linda B, b 14 Dec 1880 - d
  19 Aug 1969, UNN
Link A, b 1 Aug 1887 - d
  27 Nov 1963, EST
Marjorie E, b 15 May 1930
  - d 5 May 1932, UNN
Mrs Mary, d 11 Feb 1980,
  ae 56y, UNN
Mary Ann, b 6 Oct 1881 - d
  14 June 1911, UNN
Minnie J, b 23 May 1893 -
  d 30 June 1974, EST
Myrtle Henry, d 11 Feb
  1979, ae 74y, WRC
Nancy Belle Williams, b 5
  Aug 1877 - d 17 Jan
  1907, UNN
Nellie F Jones, b 29 May
  1896 - d 15 Oct 1974,
  UNN
Novatine, b 15 Feb 1930 -
  d 1 March 1930, EST
Riley, b 1 Dec 1878 - d 5

WOODS (continued)
Oct 1961, UNN
Robert, b 18 Nov 1910 - d
26 July 1953, NWP
Rusty, b 24 Oct 1963 - d
15 Aug 1973, UNN
Sarah Jane, b 25 June 1859
- d 1 Aug 1863, UNN
Sarah Justice, b 1 Apr
1852 - d 12 Oct 1902,
UNN
Seaberry, b 1890 - d 1967,
FLF
Stanley Lee Jr, 1972 - no
other date, LNE
W Wesley, b 26 May 1855 -
d 3 Apr 1924, UNN
William C, b 9 Apr 1895 -
d 16 Aug 1970, UNN
WOODWARD, Eugene, Tech 5
SVC Co 21 Inf WWII, b 13
July 1912 - d 27 July
1964, NWP
WOOLDRIDGE, Mary Eliza, b 6
Sept 1864 - d 7 May
1949, DRL
WOOLUM, Ben F, b 21 Apr
1875 - d 19 Oct 1946,
LBR
Betty White, b 16 Nov 1881
- d 3 Aug 1958, LBR
Joe Marie, d 8 May 1977,
ae 77y, LBR
WORKMAN, Clifford, b 9 July
1934 - d 16 Jan 1973,
BRR
Luther, b 21 Sept 1915 - d
23 Nov 1927, BRR
Zora, b 25 July 1912 - d
10 Jan 1927, BRR
WORLEY, Betty Lucile, b 29
Oct 1936 - d 31 May
1937, NWP
James E, b 9 Oct 1905 - d
16 July 1903, UNN
Jeffrey A, b&d 3 Nov 1958,
NWP
Josephine B, b 24 Oct 1963

WORLEY (continued)
- d 15 Aug 1973, UNN
Kenneth R, d 14 June 1980,
ae 21y, NWP
Mary, b 1940 - d 1963, NWP
Nannie A, b 13 Aug 1896 -
d 30 March 1937, WRJ
Richard Roscoe, b 24 Feb
1917 - d 11 Aug 1929,
CRO
Charles, b 17 Feb 1903 - d
13 Dec 1953, DVS
Delia, b 13 June 1905 - d
15 Oct 1942, DVS
Mable, b 5 June 1918 - d
16 Aug 1919, CBJ
Nancy J, b 12 Sept 1884 -
d 2 Dec 1976, CBJ
Sam G, b 24 July 1882 - d
4 Jan 1951, CBJ
Thomas, Pvt 335 Inf WWII,
b 22 July 1925 - d 2 Dec
1944, OOO
WORST, Howard David, b 8
March 1870 - d 5 Oct
1949, WRC
Lola Ann, b 10 Dec 1903 -
d 24 Aug 1970, WRC
Mrs Margaret, d 22 Dec
1978, ae 100y, WRC
WORTLEY, Randall G, d 2 Nov
1976, ae 69y, DRL
WRIGHT, Rev A B, b 3 Nov
1826 - d 9 Nov 1893, BRR
Bertha Jane, b 1887 - d
1960, SNB
Bowman, b 10 Nov 1904 - d
8 Feb 1969, CLH
Cynthia S, b 28 Nov 1824 -
d 29 Sept 1900, BRR
Debbie C, d 13 Jan 1884,
ae 20y, BRR
Elisha, b 9 March 1856 - d
8 Nov 1930, MRR
Ellen W, b 17 June 1900 -
no death date, RTT
Emily W, b 18 July 1899 -
d 3 Oct 1938, NWP

WRIGHT (continued)
Eva Jane, b 19 March 1891
- d 14 March 1912, MRR
Fred E, b 26 Aug 1913 - d
14 July 1967, RTT
Fred R Sr, b 14 Oct 1904 -
d 29 Sept 1967, NWP
Freely A, b 16 Aug 1828 -
d 5 Apr 1900, BRR
Horace M, Pvt TN USA, d 20
Apr 1909, DVS
James C, b 12 Nov 1924 - d
17 Nov 1924, DRM
Jeremiah, b 26 Feb 1814 -
d 1 Apr 1888, BRR
John H, b 19 Sept 1870 - d
16 Sept 1904, DVS
Linsy, b 11 Nov 1899 - d
27 March 1902, MRR
Mack, d 6 March 1978, ae
77y, CRO
Mary, b 10 May 1858 - d 15
Sept 1915, MRR
Mary A, b 11 Aug 1918 - no
death date, CLC
Dr Rufus, d 23 Feb 1974,
ae 70y, WRC
S Albert, b 16 Aug 1894
(?) -d 20 Jan 1857 (?),
DVS
Will, b 1875 - d 1928, BRR
William C T, b 10 Aug 1881
- d 11 Feb 1945, SNB
William W, d 24 June 1978,
ae 82y, WBB
Willis B, b 19 Sept 1903 -
no death date, NWP
YESTER, Joanna T Polson, b
1923 - d 27 Jan 1978,
PLR
YORK, Anna L, b 1874 - d
1964, BRR
Annie E Lynch, b 15 July
1878 - no death date,
BRR
Ben L, b 4 Apr 1872 - d 25
March 1875, NDK
Emert M, b 11 July 1907 -

YORK (continued)
d 10 Oct 1910, BRR
George M, b 8 May 1870 - d
1 Dec 1951, BRR
Hannah Webb, b 5 March
1908 - d 9 Nov 1962, LNE
Henry M, b 24 Feb 1837 - d
26 Dec 1930, NDK
John B, b 1868 - d 1963,
BRR
Martin G, b 9 May 1874 - d
7 Nov 1937, LNE
Mary Taylor, b 21 May 1881
- d 17 Jan 1935, LNE
Nancy, b 4 Apr 1838 - d 7
Apr 1926, NDK
Nellie, ae 87y - no other
dates, LNE
YOUNG, Abra, b 1 Apr 1850 -
d 21 May 1887, PLR
Alpha M, b 5 Aug 1913 - no
death date, MLC
Bates, b 3 Nov 1884 - d 26
Jan 1934, CLC
Bertie Bell, b 1 March
1879 - d 26 May 1960,
BRR
Beulah, b 1922 - d 1963,
CLC
Carl H, b 23 Apr 1954 - d
17 July 1963, WRC
Cassie M, b 7 May 1888 - d
14 Jan 1970, CLC
Clearisa E, b 5 Feb 1873 -
d 28 Dec 1906, UNH
Daniel C, b 22 Feb 1847 -
d 15 Jan 1935, NDK
Earl, b 30 Jan 1901 - d 3
March 1901, ALB
Eva Ray, b&d 14 Feb 1893,
NDK
F M, b 26 Nov 1857 - d 16
June 1909, MLC
Fred O, b 29 Apr 1897 - d
19 June 1945, BRR
Glenis Walker, b 28 Sept
1931 - d 17 Oct 1961,
CLC

YOUNG (continued)
Glenna Mae, b 15 Apr 1930 - d 28 June 1932, ELZ
Gus, b 2 Nov 1900 - no death date, SNB
Gus, d 16 June 1979, ae 78y, SNB
Hannah N Galloway, b 6 Dec 1851 - d 7 Feb 1942, NDK
Hillary S, b 11 July 1878 - d 12 Apr 1940, ALB
Infant Twins, b&d 10 Apr 1876, NDK
James Daily, b 6 Dec 1873 - d 1 Sept 1972, ALB
James E, b 10 March 1947 - d 14 March 1947, WRC
James Otis Jr, Cpl 46 Trans SVC Korea, b 24 June 1928 - d 27 May 1955, LNE
John, b 26 Dec 1812 - d 27 Oct 1877, NDK
John B, b 1867 - d 1904, BRR
John M, b 29 July 1872 - d 21 Aug 1874, NDK
Lefa M, b 16 Jan 1916 - no death date, FRC
Marcena M, b 10 Sept 1874 - d 10 May 1915, BRR
Margaret Rose, b&d 16 Apr 1967, ARM
Marie, b 27 June 1908 - d 23 Apr 1975, SNB
Mary Jane, b 24 Dec 1886 - d 14 Sept 1892, NDK
Maude A C, b 9 Aug 1875 - d 12 Nov 1948, ALB
Nancy, b 8 Dec 1815 - d 28 March 1881, NDK
Nola, d 10 Apr 1976, ae 85y, MLC
Ollie L, b 20 Apr 1885 - d 5 Dec 1948, ALB
Orlena, b 18 Apr 1843 - d 10 Oct 1902, BRR
Raymond H, b 23 Apr 1899 -

YOUNG (continued)
d 2 Jan 1969, FRC
Sarah Sexton, b 24 June 1874 - d 4 Nov 1952, MLC
Shirley Ann, b 9 Dec 1936 - d 9 Nov 1939, NDK
Timothy A, 13 Jan 1929 - no other date, UNH
Wanda Lee, b 10 Dec 1930 - d 21 Apr 1936, CLC
William G, b 3 June 1901 - d 15 Nov 1969, MLC
Willie, 1937, MLC
YOUNGBLOOD, George A, b 10 March 1870 - d 30 May 1948, CBJ
William, b 14 Oct 1902 - d 20 Apr 1951, WRC
YUTEMEYER, Blevins, b 3 Feb 1846 - d 3 May 1922, PNY
Juley, b 1 Apr 1845 - d 29 May 1924, PNY
ZACHARY, Ora, b 1894 - d 1972, WMG
ZALESKI, Infant Son, no dates, DRL
ZATOISKI, Alexander, b 1873 - d 1954, DRL
Antonia, b 1876 - d 1970, DRL
Theodore, b 9 Nov 1909 - d 11 Jan 1968, DRL
Vera G, b 9 Oct 1903 - d 16 July 1980, DRL
ZATOSKI, Stella, b 1884 - d 1935, DRL
ZELLER, Bertha, b 1868 - d 1952, DRL
Charles, b 1860 - d 1931, DRL
Charles David, b 18 July 1905 - d 17 March 1918, DRL
ZLATY, Casmer J, b 1914 - d 1939, DRL
ZOBRIST, Elizabeth, b -- Feb 1823 - d 24 Nov 1886, WRC

ZOBRIST (continued)
Renhart, b 1809 - d 1882, WRC

ZUMESTEIN, Caroline H, b 1826 - d 1914, WRC

Charles, b 20 Oct 1869 - d 18 Aug 1958, LNC

Charles A, b 12 May 1857 - d 21 Sept 1946, WRC

Cheryl Ann, 16 Oct 1963, DRM

Clarence F, b 4 May 1900 - d 5 Dec 1959, WRC

Cora L, b 30 June 1924 - no death date, WRC

Edward W, b 7 Nov 1889 - d 6 Nov 1964, WRC

ZUMESTEIN (continued)
Ethel W, b 10 May 1894 - d 6 May 1956, WRC

John Frederick, 31 July 1965, DRM

Lena Marie, b 4 Feb 1892 - d 29 Dec 1922, WRC

Mary A, b 24 Dec 1864 - d 15 Feb 1940, WRC

Verlinda A, b 1 Aug 1871 - d 11 Aug 1949, LNC

Violet Heidel, d 7 July 1973, ae 70y, WRC

Violet, d 6 July 1973, ae 70y, WMG

INDEX

This index lists the names of women buried in the text. Although the last names appear to be surnames, it is up to the researcher to determine if they indeed are or if they are actually middle names.

ADCOCK, Kisiah 206
ADKISSON, Hattie 96
ALLEN, Mary E 104
ALLEY, Dixie 21 Kate 37
    Lavinnah 173 Lydia 161
ALLY, Brejettie 193
ANDERSON, Ethel 48
ANDREW, Nannie 93
ARMES, Bessie 199
ARMS, Vada 100
ARNFIELD, Mary 186
ASHER, Millie 75
ASHLEY, Virginia 35
AYTES, Rebecc 56
BALES, Maud 60
BANKS, Jeanette 43
BARBELL, Louise 90
BARDELL, Minnie 15
BARDILL, Anna 16 Joyce 157
    Mrs J 157
BARGER, Betty 71 Screna 105
BARGES, Beulah 35
BARGESS, Bertha 26
BASS, Eliza 153
BATES, Rena 95
BAXTER, Mary 159
BEENE, Crystal 159
BELL, Bertie 208 Genera 145
    Grace 155 Ida 122 200
    Laura 56 Mary 154 Nora
    62
BEST, Connie 28
BINGHAM, Maggie 112
BLAIR, Bertha 28 Dora E 85
    Marcia 206
BLAKE, Linda 183 Velea M
    157
BODINE, Lucile 139
BONIFACIUS, Jane 23
BOWMAN, Delphia 89

BRAN, Lenora 10
BRANSTETTER, Mary 90 Minnie
    141 Susie 46
BRASEL, Dora 206 Jane 205
BRAZEL, Mary 67
BREEDLOVE, Bertha 73 Hopey
    31
BROCK, Minnie 191
BROOK, Maude 93
BROWN, Ainy 38 Mary Jane 92
    Maxine 28
BRUMBY, Lillian 24
BRYANT, Dora 1 Maggie 76
BULLARD, Mary 8
BUNCH, Octavia 81
BURNS, Lena 92
BUTLER, Annie 54 Bonnie L 3
BUTTRAM, Martha J 67
BUXTON, Louise 138
BYRD, Laura 63 Linda C 169
    Margaret 50 Mary L 125
    Nancy 54 75 Sarah 167
    Susan 116
CAIN, Ella 175
CARPENTER, Alphia 176
CARROLL, Nellie 139
CARSON, June 135 Lee Ellen
    160 Myrtle 169
CARTER, Addie 143 Mary 108
CASEY, Mary 33
CHAMB, Lula Ann 58
CHANEY, Emma 182 Jennie 157
    Maggie 3 Minnie 168
CHAPMAN, Martha 75 Thelma
    80
CLARK, Alta 167 Ella 102
    Ida 3
CLAY, Eltha 204
COCHRAN, Joyce 141
COLLINS, Dorothy 132

COOPER, Effie 87 Isabel 179
  Ruth 98
COX, Dorothy 56 Sarah 40
CREEKMORE, Alma 174
CRENSHAW, Amy C 44
CROMWELL, Gladys 32 Martha
  63
CROSS, Christine H 92
DAGLEY, Bonnie N 89
DAVIDSON, Malinda 123
  Patience 105 Regina 80
DAVIS, Ada 101 Clair 59
  Gertie 164 Loraine 158
  Mary Ann 79 Meredith 2
  Nancy A 122
DAYHUFF, Emma 69
DEAN, Zella 194
DELANEY, Irene 191
DELL, Mary 97
DIXON, Alta 124
DOUGHERTY, Mary E 176
DOUGLAS, Alice M 71
DOYLE, Mary 142
DRAKE, Cassie 36
DUNCAN, Abba 96 Mary 76 205
  Rivera 60
DUNN, Lucinda 178
DYER, DElilia 124
EASTRIDGE, Alma 158
EDMONDS, Gertie 36
EILLEY, Lila 52
EMERSON, Ann E 42
ENGERT, Clara 194 Martha H
  186
ENGLAND, Bettie 154 Georgia
  30 Minnie 94 Nola 90
  Polly 184
ERNEST, Pearl A 165
ESTES, Matilda 47
ESTIS, Mary J 97
EVANS, Ola Lee 37
EWING, Dorsa 29
FAGAN, Essie 158
FAWLEWIEKE, Amalie 56
FINCH, Della 84
FORSTNER, Alice 124
FOSTER, Polly Ann 139
FREELS, Mary Ann 94 Nell 59

FRENCH, Ellen 80
FRIES, Dora 139
FRYE, Sarah J 21 Wanda 71
GADNER, Lucy 113
GAFFIN, Opal 100
GALLOWAY, Hannah N 209
  Leona 183 Mary 104
  Phoenia 98
GAMBLE, Eva 34
GARRETT, Amy 11 Eliz Ann 70
  Margaret 130 Sarah Tenn
  162
GAUDEN, Lena 4
GIBBS, Ada Mae 107
GIBSON, Ina 146
GOAD, Eliza Ann 43 Emma 81
  Hazel 111
GOANS, Evelyn 202
GODDARD, Ellen S 115 Mary A
  127
GOLDBERG, Ann 204 Pauline 9
GOLDBERT, Kathlyn 117
GOLDSTON, Carnin 188 Mary
  15 112 Mona 29
GONES, Ella 28
GOUGH, Bessie 127
GRANT, Cordelia 101
GRASHAM, Ida 14
GRAVES, Vicey 57
GRAY, Ida 30
GREASY, Elsie 28
GRECULA, Susan 180
GREEN, Alta 41
GRIBBLE, Lizzie 8
GRIFFITH, Della 168 Elmira
  160 Ruth 205
GSCH, Augusta 112
GSCHWIND, Mary 113
GUNTER, Florence 73
HAAG, Catherine 193
HALL, Belvia 27 Dolly 23
  Dorine 69 Drucilla 94
  Etta 77 Gertrude 113
  Jane 40 Julia 131
  Letitia 129 Maggie 104
  Minda M 180 Rachel 167
  Sarah A 46
HAMBY, Elsie 51 Hazel 60

HAMBY (continued)
    Isa 170 Laura 60 Verna
    126
HAMMOND, Rebecca 206
HANKS, Nancy 140
HATFIELD, Eveline 134
HEADRICK, Mary 196
HEGBEE, Linda 64
HEIDEL, Violet 210
HENRY, Myrtle 206
HICKMAN, Lula 186
HICKS, Ann 143
HIGGIN, Lula 184
HINDS, Grace 163 Maud 128
HOLLADAY, Laura 144
HOLLOWAY, Louise 39
HONEYCUTT, Etta 16 Martha
    157 Mary L 37 Nellie 40
    Nora 198 Sallie 132
    Susan 203 Zenice 30
HOOD, Sybl 7
HOOKS, Lola 165 Lora 192
HORNSBY, Cora 167
HOWARD, Anna 38 Effie 92
    Ethel 16 Laura 88 Lizzie
    74 Margaret 196 Mary 154
HOWE, Sadie B 108
HUDSON, Mary F 195 Susan 98
HUMAN, Bessie 142 Beulah 30
    Lucy 59 Madelyn 180 Opal
    183
HURST, Nola 154
HURTT, Eunice 70
HUSKINS, Hattie 174
INES, Mary 136
ISHAM, Ellen 100
JACKSON, Anna 58 Margaret
    152 Martha 129 Mary 104
    128 Matilda 64 Ona 140
JAMES, Karen 159
JEFFERS, Bessie 61
JENNINGS, Ella Mae 58
JETT, Elizabeth 24 Margaret
    123
JOHNSON, Margaret 59 Pearl
    23
JONE, Clara 70 Florence 45
JONES, Anna 112 Annie 179

JONES (continued)
    Bessie R 107 Cynthia 113
    Ella 144 Ellen 53
    Gertrude 15 Gleneva 22
    Henrietta 50 Lola 52
    Lydia 205 Maggie D 18
    Mary 109 148 Mary F 59
    Mary S L 63 Milda 178
    Nellie F 206 Sallie 205
    Wanda 132
JOYNER, Annie 49 Ellen 102
    Julia B 121 Martha 150
    Mary 55
JUSTICE, Jane 54 Laura 166
    Sallie M 193 Sarah 207
KAMER, Louise 60 Minnie 82
KAUFMAN, Ida 84
KELLEY, Lena 135
KELLY, Malinda 19 Marilyn
    146 Rachel 50 Rachel A
    107
KENNEDY, Laura 53
KENWICK, Ruby E 129
KING, Nina 37
KITTRELL, Gladys 193 Lena M
    103 Sarah M 29
KOONTZ, Irene M 86
KRAMER, Rosa 83
KREIS, Augusta 84 Nina 193
LAND, Ethel 35
LANE, Edith Dora 25
LANGLEY, Celia 66 Delia 40
    Emilie 31 Emma 82 Flora
    112 Florence 132 Lula 21
    Margaret 104 Margrette
    163
LEE, Amanda 57 Annis 180
    Beulah 148 Blanche 71
    Bonnie 70 Cora 6 204
    Edna 178 Eliza 102
    Gertie 39 Ida 57 Iva 82
    Lottie 34 Mamie 17 Mary
    143 Minnie 123 190 205
    Nova 135 Rose 80 Sallie
    98
LEHMAN, Erna 145
LEON, Clara 34 Flilchea 40
LESTER, Nell 110

213

SCOTT (continued)
Edith 122 Laura 45
Louisa 74 Lucy E 94
Lydia 165 Martha 1 Mary
170 Sylvia 82
SEXTON, Easter 70 Laura 67
Maggie 150 Mary 75 Sarah
209
SHANNON, Clara 21 Dora 170
Vestie 171
SHAVER, Rebecca 78
SHELTON, Reba 60
SHOTWELL, Grace 102
SIMS, Gertie 31
SMARSH, Hannah 165
SMITH, Hilda 109
SPURLING, Allie 101
STENNETT, Bessie 41
STEPHENS, Margie 104
STEVENSON, Amanda 148
STEWART, Mary 183
STONE, Phebe A 196
STONECIPHER, Annie 63
Matilda 104 Sally 105
STRINGFIELD, Mary 27 Virgie
192
STRONG, Vivian 197
STRUTTON, Myrtle 34
STURGES, Nancy 68
SUMMERS, Mary 106
TAYLOR, Della 42 Mary 208
Pearl 162 Sarah E 88
Sybil 159 Sylvania 198
TERRY, Mildred 51
THOMAS, Bessie 124 Susie 94
THORNTON, Minnie M 75 Nancy
142 Sarah 177
TILLEY, Anna May 13
TISHNER, Fanni 8
TODD, Ada 65
TONEY, Dora 44
TOOMEY, Louise 202
TOWNSEND, Mamie 74
TRAIL, Emma 167 Rose 204
TRAMMEL, Louise 19
TRIPLETT, Irene 128
VAILES, Martha 4
VESPER, Myrtle 15

VICKERS, Eva 33
VOYLES, Dixie M 190
WALDRIP, Stella 199
WALKER, Ann 44 Glenis 208
Mary 93 Nellie 184
WALLS, Bertha 163 Elizabeth
86
WEBB, Anna 25 Annie 12
Elizabeth 92 Emma 61
Hannah 208 Juanita 130
Laura 112 Laura E 30
Margaret 120 Martha 94
Parthina 40
WELCH, Lula 29
WEST, Geraldine 94 Hazel
174
WHIT, Georgeann 94
WHITE, Betty 207
WILLIAMS, Amanda 54 Eloise
86 Lydia 132 Malinda 10
Mary E 104 Minerva 64
Nancy Belle 206 Sally
105 Sarah 90
WILSON, Ann 11 Carol Sue 60
Emily 181 Eva 88 Jenia
150 Nora 181 Ruth 109
WOODS, Ellen 107
WOOLUM, Mrs Jonnie 206 Nell
93
WORTHINGTON, Sarah 204
WRIGHT, Sarah A C 149
YORK, Mary S 152
YOUNG, Addie 188 Minnie 132

www.ingramcontent.com/pod-product-compliance
Lightning Source LLC
Chambersburg PA
CBHW070908270326
41927CB00011B/2492